Dr. J. HANNAK

EMANUEL LASKER

THE LIFE OF A CHESS MASTER

With annotations of more than
100 of his greatest games

Foreword by

ALBERT EINSTEIN

★

Translated by
HEINRICH FRAENKEL

DOVER PUBLICATIONS, INC.
New York

This Dover edition, first published in 1991, is an unabridged republication of the work first published in English by Andre Deutsch Ltd., London, and Simon & Schuster, New York, in 1959. The work was first published in German by Siegfried Engelhardt Verlag, Berlin-Frohnau, in 1952 under the title *Emanuel Lasker, Biographie eines Schachweltmeisters.* In this edition the record of Lasker's tournament and match results which was printed on the back of the dust jacket in the first English edition has been expanded and placed after the table of contents.

Manufactured in the United States of America
Dover Publications, Inc., 31 East 2nd Street, Mineola, N.Y. 11501

Library of Congress Cataloging in Publication Data

Hannak, J. (Jacques)
    [Emanuel Lasker. English]
    Emanuel Lasker : the life of a chess master : with annotations of more than 100 of his greatest games / Dr. J. Hannak ; foreword by Albert Einstein ; translated by Heinrich Fraenkel.
        p.   cm.
    Reprint. First published: New York : Simon & Schuster, 1959.
    Translation of: Emanuel Lasker, Biographie eines Schachweltmeisters.
    ISBN 0-486-26706-7
    1. Lasker, Emanuel, 1868–1941.   2. Chess players—Germany—Biography.
I. Title.
GV1439.L3H33   1991
794.1'092—dc20
    [B]   91-14487
                                                                                        CIP

CONTENTS

EMANUEL LASKER'S CHESS CAREER

Tournaments

1889: AMSTERDAM
9 competitors: *1st*, Burn; *2nd*, Lasker; *3rd*, Mason

1890: GRAZ
7 competitors: *1st*, Makowetz; *2nd*, Bauer; *3rd*, Lasker

1892: LONDON
11 competitors: *1st*, Lasker; *2nd*, Mason; *3rd*, Loman

1892: LONDON
5 competitors: *1st*, Lasker; *2nd*, Blackburne; *3rd* Mason

1893: NEW YORK
14 competitors: *1st*, Lasker; *2nd*, Albin; *3rd*, Delmar

1895: HASTINGS
22 competitors: *1st*, Pillsbury; *2nd*, Tchigorin; *3rd*, Lasker

1895–96: ST. PETERSBURG
4 competitors: *1st*, Lasker; *2nd*, Steinitz; *3rd*, Pillsbury; *4th*, Tchigorin

1896: NUREMBERG
19 competitors: *1st*, Lasker; *2nd*, Maroczy; *3rd*, Pillsbury and Tarrasch

1899: LONDON
15 competitors: *1st*, Lasker; *2nd–4th*, Janowski, Maroczy and Pillsbury

1900: PARIS
17 competitors: *1st*, Lasker; *2nd*, Pillsbury; *3rd*, Maroczy and Marshall

1904: CAMBRIDGE SPRINGS
16 competitors: *1st*, Marshall; *2nd* and *3rd*, Janowski and Lasker

1909: ST. PETERSBURG
19 competitors: *1st* and *2nd*, Lasker and Rubinstein; *3rd*, Duras and Spielmann

1914: ST. PETERSBURG
11 competitors: *1st*, Lasker; *2nd*, Capablanca; *3rd*, Alekhine; *4th*, Tarrasch; *5th*, Marshall

1918: BERLIN
4 competitors: *1st*, Lasker; *2nd*, Rubinstein; *3rd*, Schlechter; *4th*, Tarrasch

1923: MAHRISCH-OSTRAU
14 competitors: *1st*, Lasker; *2nd*, Reti; *3rd*, Gruenfeld

1924: NEW YORK
11 competitors: *1st*, Lasker; *2nd*, Capablanca; *3rd*, Alekhine; *4th*, Marshall

1925: MOSCOW
20 competitors: *1st*, Bogolyubov; *2nd*, Lasker; *3rd*, Capablanca; *4th*, Marshall

1934: ZURICH
16 competitors: *1st*, Alekhine; *2nd* and *3rd*, Euŵe and Flohr; *4th*, Bogolyubov; *5th*, Lasker

1935: MOSCOW
20 competitors: *1st* and *2nd*, Botvinnik and Flohr; *3rd*, Lasker; *4th*, Capablanca

1936: MOSCOW
10 competitors: *1st*, Capablanca; *2nd*, Botvinnik; *3rd*, Flohr; *4th*, Lilienthal; *5th*, Ragozin; *6th*, Lasker

1936: NOTTINGHAM
15 competitors: *1st* and *2nd*, Botvinnik and Capablanca; *3rd–5th*, Euwe, Fine and Reshevsky; *6th*, Alekhine; *7th*, Flohr and Lasker

MATCHES

		Won	Lost	Drew
1889	Bardeleben	2	1	1
1890	Mieses	5	0	3
1890	Bird	7	2	3
1890	Miniati	4	1	0
1890	Englisch	2	0	3
1891	Lee	1	0	5
1892	Bird	5	0	0
1892	Blackburne	6	0	4
1893	Golmayo	2	0	1
1893	Vasquez	3	0	0
1893	Showalter	6	2	2
1893	Ettlinger	5	0	0
1894	Steinitz	10	5	4
1896	Steinitz	10	2	5
1903	Tchigorin	1	2	3
1907	Marshall	8	0	7
1908	Tarrasch	8	3	5
1909	Speyer	2	0	1
1909	Janowski	2	2	0
1909	Janowski	7	1	2
1910	Schlechter	1	1	8
1910	Janowski	8	0	3
1916	Tarrasch	5	0	1
1921	Capablanca	0	4	10

FOREWORD

Emanuel Lasker was undoubtedly one of the most interesting people I came to know in my later life. We owe a debt of gratitude to those who have troubled to acquaint contemporary and future generations with his life-story. For few indeed can have combined such a unique independence of personality with so eager an interest in all the great problems of mankind.

I am no chess player myself, so I am not in a position to admire his mental powers in the sphere of his greatest intellectual achievements; indeed I have to confess that I have always disliked the fierce competitive spirit embodied in that highly intellectual game.

I met Emanuel Lasker in the house of my old friend Alexander Moszkowski, and I came to know him well during the many walks we took together, discussing ideas on a variety of subjects. It was a somewhat unilateral discussion in which, almost invariably, I was in the position of listener for it seemed to be the natural thing for this eminently creative man to generate his own ideas rather than adjust himself to those of someone else.

Whenever we met I seemed to detect a somewhat tragic note in his personality, in spite of a fundamentally optimistic inclination always to seek some positive meaning in life. His mind which had that exceptional elasticity characteristic of chess players was imbued with chess to such an extent that he could never quite rid himself of the spirit of the game, even while dealing with philosophical and human problems. Nevertheless, I had the impression that to him chess was a means of livelihood rather than the real object of his life.

What he really yearned for was some scientific understanding and that beauty peculiar to the process of logical creation, a beauty from whose magic spell no one can escape who has ever felt even its slightest influence. Spinoza's material life and economic independence were based on the grinding of lenses; in Lasker's life chess played a similar part. But Spinoza was luckier, for his business was such as to leave his mind free and independent; whereas master-chess grips its exponent, shackling the mind and brain, so that the inner freedom and independence of even the strongest character cannot remain unaffected. This I became aware of whenever I talked to Lasker or read one of his philosophical books. Of these I was most interested in his *Philosophie des Unvollendbar*, a highly original work and very revealing of its author's personality.

Finally, I should like to add a word of explanation as to why I never attempted, either in writing or in conversation, to deal with

Lasker's criticism of the theory of relativity. Since even in this biography, with the emphasis on the man and the chess player rather than the scientist, a slight reproach seems noticeable in the passage mentioning that essay, I had better say a word about it.

Lasker's keen analytical brain had immediately and clearly recognised that the entire problem hinged on the constancy of the velocity of light in empty space. He clearly saw that, once such constancy was admitted, the relativisation of time was unanswerable, whether one liked it or not (and he did not like it at all). What then was to be done? He tried to emulate what Alexander the (so called) 'Great' did when cutting through the Gordian knot.

Lasker's argument could be summarized thus: No one has any direct and immediate knowledge about the velocity of light in absolutely empty space; for even interstellar space contains a certain if infinitesimal quantity of matter, and this applies even more to space from which the air has been pumped by imperfect human agencies. Who then can presume to deny that the velocity of light in absolutely empty space would be infinite?

That is the gist of Lasker's argument, and it could be answered in this way: True enough, no one can tell from any direct and experimental knowledge precisely how light would move in absolutely empty space. But it is virtually impossible to think of any reasonable theory of light based on the notion that infinitesimal traces of matter, while influencing the velocity of light to a remarkable extent, would yet remain almost independent of the density of such matter.

Pending the proposition of such a theory, which, incidentally, would have to accord with well known optical phenomena in *almost* empty space, any physicist must consider this particular Gordian knot to be still unravelled and unravellable, unless he is content with the existing extent of the unravelling. And the moral? A keen brain and a powerful mind is no substitute for the deft touch of nimble fingers. However, I rather liked Lasker's stubborn intellectual independence, a most rare quality in a generation whose intellectuals are almost invariably mere camp-followers. And so I let the matter rest.

I am glad that the readers of this sympathetic biography will get to know a man who was so strong a personality and yet so sensitive and lovable a person. As for myself, I shall remember with gratitude the pleasing conversations I enjoyed with that incessantly eager, truly independent and yet most modest of men.

Princeton, N.J., October 1952   ALBERT EINSTEIN

CHAPTER ONE

Childhood in the Backwoods

Chess, a hobby, a mere pastime may well have the poisonously inspiring effect of a drug; it may well be as intoxicating as wine, a thoroughly enchanting vice; but surely—we may well ask—it cannot be worth a great man's while to devote his life to it! After all, it is merely a game, and while its heroes may well claim such fame among their devotees as Tilden and Dempsey did in the realms of tennis and boxing, surely there can be no cause to write the life of a chess master, however great his prowess! What on earth can be the meaning of such a life to any wider public? And was not Diderot right to say: 'It is quite possible for a wise man to be a great chess player, but it is equally possible for a great chess player to be a fool'?

Such doubts are thoroughly justified. To describe the life of one of the heroes of the chessboard, to write the *Don Quixotiade* of a chess-crusader may be quite interesting, if may be fascinating for the devotees of the game, but it could hardly be important enough to command the attention of a wider public. As for the man Lasker, what is so remarkable about him is hardly the fact that he is reputed to have been the greatest chess player of all time. The remarkable thing is that all his life he has been striving desperately to get away from chess, towards his very own conception of *ultima ratio*. Chess to him merely meant a means of livelihood, a potboiler; and yet, it exercised a spell over him, of which he could never rid himself while using it as a mere point of departure for far wider fields and far greater adventures of the mind.

Lasker was chess player, philosopher, mathematician, poet; he wrote a good many books (least of all on chess); he knocked about the world a good deal, seeing many people, many lands, and a bewildering change of epochs; and his long and restless life—two years beyond the biblical span of three score and ten—was full of struggle, full of love and spite, full of triumph and disappointment, full of achievement and spleen, and crammed full with adventures of the spirit.

He was for ever striving to get away from chess, and for ever destined to return to it. Chess was Emanuel Lasker's greatness and triumph no less than his inner humiliation and tragedy. All his life he was loath to be restricted to thinking in terms of thirty-two wooden symbols, and yet he was obsessed by them. His was the life of a fighter, but his most exciting struggles were fought far away from those sixty-four squares on which he was hailed as invincible; they were fought in that wider realm of metaphysics in which there can be no victory but only doubt and the agonising bliss of doubting one's own doubts.

* * *

It was from almost ludicrously humble circumstances that Emanuel Lasker was called upon to rise towards his destiny. Everybody, of course, has heard of Berlin. But Berlinchen? What on earth can be the meaning of that funny diminutive for Germany's capital city? Could it be a district, or, may be, a particularly small suburb of Berlin? No, it is much less and very much smaller, it is a humble little township some four or five train-hours from Berlin, in the wilds of the province of Brandenburg. It never had more than seven thousand inhabitants. It is surrounded by woods which provide some timber-trade, and its main attractions are a rather pretty lake and some quaint old cottages. In the Thirty Years War Berlinchen was razed to the ground, but it was built up again. In 1811 Napoleon passed through. That is about all that might be noteworthy about Emanuel Lasker's home town.

At all times and through all the vagaries of history it was borderland with a considerable conflux of Germans, Poles, Balts, Russians, Jews. The Jewish community was relatively large, and while the social upper-crust of the town consisted of the higher civil servants, the notary, the doctor, the chemist, and a few timber-merchants; while the solid German middle-class was made up by the minor officials, the small-time farmers and the shopkeepers, it was left to the Jews to look after the shabbier by-products of the town's economic life, such as the pawnshop, smalltime business, hawking, agenting. At best it yielded them a poor living, and even the poorest of them, unlike their sedentary German fellow-citizens, would longingly cast their minds beyond the narrow confines of the town.

Nothing, indeed, could be more significant than the location of the churchyard and the Jewish cemetery. The church right in the centre of the town, its neat spire towering over that cluster of tidily tiled houses like a big hen anxiously keeping her chicks under her wing lest any of them be tempted to stray abroad; and the Jewish cemetery right on top of the hill overlooking that pretty lake and giving a view far beyond the confines of the town, as far indeed as the eye could see.

Young Emanuel's eyes could see far enough, but his mind could see even further when he climbed up to where the dead were laid to rest and whence one could look out towards the great big world beyond his town, where great adventure and fame might be won. Had not his own grandfather been a famous man? He was the Rabbi of Lessen, a small town near the Russian border; but he wasn't just an ordinary Rabbi, he was a *Wunder-Rabbi* whose prophetic gifts were highly honoured by Jews many miles beyond his humble town. Nor indeed was it the town of his ancestors; they had come from a small place called Lask, and that was evidently where the family name was derived from.

The Rabbi's eldest son Adolf had gone to Talmud-School, and having been duly appointed cantor at the small synagogue of Berlinchen he had taken as his wife pretty young Rosalie Israel-sohn, who also came from a cantor's family in nearby Soldin. They had two boys and two girls, Berthold being the firstborn and Emanuel the youngest. In between came their sisters Theophila and Amalia. Emanuel was born on 24 December 1868, on the very eve of the Bismarck epoch in Germany's history, an epoch of rapid industrial and imperialist expansion. We have yet to see how Lasker's life was to be influenced by the growth of that epoch (and its aftermath), but meanwhile we can still watch young Emanuel in his quaint little home-town and in the relative security of a family life which, in spite of dire poverty and many privations, was by no means unhappy.

Father Adolf barely earned enough to feed his family, but the trouble was that he was too kindhearted and never able to say 'no' to the *schnorrers* who would line his path on pay-day before he had put his salary in Rosalie's capable hands. One early morning one of them knocked at his door and asked for a pair of shoes. 'Look under the bed', said the cantor drowsily and went to sleep again. When he got up to dress he found two left shoes only. He had to go to synagogue in slippers. He always was a bit of a dreamer and but for Rosalie's common sense and thrift his family may well have been even hungrier than they were.

Berthold was eight years older than Emanuel and, naturally, his protector and mentor as they roamed through the woods and around the lake. Berthold was the more sensitive of the two whilst Emanuel, at a surprisingly early age, proved to be a realist and a fighter. One early childhood experience may have influenced him profoundly. When he was about five years old he was considerably overawed by a woman next door who would bang away all day long, screaming invective at everybody and everything and on the slightest provocation (or without any provocation at all). Young Emanuel used to think of her as a living *donnerwetter* (thunderstorm) and he observed her with a mixture of fear and admiration. One day they had an unusually severe thunderstorm. The rain came pelting down in torrents, streaks of lightning flashed all over the darkening sky, and the claps of thunder sounded more menacing than ever. Still, young Emanuel wasn't afraid, or not much anyhow, for his long forest-walks with big brother Berthold had accustomed him to the changing moods of nature. But all of a sudden, the woman from next door came running in. She wasn't, this time, screaming like a demon, she was sobbing like a child; she wasn't shaking her fist at anybody, she was trembling like a leaf as she buried her head in Mamma Rosalie's lap.

For young Emanuel this was a revelation. 'What!' he piped: 'You, the *donnerwetter* are afraid of a *donnerwetter!?*'

It was his first experience in debunking or, for whoever prefers to have it put that way, his first lesson in relativity.

It was grandfather Israelsohn he had to thank for a less melo-dramatic but none the less impressive and lasting lesson in relativity. One day, little Emanuel felt he hadn't had enough sugar for his coffee, and he began to cry. His grandfather made no fuss at all about the child's tantrums. Feigning absentmindedness the shrewd old man took one of the sugar-lumps from the boy's saucer and nibbled off a bit. Emanuel went on complaining, and his grand-father repeated the procedure until it dawned on the future philo-sopher, mathematician and chess master that, if he carried on talking instead of acting there would be less and less sugar rather than any more of it. So he stopped moaning and started to consume what there was of it.

It was certainly a useful object lesson in what was to be his theory of 'machology', his very own philosophy of the struggle of life.

CHAPTER TWO

The Hungry Schoolboy

When Berthold went to the big city of Berlin to study, the happiest part of Emanuel's childhood came to an end. As for Berthold, he had to make a living somehow. His parents were to poor to make him even the most modest allowance, and yet so proud were they of their son's cleverness that it would never have occurred to them that he could go in for anything less than an academic career.

He had to go to grammar school first for matriculation, and then went on to the university to study medicine. He managed to earn a pittance here and there by tutoring and by all manner of odd jobs, but he rarely had enough to eat. Yet, he was an excellent scholar, much admired by his 'landlord', a poor East-end tailor who had numerous children of his own, usually too hungry to bother about any kind of learning. Whenever Berthold brought home one of his model reports it was a black day for the tailor's family, for he would spank one after the other of his offsprings, shouting to each of them in turn: 'Such a brain you should have, you *chammer*, such a brain as Berthold's!'

Indeed there was nothing wrong with Berthold's brain, but his stomach left much to be desired. It was therefore a lucky break for the hungry young student to learn that two old ladies had opened a tea-room and were looking for someone to teach chess and certain card games. Berthold's prowess at both chess and *skat* was not inconsiderable, and he did quite well in the tea-room, making as much as a mark or two in a few hours.

He felt immensely rich and on the threshold of even greater affluence, and he wrote home about his stroke of luck. He may have exaggerated a little, and he was somewhat vague about the precarious source of his earnings, but his letter certainly served to make the parents even prouder of their clever son; and presently, *tout* Berlinchen—or at any rate its Jewish community—was gossiping about young Berthold up in Berlin being practically a millionaire.

In such pleasing circumstances nothing could have seemed more natural than to pack off young Emanuel, now eleven years old, to go to school in the big city. Surely, his rich brother would take good care of him and see to it that he too was safely set on the high-road to wisdom and success. Father Adolf, as gullible as ever, was quite exuberant about the prospects, and almost angry when mother Rosalie ventured to voice some misgivings.

'Who is to look after the little boy in the big city?'

'Who is to look after him? Why, Berthold of course! Who else should look after him but his own brother?'

'And who is to cook?'

'Cook? Cook!' Father Adolf was quite indignant about so typically female a question. 'My dear Rosalie', he said, 'it may be important to eat; but it is far more important to learn!'

So it came to pass that Emanuel, aged all of 11, left his native Berlinchen to go to Berlin. For Berthold it meant quite a shock and a staggering responsibility. Yet, he was happy to have little Emanuel around, so happy indeed that in the first flush of excitement he forgot all about making the proper application for his brother's test in school. When he took him there it appeared that no more applications were acceptable that term. Emanuel cried bitterly, but Berthold got very busy and discovered a school where the tests for the forthcoming term were still open to application.

Moreover, Emanuel was particularly lucky in his test. They happened to give him the very 'sums' he had been swotting up the day before, and of course he passed with ease. But he could well have done without that stroke of luck, for his mathematical talent had been evident even in early childhood. At the age of five he had greatly astonished Herr Ludwig, the head of the local school, by doing multiplications such as 7×53 or 18×96 in his head. When the doubting teacher suggested that the child had been specially coached, young Emanuel protested vehemently and demanded to be asked 'something more difficult'. He was asked, and he coped just as promptly, thereby achieving some local fame before he was old enough to go to school. A few years later his teacher Fräulein Ludwig (the head's daughter) would say that Emanuel was far and away the best pupil they ever had in Berlinchen.

And now, in the big city of Berlin, he did equally well, his entry test being so brilliant that he was put two classes above his age-group. He was blissfully happy; but alas, he went down with measles, was more than usually feverish, and had to go to hospital.

Young Emanuel was pining for school and unhappy to be kept away from it in the idleness of a sickbed. Yet, it so happened that here was the point of departure for the very career that was to make him world-famous. At his wit's end as to how to keep that eager young mind adequately occupied, Berthold thought of teaching the restless patient to play chess. The boy grasped it with just the same avid eagerness he would apply to any mental exercise; he asked for some chess books, devoured them like all his other books, and soon turned out to be a quite proficient chess player for his age. But there was nothing extraordinary about it; he certainly wasn't a prodigy, nor did he take chess very seriously at that time; it was merely a hobby and a stimulating pastime. His real ambition aimed rather higher. The schoolboy Emanuel dreamed of becoming a great mathematician, a philosopher, a physicist, a biologist.

To some extent the dream was to come true, but not without some detours forced upon him by grim necessity and the hard facts of the struggle to keep alive. When a boy has one pair of boots only which badly need soling and when no money is available for that purpose it is not easy to march along the direct route to one's dreamland. Without boots one cannot march, one can only sit at home until the brother, teaching chess and playing *skat* in the old ladies' tea-room, has earned enough pfennigs to collect the boots from the cobbler and to bring home a bit of food too. Such experience, frequently repeated, may have been enough to make a boy bitter; but it would make him tough too, not easily cowed by anybody or any argument.

In the long run the wretched circumstances of the two boys could not be kept from their naively guillible parents. When Rosalie learned that Berthold's alleged affluence was mainly based on gambling in a tea-room and that little Emanuel was also knocking about there, so as to scrounge a snack from time to time, she resolutely decided on a radical change. What mattered, she thought, was to separate the boys, so that Berthold would find it less difficult to make ends meet, while Emanuel would be saved from the temptations of the tea-room. Rosalie dug out an elderly acquaintance living miles away from Berthold, and the old woman agreed to give Emanuel board and lodging and to look after him. He had to be changed to another school too, nearer his new abode.

As a matter of fact, the boy's new home wasn't any better than the old one. He wasn't looked after at all nor did he have any more to eat than he used to have; above all, he was pining for his brother and the free and easy life he had got used to. But then he was miles away, almost at the other end of the great city. To go there by tramcar and horse-bus would cost ten or fifteen pfennigs, and who could think of wasting so much money! But, given a few hours, one can walk even a capital city from end to end. So, night after night Emanuel set out on the long journey to the tea-room, to see his brother and to watch the games. All day he passed diligently at school and at his homework, and much of his nightly sleep he gave up for what to him was the romance of his young life: watching the games in the carefree atmosphere of the tea-room.

He met many interesting people there, including an undergraduate by the name of Siegbert Tarrasch who was to be his antagonist for a life-time. But in those days, it was beneath the dignity of a university student and a budding chess master to pay much attention to a wretched little boy who, often enough, would annoy his elders by sinning against the basic rule of *kibitzing:* to watch in silence and, above all, to refrain from voicing personal opinions and suggestions. Young Emanuel's piping voice wasn't easily silenced when he thought he knew best; and as often as not he was right, for his prowess at chess was steadily improving.

To make up for so much hunger, cold and lack of sleep, the boy's will-power must have been quite remarkable; even so, it wasn't a state of things that could last in the long run, and once again a radical change had to be initiated from the parental home. This time Adolf put in a personal appearance to remove his younger son from the dangers of Berlin. He took him to Landsberg, a small town where a friend of the family, one Cohen, was to look after the boy while he went to the local grammar school.

If indeed it was his father's intention to save Emanuel from the temptations of chess that laudable purpose was somewhat thwarted by the fact that Emanuel's favourite teacher at the Landsberg school happened to be a keen chess player. It was the mathematics master, Professor Kevitz, and many years later (when Lasker's fame had spread round the world) the Professor published an interesting report about Emanuel's 'matric' in April 1888, particularly about his prowess at mathematics, all the more remarkable since the mathematical test at the Landsberg school happened to be rather more difficult than anywhere else. Here it is:

'1)   Find the largest cone circumscribed to, and the smallest cone inscribed in, a given sphere,

2)   Find the common tangents to an ellipse and the concentric hyperbola with the same lengths of the axes.

3)   Construct a triangle, and calculate its sides and angles trigonometrically, if the side $c = 273$, the perpendicular on it $h^4 = 156$ and the difference of the two remaining sides $a - b = 91$ are given.

4)   Find the partial fractions of

$$\frac{7x^2 + 7x - 176}{x^3 - 9x^2 + 6x + 56} \text{ and } \frac{5x^3 - 11x + 5x + 4}{(x - 1)^4}$$

Prof. Kevitz reports that almost all the boys (most of them aged eighteen or nineteen) fully needed the five hours allotted for this task—all except young Lasker who made a perfect job of it within a couple of hours. The Professor says he was amazed, and so as to keep the boy occupied for the remaining three hours he gave him an even tougher nut to crack: this one:

If a tangent is drawn to a circle, and if secants are drawn from the endpoint of the diameter perpendicular to the tangent, and if the lengths of the chords of the circle are cut off on these secants backwards from the point of intersection with the tangent then the locus of all the points so obtained is a curve which is called the 'cissoid of Diocles'. This curve enables us to solve geometrically cubic equations in the reduced form $x^3 + px = q$.

Find the equation of the curve.

Describe the shape of the curve.

Explain the significance of the tangent to the circle for the curve.

Find the ratio of the area between the curve and the tangent to the area of the circle.

Find the length of arc of the curve inside the circle.

If the cissoid is rotated about the diameter of the circle, a solid of revolution is obtained whose volume and surface area tend to infinity. Calculate its volume and surface area between the limits $x=q$ and $x=r$.

If the cissoid is rotated about its asymptote, show that the volume of the solid of revolution so obtained is finite, although its vertex is at an infinite distance.

Determine the centres of gravity of these two solids of revolution and also the area bounded by the two branches of the curve and its asymptote.'

Here is the Professor's comment and the rest of his report:

'Incredible as it seemed, Lasker coped with this one too. I might add that he shone in arithmetics rather than geometry. His drawing was shoddy, but his combinative powers were uncommonly developed.'

Now, as for chess, it so happened I was the President of the Landsberg Chess Club and also the Club Champion. Lasker would have loved to join the Club, but being a schoolboy he could not be admitted.

"Won't you play me a game, sir?" he would say more than once, but I had to tell him: "My dear Lasker, business before pleasure! You have to do your homework first, and not in maths only!"

He wasn't used to discipline, and he worked haphazardly; sometimes not at all, and then again for nights on end. He evidently felt cramped by rules and regulations and I frequently had to intercede for him when he got into trouble with one of the other masters.

It was when we went for the usual annual summer outing that he approached me again with the request for a game, adding eagerly that he had brought a pocket-set along, i.e. a small card-board with slits to hold the chessmen. This time I readily agreed, and we started to play, as we were hiking through a wood, with the small board constantly changing hands. As the first game proceeded I soon saw that I was doomed, and in the second game I was determined not to under-rate my young opponent. But I lost that one too, and after lunch I lost a third and a fourth game. Thereupon I offered the young man my best wishes for his future victories. I recommended Bilguer's *Handbuch*([1]) for further study, and I warned him not to spend too much time on chess and never to forget that, once he got to the University, his mathematical studies must command his main attention. Maybe he would have lived up to such good advice had he not been forced by economic needs to use chess as a means of livelihood. I said 'maybe', for even then I could detect in him an ambitious streak, and indeed one of public ambition . . . .'

How right he was, the kindly if somewhat pedantic old schoolmaster, how well he knew his pupil! Lasker certainly did not want to become a chess master. His 'public ambition' aimed at altogether different targets, but his social and economic circumstances forced him to go the way he went.

Lasker had been looking forward impatiently to the end of his Landsberg 'exile', and as soon as he had passed his exam, he went back to Berlin, back to the familiar atmosphere of the tea-room where he would spend half the night to earn a few coins at the chess board or card table.

Lasker wanted to study philosophy and mathematics, and his young and eager mind was bent on tackling the great unsolved riddles of the Universe. As for chess and card games they were merely a handy means of making just enough for rent and food, for college fees and books. He deeply resented and bitterly hated the way he had to make his living, but he knew no other. It wasn't a passionate desire for the game that made him a chess master, it was bitter need and harsh economic necessity: and while he gained world-wide fame by playing chess, he rather resented it and he grudged the time it cost him.

([1]) P. R. v. Bilguer (v. d. Lasa): *Handbuch des Schachspiels*, for well over a century the standard work of German chess literature. It may be assumed, though, that young Emanuel was well aware of it even before the Professor's recommendation.

In those early days he felt deeply humiliated by looking so down-at-heel and shabby. There were times when Berthold and he were unable to go out together because they had only one pair of trousers between them; and since both of them earned some of their money by tutoring schoolboys, such lessons involved intricate problems of timing until another pair of trousers could be purchased.

One of Emanuel's benefactors in those days was Jacob Bamberger who gave him ten marks a month: half a sovereign, a princely sum in Lasker's circumstances. But neither donor nor beneficiary could have imagined their closer links twenty years later, when Lasker was to marry Bamberger's daughter.

Fortunately, Berthold by now was near the end of his studies. He soon became a highly renowned doctor and scientist and his new treatment of thrombosis caused quite a stir in the medical profession. (Much later in life he married Else Lasker-Schüler the poetess who has an imperishable niche in German literature).

As for Adolf, naturally he gloried in the success of his clever sons, both of them soon to become quite famous; and it is significant of that family's amazing thirst for knowledge that the old man, well in his sixties, took up the study of Latin and Greek with youthful zest.

As for the sisters, Theophila was highly sensitive, a dreamer mitigated by a strong sense of humour. She married and bore five children, three of whom survive, each in a different continent. When the Nazis came to power she found sanctuary with a friend of Emanuel's in Holland. She was eighty years old when taken to the gas-chambers of Auschwitz or Maidanek, (no one will ever know where).

Amalia, the younger sister was a woman of the world, strong willed and not without some influence on her brother Emanuel in his earlier years. She too married and had five children. In later life she was an indispensable helpmate in brother Berthold's clinic. She died in 1939.

CHAPTER THREE

The Lure of Professional Chess

But in the late eighties it was still a far cry to Berthold having a professorship and a clinic of his own and to Emanuel being world famous and rid of material worries.

He had finished grammar school, to be sure, and he had entered the university, but in his School of Life he was still having a hard time in one of the lower forms. He was sick and tired of spending hours in the tea-room to earn some miserable pittance; and he was duly impressed when someone told him that the great Café Kaiserhof was about to stage its annual chess tournament, open to all comers and renowned for its fairly generous prizes.

Young Lasker plucked up courage and entered the pompously furnished and brilliantly lit Café, its huge mirrors cruelly reflecting the contrast of his own shoddy clothes and the elegance and comfort of carefree Berliners and tourists sipping their coffee and chocolate and munching huge cakes with lashings of whipped cream.

Shyly he slouched through this unaccustomed atmosphere of palatial luxury, and diffidently approached the door of the large room reserved for the Chess Fraternity. And lo and behold: here he found people looking just as shabby and starved as he was; but they seemed to be quite unaware of their sartorial shortcomings and pinched faces; they were, all of them, completely absorbed by those thirty-two pieces of wood cunningly aligned on sixty-four squares.

Forthwith, young Lasker felt at home and at ease, felt happy and secure in having something in common with all these people in that large and smoky room: their common knowledge about those sixty-four squares, their common ambition in guiding those thirty-two pieces. He felt the bliss and power of solidarity, and he learned that even the Pariahs of Life can achieve something by collective effort.

Another revelation was in store for him: he was surprised to realise that he had come to be a very strong chessplayer. He had never taken the game seriously enough to bother about his own standing, but now it appeared that no one in that tournament was his equal; no one even managed to draw against him; he won every single game. No one had ever won that annual event at the Café quite so convincingly.

Best of all, there was quite a generous prize, enough to appease the constant rumbling of Emanuel's stomach for a week or two. But then what? Back again to the old grind, back to the constant worries of how to provide for the most primitive needs. It was all very well sitting in one's quiet little attic, surrounded by books and wrestling with serene philosophical and mathematical problems; but it was hard going on an empty stomach.

Once again the temptation of a chess tournament approached him, one much bigger and more important than the amateurish event in the Café Kaiserhof. Someone told Emanuel that there was such a thing as the German Chess Federation, a huge and nation-wide organisation which, once every other year, organised quite a string of tournaments in some big city. It was in Berlin in 1881, in Nuremberg in 1883, in Hamburg in 1885, in Frankfurt in 1887, and this time it was to be in Breslau. Siegbert Tarrasch, who used to be an *habitué* at the old ladies' tea-room, was going, and surely, after his sensational success in the Kaiserhof tournament, young Lasker could be sure of an invitation as well.

Emanuel yielded to the temptation; and deep down in his heart he knew that if he was successful—and he would be successful—it meant chess as a profession; it meant goodbye to the university and to philosophy and to mathematics; for quite some time at any rate. But had he any other choice? He could not see one. Emanuel went to Breslau. Lasker's star was about to rise on a firmament studded with chess celebrities. Emanuel Lasker was set on his peculiar way of life.

Those who have never seen a chess tournament—and most people haven't—may have a very wrong conception of it. It is certainly nothing like some big football match or tennis tournament where every minute, every second may bring some sensational development breathlessly watched by an excited crowd. When reading a newspaper report about some particularly sensational chess event it may seem to be very much like it, but it isn't.

Whoever first enters a tournament hall will be disappointed by the paucity of the onlookers. But then, the vast majority of devotees —and there are far more of them than any 'Cup Final' crowd— will wait for the game to be published in their Sunday paper or chess magazine, quietly to play it over at their own fireside. Those who go to watch the actual game will be attending rather than watching, the simple reason being that, once one has seen the masters brooding over their boards, there is nothing much to watch: not, at any rate, until another move is made. And that may take quite a while, and one might as well watch it on the big wall-board next door where one can carry on a conversation in more than a whisper.

Watching the masters actually make their moves is like standing in a cave waiting for a stalactite to drop. There may be one every ten or twenty minutes, and then there is solemn silence again, and we can imagine we are listening to the heartbeat of eternity while feeling slightly embarrassed and irritated by the apparently inactive and uneventful passage of time.

Of course, it is far from being inactive and uneventful. Just as the lime in the cave takes its ten or twenty minutes for the next stalactite, atom by atom, to grow and fatten until it is ready to drop, so the next move is being generated cell by cell in the master's brain until it is ready to be made.

It is an uncanny and rather awkward thing to watch, and it makes us uncomfortable to feel the loneliness of the thinking brain, its splendid and total isolation from the rest of the world, indeed from everything except the evolution of certain ideas on the board and the silent passage of time.

Not so silent either; for this lapse of time is registered by a very special device called a 'chess-clock'; in point of fact, two clocks linked in a case. Having made his move the player presses a button at his end of the double-clock, thereby causing his clock to stop and the other one to start. When the opponent has made his move he reverses the procedure by pressing the button at his end, thereby causing time to stand still for himself while for the opponent it ticks on audibly enough.

It is this constant ticking that acts as a spur no less than as additional labour-pains in the birth of ideas. Incessantly and inexorably the ticking warns: Act! Act quickly! Come to a decision! For if you overstep your time limit by as much as a second([1]) you forfeit your game, however good your position. Hence, while the brain functions as a brake for hasty action the clock acts as a spur for activity; and when adding the positional and combinative deliberations demanded by the actual position on the board, we can well imagine the turmoil of conflicting thoughts and emotions raging in the players' minds, even though we onlookers see nothing but two men deep in thought and taking a long time to get a move on: a good enough reason for the difficulties of making a chess tournament a spectacle sufficiently attractive for mass audiences. (The only exception to the rule — as we shall see — seems to be Russia).

([1]) In modern international tournaments the usual time limit is $2\frac{1}{2}$ hours for the first forty moves and one hour each for successive sixteen moves.

Naturally it is the very fact of a game of chess being so 'unspectacular' which causes the difficulties of financing such a 'spectacle'. To stress the point Lasker liked to tell a story concerning a chess player's pretty young wife who had come along with her husband to watch a tournament. She was intrigued by one of the masters being particularly deep in thought and taking an uncommonly long time over his move. The young lady was fascinated by so much concentration and she patiently persevered at that particular board; she seemed to think that something gigantic must result from so much thought. When half an hour had passed and the master still sat brooding over the board the lady was almost trembling with the sort of thrill she would feel watching a particularly exciting rally in the finals at Wimbledon. At long last the master stirred from his reverie, and as he slowly lifted his hand the lady's glance followed it in feverish excitement. What he did was to move a pawn one step forward. It was an excellent move which while seeming to involve certain risks (each of them tractable) would secure a small but decisive advantage many moves later. But the lady was bitterly disappointed and complained to her husband: 'Forty minutes he took, thinking and thinking! And all for such a tiny move! Why, this *must* be a crazy game!' She turned her pretty back and never went near another chess tournament.

It is this lack of appeal to the more primitive spectator that makes chess tournaments an inevitably poor proposition in a commercialised age. Let us, then, glance at the epoch in which Lasker rose to fame.

It was the age of Wilhelm II, the end of the Victorian era, a time in which the type of modern *conquistador* was predominant, men such as Cecil Rhodes, Leopold of Belgium, Rockefeller and a new generation of industrial magnates. What mattered was colonial enterprise and the acquisition of more and more rubber, silvermines, iron ore and steel, more and better electrification and combustion engines. Huge undeveloped areas were 'civilised' more quickly and efficiently than Columbus and Vasco da Gama could ever dream of.

The result was an enormous agglomeration of wealth and a substantial feeling of security. Never had mankind been as 'pacifistic' as in the couple of decades round about the turn of the century. True enough, there were rows about colonial possessions, a mailed fist vied with invincible dreadnoughts, there was a good deal of espionage and commercial jealousy, there was a spot of war in China, in South Africa, in the Philippines. But in Western Europe and the USA it merely added to the spice of life and to the satisfaction of being wealthy and getting more so every year.

Some crumbs from that very rich table inevitably came to the chess masters too; not many crumbs, to be sure, nor very fat ones, but just enough for a number of masters to make some sort of a living. To be a chess master had become a profession like being an actor, a singer, a trapeze-artist; but it was rather more precarious. Many came and were gone with the wind, but a few reached the pinnacle and stayed up for quite some time.

A good many of the international tournaments were sponsored by famous watering resorts which would gain ample publicity value for the relatively small financial outlay involved. But in most of the other tournaments organised by National Federations the financial basis was a more or less modest collection of funds from clubs and individuals. At best it would provide enough to pay for the expenses of the competing masters and to send the six or eight prize-winners away with enough to live on for periods ranging from a few weeks to several months.

Anyway, by then (so long as they were successful) they could safely rely on being invited to some other tournament; and in between tournaments there were other ways for a successful and industrious chess master to make a living. He could give 'simultaneous' performances, playing twenty or thirty (or rather more) games by hustling from board to board and making his moves at a moment's notice—a gruelling job of many hours' work. Moreover, if so inclined (and trained) he could give 'blindfold' performances, playing a number of opponents who would have plenty of time to study the position on the board while the performing master, sitting in splendid isolation and deepest concentration, must memorize all the games and call out his own moves as soon as the opponent's move had been announced.

If booked for a regular tour of such performances the master could earn a few fees, get a little publicity, and sell some of his books. But it was a hard life. It meant getting around a bit too; but the trouble with most chess masters is that they get little change out of all their travels. No matter whether they happen to be in Sweden or in some Mediterranean resort, in South America or in Moscow, they rarely see more than a large room filled with chess-boards, and for most of them life has little meaning beyond the infinite adventures of those thirty-two wooden symbols moving about their sixty-four squares.

One may well ask: why all these exertions, why all this trouble and heartbreak for a mere game? Why, if at best its leading protagonists can wrest from it a modest and precarious livelihood? Why indeed? But then, why do men risk their lives to climb a mountain; why do they kill one another for some religious or political idea; why do they commit suicide, murder or other inexplicable follies when touched, moved, and driven by that finest and most inexplicable of human emotions: love?

The answer is that life *is* irrational, life is inconsequential, contradictory, impenetrable and unfathomable. It is risky too, and only he who dares to tackle life can 'play for a win', to use a term of the chess player's own vernacular. He mustn't be afraid, though, to move around the quagmire of irrationalism. He who will have nought but cool sobriety and common sense may well have a long life, but it might be a pretty dull one. As for the chess master, let us praise him for his courage to live for a mere dream, a Queen's sacrifice, a mate in three moves.

Readers may now have an inkling of how and why it was so decisive a crossroad in Emanuel Lasker's life when he failed to resist the temptation of going to Breslau in the summer of 1889 to compete in the congress organised by the German Chess Federation. Apart from minor tournaments for various groups of amateurs there was one for recognised masters and one for those aspiring to such honour. The winner of that tournament would be awarded the official title *Deutscher Schachmeister*, a dignity achieved by Siegbert Tarrasch in the preceding congress, a couple of years earlier. Hence, at Breslau, he played in the master-tournament, while young Lasker, a newcomer to the congress, had to earn his spurs in the aspirants' tourney.

Lasker did earn them. He won the tournament, but only by the narrowest margin possible. And, indeed, by a fluke entirely outside his own control. Thereby hangs a tale, and since it happens to be very odd and never yet published in its entirety (not even in the original edition of this book); and since it certainly made or helped to make chess history, it may as well be given some space here.

That particular *Hauptturnier* (meaning the 'candidate's tournament', the victor of which would obtain the 'Master' title conferred by the German Federation) was a specially strong one, the competitors, apart from young Lasker, including Lipke, who later became quite a well-known Master, as well as another highly gifted player called von Feyerfeil. As a matter of fact, Feyerfeil beat Lasker in their individual game, and since Lasker dropped another point (against a rank outsider) he was very lucky to come out equal with von Feyerfeil who had lost only one game (to Lipke) and drawn two others.

Now the odd thing was that Feyerfeil should never have lost that game. What happened was that when he and Lipke put up the position after the adjournment, they did so from memory-without bothering to play through the whole game, and it so happen, ed that they forgot to put up Feyerfeil's RP, with the result that his first move after the adjournment was an illegal one. In point of fact he moved his R to where his P was supposed to be.(*)

Now, according to the rules, as soon as the mistake was discovered and claimed, all the moves played after the adjournment should have been considered illegal and a replay would have had to be ordered by the tournament director. But as it happened, the mistake was not claimed while the game was still on, and it only came to be mentioned long after the end of the tournament. What happened was that poor Feyerfeil, who should have drawn the game with ease, lost it after a gruelling battle of over a hundred moves.

Now, so far as chess history is concerned, the intriguing if some-what speculative point is this that a proper outcome of that odd game may well have finished Lasker's chess career before it ever began. Of course, if Feyerfeil had drawn that game he would have been half a point ahead of Lasker, and the undisputed winner of the tournament. And it may well be that Lasker, had he failed to achieve the Master title at that first attempt, would have given up chess altogether. In fact, he had repeatedly told his brother Berthold that he would do so.

Hence, the odd and somewhat fishy circumstances of that Feyerfeil-Lipke game may well have turned out to be one of the greatest blessings in disguise for chess history and chess literature. Since Feyerfeil lost the game, he was level with Lasker; they had to 'play off' and Lasker won the decisive game quite convincingly,(†)

(*) *Translator's note:* Here is the adjourned position of that crucial game. According to the official report of the tournament committee (dug out by J. Gilchrist & K. Whyld for their complete score of Lasker's games), White's illegal 53rd move was R–KR2.

(†) *Translator's note:* Since this game, having never been published except in the records of the Breslau Congress, is practically unknown and yet of some historical significance, as it were, I have included it in the Games Section of this book. See GAME 3a, page 41.

thereby winning the title which enabled him to compete in master tournaments.

In the concurrant principal event of the congress, the International Master-Tournament, young Tarrasch was equally successful. Out of seventeen games he scored thirteen points, well ahead of quite a bevy of famous masters, such as Burn, Mieses, von Bardeleben, Bauer, Gunsberg, Paulsen, Blackburne, Mason. Thus, the young undergraduate and the small boy who had met in the old tea-room had made some headway. Tarrasch had emerged as one of the top-ranking masters of Europe, but Lasker had only just earned the title; he had merely put his foot on the bottom-rung of the ladder while Tarrasch was already very near the top. Lasker was at the start of his climb; but even at that early stage Samuel Hoffer, Chess Editor of *The Field*, England's most important chess column, had this to say about him: 'Herr Lasker, a rising player from Berlin shows considerable talent for the game and will probably be the future master.'

For the time being, though, Hoffer's prophecy still seemed far from being vindicated. Immediately after the Breslau Congress the young *Meister* was honoured by an invitation to compete in a small International master-tournament at Amsterdam. For the first time in his life Lasker crossed the German border and got the thrill and experience of being abroad in a foreign land. In the tournament he won the brilliancy prize for his stunning sacrifice of both bishops against J. H. Bauer, (see p. 37), one of the gems of chess literature which was to be reprinted over and over again in almost every anthology of such master-strokes. But he lost the decisive game against the British master Burn who had been runner-up to Tarrasch in the Breslau tournament and who went ahead to win the Amsterdam event with seven points out of eight games. Lasker scored only six points and had to be content with the second prize. Certainly a gratifying success for one so young, but nothing very sensational.

Back in Berlin, Lasker soon gave a few simultaneous performances, and then played a short match against C. von Bardeleben who had come fourth at Breslau and who, at that time, was considered one of the 'aces' of the Berlin chess fraternity. Lasker won two games, lost one and drew one; certainly a remarkable success, though again not exactly magnificent. Nor was he to fare any better when, early in 1890, he went to compete in a small Austrian tournament at Graz. True, he didn't lose a game, but his three wins and three draws only sufficed for third prize, Makovetz and Bauer (his Amsterdam victim) being ahead of him.

Somewhat depressed Lasker returned to Berlin, and it was a

lucky chance for him that the veteran British master Bird was
prepared to play a match against the budding German master.
Bird himself (and most of the experts) expected that, while it would
be a stiff and fairly even contest, the odds were still on the older
man. Yet Lasker won the match convincingly with seven wins,
two losses, and three draws.

Soon afterwards he played a match against J. Mieses, a highly
renowned master of the younger German generation and the third
prize-winner at the recent Breslau Congress. Lasker won that match
even more convincingly by 5 : 0, with three draws, and now indeed
Sam Hoffer's prophetic words of the year before seemed to be nearer
vindication, as the entire chess world began to keep a watchful eye
on that dangerous young man.

CHAPTER FOUR

Professional in England and America

In London they were planning a World Exhibition, and someone had sensibly decided that so comprehensive a show of human endeavour would not be complete without a Chess Pavilion. Naturally, once that decision was taken the need to offer the public a special attraction was evident and so the manager of the pavilion hit upon the idea of inviting that rising young chess master Emanuel Lasker to London and hiring him as the star attraction of the show.

It wasn't a very exacting task. Lasker's duties included the readiness to play 'all comers', and since most of the visitors were mere 'duffers' it did not require much of an effort on the master's part; it was, indeed, rather dull work. But the pay was good, by the young man's very modest standards it was almost magnificent. There was a constant crowd of male and female admirers and for the first time in his life Emanuel Lasker could enjoy — or, at any rate, experience—the sweets of being the object of hero worship.

Very soon he could save as much as £10 to be sent to his parents at Berlinchen, and presently the news of an enormous cheque from London spread like wildfire. Why, what great good luck! Fancy, Cantor Lasker's Emanuel being a millionaire, and in England too!

In point of fact, he could soon spare another £10, enough to facilitate his parents' move to Berlin where Berthold was now safely established as a doctor: happily, and very proud of their clever sons, the old people were settled in a small flat, conveniently near the elder son's fast growing practice. But as for Emanuel, it would take a long time for them to see more of him than his loyal contributions to their small household. His stay in London dragged on and on. Just like Steinitz thirty years earlier, so Lasker had come to London for what was meant to be a few weeks; and just like Steinitz he stayed on for years.

The young German chess star got plenty of engagements for matches and tournaments, and in every one of them he triumphed. He played a couple of games against the British master Lee, winning one and drawing the other; he beat the Austrian master Englisch in a short match by 2 : 0, with three draws: he gave Bird a return match of five games, winning every one of them. Then came the biggest test of all: J. H. Blackburne, for many years British Champion, and the battle-tried hero of many a tournament and match; not so long ago, in the great Manchester Tournament of 1890, he had been runner-up to Tarrasch who had come to be regarded as almost invincible: but Blackburne's second prize had left him well ahead of Bird, Mackenzie and quite a cluster of renowned international masters. Surely he would put a stop to young Lasker's uninterrupted run of triumphs in the British Isles!

He didn't. The young man seemed as little overawed by the great Blackburne as by anybody else; out of ten games he won six and drew four. Further successes were to come in the annual tournament of the British Chess Federation and in the subsequent 'Quintangular'. In the B.C.F. tournament Lasker had the fine score of nine points out of eleven games, and in the Quintangular, a double-round affair, Lasker won five and drew three games, well ahead of such formidable opponents as Bird, Blackburne, Gunsberg, Mason. Within the brief span of less than two years Lasker had gone a long way towards challenging the hegemony of Tarrasch in European chess. Possibly Tarrasch was beginning to feel slightly embarrassed by the growing fame of young Lasker; but neither he nor Lasker himself, at that time, could have guessed how soon and how much more deeply the older master would be embarrassed by his competitor, long before they were to meet over the board in a tournament, let alone in the more convincing contest of a match.

As for the next phase in Lasker's life, it is odd that once again he followed in Steinitz's footsteps. Steinitz had come to London in 1862, merely to play in a tournament; he had meant to return to Vienna at once, but he stayed on for twenty years. Then he had moved on to America, again for what was meant to be a brief visit; but once again he stayed for nearly twenty years, very rarely interrupted by visits to Europe. In Lasker's life we have much the same pattern, even if compressed in shorter spans of time, with changes more frequent and more rapid as befitted the faster heart-beat of a more modern age. He too had come to London for a short engagement, but he stayed on for two years; he too went on to America, and stayed there for years rather than the few months originally intended.

In the USA he had an uninterrupted run of successes to confirm and enhance the reputation built up in England. In the New York tournament of 1893 he won all his thirteen games, far ahead of such renowned masters as Albin, Hodges, Showalter and young Pillsbury; in matches he disposed of Golmayo by 2 : 0, with one draw; Vasquez by 3 : 0, Ettlinger by 5 : 0; and finally he beat Showalter, probably the strongest American master of the time, by 6 : 2, with two draws. But results such as these were no longer considered sensational; one had come to expect them from Lasker.

The American Chess Fraternity was delighted. Now they not only had Steinitz in the country, the world champion, the 'grand old man' of chess; they also had that lean young man Lasker who seemed all set for divesting the old man of his crown. And why indeed shouldn't he? Of course, there was Dr. Tarrasch over in Europe. What with Breslau 1889, Manchester 1890, Dresden 1892, he had won three great International Tournaments in a row, and he had proved equally invincible in match-play. But he had never yet dared to challenge Steinitz. On the other hand, Lasker had repeatedly declared his readiness to cross swords with his famous compatriot, but Tarrasch had haughtily declined the challenge, declaring himself utterly unimpressed by Lasker's long string of successes in relatively minor tournaments and matches. 'The young man', he said, 'should first prove his worth by attempting to win one or two major international events; he is not entitled yet to play a match against someone like me!'

Lasker's answer was characteristic: he challenged the world champion, Wilhelm Steinitz. For the first time, at one of the decisive moments of his life, he gave public evidence of his almost infallible instinct to strike at the right time and then to put all his strength and courage into staking everything he had.

To be accepted as a challenger by the world champion and to fight for his crown was high honour indeed, and to be beaten by the world champion would have been nothing to be ashamed of by anybody. Yet, had it happened to the 27-year-old Lasker at the hands of a tired and ailing Steinitz, more than twice his age, it would have been too much to bear, even for one steeled in so hard a school of life as Lasker's. Never content to aim at any but the highest peak it is probable that Lasker, had he lost the match, would have turned his back on chess for ever, seeking fulfilment in what at all times he considered his real spiritual home—the realm of philosophy and mathematics.

It was not to be. He was fated to reach the highest peak of chess at the age of 27, and to stay up there for another twenty-seven years. Even then and up to the end of his days he was never quite to get away from chess, and it was only during interludes that he could return to his true love in the rarified atmosphere of philosophical argument and abstract mathematical thought.

CHAPTER FIVE

Playing the Man or the Board?

When Tarrasch first met Lasker in that little Berlin tea-room he was bound to assume a somewhat patronising air, so far as he deigned to notice him at all. After all, he was six years older, a prosperous undergraduate at the University and a budding master at chess while Lasker was a mere schoolboy.

Tarrasch graduated as a doctor in 1885, set up as a general practicioner in his native Nuremberg, and married a comfortably dowered young lady. Even in his mid-twenties he was very much the man of substance, very respectable and dignified, very much the solid, correct *bourgeois gentilhomme* of his time: a man of order and discipline and thoroughly immune to those hazardous adventures of body and soul that haunted poor Steinitz.

The young doctor had all the virtues of the model German citizen: his diligence, his solidity and his reliability; but he had his faults too: his righteousness and pedantry, his conceit and stubborn dogmatism. He strove to be, and indeed he was, the mentor of an entire generation of chess players: *praeceptor Germaniae* they used to call him, and he rather liked to hear it; indeed, he took it for granted. He was very much the schoolmaster.

Tarrasch's interpretation of chess laid claim to eternal and inviolable validity. He would solemnly pronounce his theses as if they were edicts of a King or a Papal Bull. Yet, a good many of them were disproved, even in his own life-time. Let us open, at random, one of the best of his numerous books, the one about the great St. Petersburg Tournament of 1914, and in the very first game we find this comment: 'A Queen's Gambit with the inferior defence P—QB3.' But it so happened a mere twenty years later that this 'inferior' line, (the 'Slav Defence') was all the rage for years, almost exclusively adopted by both Alekhine and Euwe in the sixty games they played in their two contests for the World Championship.

It was by no means the only one of Tarrasch's peremptory statements to be proved wrong. But then, that was inevitable, it was logically rooted in his character. His theory of chess was meant to be as precise and as infallible as a machine. He looked for the *absolutely* right move, but what he overlooked was that a human being is neither a machine nor infallible. Tarrasch was the typical product of an era so satiated with wealth and self-assurance that it would cheerfully venture to solve all the riddles of the Universe once and for all. That is how Tarrasch set about tidying the dynamic of Steinitz's ideas; that was how he strove to regulate the maelstrom of their dark and dangerous torrents by a meticulous system of locks and dams, thereby giving the world a Steinitz, properly tamed, systematized and, above all, teachable and in much the same apple-pie order as the regulations of German Army drill.

It was a mighty undertaking, and a very meritorious one; for it was certainly Tarrasch who popularized Steinitz and made him digestible for mass consumption. He was his greatest interpreter; it was he who, for many a decade, as author, teacher, commentator, lecturer, and practising master did most to elucidate the mechanics of modern chess. He was certainly the founder and one of the leaders of a school of thought that gave chess a galaxy of great masters, a multitude of talent, and an ever growing record of erudition. But by the same token, Tarrasch barred his own way to the real greatness of doubting one's omnipotence and wrestling with such doubts in one's own soul. He who presumes to know all, he who feels equal to solving his every doubt and problem may well enjoy a comfortable life, eased by self-satisfaction. But the really great men who walk this earth are made of different stuff.

How does Emanuel Lasker fit into the picture? What is so peculiar and unique about *his* achievment as a chessplayer? Why was it greater than Tarrasch's and indeed anybody else's?

True enough, Lasker was world champion, and Tarrasch wasn't; Lasker vanquished old Steinitz, and much later he twice defeated the ageing Tarrasch. But surely, we mustn't assess a person's worth on the strength of material success only; there are many other circumstances to be considered, and in due course we shall get to know them. But there is one thing to be said and considered at once, so as to clarify matters even for those who know little or nothing about chess. It is that Lasker's very own 'Chess Philosophy' did not emerge as ready-made as Pallas Athene stepped forth from the head of Zeus. It took a lifetime to mature, and once he had accomplished it he applied and handled it masterfully up to the end of his days. But even young Lasker whose worldly wisdom was still small and who had yet to live and to learn—even he showed unmistakeable traces of the very notions that were to make him so unique a chess player.

What then were these unique notions? What made him so different from Tarrasch, and indeed from any other master?

One thing certainly both Lasker and Tarrasch had in common: both would be unthinkable without Steinitz. Yet, they went in

diametrically opposing ways. What Tarrasch had in common with
Steinitz was that both were looking for Truth absolute. Yet, while
Steinitz knew only too well that there is no such thing as absolute
truth and that all one can do is to strive for it, while Steinitz
suffered deeply from his awareness of the relativity of all human
knowledge, Tarrasch was the perennial optimist, firmly convinced
of his own permanent security no less than of absolute truth being
well within his reach. To him all his own notions and theories were
invariably and eternally valid.

That is where he differed from Steinitz and very much more so
from Lasker. As for Lasker's own incomparable greatness as a
chess player it rests in the very fact that he went on to carry Steinitz
relativism far beyond the point where the older man had come to a
standstill. Steinitz did look for Chess Absolute, for the absolutely
right move, even though he felt that it could only be found in
Utopia. Lasker did not even bother to look for it; he kept his eyes
open and looked for flesh and blood.

Both Steinitz and Tarrasch were mainly concerned with their own
reasoning, and out of their own brains they endeavoured to approach
their conception of ultimate truth. But it never occurred to them,
or at all events they never seriously considered that in every contest
over the chessboard there is yet another brain, another mind at
work. They never considered their opponent, to them it was utterly
irrelevant whoever happened to sit on the other side of the board.([1])
To Lasker it was vitally important.

Steinitz always *looked* for the objectively right move, Tarrasch
always claimed to have *found* the objectively right move. Lasker did
nothing of the kind. He never bothered about what might or might
not be the objectively right move; all *he* cared for was to find
whatever move was likely to be most embarrassing for the specific
person sitting on the other side of the board. He did not care whether
that move was 'objectively' right or wrong. He thought that there
may well be quite a few 'right' moves, exactly as many indeed as

([1])   Steinitz said so himself in a most significant interview published in the
'British Chess Magazine' of 1894 (p. 366). In the course of giving his opinions on
Morphy he said:

'Another remarkable gift was his intuitive knowledge of human nature.
I think he played the man rather than the board.'

Here Steinitz was interrupted by the interviewer asking him if that did not
apply to every chessplayer. Steinitz answered emphatically:

'Not to me! Certainly not! I am fully and entirely concentrated on the board.
I never even consider my opponent's personality. So far as I am concerned my
opponent might as well be an abstraction or an automaton.'

the number of opponents psychologically differing from one another. Steinitz and Tarrasch played chess in the vacuum of an abstraction, Lasker played the man rather than the board.

Hence, Lasker's unique achievement was his ability to reflect the struggle of life on the chess-board: and since he knew more than his opponents about life and its riddles and contradictions, since he had an infinitely deeper knowledge than most of them about the complexities of the human mind, he reached his dominating position and maintained it even in old age.

Certainly, to play chess as 'psychologically' as Lasker did, required strength of character and the 'super-human' will-power of Nietzsche's Zarathustra. Indeed it meant 'living dangerously', it meant fighting near the abyss rather than on less exacting and far less dangerous well-trodden paths in comfortable lowlands; it meant dragging the opponent through treacherous ravines, on to dizzy peaks, and across uncharted seas. One can easily falter that way; but so can the opponent. Let the better morale, the stronger character win—that was the basic maxim in Lasker's life.

But what about those eminently logical principles established by Steinitz? Does not Lasker's conception of chess—one may well ask—does not such style and tactic revert to the very romanticism brushed away by Steinitz? Did not the romanticists too indulge in eaching out for dizzy heights and taking a glorious gamble on triumph or disaster?

To ask such questions is to misunderstand Emanuel Lasker. For his game rests on the solid foundations of logic and reason as taught by Steinitz, but it rests on more than the mere logic of thirty-two symbols moving around sixty-four squares; it includes in reasoning some deep knowledge of the human mind and all ts vagaries. It is more than mere logic; it is 'Psycho-Logic'.

To be able to think and to act and to play like that, one must needs be a man of the world, one who knows many facets of life, one who has seen (and seen through) all manner of people, one who has knocked about this globe a bit. Lasker, just like Tarrasch, was born in Germany. But while Tarrasch, with all his voyages to tournaments and matches far afield, somehow never got beyond the city boundaries of Nuremberg or Munich and remained a solid German burgher all his life, Lasker really moved about, for ever driven by the insatiable curiosity of the true vagabond, that unquenchable thirst for more knowledge, novel notions, new faces in yet another land. While Tarrasch, a true representative of his time, was a firm believer and guardian of all its values and always upholding and praising them, Lasker represented the other side of the medal, never content

with existing values and always sceptical about them. For Tarrasch
life was static and the existing order inviolable; for Lasker it was
dynamic and for ever in flux.

There is nothing very remarkable about such contrast. At all
times there has been and there must be the Conservative and the
Progressive. It takes both these elements of maintenance and drive
to make a world. As for the world of chess in the twenty years
before World War I, it would be unthinkable without Tarrasch,
the Conservative and Lasker, the Revolutionary. We need them
both to give the picture its proper colour and perspective; and both
of them hailed from the same progenitor—Steinitz.

PREFATORY NOTE ON THE GAMES' SECTIONS

Apart from one or two deletions and two or three addenda, I have
followed the excellent choice of games in the original edition.

With more than 500 recorded games to choose from it seemed
wise to limit the selection to round about 100; and then again not
merely to pick such obvious choices as the master's most celebrated
triumphs, but also some of the lesser known games and certainly
a few of his losses, so far as they happen to be of some special
significance for the personality of our hero or for the circumstances
and the psychological background of the games concerned.

A problem was offered by the annotation no less than the selection
of the games. Considering that many of them were played in the last
century and some of the most important ones as long as forty to
fifty years ago, it seemed tempting to have the games completely
re-annotated in the light of the most modern development of opening
theory. I toyed with the idea, but I am glad I rejected it just as the
author and the original publisher had done before me. I think they
were wise in doing so because, what matters in this book is not to
add just another one to many excellent and up-to-date treatises on
modern opening theory; what mattered in these pages is to bring
the man Emanuel Lasker to life; and so far as his games are concerned, the best course obviously is to look at them in the light
of their origin, to see them as Lasker himself and his opponents
and contemporaries saw them. After all they included some of the
finest annotators of all times.

Only the pick of such contemporary comment (including, often
enough, Lasker's own) was selected, and wherever it happens to
have been disproved by more modern experience and analysis this
was duly noted by Rudolf Teschner. In securing the services of
so erudite and modern a theoretician, the author and the original

publisher struck a very happy balance in making the games' sections sufficiently up-to-date and yet maintaining the background and atmosphere of Lasker's own epoch. Teschner's comments are sparing and to the point, and while using every one of them—they are marked R.T. and italicised—I have ventured, here and there to add some further comment from various modern sources.

Considering that a good many readers, knowing little or nothing about chess, would be mainly interested in Lasker's achievments in other fields and in his fascinating personality, it seemed a plausible idea to separate the games' section from the biographical text. It would be very wrong, though, for whether he liked it or not—and most of the time he didn't like it—his addiction to chess was an integral part of Lasker's personality; and just so the pattern of his chess career, (complete with his frequent escapes from it and his inevitable return), is inextricably interwoven with the growth of that interesting personality, glittering in so numerous and so divers facets.

For a chess player—and after all, many thousands of readers are bound to be chess players—to comprehend the growth of Lasker's fascinating personality he will want to play over his games, and he will want to do it chronologically. Hence, the games selected and the appropriate tournament-tables have been spread all over the book in various sections placed in whichever part of the narrative they happen to belong. H.F.

GAME 1

BIRD'S OPENING

LASKER–BAUER Amsterdam
26 August 1889
International Tournament

1) P—KB4
The only recorded instance of Lasker's adoption of this rarely played opening
1) ..... P—Q4
2) P—K3 Kt—KB3
3) P—QKt3
Not the most precise continuation. 3) Kt—KB3 would have been better, for now Black could play 3) ...P—Q5, completely disorganising his opponent's plan.

3) ..... P—K3
4) B—Kt2 B—K2
5) B—Q3
Clearly revealing his intention of obtaining a K side attack, and doubtless better than B—K2 or P—Kt3 followed by B—Kt2
5) ..... P—QKt3
6) Kt—QB3 B—Kt2
7) Kt—B3 QKt—Q2
8) 0—0 0—0
9) Kt—K2
Reinforcing the projected attack by opening the QB diagonal and bringing the Kt to the other wing
9) ..... P—B4
Here Black should have seized

the opportunity of ridding himself of one of the dangerous Bs by Kt—B4 etc. (*Deutsche Schachzeitung*)

10) Kt—Kt3   Q—B2
11) Kt—K5   Kt×Kt

This is rather risky and demands careful play on Black's part. P—Kt3 would have been safer despite the weakening of the diagonal.

12) B×Kt   Q—B3

with the transparent threat of ...P—Q5

13) Q—K2   P—QR3?

In order to play ...Kt—Q2, without having to fear B—Kt5. But 13) ...Kt—Q2 *was* imperative.

Position after Black's 13th move

14) Kt—R5!

After this there is no saving the game for Black.

    I: 14) ...Kt—K1 15) B×P, Kt×B 16) Q—Kt4

    II: 14) ...P—R3 15) B×Kt, B×B 16) Kt×B ch, P×Kt 17) Q—Kt4 ch, K—R1 18) Q—R4, K—Kt2 19)

R—B3, KR—Q1 20) R—Kt3 ch etc.

    III: 14) ...P—Q5 15) B×Kt, B×B 16) Q—Kt4, K—R1 17) R—B3, R—KKt1 18) B×KRP, KR—Q1 19) Q—R3, B—K2 20) B—K4! etc.

14) .....   Kt×Kt

Leading to a brilliant refutation which has since served as a classic example of the power of united Bs.

15) B×P ch!

Black no doubt expected 15) Q×Kt, P—B4 etc.

15) .....   K×B
16) Q×Kt ch   K—Kt1
17) B×P!!

A really beautiful move which adds lustre to Lasker's combination.

17) .....   K×B

P—B3 would lose quickly because of R—B3—Kt3.

18) Q—Kt4 ch!   K—R2
19) R—B3   P—K4
20) R—R3 ch   Q—R3
21) R×Q ch   K×R
22) Q—Q7

This move crowns the combination begun on the 14th move.

22) .....   B—KB3
23) Q×B   K—Kt2

Not 23) ...P×P 24) Q×KtP, K—Kt2 25) R—KB1. But Black's game is hopeless anyway.

24) R—KB1   QR—Kt1
25) Q—Q7

Rightly disdaining the Q-side Pawns in favour of the attack

25)	.....	KR—Q1
26)	Q—Kt4 ch	K—B1
27)	P×P	B—Kt2

B×P would, of course, lose the B, on account of Q—B5

28) P—K6
This settles matters.

28)	.....	R—Kt2

29)	Q—Kt6	P—B3
30)	R×P ch!	B×R
31)	Q×B ch	K—K1
32)	Q—R8 ch	K—K2
33)	Q—Kt7 ch	resigns

(Notes by FRED REINFELD in *Dr. Lasker's Chess Career*)

GAME 2

VIENNA GAME

MIESES–LASKER

Match game at Berlin 1889

1)	P—K4	P—K4
2)	Kt—QB3	B—B4
3)	P—KKt3	Kt—QB3
4)	B—Kt2	P—Q3
5)	Kt—R4?(Kt—K2!)	B—K3
6)	Kt×B	P×Kt
7)	P—Q3	Kt—B3
8)	Kt—K2	Q—Q3!

After the routine 8) ...0—0 9) 0—0, followed by P—KB4, White would obtain a strong attack.

9) P—KB4   P—KR4
To discourage White from castling K-side.

10) P—B5
Blocking the position does not appreciably help White. He should rather have continued with P—KR3, followed by B—K3, Q—Q2 and (eventually) 0—0—0.

10)	.....	B—Q2
11)	B—Kt5?(B—K3!)	Kt—R2
12)	B—K3	0—0—0
13)	Kt—B3	

Planning a risky attack against Black's K which is not justified by White's insufficient development. 13) Q—Q2 could have been played quite safely

13)	.....	Kt—B3
14)	Kt—Kt5	Q—K2
15)	P—B3	P—B5!?

15) ...P—R3 was more prudent

16) P—QKt4?
For here 16) Q—R4, and if ...P—R3, 17) P×P! would have yielded a powerful attack

16)	.....	Kt×KtP!
17)	Kt×P ch	K—Kt1
18)	P×Kt	

Declining the sacrifice would leave White with a hopelessly disorganised game

18)	.....	Q×P ch
19)	K—B1	Kt—Kt5
20)	B—Kt1	B—R5
21)	R—Kt1	Q—R6
22)	Q—K2	R×P
23)	P—R3	

Despite his material advantage, White's position is untenable; if for example 23) Q—Kt2, R—Q8 ch 24) R×R, Q×Q

23)	.....	KR—Q1!!

White probably expected ...Kt—K6 ch 24) B×Kt, R×B 25) Q×BP, K×Kt 26) Q×QBP with counterplay.

Position after Black's 27th move

24)	P×Kt	P—B6!
25)	Kt—B6 ch	B×Kt
26)	B—K3	P—B7!

GAME 3

VIENNA GAME

BLACKBURNE–LASKER

London Tournament of the B.C.F., March 1892

1)	P—K4	P—K4
2)	Kt—QB3	Kt—KB3
3)	P—B4	P—Q4
4)	BP×P	Kt×P
5)	Q—B3	P—KB4

More usual is the line of play recommended by Steinitz: 5) ...Kt—QB3 6) B—Kt5, Kt× Kt 7) KtP×Kt, Q—R5 ch 8) P—Kt3, Q—K5 ch etc. The text leads to more complicated play

6) Kt—R3

This is too slow. 6) P—Q3 seems best, with the continuation ...Kt×Kt 7) P×Kt, P—Q5 8) Q—Kt3 with good prospects

| 6) | ..... | P—B3 |

But not 26) ...R×B? 27) Q×R, P—B7 28) R×P ch! and wins

| 27) | Q×P | R×B |
| 28) | K—B2 | |

28) Q×B is refuted by ...R—Q8 ch etc.

| 28) | ..... | R—B6 |

White resigns: if 29) Q—Kt2, Q—B4 ch, followed by ...R—B7. A spirited game in which the youthful Lasker carries out the attack in the most elegant style.

(Notes by FRED REINFELD in *Dr. Lasker's Chess Career*)

Rather conservative. On 6) Kt—B3 Tarrasch gives 7) B—Kt5, Q—R5 ch 8) K—B1 as best for White

7) Kt—K2?

Blackburne wishes to dislodge Black's Kt by P—Q3 without allowing an exchange. But this is not an unmixed blessing, since White's minor pieces are so badly posted. 7) P—Q3 was essential, instead of the time-wasting text.

7)	.....	B—K2
8)	P—Q3	Kt—B4
9)	P—R3?	0—0
10)	B—K3	QKt—Q2
11)	B×Kt	

If instead 11) P—Q4, Kt—K5, followed by ...Q—Kt 3.
11) Q—B4 would lose the KP after ...Kt—K3 [12) Q—Kt3?, B—R5]

| 11) | ..... | Kt×B |
| 12) | Kt(3)—B4 | Q—Kt3! |

Very strong! White's best reply would have been 13) P—QKt3

13) P—QKt4

Creating a new weakness which enables Black to institute an energetic attack.

13) .....   Kt—Q2
14) P—Q4   P—QR4!
15) R—QKt1

15) P—B3 would, of course, be useless: ...P×P 16) BP×P, B×P ch etc.

15) .....   P×P

Position after white's 16th move

16) P×P   B×P ch

This is not so much a sacrifice as a profitable investment.

17) P—B3   B×P ch
18) Kt×B   Q×P

The ultimate result cannot be in doubt. Black gets four Ps for the piece, open lines for the attack, and White's K is dangerously exposed.

19) Kt(B4)—K2

he must provide for ...R—R6

19) .....   Q×P
20) Q—B4   Q—B3
21) Kt—Q4   Kt—B4!

Threatening to win a piece by ...Kt—K3.

22) Q—Q2   Kt—K5
23) Kt×Kt   BP×Kt
24) Q—K3   R—R5
25) Kt—B2

White must give way. A plausible continuation after 25) R—Q1 would be ...P—B4 26) Kt—B2, P—Q5 27) Q—Q2, P—K6 28) Q—K2, B—Kt5

25) .....   R—R7
26) R—B1   B—Kt5
27) B—K2   B×B
28) K×B   Q—Kt7
29) K—Q1   Q—Kt4!
30) R—K1

if 30) K—K1, Q—Q6 31) Q—K2, P—Q5 wins easily

30) .....   R—Kt7!

Not 30) ...Q—Q6 ch 31) Q×Q, P×Q at once because of 32) Kt—Kt4. Blackburne misses the point and loses at once.

31) Q—K2   Q—Q6 ch
32) Q×Q   P×Q

White resigns as he must lose a piece. Lasker's play throughout is characterised by superb vigour.

(Notes by FRED REINFELD in *Dr. Lasker's Chess Career*)

GAME 3*a*

v. FEYERFEIL–LASKER

Breslau (Hauptturnier) 27 July 1889

Queen's Pawn

1) P—Q4   P—Q4
2) B—B4   P—QB4
3) P×P   Kt—QB3
4) Kt—KB3   P—B3!

5)	P—K3	P—K4		
6)	B—Kt3	B×P		
7)	P—B3	Kt—K2		
8)	QKt—Q2	B—K3		

What with his firm grip on the centre Black has got much the better of the opening

9)	Q—R4?	P—QR3
10)	R—Q1	P—QKt4
11)	Q—B2	Q—B1!
12)	P—QR3	O—O
13)	B—K2	B—B4
14)	Q—B1	R—R2
15)	O—O	P—Kt4
16)	KR—K1	K—R1
17)	Kt—B1	Q—K3
18)	R—Q2	R—Q2
19)	KR—Q1	Kt—R4!
20)	P—Kt4	Kt—Kt6
21)	Q—Kt2	Kt×R
22)	R×Kt	B—R2
23)	P—QR4	R—Kt2
24)	P×P	P×P
25)	R—Q1	Q—B3
26)	Kt(1)—Q2	B—K3
27)	P—R3	R—B1
28)	R—QB1	Kt—B4
29)	B—R2	P—K5

Position after White's 30th move

30)	Kt—K1	P—Q5!

An elegant way of clinching the issue, but White was lost in any case.

31)	Kt×P	P×KP
32)	P—B3	B—B5
33)	K—R1	B×B
34)	Q×B	B—Kt1!
35)	B×B	R(2)×B
36)	K—Kt1	Q—Kt3
37)	Kt—Q3	R—K1
38)	Kt(4)—B5	R—Q1
39)	P—Kt4	Kt—R5
40)	Q×P	Q—B2
41)	R—B1	Kt—Kt3
42)	Q—B2	Kt—B5
43)	Q—KR2	Q—K4
44)	R—Kt1	Q—Q4
45)	Q—QB2	Kt×P ch
46)	K—R2	Kt—B5
	resigns	

This game is practically unknown, having been published only in the book of the tournament and then, nearly 70 years later, in the Whyld–Gilchrist collection. Yet, the game, undistinguished though it is, has some very considerable importance in the history of chess. It was the 'decider' of the tie for 1st prize in the *Hauptturnier* and by winning the game, young Lasker got the coveted title of *Deutscher Meister*, thereby being set for his career. Had he lost the game the title would have gone to Feyerfeil, and it is more than probable that Lasker would have given up chess altogether. Hence, this game may well be considered the most important in his career.

CHAPTER SIX

Winning the Title

At last we approach the great contest that was to end the supremacy held by Steinitz for nearly three decades. Long and complex negotiations preceeded the event. The audience, naturally, is merely intent on the spectacle presented on the stage; the spectator is only too likely to forget that for the actors their livelihood depends on it. The chroniclers of any creative effort are merely concerned with the accomplished work, and they may well rapsodize about its grandeur and beauty; but those who created it, however entranced by the intoxicating thrill of creation, had to have their daily bread.

As often as not, they hadn't, and alas, Mozart was not the only creative genius to perish in penury. As for chess masters, it used to be the rule rather than the exception to suffer hunger and destitution. We shall see, in due course, the circumstances in which great Steinitz had to die. How did he live? Not much better than he died. And yet he wore the crown of the chess world for twenty-eight years.

How then, in those days, was a chess match financed? Certainly not by offering both masters an adequate fee. They were treated like race-horses, the only difference being that those noble animals are better fed and looked after. The chess masters first had to find some backers prepared to risk a stake on their respective prowess, and it was only after they had managed to secure a sufficiency of backers that actual preparations for organising the match could be started. When it was all over the winning group of backers would dole out prizes, giving the lion's share, of course, to their own favourite and a more or less generous consolation prize to the loser. Hence, the contending masters were merely servants of a betting agency, unpaid servants as it were, to be dismissed with a tip. Steinitz who was a sensitive man suffered deeply under such humiliating conditions, but he had to accept them all his life.

Young Lasker had to accept them too at the beginning of his career. He loathed it and was determined to bring about a change. But he knew that, before he could do so he would first have to reach the top and to make himself indispensable. He did, and in due course we shall hear more about his 'extravagant demands' which used to annoy people quite a lot. Still, he brought home to them the unpalatable truth that the existence of a chess master is a social and economic problem no less than an artistic and sporting one.

As for the first Lasker-Steinitz match, it still had to be organised on the lines of similar events from time immemorial: which meant that the two heroes first had to set themselves up as a sort of book-makers' agency, acting as their own touts. Thus to hunt around begging for backers is a humiliating business, and it takes a lot of time too. It took many months until, at long last, a sum of $3000 had been collected to finance an event eagerly expected by millions of chessplayers in five continents. Even so, it was much the largest amount ever yet collected for a chess match. Moreover, the contenders this time were not to be dependent on a 'tip' from their backers; a guaranteed fee was fixed: $2250 for the winner and $750 for the loser. The match was to be played at New York, Philadelphia, and Montreal, and it was to begin on 15 March 1894.

All the world knew that Steinitz had aged. He was tormented by gout and hobbled about painfully with stick and crutches. To give his opponent the odds of thirty years and good health seemed an excessive handicap. Even so—and nothing could be more significant of the dominating personality of Wilhelm Steinitz—even so and though no one really liked him much, almost everybody expected the sick old man still to be unconquerable and to stand at least an even chance against his ambitious young opponent. That no one really liked him was due to his queerly impenetrable style at chess, no less than to his being a grouchy old man. Steinitz had come to be almost a nightmare for his contemporaries, but he had come to be a legend too. Certainly his fame was legendary, and people simply would not see that the poor creature was merely a mortal, subject to the iron law of time, however long and grandly he had resisted it.

In the first phase of the match Steinitz still managed to put up some real resistance. He built up his games as carefully as he knew how, and with that immense positional judgment and experience which, over the decades, he had made his very own tradition. In almost every game he secured some positional advantage and sooner or later, almost invariably, he could claim to have the 'better position'. But his opponent had better nerves, stronger stamina, more flexibility, shrewder tactics, and above all he was a psychologist. He sought uncommonly difficult complications and deliberately went on dangerous ground near the precipice. By rights he should have faltered and fallen. But it wasn't Lasker who faltered, it was Steinitz who fell into the abyss. It wasn't the theoretical pros and cons of certain opening variations, it wasn't sound strategy that decided the struggle; it was rather a matter of tactics, and even more the *élan vital* of the younger and shrewder man, his mental power of resistance, his greater self-control, his deeper knowledge of human nature.

Lasker won the first game, Steinitz the second, Lasker the third, and Steinitz again the fourth. The fifth and sixth game remained undecided, and since draws were not counted in that match the score after six games was still 2 : 2.

But now Lasker's tactic of psychologically undermining his opponent's confidence began to take full effect. The next phase of the match was a landslide, and for Steinitz it seemed to indicate total collapse. Still in New York, Lasker won the seventh and eight game, so that he could start with the advantage of 4 : 2 when the match was continued at Philadelphia. All the world now expected a counter-thrust from Steinitz, but it did not materialise. Lasker won all three games played at Philadelphia. Thus, after eleven games the score was 7 : 2, and since the match was to be decided by the win of ten games Lasker had already gone more than two thirds of the way. It seemed that he would have to play barely half of the thirty games which most experts had forecast as the minimum number required to reach the decision.

It was under such desperate auspices that Steinitz went into the third phase of the match at Montreal. He had lost five games in a row, a débacle never experienced in the whole of his career. He seemed to be doomed. It was all the more amazing and admirable that the tired and unhappy old man could rise to a last and truly heroic effort. All of a sudden the younger man, so confident of success, so sure of speedy triumph, was badly mauled by the sick old lion. These were indeed anxious days for Lasker. The twelfth game was a draw, but in the thirteenth and fourteenth Steinitz was the winner. The score now stood at 7 : 4 and since there was to be a week's break which would give the older man some much needed rest a surprising turn of fate seemed by no means out of the question.

But the interruption of the struggle had failed to give Steinitz the expected revigoration: it may well have had the opposite effect. At any rate, Lasker was now definitely 'on top', and he seemed bent with inexorable energy on making an end of it. He won the fifteenth and sixteenth game, reaching the score of 9 : 4. Only one more game to be won, and the triumph of the world championship would be his. But still, Steinitz was not to be denied, still the old giant fought tooth and nail. He won the seventeenth game, perhaps the best of the whole match, conducted by Steinitz in the grand style of his hey-day.

After that game Lasker was a little 'groggy'. Was the incredible old man unbeatable after all? Was there some magic spell that made the giant unconquerable? Was his almost certain victory to elude the younger man at the last moment? The world stood aghast when the next game too could not be won by Lasker. For once he had the superior position all along, but the old man fought back with unbelievable tenacity, defending himself with indomitable persistence and infinite patience, and once again wresting a draw from his opponent.

But then came 26 May 1894, the day that was to see the end of it. For fifty-two moves Steinitz held on, delaying the end, fighting back to the last. But then the inevitable happened, the game was lost. Lasker had scored his tenth point, deciding the match by 10 : 5, with four draws. Laboriously reaching for his stick Steinitz rose from his seat and called for three cheers for the new World Champion. Then he hobbled to the room next door, to darkness and solitude.

As for the quality of individual games in that match, expert opinion has differed. The contemporaries certainly attributed the result of the match to Steinitz's senility rather than to Lasker's supremacy. This is what Curt von Bardeleben, one of the leading authorities of the time, had to say about it in the *Deutsche Schachzeitung* (Vol. 1894):

'Lasker lacks the depth of Steinitz's conception, but he makes up for it by his extraordinary self-control. His game is almost faultless, and that is the main reason for his victory. No less significant for Lasker's style is the fact that he knows how to defend precarious positions with considerable calm and circumspection, thereby making his opponent's task as difficult as possible, whereas lesser players in equally bad positions would lose heart and make mistakes hastening the end. As for Lasker's treatment of openings it is usually correct, but never particularly dominating. Generally speaking, Lasker represents the Modern School. His style is not particularly aggressive, his combinations are lacking in brilliance, but his positional judgment is sound. Moreover, he is extremely cautious and it is difficult indeed to attack him successfully. In defence he is much stronger than in attack; indeed, he will only attack when his own advantage is obvious and decisive, or again when his position is so precarious that a mere passive defence would no longer offer any chance.'

The consensus of public and expert opinion among the contemporaries was much the same, and very understandably too. In those days people could not possibly understand that when Bardeleben spoke of a position 'so precarious that a mere passive defence would not do' he was really, even if unwittingly, pointing to the very core of Lasker's philosophy as applied to chess. Bardeleben (and others) could not yet see that the very 'precariousness' of such a position was deliberately sought by Lasker, being the very precipice to the edge of which he would lure his opponent. It took a long time for the experts to get away from their erstwhile notion that Lasker's play was 'correct, but not very trenchant'. In point of fact, it was anything but 'correct' in terms of erudite book knowledge, and it was 'trenchant' in a very much deeper sense than the non-psychologists of the Tarrasch School could possibly grasp in those days.

It was a pity that Steinitz too could not see how deeply rooted Lasker's supremacy really was; it was a pity that, rather than resigning with a grand gesture, the old man fanatically persisted in his belief that one day he would get his own back and that his first defeat was merely due to physical infirmity. That was an opinion shared by Dr Tarrasch who made no secret of his conviction that the new world champion would fail to stand up to a really serious test, particularly if he was to be tested by himself.

It is only fair to add that the widespread doubts about Lasker's real prowess were largely based on the fact that, prior to the match with Steinitz, the young man, however successful in several minor events, had never yet been tested in a great International Tournament; except perhaps at Amsterdam in 1889, his first tournament where, after all, he had been merely runner-up to Burn. In the meantime, had not Tarrasch won as many as four major events, (Breslau, 1889; Manchester, 1890; Dresden, 1892 Leipzig 1894), all in a row? And were there not quite a number of other newcomers, such as Lipke, Teichmann, Janowski, Marco, Walbrodt—each one of them perhaps no less talented than young Lasker? True enough, no one of them had beaten Steinitz, but who could deny that they might have, if given the chance?

Evidently, public opinion after the match was inclined not to think too highly of Lasker's victory; which seems odd enough, considering that before the match the same public opinion refused to believe that the legend of the old man's invincibility could be destroyed by his young challenger. What most of the experts now expected was that young Lasker was merely a stop-gap until someone greater—probably Dr. Tarrasch—would rightfully assume Caissa's coveted crown.

CHAPTER SEVEN

Set-back at Hastings

By the rules of poetic justice young Lasker should have now been given an opportunity to uphold his glorious title, thereby silencing his critics once and for all. But poetic justice, alas, appears only in novels; real life usually tends to follow a more prosaic course. Lasker's life certainly did. He was indeed given an immediate opportunity to confound his critics; but he muffed it: at any rate, it wasn't nearly as glorious as poetic justice demanded.

Opportunity certainly knocked at once. Lasker was called to Europe, invited to compete in a tournament which, to this day, ranks as one of the greatest in the history of chess: Hastings 1895.

In that last decade of the nineteenth century, England, apart from Germany, seemed to be the only country capable of financing and organising a string of chess tournaments in the grand manner. There had been the Bradford Tournament of 1888, Manchester in 1890, and the great London Tournament of 1899 was still to come. Nearly four decades were to elapse after this until, at Nottingham in 1936, there was to be another British Tournament comparable with the first of many staged at Hastings.

That first one in 1895 is still as noteworthy as ever, because never before and seldom since has it been possible to assemble so complete an array of all the leading masters of the day. Naturally Lasker, the new World Champion, was asked, along with his predecessor Steinitz and their most improtant rival Dr Siegbert Tarrasch. From Russia came Tchigorin, victor of the great New York Tournament of 1889 and twice Steinitz's challenger in a match; from France came Janowski, a fast rising star, from Central Europe the entire young generation of budding grandmasters, such as Schlechter, Teichmann, Mieses, v. Bardeleben, Marco, Walbrodt. As for the 'home-side', naturally the flower of British Chess was fully assembled: famous old Blackburne, a grandmaster of many years' standing; Bird and Burn, well tried in many an international contest; and, of course, Gunsberg and Mason.

These were the 'names', and indeed every one of them was famous; but there were three or four 'outsiders' too, among them a twenty-two-year-old American hardly any one in Europe had ever heard of, one Harry N. Pillsbury. It was he who won the tournament.

Lasker was not in good physical shape when he entered that

greatest of all chess competitions. He had come to Europe in good time, and he had gone to see brother Berthold and the parents in Berlin. It turned out to be a much longer visit than contemplated, for Emanuel fell ill and was bed-ridden for weeks. In spite of Doctor Berthold's expert and loving care convalescence took a long time; longer perhaps than it might have taken if the patient had not been fretting about the masses of commissioned work waiting to be dealt with even before the start of the tournament.[1]

Lasker's prior assignment was a lecture tour in England, the subject being the Principles of Chess, and he took it very seriously. It was not his way to fill such an assignment by dispensing some facile platitudes; indeed, he would prepare for such lectures rather more thoroughly than for a match. Even though not quite recovered yet (and disobeying doctor's orders of a few weeks' complete rest), he started on his lecture tour in the spring of 1895; and so far as these lectures are concerned we are certainly in a position to assess their quality and significance; for an extract from them was to be Lasker's first book, which may be considered the essence of his chess philosophy—a book which has been an invaluable guide to generations of chessplayers and which even now, more than sixty years after its publication [2] is as fresh and 'modern' as ever. It is a slim volume entitled *Common Sense in Chess*, a most fitting title, for the book deals with 'common sense' not in terms of offering 'common or garden' recipes, but rather in the basic meaning of the term. To have 'common sense', according to Lasker, means not to be content with a superficial glance, but to look into the meaning of things and then to do the natural thing. That applies to chess no less than to any form of activity. The ostrich shows common sense by burying his head in the sand, the eagle shows it by nesting on a lofty rock. For the timid and sick it is common sense to shut their window tightly against any perilous draught; for the mountaineer it is common sense to open his window wide so as to enjoy a deep breath of fresh air. Every person indeed must apply his very own common sense to his very own problems; and if we must have a

[1]   The Hastings Tournament began on August 5th and finished on September 3rd, (the 1st prize, incidentally, being £150). As for Lasker's illness and the serious concern caused by it, here is a quotation from the August number of the *British Chess Magazine:* 'We were sorry to learn that Herr Lasker's state of health leaves much to be desired. It is to be feared that the considerable physical effort involved in the International Tournament may bode ill for Lasker's chances of success.

[2]   *Emanuel Lasker: Common Sense in Chess.* Published 1896 by Bellairs & Co, London, Mayer & Müller, Berlin, and British Chess Co., London.

simple formula for it we might do worse than quoting from the Persian epigrams of Omar:

> *Of all the many sorts of folk I rated,*
> *I found but two in state of bliss supreme:*
> *Him who had tasted wisdom to the brim*
> *And him who is a fool unmitigated.*

So as not to tire readers who know little or nothing about chess we must refrain from quoting technicalities; but whoever has mastered a little more than the rudiments of the game will find it most rewarding to study Lasker's *Common Sense in Chess*. It is and will remain one of the standard works, no matter whether one has the first edition or one of the later ones in which the ideological opposition to Tarrasch is clearly outlined.

Lasker wrote the preface to the first edition on July 25 at Ilkley, and less than two weeks later he was at Hastings for the start of the great tournament. It was to be a disappointment for him even more than for the entire chess world excitedly following the thrilling event. More than once in the course of that gigantic struggle Lasker was on the point of taking the lead; but again and again he would suffer a reverse and lose the ground gained or recovered. Right up to the last rounds Lasker had a chance of winning, but at no time during the tournament did he show the degree of real supremacy to be expected from the world champion.

With a bit of luck—a couple of half points making all the difference—he might still have won the tournament; but at best, it would have meant being *primus inter pares*. He wasn't even that.

It was Pillsbury, the rank outsider, the American youth completely unknown in Europe, who shot up from obscurity to world fame by dint of a triumph so great that he could never quite live up to it. Even so, during the brief span of life left to him—he died in his early thirties—he was the delight of every tournament he graced by his presence. Pillsbury played Morphy-games with Steinitz's lucidity: in him the sombre old man's profoundness was tempered by the cheerfulness of youth. As for that great event of Hastings 1895—great by any standards—it had been given the additional boon of discovering a new darling of the gods. Naturally it was he who was the hero of the day, jubilantly acclaimed by the crowd.

His most dangerous rival was not Lasker, nor Tarrasch, nor Steinitz. It was the Russian Tchigorin, one of the old swashbucklers of the 'Romantic School', and a convinced opponent of the Steinitz school of thought. He was hard on the winner's heels, and Lasker just as hard on his, with merely a half point between each of them.

HASTINGS 1895

		1	2	3	4	5	6	7	8	9	10	11	12	13	14	15	16	17	18	19	20	21	22	
1	Pillsbury	×	0	0	1	1	1	1	1	0	½	½	1	1	1	1	1	1	½	1	1	1	1	16½
2	Tchigorin	1	×	1	1	0	0	1	1	1	1	½	1	0	1	½	1	½	1	1	½	1	1	16
3	Lasker	1	0	×	0	1	1	0	1	1	0	1	1	1	½	1	1	½	1	1	½	1	1	15½
4	Tarrasch	0	0	1	×	1	1	½	0	½	1	1	1	1	0	1	½	1	1	0	½	1	1	14
5	Steinitz	0	1	0	0	×	1	1	½	½	1	1	½	0	1	0	1	1	1	0	½	1	1	13
6	Schiffers	0	1	0	0	0	×	½	½	0	1	1	½	1	½	1	1	0	½	1	½	1	1	12
7	von Bardeleben	0	0	1	½	0	½	×	½	½	0	0	1	½	1	½	1	½	1	1	1	0	1	11½
8	Teichmann	0	0	0	1	½	½	½	×	½	0	0	1	½	1	1	0	½	1	½	1	1	1	11½
9	Schlechter	1	0	0	½	½	1	½	½	×	½	½	1	0	1	½	½	½	½	½	½	1	0	11
10	Blackburne	½	0	1	0	0	0	1	1	½	×	0	1	1	0	½	0	1	0	1	0	1	1	10½
11	Walbrodt	½	½	0	0	0	0	1	1	½	1	×	0	0	½	½	½	0	½	½	1	1	1	10
12	Burn	0	0	0	0	½	½	0	0	0	0	1	×	1	0	½	0	1	1	1	1	1	1	9½
13	Janowski	0	1	0	0	1	0	½	½	1	0	1	0	×	½	½	0	0	1	½	1	0	1	9½
14	Mason	0	0	½	1	0	½	0	0	0	1	½	1	½	×	1	0	½	0	1	1	0	1	9½
15	Bird	0	½	0	0	1	0	½	0	½	½	½	½	½	0	×	1	1	½	0	½	½	1	9
16	Gunsberg	0	0	0	½	0	0	0	1	½	1	½	1	1	1	0	×	1	½	0	1	0	0	9
17	Albin	0	½	½	0	0	1	½	½	½	0	1	0	1	½	0	0	×	0	0	1	1	½	8½
18	Marco	½	0	0	0	0	½	0	0	½	1	½	0	0	1	½	½	1	×	1	1	0	½	8½
19	Pollock	0	0	0	1	1	0	0	½	½	0	½	0	½	0	1	1	1	0	×	0	0	1	8
20	Mieses	0	½	½	½	½	½	0	0	½	1	0	0	0	0	½	0	0	0	1	×	1	1	7½
21	Tinsley	0	0	0	0	0	0	1	0	0	0	0	0	1	1	½	1	0	1	1	0	×	1	7½
22	Vergani	0	0	0	0	0	0	0	0	1	0	0	0	0	0	0	1	½	½	0	0	0	×	3

Clearly these three were a class by themselves. Then came a gap of one and a half points before Tarrasch, the fourth prize-winner, came to lead the rest of the field, with Steinitz close behind him.

Tarrasch, of course, was very disappointed too. True enough, he had won his individual game against Lasker, but in the tournament he could never do better than trail just behind the leaders. It was a bitter set-back after six years of uninterrupted and glittering success.

As for Lasker, though he had beaten Pillsbury in their individual encounter he was deeply dissatisfied: not so much because he had failed to win the first prize, but even more so because very few of the games he played at Hastings had come up to the high standard he had set himself. Oddly enough, the one really 'smashing' game he won at Hastings was against none other than poor old Steinitz.

CHAPTER EIGHT

Triumph at St. Petersburg

Lasker was not the sort of man to let grass grow under his feet. For him to be dissatisfied with himself meant to do something about it, to do better, and to do it at once. He was lucky enough to be given the chance almost immediately, and he owed it to the very fact that had proved so disturbing to him during the tournament: Tchigorin's excellent achievement at Hastings. Naturally, that had caused quite a stir in Russia; indeed, the master's compatriots were so delighted that, there and then, they sent a telegram to Hastings, asking Tchigorin to invite the first five for a real grandmaster-tournament (¹) to start before the year was out. Tarrasch declined, claiming pressure of professional work—he had his doctor's practice in Nuremberg to attend to—but Lasker, Pillsbury and Steinitz, while still at Hastings, immediately accepted the challenge to meet Tchigorin on his home-ground.

Thus, towards the end of 1895, four 'grandmasters' (¹) met in St. Petersburg, each of them to play six games against one another. It therefore might be called a combination of match-play rather than a tournament. The contest started on 13 December and lasted nearly seven weeks, the wealthy organisers being very generous in allowing for some days of rest in between the eighteen games to be played by every competitor.

At first, fortune once again seemed to favour young Pillsbury; but when he came to play his third game against Lasker he was heading for trouble. It was the game (see p. 66) which Lasker himself considered the best he ever played. On his seventeenth move, playing Black in a Queen's Gambit, he embarked on a sacrificial combination of incomparable depth, and in a maze of complications, with every successive move beckoning to triumph or disaster, he

---

(¹) In those days (and until fairly recently) the title 'grandmaster' was more or less unofficially and by tacit agreement accorded to those masters who had won at least one major international event. Some time ago matters were properly organised by the *Fédération Internationale des Echecs* officially granting the title, (though much on the strength of the same kind of qualification formerly demanded). At present there are some fifty officially recognized grandmasters, a great deal more than there used to be in the first quarter of the century before organised chess began to get substantial official encouragement in the USSR and other countries of Eastern Europe.

groped his way to victory with the somnambulistic assurance of a tight-rope walker. Once again Lasker methodically walked on the edge of the precipice, but it was the opponent who tumbled into the abyss. And once and for all, after that game, Bardeleben and other critics had to revise their opinion that Lasker's style was 'not particularly aggressive' and that his combinations 'lacked brilliance'.

Lasker now took the lead and held on to it with iron energy until, in the last week of January, the final result was established: Lasker 11½, Steinitz 9½, Pillsbury 8, Tchigorin 7. Lasker and Steinitz had reversed the result of Hastings by deflating the two first prize-winners of that great tournament. Lasker has done it so convincingly that no one, any longer, would doubt his real supremacy. After all, his opponents were indubitably the strongest of the time, and for anyone to show such decisive superiority in so many match-games clearly proved that he was no mere stop-gap soon to be relieved by someone greater, but the greatest of all, the one most worthy to wear the crown.

But there was one other man who had emerged from that gruelling test of truly 'grandmasterly' chess with new hopes, and that was Steinitz. After his defeat by Lasker and his relatively poor showing at Hastings he had been written off as utterly *passé*—and well he knew it—but he had now shown them that he was anything but done for. His highly creditable score in that great test of Petersburg had surely given him the moral right to demand a return-match with Lasker.

Had his wisdom been equal to his years he would have been loath to challenge fate once again, he would have retired there and then in the haze of glory achieved at Petersburg. But for one thing,

ST. PETERSBURG 1895/96

	1	2	3	4	
1 Lasker		11½01½	00½1½½	1½11½1	11½
2 Steinitz	00½10½		1½½111	01100½	9½
3 Pillsbury . . .	11½0½½	0½½000		11100½	8
4 Tchigorin . . .	0½00½0	10011½	00011½		7

having eked out a meagre hand-to-mouth existence all his life he just couldn't afford to retire; and for another, his was not the wisdom to recognise his own limitations. Old in years, he was still driven by the demons of youthful ambition. He was not wise enough to see that an old person must conform to the physical demands of his own age.

As for the return match with Lasker, it was duly arranged, and for once it could be done with practically no fuss or trouble; for the same wealthy patrons who had financed the Petersburg event were proud and delighted to have a match for the world championship on Russian soil. Negotiations were completed in practically no time, November 1896 was agreed on as a convenient time for starting the match, and Moscow was chosen as the venue.

CHAPTER NINE

Going from Strength to Strength

If only Steinitz had allowed himself some rest, so badly needed prior to the match! But he could not get enough of throwing his newly established weight about; he would not pass up any chance of exhibiting his prowess; he seemed to be whipped by furies on the way to what he fondly imagined to be his great resurrection.

It so happened that a few months after the end of the Petersburg event another great International Tournament was in the offing: it was to start on July 19th at Nuremberg and it was to assemble almost if not quite the galaxy of masters that had made so memorable an event of the Hastings Tournament just a year earlier. Lasker had accepted the invitation, and Steinitz of course was not to be denied. There was Tarrasch, burning with ambition to triumph in his own hometown. There was Pillsbury and Tchigorin too, the heroes of Hastings; Schlechter came from Vienna, old Blackburne from London, and from Budapest came Maroczy, a rising young star.

It certainly was a grand field, but this time Lasker was considered 'hot favourite' by all the experts, except the Tarrasch-'fans' hoping and praying for their hero to regain his claim to supremacy. As for Lasker, it was the first time he played in a really important tournament in his own country, and since he was in perfect physical shape, he justified world-wide expectations. He took the lead soon after the start and never let go of it. After eighteen rounds the result was: Lasker $13\frac{1}{2}$, Maroczy $12\frac{1}{2}$, Pillsbury and Tarrasch 12 each, Janowski $11\frac{1}{2}$, Steinitz 11. Tarrasch again $1\frac{1}{2}$ points behind his great rival, and this time beaten in their individual encounter too! Surely, Lasker must stay world champion! But Tarrasch did not see it that way, yet.

Steinitz sixth! In a field of such quality it was still a remarkable achievement for anybody, the more so for an old man in bad health. But Steinitz did not have the wisdom that Lasker was to show in similar circumstances nearly forty years later, when he was some years older than Steinitz had been at the time of the Nuremberg tournament. Not that Lasker at that time of life and in normal circumstances would have considered competing in any tournament at all. But the circumstances weren't normal. Hitler had just come to power, and the Laskers were deprived of their property and forced to leave the country; it was merely because he had to earn some money that Lasker accepted the invitation to play in the

NUREMBERG 1896

		1	2	3	4	5	6	7	8	9	10	11	12	13	14	15	16	17	18	19	
1	Lasker	×	½	0	1	0	1	½	½	1	1	1	0	1	1	1	1	1	1	1	13½
2	Maroczy	½	×	1	½	1	0	½	½	½	½	½	1	½	1	1	1	1	1	½	12½
3	Pillsbury	1	0	×	1	½	1	0	½	1	0	0	½	1	1	1	½	1	1	1	12
4	Tarrasch	0	½	0	×	1	1	½	½	1	1	0	1	1	1	1	½	½	½	1	12
5	Janowski	1	0	½	0	×	1	1	1	0	1	½	0	1	½	1	1	0	1	1	11½
6	Steinitz	0	1	0	0	0	×	½	1	1	½	1	1	1	0	0	1	1	1	1	11
7	Walbrodt	½	½	1	½	0	½	×	½	1	½	0	0	½	1	1	1	1	1	0	10½
8	Schlechter	½	½	½	½	0	0	½	×	1	½	½	½	½	1	1	½	½	1	1	10½
9	Tchigorin	0	½	0	0	1	0	0	0	×	½	1	1	½	1	1	1	0	1	1	9½
10	Schiffers	0	½	1	0	0	½	½	½	½	×	0	½	½	1	½	½	1	1	1	9½
11	Blackburne	0	½	1	1	½	0	1	½	0	1	×	0	0	0	1	0	1	1	½	9
12	Charousek	1	0	½	0	1	0	1	½	0	½	1	×	½	0	½	1	1	0	0	8½
13	Marco	0	½	0	0	0	0	½	½	½	½	1	½	×	½	1	½	½	1	½	8
14	Albin	0	0	0	0	½	1	0	0	0	0	1	1	½	×	0	½	½	1	1	7
15	Winawer	0	0	0	0	0	1	0	0	0	½	0	½	0	1	×	1	1	1	½	6½
16	Porges	0	0	½	½	0	0	0	½	0	½	1	0	½	½	0	×	½	0	1	5½
17	Showalter	0	0	0	½	1	0	0	½	1	0	0	0	½	½	0	½	×	0	1	5½
18	Schallopp	0	0	0	½	0	0	0	0	0	0	0	1	0	0	0	1	1	×	1	4½
19	Teichmann	0	½	0	0	0	0	1	0	0	0	½	1	½	0	½	0	0	0	×	4

Zürich tournament of 1934. We shall hear more about it when we get to that part of the story, but the significant point of comparison is this that old Lasker when he went to the Zürich tournament (which was about as strong as the one at Nuremberg 1896) had no such illusions as old Steinitz had in the earlier event. Assessing precisely the enormous strength of his opponents and his own handicap of old age and infirmity he predicted that he might do quite well in the first week, that he was likely then to feel the physical strain and that he would probably still be good enough for the fifth prize. That was exactly what he achieved, not without playing one or two magnificent games and beating Euwe (who was to win the World Championship in the next year). It was certainly a remarkable achievement and while old Lasker wasn't particularly elated about it he wasn't disappointed either; he knew that it was about the best that could reasonably be expected.

But Steinitz, thirty-eight years earlier, was deeply disappointed by being merely sixth at Nuremberg. He could not see that, for a man of his age, it was quite an achievement; he considered himself a failure and felt he had utterly wasted the nervous energy lavished on that contest. He was a nervous wreck when a few months later, on November 7th, the return match with Lasker was started.

Lasker won the first game quite easily, then the second, the third, the fourth, and the fifth. With a score of 5:0 and half his task accomplished Lasker let up a bit. The next three games were drawn, then another two wins for Lasker, and one more drawn. Then at long last, in the twelfth and thirteenth game Steinitz managed to score his only two points. Yet another draw followed, and then Lasker made an end of it by winning three games in a row. Result 10:2, with five draws. Total collapse for Steinitz. His life had lost its meaning. The last game was played on January 14th 1897. Exactly four weeks later they had to take the old man to the psychiatric clinic in Moscow.

Once again he recuperated. He returned to his second home—if he ever had a home—in the USA. He made one more trip to Europe, and in the Vienna Tournament of 1898 he actually scored a very handsome fourth prize, with only Tarrasch, Pillsbury and Janowski ahead of him and sixteen other masters behind him. That was the last flicker of the bright flame that was Wilhelm Steinitz. In the great London Tournament of 1899 he was nowhere near the prize-winners; not even the minor ones. For the first and last time in his life he was 'unplaced'. Soon after, he was found to be hopelessly demented. He had to be taken to a clinic, and on August 12th, 1900 he died, leaving behind a family in sorrow and in need.

Such, in the last analysis, was the melancholy result of that rather superfluous second match between Lasker and Steinitz. It made a deep impression on Lasker's sensitive mind, and while his own position in the chess world was more secure than ever, he could not forget the question that had worried him when, as a youngster, he was first drawn to professional chess by economic necessity rather than the lure of the game. What's the good of it? What's the use of being a mere chess player? He was world champion, the supreme arbiter and idol of a world-wide movement. But when all was said and done, was it not still a mere game? The 'Royal Game', to be sure, but still no more than a game! Was not its own great historian Tassilo von Heydebrandt und der Lasa quite right in saying about chess: 'An art in its form, a science by treatment but in essence a game'? And was not Moses Mendelssohn, the great philosopher of the eighteenth century (and no mean chess player himself) equally right when he remarked: 'Too playful to be taken seriously, and rather too serious for a game.' Was a man morally justified to give—nay, to waste—his life for such a thing?

Much later, in his *Philosophie des Unvollendbare*, Emanuel Lasker was to think out and to formulate such ideas: but now he had to wrestle with the problem in his own soul: What is victory? —No satisfaction, but merely a commitment for further effort. What is a goal?—Nothing finite, but merely a glimpse of the infinite.

For five years, with single-minded determination, Lasker had driven himself towards that one goal: the world championship in chess. Now that the goal was reached it failed to give Lasker satisfaction, let alone contentment. Life was so rich. There was so much to be learned and to be done. Some new goal had to be sought, some new peak to be reached, a higher one, worth a man's while.

At that time Lasker immersed himself more and more in philosophical and mathematical thought, for ever trying to 'transcend' from chess to those greater realms. He was rather modest about it, and he liked to contrast himself as a mere 'player' with Steinitz, the 'thinker'. Such a statement needs some qualification. There was certainly a bit of the 'player' and the 'thinker' in both of them, but in Steinitz's mind it was the player who got the better of the thinker and drove the man to perdition. But Lasker was fortunate enough often to tire of 'playing' and to seek refuge in a realm of thought far beyond chess. Steinitz exhausted himself in chess and died of it. Lasker rose above chess to live another life in all the riches of the spirit. Steinitz was unhappy whenever he lost a game of chess. Lasker was unhappy whenever he failed to get away from the game.

GAME 4

RUY LOPEZ

LASKER–STEINITZ

9th game of the 1894 match, played Apr. 14 at Philadelphia

1) P—K4   P—K4
2) Kt—KB3   Kt—QB3
3) B—Kt5   P—Q3
4) Kt—B3

Not quite so good as 4) P—Q4, B—Q2 5) Kt—B3 which Lasker had played previously in this match. While 4) P—Q4 threatens to win a P the text is relatively innocuous, so that Black can equalize quickly.

4) . . . . .   P—QR3
5) B—B4   B—K3
6) B×B   P×B
7) P—Q4   P×P
8) Kt×P   Kt×Kt
9) Q×Kt   Kt—K2
10) B—Kt5   Kt—B3
11) B×Q   Kt×Q
12) 0—0—0   Kt—Kt4?

Here Steinitz shows poor judgment, since he will be left with a doubled isolated QKtP and a weak QP. 12) ...P—QB4 13) B—Kt5 would also be unfavourable for Black, but he could simply have played 12) ...R×B 13) R×Kt, B—K2 with an even game.

13) Kt×Kt   P×Kt
14) B×P   R×P

Black could have won the KP by 14) ...R—R3, forcing 15) P—K5 (else ...K—Q2) P—Q4 16) P—QR3, K—Q2, although even then White would still have the better game. Now

Black threatens to come out a P ahead by ...R—R3

15) B—Kt6   B—K2
16) P—QB3   K—B2
17) K—B2   R(1)—R1
18) K—Kt3   R(7)—R5
19) P—B3   R(1)—R3
20) B—Q4   P—KKt3
21) R—Q3   K—K1

Position after White's 22nd move

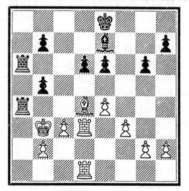

22) R(1)—Q1   P—K4

Obviously a very bad move, but a difficult one to avoid in view of Black's P position. The QP is now permanently weakened, and White can attack the QKtP as well

23) B—K3   K—Q2

Enables White to post his B on the diagonal QR3—KB8. But Black must protect the KtP, for White already threatens R—Q5

24) B—B5!   R—R8
25) R(1)—Q2   K—K3
26) B—R3   P—Kt4
27) R—Q5   R—Kt3
28) K—Kt4   P—Kt5

In contrast to his weak and colourless play in the early

part of the game, Steinitz plays now with great energy. Lasker's play however is also on a high level. The object of the text is, of course, to weaken White's K side Ps

29) K—R5

Lasker suggested the following variation as superior to the text: 29) P×P, R—K8 30) K—R5, B—Q1 31) R×P, R—R3 ch 32) K—Kt4, R×P ch 33) K—Kt3. The move actually played has the merit of simplicity

29)	.....	R—R3 ch
30)	K×P	P—R4
31)	R—Q1	R×R
32)	R×R	P×P
33)	P×P	R—R1
34)	K—Kt6	R—KKt1
35)	K×P	R—Kt7
36)	P—R4	R—R7
37)	K—B6	B×P
38)	R×P ch	K—B2
39)	K—Q5	B—B3

if 39) ...R—Q7 ch 40) K×P, B—Kt6 ch 41) P—B4, R×R 42) B×R, P—R5 43) B—B5, P—R6 44) B—Kt1 and White wins easily (Lasker's own notes)

40)	R—Q7 ch	K—Kt3
41)	K—K6	P—R5
42)	R—Q1	P—R6
43)	R—Kt1 ch	R—Kt7

Or 43 ...B—Kt4 44) B—K7, R—Kt7 45) R×R, P×R 46) B—B5 and wins

44)	R×R ch	P×R
45)	B—B5	B—Q1
46)	P—Kt4	K—Kt4
47)	K—Q7	B—B3
48)	P—Kt5	K—B5
49)	P—Kt6	Resigns

Lasker's best game in this match (Notes by FRED REINFELD in *Dr. Lasker's Chess Career*)

GAME 5

RUY LOPEZ

LASKER–STEINITZ

13th game of the 1894 match

1)	P—K4	P—K4
2)	Kt—KB3	Kt—QB3
3)	B—Kt5	P—QR3
4)	B×Kt	QP×B
5)	P—Q4	

Logical play, for only in the end-game can White turn his extra P on the K side to account

5) ..... P×P

Accepting the challenge of 'having it out in the centre'.

An interesting idea (due to Frank Marshall) is 5) ...B—KKt5 6) P×P, Q×Q ch 7) K×Q, 0—0—0 ch 8) K—K1 (best), R—K1 recovering the P

6)	Q×P	Q×Q
7)	Kt×Q	P—QB4
8)	Kt—K2	B—Q2
9)	QKt—B3	

Instead of the simple development, a more astute mobilisation results from 9) P—QKt3

9) ..... 0—0—0

After his rapid and straightforward development, Black has already overcome all the difficulties of the opening

10)	B—B4	B—B3
11)	0—0	Kt—B3
12)	P—B3	

Thus White's majority in the centre is held for a long time to come

12)	.....	B—K2
13)	Kt—Kt3	P—KKt3
14)	KR—K1	Kt—Q2
15)	Kt—Q1	Kt—Kt3
16)	Kt—B1	

With the idea of controlling his Q2, but all this regrouping behind the front demonstrates that all is not well with White

16)	.....	R—Q2
17)	B—K3	R(1)—Q1

Black has massed his troops on the critical sector and, in the sequel, will demonstrate that, in spite of the exchange of Queens, the end-game is not yet, and the play shows the sacrifices and other conceptions germane to the middle game

18)	P—QKt3	P—B5!
19)	B×Kt	P×B
20)	P×P	B—Kt5
21)	P—B3	B—B4 ch

Position after White's 24th move

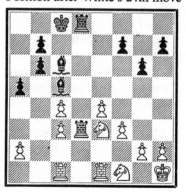

22)	K—R1	R—Q6
23)	R—B1	P—QR4
24)	Kt(Q)—K3	

Making for Q5. He should have tried to perturb his adversary with 24) Kt—Kt2

24)	.....	P—B4!

A magnificent conception, breaking down the King's defences

25)	P×P	P×P
26)	P—KR3	R—Kt1
27)	Kt—Q5	B×Kt
28)	P×B	R×QP
29)	QR—Q1	R×R
30)	R×R	P—B5!

This resplendent Pawn blockades not only the adverse Kt but the whole trio of White Pawns on the K side

31)	K—R2	R—K1
32)	P—QR4	K—B2
33)	P—R4	K—B3
34)	P—B4	B—Kt5
35)	K—R3	R—K8

Masterly liquidation. In the ensuing ending Black holds the trump cards.

36)	R×R	B×R
37)	K—Kt4	K—B4
38)	K×P	K×P
39)	K—K4	B×P
40)	P—Kt3	B—Q1
41)	Kt—K3 ch	K—Kt5
42)	K—Q3	K×P
43)	K—B2	K—Kt4
44)	P—B4	K—B4
45)	P—B5	K—Q3
46)	P—Kt4	P—Kt4
47)	Kt—Q1	K—K4
48)	Kt—B3	P—Kt5
49)	Kt—R4	K—Q5
50)	Kt—Kt2	P—Kt4

51)	K—Kt3	B—K2
52)	P—Kt5	P—R5 ch
53)	Kt×P	P×Ktch
54)	K×P	K—K4
55)	K—Kt3	K×P
	Resigns	

A game which is impressive, not only in the singleness of purpose with which Black carries out the main ideas of the defence, such as pressure on the open Q file and co-operation of the two Bishops, but also by the economy of means employed.

(Notes by TARTAKOVER and DU MONT (from 500 *Master Games of Chess*)

GAME 6

RUY LOPEZ

LASKER–STEINITZ

Hastings 1895

1)	P—K4	P—K4
2)	Kt—KB3	Kt—QB3
3)	B—Kt5	P—QR3
4)	B—R4	P—Q3
5)	0—0	Kt—K2

One of the many defences which Steinitz invented, but which have not found favour with other masters. Nowadays the usual reply is 5) ...B—Q2 6) P—B3, P—KKt3, or 5) ...P—B4 (*More recently, though, Steinitz's old line has been repeatedly tried in tournament games, such as Euwe–Keres, Hague 1948 R.T.*)

6)	P—B3	B—Q2
7)	P—Q4	Kt—Kt3

Black gets an easier game with 7) ...P—KKt3

8)	R—K1	B—K2
9)	QKt—Q2	0—0
10)	Kt—B1	

The manoeuvre with the QKt was invented by Steinitz himself

10)	.....	Q—K1

The critics are unanimous in applying to this move such epithets as 'bizarre', 'typically Steinitzian', 'peculiar', and the like. In reality the text begins a profound manoeuvre. Black wishes to force his opponent to play P—Q5. Once the centre is stabilised by this advance, Black can undertake a promising attack on the Q side. Unfortunately Black's KKt is not very well placed for the execution of this plan. But as we shall see, it is not on account of his 'bizarre' moves that Steinitz loses this game.

11)	B—B2	K—R1
12)	Kt—Kt3	B—Kt5
13)	P—Q5	

Black has finally forced the advance of the QP and should now continue ...Kt—Q1, (as he did, more successfully, in one of his match games against Lasker).

13)	.....	Kt—Kt1
14)	P—KR3	B—B1
15)	Kt—B5	B—Q1
16)	P—KKt4	Kt—K2

17) Kt—Kt3   Kt—Kt1
The *Deutsche Schachzeitung*
inclined to the opinion that
Steinitz allowed his sense of
humour to get the better of
him in bringing about the
present position. This impu-
tation of humorous intent is,
however, merely a sign of the
annotator's laziness. It is clear
that after ...P—KKt3, followed by ...B—B3—Kt2,
...Kt—K2 and ...P—KB4
Black will have a promising
game.

Position after Black's 17th move

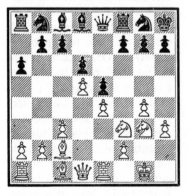

18) K—Kt2   Kt—Q2
Again Steinitz changes his plan
19) B—K3   Kt—Kt3
The Kt is, of course, quite
ineffective on this square, but
it is to be brought to K2.
20) P—Kt3   B—Q2
21) P—B4

Now White has the initiative
on both wings
21) .....   Kt—B1
22) Q—Q2   Kt(B1)—K2
23) P—B5   P—KKt3
24) Q—B3!   P—B4?
Overlooking the threatened
sacrifice. 24) ...P—B3, followed by Q—B2—Kt2 was
indicated.
25) Kt×KP!   P×Kt
26) Q×P ch   Kt—B3
27) B—Q4!
But not 27) P—Kt5?, Kt×QP!
27) .....   P×KtP
28) P×P   B×P
29) Q—Kt5   Q—Q2
30) B×Kt ch   K—Kt1
31) B—Q1   B—R6 ch
32) K—Kt1   Kt×P?
This sacrifice loses quickly.
The only way of putting up
any fight at all was 32)
...R×B 33) Q×R, Kt×P
33) B×B   Kt—B5
34) B—B6   Q—Q7
35) R—K2!
The simplest method of putting
an end to Black's demon-
stration
35) .....   Kt×R ch
36) B×Kt   Q—Q2
37) R—Q1   Q—B2
38) B—B4   B—K3
39) P—K5   B×B
40) Kt—B5   Resigns

(Notes by FRED REINFELD in
Dr. Lasker's Chess Career)

GAME 7

QUEEN'S GAMBIT DECLINED

STEINITZ–LASKER

St. Petersburg Tournament
19. Dec. 1895

1)	P—Q4	P—Q4
2)	P—QB4	P—K3
3)	Kt—QB3	Kt—KB3
4)	B—B4	B—K2
5)	P—K3	0—0
6)	R—B1	P—B4
7)	QP×P	B×P
8)	P×P	P×P

Not ...Kt×P?, or account of
9) Kt×Kt, with an attack on
the B. After the text-move,
though, 9) Kt×P would be
ineffective.

9)	Kt—KB3	Kt—B3
10)	B—Q3	P—Q5
11)	P×P	Kt×P
12)	0—0	

It would be safer to exchange
on Q4, prior to castling

12)	.....	B—KKt5
13)	Kt—QKt5?	

This 'attack' is uncalled for;
after 13) B—K2 White would
have had a tenable game.

13)	.....	B×Kt
14)	P×B	Kt—K3!
15)	B—K5	Kt—R4
16)	K—R1	Q—Kt4
17)	B—Kt3	QR—Q1!

Typical for Lasker: a positional
manoeuvre combined with a
tactical threat.

18) Q—B2   Q—R3

The point of Lasker's trap is
this that the natural move
19) KR—Q1 would now be
faulty, in as much as ...R—

QB1 would give Black a win
in every variation.

Position after Black's 18th move

19) QR—Q1   R—B1!

Having interfered with the
opponent's natural development Lasker now regroups his
forces. For much the same
manoeuvre see his games
against Janowski (Petersburg
1914) and Rubinstein (Moscow
1925). (See pp. 181 and 250).

20)	Q—Kt3	P—QR3
21)	Kt—B3	Kt—Q5!

A P-sacrifice which should
secure at least a draw.

22)	Q×P	Kt×B ch
23)	P×Kt	R—Kt1
24)	Q×P	R—Kt3
25)	Q—B4	R×P
26)	P—KR4?	

By 26) Kt—K2 White could
have forced a draw, but
Steinitz evidently means to
play for a win. Indeed, his
position looks fairly secure

26) .....   B—R2
27) B—K4   Q—Q3!

Stopping Kt—K2 for good

and all and practically forcing the next move.

28) P—B4   Q—Q2
29) B—Kt2   Q—Kt5!

Very pretty, since 30) R×Kt can now be countered by ... Q×KtP etc.

30) Q—Q3   Kt—B4
31) Kt—K4   B—K6

Much better than ...Kt×RP and putting paid to Steinitz's excellent defence.

32) R—B3(best)   R×B!

GAME 8

QUEEN'S GAMBIT DECLINED

PILLSBURY–LASKER

St. Petersburg Tournament,
4. January 1896

1) P—Q4   P—Q4
2) P—QB4   P—K3
3) Kt—QB3   Kt—KB3
4) Kt—B3   P—B4
5) B—Kt5

The most aggressive continuation. If 5) BP×P, Kt×P with approximate equality

5) .....   BP×P
6) Q×P   Kt—B3
7) Q—R4

Here, White misses the best line. Pillsbury subsequently subjected the variation to rigorous analysis for many years and found that 7) B×Kt gives White the better game. This he demonstrated in his Cambridge Springs encounter with Lasker. [See game 26]. (According to more recent analysis White's advantage is open to doubt. R.T.)

33) K×R   Kt×P ch
34) K—R2   Kt×R ch
35) K—Kt2   Kt—R5 ch
36) K—R2   Kt—B4
37) R—QKt1   P—R4
38) R—Kt4   R—R1
39) P—R3   R×P!

Resigns

If 40) Q×R, Black mates in 4; nor could White save himself by Q—Q8 ch.

(Notes by FRED REINFELD in *Chess Strategy and Tactics*)

7) .....   B—K2
8) 0—0—0

A risky move which is difficult to avoid, for if 8) P—K3, Q—Kt3 9) QR—Kt1, P—KR3 10) B—Q3, P×P 11) B×BP, 0—0 12) B×RP, P×B 13) Q×P, Q—B4!

8) .....   Q—R4
9) P—K3   B—Q2
10) K—Kt1   P—KR3 !

An excellent move. The Q must now remain at KR4 until the B is exchanged

11) P×P   P×P
12) Kt—Q4

If 12) B—Q3, 0—0—0 would win at least a P and expose White's K to attack.

12) .....   0—0
13) B×Kt   B×B
14) Q—R5

White is pursuing a will o' the wisp (K side attack). The sequel clearly reveals the inadequacy of this plan. Either 14) Q—B4 or Q—Kt3 would therefore be better

14) ..... Kt×Kt
15) P×Kt B—K3
16) P—B4

Intending P—B5, P—KKt4, P—KR4, followed by B—R3 and P—Kt5

16) ..... QR—B1
17) P—B5

He can hardly be blamed for overlooking Lasker's magnificent combination, but here 17) Q—B3 was in order

17) ..... R×Kt!
18) P×B

Best. If 18) P×R, Q×BP

Position after White's 18th move

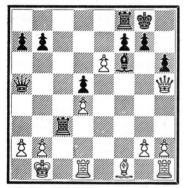

18) ..... R—QR6!!
19) P×P ch

Alternatives are:

I: 19) P×R, Q—Kt3 ch 20) K—R1, B×P ch 21) R×B, Q×R ch 22) K—Kt1, P×P 23) B—K2, Q—K5 ch 24) K any, R—B7 and should win

II: 19) P—K7, R—K1 20) P×R, Q—Kt3 ch 21) K—B2, R—B1 ch 22) K—Q2, B×P 23) P—K8(Q) ch,

R×Q 24) B—Q3, Q—R4 ch 25) K—B1, R—B1 ch 26) R—B2, R×B ch and wins. This variation was given by the players in post-mortem analysis.

19) ..... R×P
20) P×R Q—Kt3 ch
21) B—Kt5 (forced) Q×B ch
22) K—R1 R—B2
23) R—Q2 R—B5
24) KR—Q1 R—B6

The concluding moves were played under fearful time-pressure

25) Q—B5

The alternative 25) Q—K2 is refuted by ...R—B8! ch 26) R×R, B×P ch 27) R×B, Q×Q 28) R—KKt1, Q—KB7! 29) R(Q4)—Q1, P—Q5 and Black has good winning chances. But it is not easy to see that after the text White must lose.

25) ..... Q—B5
26) K—Kt2? R×P!
27) Q—K6 ch K—R2
28) K×R Black mates in 5 moves

By 18) ...Q—B6 ch 29) K—R4, P—Kt4 ch 30) K×P, Q—B5 ch 31) K—R5, B—Q1 ch 32) Q—Kt6, P×Q mate Lasker's outstanding combinative game. So competent a judge as Amos Burn said of the combination begun on the 17th move: 'One of the finest ever made'.

(Notes by FRED REINFELD in *Dr. Lasker's Chess Career*)

GAME 9

RUY LOPEZ

LASKER–STEINITZ,

St. Petersburg Tournament
14th January 1896

1) P—K4   P—K4
2) Kt—KB3   Kt—QB3
3) B—Kt5   P—Q3
4) P—Q4   B—Q2
5) Kt—B3   KKt—B3
6) P×P   P×P
7) B—Kt5!

An excellent move which completely refutes Black's opening strategy; either he remains with a weak, doubled and isolated QBP or else he must weaken his K side with ...P—R3

7) .....   P—KR3
8) B×QKt   P×B
9) B—K3

The attack on Black's weak QB4 will serve as the motif of the ensuing play.

9) .....   Kt—Kt1
10) Q—Q3   B—Q3
11) Kt—Q2   Kt—K2?

Black has a bad game, but this

Position after Black's 14th move

move makes it even worse.

12) Kt—B4   Kt—B1
13) O—O—O   Q—K2
14) P—B4!

Opening the KB file as a basis for future operations

14) .....   P—B3
15) P×P   P×P

The alternative ...B×P would lose very quickly: 16) Kt×B, P×Kt 17) B—B5!, Q—K3 18) Q—Kt3, R—KKt1 19) KR—B1, Kt—K2 20) B×Kt, Q×B 21) Q—Kt6 ch, K—Q1 22) R—B7 etc.

16) KR—B1

By means of the foregoing exchange, Lasker has not only opened another file for his pieces, but has induced a new weakness in Black's Pawn position.

16) .....   Q—K3
17) Kt—R4   Q—K2

Black is lost. He has no adequate defence to B—B5. If, e.g., 17) ...R—B1 18) Kt—B5, B×Kt 19) B×B, R×R 20) R×R, Kt—K2 21) Q—QB3, Kt—Kt3? 22) Kt×P! Steinitz had, to be sure, the inferior game after the opening; but that his position should be definitely lost on the 17th move is quite a tribute to Lasker's energetic play.

18) B—B5   B×B
19) Kt×B   B—Kt5
20) R—Q2   Kt—Kt3
21) Kt—R6   R—KB1
22) Kt—R5

The play with the Knights is very pretty.

22)	R×R ch	38)	P—B4	B—Kt7
23) Q×R	R—Q1	39)	P—QKt4	P—R4
24) Kt(5)×P	R×R	40)	P—Kt5	P—R5
25) Kt×Q	R—Q8 ch	41)	P×P	P×P
26) Q×R	B×Q	42)	P—B5 ch	K—Q2
27) Kt—B6	B—K7	43)	P—R4	K—B1
28) Kt—B5	B—B8	44)	P—B6	K—Kt1
29) P—KKt3	Kt—B5	45)	Kt—K5	K—R2
30) Kt×RP	B—Kt7	46)	K—B5	B—R6
31) Kt—B6	Kt—Q3	47)	Kt—Q7	Resigns
32) Kt×P	Kt×P			
33) Kt×Kt	B×Kt			
34) Kt—Q3	K—Q2			
35) K—Q2	K—Q3			
36) K—B3	B—Q4			
37) K—Q4	P—Kt4			

Lasker's exploitation of weak squares—a 'hypermodern' stratagem—is once more in evidence in this elegant game.

(Notes by FRED REINFELD in *Dr. Lasker's Chess Career*)

GAME 10

RUY LOPEZ

PORGES–LASKER

1st round of Nuremberg Tournament July 20th 1896

1)	P—K4	P—K4
2)	Kt—KB3	Kt—QB3
3)	B—Kt5	Kt—B3
4)	0—0	Kt×P
5)	P—Q4	B—K2
6)	Q—K2	Kt—Q3
7)	B×Kt	KtP×B
8)	P×P	Kt—Kt2

If a Kt has spent four of the first eight opening moves, merely, so as to be displaced at so incredible an 'outpost' as QKt2, I for one cannot but consider this utterly ludicrous; nor can I see why such a mode of development should have been accepted as normal for many a year. Anyway, I consider it better for Black to capture with his QP on his 7th move, since White's attack after 8) P×P, Kt—B4 9) R—Q1, B—Q2 10) P—K6, P×P 11) Kt—K5 is short-lived and may well lead to a quick counter-attack.

(*But an analysis of Showalter's has proved that White can obtain lasting advantage by playing 10) P—KKt4 instead of P—K6., such as 10) ...Kt—R3 11) P—Kt5, Kt—B4 12) P—K6, P×P 13) Kt—K5, B—Q3 14) Q—R5 ch, P—Kt3 15) Kt× KtP, Kt—Kt2 16) Q—R6, Kt—B4 17) Q—R3, R—KKt1 18) Q×P, R—Kt2 19) Q—R5 R. T.*)

9) P—QKt3

First played by Lasker in a little known game against O. C. Müller.

9)	.....	0—0
10)	B—Kt2	P—Q4

11) P×P e. p.

This gives away White's opening advantage by consolidating the opponent's game. 11) QKt—Q2 was indicated.

11) ..... P×P
12) QKt—Q2 R—K1!

The R here threatens the White Q, and it is interesting to see how quickly that indirect menace gives Black some decisive advantage.

13) KR—K1 B—Q2
14) Kt—K4

This turns out to be ineffective. It would have been relatively best to retreat the Q to KB1, the only if modest place where she could enjoy a little peace.

14) ..... P—Q4
15) Kt(4)—Q2

The Kt mustn't go to KKt3, since B—Kt5 would cost the exchange.

15) ..... B—QR6
16) B—K5 P—B3
17) Q—R6

White just manages to avoid the loss of a piece.

17) ..... P×B
18) Q×B P—K5
19) Kt—Q4 Q—B3
20) P—QB3 R—KB1
21) P—B3 Q—Kt4

One blow after another! Lasker

plays the attack with great strength.

22) Q—B1 Kt—B4
23) Kt—B1 Q—Kt3
24) R—K3 Kt—Q6
25) Q—Q1 Kt—B5
26) Kt—Kt3 P—KR4

Position after White's 27th move

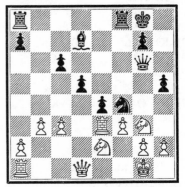

27) Kt(4)—K2 Kt×P!

Forcing the issue with an elegant combination.

28) K×Kt P×P ch
29) R×P B—R6 ch
30) K×B Q—Kt5 ch
31) K—Kt2 Q×R ch
32) K—Kt1 P—R5
33) Kt—R1 Q—K6 ch

Resigns, since K—Kt2 is punished by the pretty mate P—R6.

(Notes by Dr. TARRASCH in the Book of the Tournament)

GAME 11

FRENCH DEFENCE

STEINITZ–LASKER

Nuremberg Tournament, July 22nd 1896

1) P—K4 P—K3
2) P—Q4 P—Q4
3) Kt—Q2

Introduced by Tarrasch in the early eighteen-nineties, and quite fashionable again in (and since) the nineteen-forties. R. T.

3) ..... P—QB4

4) QP×P

White presents his opponent with a tempo as well as the centre. P—QB3 was preferable. (*Nowadays one prefers 4) KP×P R. T.*)

4) .....   B×P
5) Kt—Kt3   B—Kt3
6) P×P   Kt—KB3

There's not the least objection either against ...P×P. The centre P is an advantage, even though isolated.

7) B—Kt5 ch

White can neither play P×P nor B—KKt5, on account of 7) ...B×P ch

7) .....   B—Q2
8) B×B ch   Q×B
9) P—QB4   P×P
10) P—B5

Presenting Black with the advantage of a passed Pawn. But Steinitz evidently considered the isolated QP a source of weakness.

10) .....   B—B2
11) Kt—B3   Kt—B3
12) 0—0   0—0
13) Kt(Kt3)—Q4   Kt×Kt
14) Q×Kt

Since he cannot maintain the Q on Q4 he should have recaptured with the Kt.

14) .....   KR—K1
15) B—K3   R—K5
16) Q—Q3   QR—K1

Black has a splendidly developed game and will soon be ready for a K side attack

17) KR—Q1   P—KR3
18) P—QR3   Q—Kt5
19) P—QKt4   P—KKt4

20) Q—B3   Q—B4
21) Q—Q3

It is astonishing how half-heartedly Steinitz almost invariably played when facing Lasker.

21) .....   Q—Kt3
22) Q—Kt5

No matter whether White does or doesn't risk this adventure, Black still has a very strong attack

22) .....   Q—R4

Steinitz fails to see the menace of this move. But P—KR3 would further weaken his position.

Position after White's 23rd move

23) Q×P   B×P ch!
24) Kt×B

K—B1 was the lesser evil.

24) .....   R—R5
25) P—B3

If 25) Q—B7, Kt—Kt5! (F. Reinfeld)

25) .....   R×Kt
26) Q—B7   R—R8ch
27) K—B2   Q—R5 ch
28) Q—Kt3   Q×Q ch

He could have played 28)

P—Q5, so as to capture the QR after 29) R×P; whereas 29) B×P would have led to the brilliant ...R—B8 ch!!, resulting in either the capture of the Q or mate. But White could have played 29) Q×Q which would have been no more profitable for Black than the continuation actually chosen.

29)	K×Q	R×R
30)	R×R	R×B

The rest is mere routine.

31)	R—QB1	Kt—K1
32)	P—R4	R—R6

33)	P—Kt5	R×P
34)	R—QKt1	R—QB5
35)	P—Kt6	P×P
36)	P×P	R—B1
37)	K—Kt4	Kt—Q3
38)	K—R5	K—Kt2
39)	P—Kt7	R—QKt1
40)	R—Kt6	Kt—B4
41)	P—B4	P×P
42)	K—Kt4	Kt—K6 ch
43)	K×P	Kt—B5
44)	R—Kt4	K—B3
	Resigns	

(Notes by Dr. TARRASCH in the Book of the Tournament)

GAME 12

RUY LOPEZ

WINAWER–LASKER

Nuremberg Tournament
August 4th 1896

1)	P—K4	P—K4
2)	Kt—KB3	Kt—QB3
3)	B—Kt5	Kt—B3
4)	0—0	Kt×P
5)	P—Q4	B—K2
6)	Q—K2	Kt—Q3
7)	B×Kt	KtP×B
8)	P×P	Kt—Kt2
9)	Kt—Q4	0—0
10)	Kt(1)—B3	B—B4

The usual move here is ...Kt—B4 (*No longer recommended because White gets the advantage by 11) R—Q1, Q—K1 12) Kt—B5, P—B3 13) B—R6, Kt—K3 14) Q—Kt4 R. T.*)

11)	Kt—B5	

This attack hardly ever pays dividends. Simpler and stronger

is B—K3. (*Best is 11) R—Q1, Q—K1 12) B—B4, or 11) ...B×Kt 12) R×B, P—Q4 13) P×P e.p., P×P 14) P—QKt4!, such as Schlechter–Reti, 1914, R. T.*)

11)	.....	P—Q4

In this variation this moves always gives Black a good game.

12)	Q—Kt4	B×Kt
13)	Q×B	R—K1
14)	B—B4	B—Q5
15)	KR—K1	

Owing to Black's threat of P—Kt3 the KP required further support.

15)	.....	Kt—B4
16)	QR—Q1	

Had White tried to avoid the disrupture of his Q wing pawn-skeleton by 16) Kt—Q1 he would have lost his KP after 16) ...Kt—K5 17) P—QB3, P—Kt3.

16)	B×Kt
17) P×B	Q—B1
18) Q—R5	

White should have swopped Queens and continued R—Kt1. By relinquishing his Q wing for the sake of his K side attack he goes in for a reckless gamble.

Position after Black's 17th move

18)	Q—R3
19) R—K3	Q×P
20) R—QB1	Q—B5

It is most interesting and instructive to see how Black consistently disturbs the development of the opponent's attack and finally gets his own passed P to decide the issue.

21) R—B3	Kt—K3
22) B—Q2	R—K2
23) R—R3	Q—K5
24) P—B3	

White loses too much time. Stronger would have been 24) P—KB4, Q—Kt3 25) Q—R4, R—Q2 26) P—Kt4

24)	Q—Kt3
25) Q—R4	R—Q2
26) P—KB4	Q—K5

27) P—Kt4	

He might have continued the attack more advantageously by 27) R—Q3, followed by R—K1 and an advance of the Pawns.

27)	Kt—B1

Forestalling P—B5

28) Q—B2	P—QR4
29) R—K3	Q—B5
30) P—B5	

At long last White gets his Pawns going, but by now his pieces are displaced and the Black passed P has got moving.

30)	P—R5! (Q×KtP?)
31) R—B1	P—R6
32) R(3)—K1	P—R7
33) P—R3	P—B4!
34) K—R2	P—Q5
35) Q—B3	P—QB3

So as to double the rooks. The P is taboo on account of P—R8, followed by Q—K7 ch.

36) P—K6	P×P
37) P×P	Kt×P
38) Q×P	R(2)—R2
39) R—R1	R—KB1
40) R(B1—K1)	Kt—Q1
41) Q—Kt6	

The Q had better go back to the K wing

41)	R(2)—KB2
42) B—Kt5	R—B7 ch
43) K—Kt3	Q×P ch

Resigns

44) K—R4 would be punished by Q×RP ch, followed by a mate in two. A flawless game of Lasker's.

(Notes by Dr. TARRASCH in the Book of the Tournament)

GAME 13

RUY LOPEZ

LASKER–TARRASCH

Nuremberg Tournament, final
(18th) round 8th August 1896

1) P—K4   P—K4
2) Kt—KB3   Kt—QB3
3) B—Kt5   P—QR3
4) B×Kt

If White can do this with
impunity, (as indeed seems
likely), P—R3 would be a
pointless move.

*(The 'exchange variation' was
Lasker's favourite, and logi-
cally, when defending a Ruy
Lopez he favoured the Rio de
Janeiro variation avoiding 3)
...P—QR3). Translators note*

4) .....   QP×B
5) Kt—B3   B—B4
*(Preferable is 5) ...P—KB3
R. T.)*
6) P—Q3   B—KKt5
7) B—K3   Q—Q3
8) B×B   Q×B
9) Q—Q2!   B×Kt?

A grievous misjudgment, bringing disadvantage to Black.
P—KB3 was indicated.

10) P×B   Kt—K2
11) 0—0—0   Kt—Kt3
12) Q—K3!   Q×Q ch

Not good because it strengthens
White's centre. But after 12)
...Q—K2 Black could not
have castled Q side on account
of Q—R7, whereas castling K-
side would have been dangerous
on account of the open Kt-file.
Black is paying the penalty
of his mistake on the 9th move.

13) P×Q   R—Q1
14) Kt—K2   P—B3
15) KR—Kt1   K—B2

Castling was preferable.

16) QR—B1   KR—K1
17) Kt—Kt3   Kt—B1
18) P—KB4   P—QB4

The game is untenable. Black
tries to provide against 19)
P×P, R×P 20) P—Q4, fol-
lowed by P—K5; but there is
even worse to come.

Position after Black's 18th move

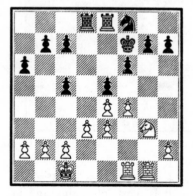

19) Kt—R5   P—KKt3
20) P×P!   R×KP

To take the Kt would allow
a mate in two

21) Kt×P   K—Kt2
22) R—B2   P—KR4
23) Kt—Q5   P—B3
24) Kt—B4   P—B5
25) R(2)—Kt2   R—Q3
26) P—KR4   P×P
27) P×P   K—B2
28) R—Kt5   R×R
29) R×R   R—B3
30) P—K5   R—B4
31) R×R ch   P×R
32) P—Q4

Better than Kt × P which would be good enough too.

32) .....   K—K2
33) K—Q2   P—B4
34) K—Q3   P × P
35) P × P   K—Q1
36) P—Q5   K—Q2

37) K—Q4   K—B2
38) P—Kt4   K—Q2
39) K—B5   K—B2
40) P—Q6 ch   K—Q2
41) K—Q5   Resigns

(Notes by Dr. TARRASCH in The Book of the Tournament)

GAME 14

RUY LOPEZ

LASKER–STEINITZ

2nd game of 2nd match, Moscow 1896

1) P—K4   P—K4
2) Kt—KB3   Kt—QB3
3) B—Kt5   B—B4
4) P—B3   KKt—K2
5) 0—0   Kt—Kt3
6) P—Q4   P × P
7) P × P   B—Kt3
8) Kt—B3   0—0
9) P—QR4   P—QR3
10) B—QB4   P—R3

10) ...P—Q3 would have been preferable

11) P—R3   P—Q3
12) B—K3   Kt(B3)—K2
13) R—K1   P—B3
14) Q—Kt3   B—B2
15) Kt—Q2   R—Kt1
16) QR—B1   P—Kt4
17) P × P   RP × P

All that Black has got to show for his pains is a weakening of his QBP

18) B—Q3   K—R1

He wants to push his KBP, but it would have been better to play ...B—K3

19) Kt—K2   P—KB4
20) P × P   B × P

21) B × B   R × B
22) Kt—Kt3   R—KB1
23) Q—K6   Q—B1
24) Q × Q   KR × Q
25) Kt—Kt3   K—Kt1
26) Kt—K4   K—B2
27) P—Kt3   K—K1
28) R—K2!

Lasker has methodically cramped the opponent's game, his immediate aim being to push his KRP so as to gain the square KB4 for his B.

28) .....   K—Q2
29) R(1)—K1!

Out of a seemingly harmless position Lasker has conjured up some mating threats, but by ...Kt—B4 on the next move Black might still put up an adequate defence

Position after White's 29th move

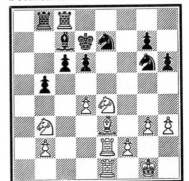

29) .....   B—Kt3?
30) B—B4   B—B2
   Obviously, Black mustn't take
   the B on account of Kt—B6 ch!
31) P—R4   P—R4
32) B—Kt5
   The threat of P—R5 has
   gained White a valuable post
   for his B. Now ...Kt—B4
   would no longer be adequate
   defence on account of 33)
   P—Kt4, P×P; 34) P—R5 etc.
32) .....   B—Q1

33) P—Kt4   P×P
34) P—R5   Kt—B1
35) Kt(4)—B5 ch!   P×Kt
36) Kt×P ch   K—Q3
37) B—B4 ch   K—Q4
38) R—K5 ch   K—B5
39) R—B1 ch   K×P
40) R—K4 ch   K—Q4
41) R—Q1 ch   K×Kt
42) B—K3 mate

(Notes by FRED REINFELD in
Lasker's Chess Career)

GAME 15

RUY LOPEZ

LASKER–STEINITZ

4th game of the 2nd match
(Moscow 1896/7)

1) P—K4   P—K4
2) Kt—KB3   Kt—QB3
3) B—Kt5   B—B4
4) P—B3   KKt—K2
5) P—Q4   P×P
6) P×P   B—Kt5 ch
   Unsatisfactory, for later on
   Black's QB4 becomes weak;
   but 6) ...B—Kt3 would be
   even worse: 7) P—Q5, Kt—
   QKt1 8) P—Q6, P×P 9)
   B—KB4, 0—0 10) Kt—B3
7) B—Q2   B×B ch
8) Q×B   P—Q4
   If 8) ...P—QR3; 9) B—R4,
   P—Q4 10) P×P, Q×P 11)
   Kt—B3, Q—K3 ch 12) K—B1,
   Q—B5 ch 13) K—Kt1 with
   advantage for White (Alekhine–
   Bogoljubov 1914)
9) P×P   Kt×P
10) B×Kt ch   P×B

In his notes to the game Reti-
Marshall in the monumental
New York 1924 Tournament
Book, Alekhine comments on
the remarkable similarity of
the two games up to this point

11) 0—0   0—0
12) Kt—B3   P—B3
   Sooner or later the possibility
   of Kt—K5 will force this
   move.
13) KR—K1   R—Kt1
14) P—KR3   B—B4
15) QR—B1   Q—Q3
16) Kt—KR4   B—Q2
17) Kt—K4   Q—B5
   A weak reply. 17) ...Q—Kt5
   would have given Black
   counterplay.
18) Q×Q   Kt×Q
19) Kt—QB5   B—B1
20) P—QKt3   K—B2
21) Kt—B3   KR—K1
   The exchange of rooks is ill-
   advised, for White is enabled
   to obtain control of the K file.
   21) ...R—Q1 would have set
   White a more difficult problem.

Lasker's handling of this end-game is classic throughout.

22) R×R   K×R
23) R—K1 ch   K—B2
24) Kt—Q2   Kt—K3?

A strategical blunder: Black rids himself of his only active piece. Correct was 24) ...R—Kt5 25) Kt—B4, B—K3! with good chances.

25) Kt×Kt   B×Kt
26) Kt—K4   B—Q4
27) Kt—B5   R—Kt5
28) R—Q1   K—K2
29) P—B3   K—Q3
30) K—B2   R—Kt1

Black's inelastic pawn structure cramps his position badly; and his B can force no weakness in White's Pawn structure.

31) R—K1   B—B2

Position after White's 32nd move

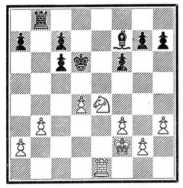

32) Kt—K4 ch   K—Q2
33) K—K3   B—Q4
34) Kt—B5 ch   K—Q3
35) K—Q3   P—KR4?

The Q side was already weak; now he ruins the K side as well. Passive resistance was in order.

36) P—KR4   R—KR1
37) K—B3   R—QKt1
38) P—B4   R—Kt1

If 38) ...B×KKtP; 39) R—K6 ch, K—Q4 40) R—K7 regains the P with advantage.

39) P—Kt3   P—Kt4?

Again Steinitz misjudges the position. There was no direct threat and hence no need for immediate action. Against passive resistance White would probably have played P—B5 and Kt—Q3—B4.

40) BP×P   P×P
41) R—K5   P×P
42) P×P   R—Kt6 ch
43) K—Kt4   R—Kt5

Black's moves are all forced. If 43) ...B—B6; 44) R×P!, B×R 45) Kt—K4 ch

44) Kt—Kt7 ch   K—Q2
45) R×P   R×P ch
46) K—R5   B—B2

White is virtually a P ahead, Black's doubled QBP being useless.

47) R—R6   R—Q7
48) Kt—B5 ch   K—K2
49) P—R4   R—Q3
50) R—R8   R—Q4
51) P—Kt4   B—K1

To prevent R—R8. If 51) ...R—Q1; 52) R×R, K×R 53) K—R6 with an easy win.

52) R—R6   R—B4

If 52) ...R—K4; 53) K—R6; whereas 53) K—R6 is now answered by R—B5.

53) R—K6 ch   K—Q1

The Black K must go to the Q side, for it is obvious that White will soon win the QRP.

54)	R—K4	B—B2	63)	R—R4	B—R7

54) R—K4   B—B2
55) K—R6   B—Q4
56) R—Q4   K—B1
57) K×P   R—R4
58) R—KB4   R—R1
59) P—R5   B—R7

The ending is pretty; If 59) ...K—Q1; 60) K—Kt7, R×P 61) P—R5, followed by P—R6—R7—R8=Q.

60) P—R6   B—Q4
61) P—R7   B—R7
62) R—K4   B—B2

63) R—R4   B—R7
64) Kt—K4   B—Kt6
65) P—R5   B—B7

Or 65) B—Q4 66) Kt—B6

66) R—Kt4!   Resigns

For if 66) ...R×P; 67) R—Kt8 ch, K—Q2 68) Kt—B6 ch etc. Or 66) ...B—Kt6 67) Kt—B6

A much admired ending.

(Notes by FRED REINFELD in *Dr. Lasker's Chess Career*)

CHAPTER TEN

Fads and Fancies

Thus, from 1896 on we have the first of those long 'intervals' in his chess activities which, as we shall see, were to occur again and again in Lasker's life. He could well afford now to decline invitations to tournaments and to accept only such lecture—and exhibition assignments as would please him or conveniently fit into his other work. As for declining competition in tournaments and matches, his position in the chess world was so secure that he need not fear the accusation of shirking competition. Indeed, the rarer he made himself as a chess performer the more popular he became; although still in his thirties, he was beginning to become almost a legend and countless anecdotes were circulating about him. Here are a few of them.

Before his first match with Steinitz, one of Lasker's admirers sent him a box of cigars with this note: 'Do please smoke them during the match; they will bring you luck.' Lasker tried one of them, found it abominable and threw the lot away. Soon after the match he happened to meet that admirer who congratulated the new champion. 'Well', he said, 'wasn't I quite right? My cigars did bring you luck, didn't they?'

'Indeed they did', said Lasker.

'So you did smoke them all during the match?' asked the delighted admirer.

'Oh no', said Lasker; 'I gave them to my opponent. He smoked them, and that was very lucky for me.'

Lasker's notorious absent-mindedness got him into some amusing trouble one day when he went to Paris. He arrived after dusk and rented a room recommended by a friend in London. He dropped his luggage there and hurried to the Café de la Régence, the most famous chess-café in the world which used to be frequented by Philidor and Labourdonnais (and even by Napoleon) and which for centuries had been the centre of chess-life in Paris. Lasker met a good many friends and spent an enjoyable evening. It was long after midnight when he thought of going home, but alas, he had forgotten his address; he could not even remember the name of the street. Still, it did not seem much to worry about. Lasker simply went home with one of his friends to stay the night, and before he did so he made a combination worthy of a chess master. He sent a

telegram to the London friend asking for the address he had recommended. Unfortunately, though, the combination had a 'flaw' of
which Lasker would never have been guilty on a chess board. In his
telegram he forgot to mention the address where he was spending
the night. Worse than that, by next morning Lasker had forgotten
that he had not included this vital information. Getting no reply
from London, he was deeply annoyed that his friend had let him
down, and wouldn't send him another wire.

But the situation was now getting serious; he was separated from
all his luggage. So there was nothing for it but systematically to
comb entire quarters of Paris, in the hope of recognising the street
and the house where he had put up. The search took many hours,
and at long last—being now extremely methodical about it—
Lasker was lucky enough to find the place. His landlady was pleased
to see her new tenant. There was a telegram for him. It turned out
to be from the London friend who, for lack of another address,
had sent it to the one Lasker was asking for. (I for one cannot help
thinking that, had the London friend been gifted with the combinative powers of a chess master, he would have sent the wire to the
Café de la Régence).

Lasker had certain idiosyncrasies. He could not bear bad table-
manners, and it drove him almost frantic to see (and hear) people
smack their lips while eating. One day, at a restaurant in Budapest
his neighbour at table was smacking away so lustily that Lasker,
his nerves on edge, was on the point of leaving the place. But he
was very hungry and he had ordered his meal, so he tried to bear it.
But when his neighbour began to shovel the food into his mouth
with the knife Lasker's patience was exhausted.

'Sir', he said icily, 'aren't you afraid of cutting your mouth?'

Knowing how hot-tempered Hungarians can be Lasker fully
expected to be challenged to a duel, but he was beyond caring.
The neighbour, though, did not resent the question.

'Oh no, sir', he answered, 'these table-knives are frightfully blunt.'

Lasker could, indeed, be quite short-tempered, and he had no
patience with fools. Any student of his books can see even now
that he was an excellent teacher; he used to lecture a good deal
(on mathematics as well as on chess), and in the years when he
more or less retired from playing chess in public, a substantial part
of his regular income was provided by private tuition. Such lessons
were very well paid, but when pupils annoyed Lasker by lack of
attention or by stupid questions he would throw the pre-paid fee on
the table, brusquely terminating the lesson.

Another thing Lasker simply would not stand for was being

kept waiting. If a guest was as little as a minute late, Lasker would order dinner to be served before his arrival. When his wife or friends reproached him for such lack of courtesy, his invariable answer was: 'It would be far more discourteous to be ill-tempered when receiving my guest; and I could not help being ill-tempered if I had to receive him with a rumbling stomach. Hence, even for the guest's sake I had better start eating. He shouldn't be late anyway.'

Food, indeed, became an important factor in Emanuel's life. He was a glutton for quality rather than quantity, undoubtedly a compensation for the privations of his wretched youth. If he was invited anywhere he did not mind if nothing was offered; after all he came for conversation rather than food. But if he was offered something not up to his own taste and standards, he would consider it a personal affront and as likely as not would never set foot in that house again.

He was competent at various sports, an excellent shot, and not lacking in physical courage. But when he had to go to the dentist he behaved like a silly child; he was even known to faint before the doctor had a chance to lay hands on him. He was allergic to dark rooms too, and whenever he went out in the evening the light had to be left on in his study. Nor could he bear to hear anyone walking behind him in the street, particularly at night. He had an explanation for that. It was because one day as a child he had been hit over the head by the stick of a tipsy student walking behind him.

Lasker could be most impatient should a lady in his company stop to look at shop windows, inspecting hats and fashions. Yet, he was quite capable, with utter disregard of his companions, of spending half an hour contemplating the windows of a bookshop or the cigars exhibited at a tobacconist's.

His consumption of cigars was enormous. It was the only luxury he indulged in. But he wasn't a bit interested in the clothes he wore; in due course we shall hear about some amusing trouble caused by his sartorial indifference at the time he wooed and married his wife.

Lasker's first long rest from chess lasted from 1896 to 1899, and at that time he was predominantly concerned with mathematical studies. At Manchester he delivered a series of crowded and highly praised lectures on the subject. He was determined to achieve his doctorate, and the research and study involved in these lectures provided part of the basis for his doctor-thesis and some subsequent academic work.

From time to time such studies would be interrupted by minor chess activities, such as simultaneous performances, lectures on chess theory, and a certain amount of journalistic work. Lasker accepted such assignments primarily and admittedly for material considerations, and he would insist on adequate fees. 'I don't want to die like Steinitz', he used to say,' nor live on charity like a beggar.' Again and again he stressed the chess master's right to be properly paid for his work, for the immense amount of pleasure he gave to an immense number of people. It was a point of principle with him, and he was a stickler for seeing to it that chess masters were less exploited financially than they used to be.

He did not have much support in these efforts from his colleagues in the ranks of master-chess, and whenever he pleaded for the need to establish some sort of copyright in published games and problems, his fellow masters—most of them in a very much weaker economic position than Lasker and hence very poor bargainers indeed—would raise the timid objection that the Press would stop giving them any publicity at all if asked to pay even a pittance. This unjustified timidity has prevailed to this day.

Lasker had little patience with colleagues who, while versed in the principles of attack and defence on the chess-board, refused to show equal courage and determination when it was a question of safeguarding their own professional interests. He demonstrated that the courage and devotion exercised in the game must also apply to the struggle of life; and although the material and social status of chess masters still leaves a great deal to be desired nobody had done so much to raise it as Emanuel Lasker did most stubbornly and consistently all his life.

Personally, he was anything but acquisitive. Having known dire poverty himself he had a soft spot for anyone in need, and there were enough of them to flock to him all the time. Time and again he would bring home two or three acquaintances picked up in the street or in a café and surprise his wife with the announcement that they were to stay for dinner. He had an infinite capacity for understanding life in the raw; he was deeply and somewhat uncomprehendingly shocked whenever he encountered callousness, rapaciousness, vanity, and conceit. He had much pride, and a wholesome loathing for anything bogus or pretentious or second-rate.

CHAPTER ELEVEN

Triumph in London and Paris

The three years of abstinence from chess had been usefully employed; but now Lasker felt the time had come to face some new test of his supremacy. He had been living in England most of that time, and when the great London Tournament of 1899 was in the offing he readily accepted the invitation to compete. It was almost as great an event as Hastings or Nuremberg, with only Dr Tarrasch missing among the fifteen famous masters assembled. It was a double-round affair, which meant that competitors had to play two games each against one another: and with twenty-eight rounds to be accomplished the tournament involved quite a test of physical endurance.

Having been out of practice for so long Lasker did not start too well, and in the fourth round he lost a game to Blackburne, the famous British master whom he had defeated so decisively seven years earlier. It was to be his only reverse in the whole long tournament; for from then on he simply ran away with it, his victory being a mathematical certainty almost half a dozen rounds before the end. He achieved the magnificent score of 23½ points, 4½ points ahead of Janowski, Maroczy, and Pillsbury who shared second to fourth prize, and of Schlechter (18), Blackburne (16½), Tchigorin (16) etc.

Lasker not only won the first prize by a record margin, but also the first brilliancy-prize for a magnificent game, (see p. 93); and the victim, of all people, was his great rival Steinitz who was playing in the very last of his innumerable tournaments, the first and only one in which he was to finish 'unplaced', well behind even the last prize winner. It seems somehow pathetic as well as significant that the last of so many games these two men played against one another should bring about so spectacular a triumph for Lasker and so humiliating a disaster for the older man.

The wins against Lee and Tchigorin—see pp. 89 and 92 — were among some other particularly fine games played by Lasker on that occasion, and he enjoyed it so much that soon after he accepted another invitation to compete in a great International Tournament. It was held in Paris in 1900, and the competition was almost as strong as in London the year before. Tarrasch was missing again, but apart from him most of the world's leading masters were assembled.

LONDON 1899

		1	2	3	4	5	6	7	8	9	10	11	12	13	14	15	
1	Lasker	×	1½	½1	½1	½1	01	11	11	1½	1½	½1	11	11	11	1	22½
2	Janowski	0½	×	01	10	11	1½	11	½1	00	11	10	11	01	1½	1	18
3	Maroczy	½0	10	×	½½	½½	½1	01	1½	10	11	½1	½1	1½	11	1	18
4	Pillsbury	½0	01	½½	×	½1	00	10	½½	11	11	11	11	1½	11	½	18
5	Schlechter	½0	00	½½	½0	×	1½	10	½1	½1	0½	11	11	11	11	1	17
6	Blackburne	10	0½	½0	11	0½	×	½0	01	1½	01	10	1½	11	11	½	15½
7	Tchigorin	00	00	10	01	01	½1	×	1½	1½	01	½1	10	11	10	1	15
8	Showalter	00	½0	0½	½½	½0	10	0½	×	0½	0½	1½	11	11	01	1	12½
9	Mason	0½	11	01	00	½0	0½	0½	1½	×	00	01	00	11	½1	1	12
10	Cohn (W)	0½	00	00	00	1½	10	10	1½	11	×	0½	1½	10	00	1	11½
11	Steinitz	½0	01	½0	00	00	01	½0	0½	10	1½	×	½0	½1	11	1	11½
12	Lee	00	00	½0	00	00	0½	01	00	11	0½	½1	×	½1	½½	1	9½
13	Bird	00	10	0½	0½	00	00	00	00	00	01	½0	½0	×	11	1	7
14	Tinsley	00	0½	00	00	00	00	01	10	½0	11	00	½½	00	×	0	6
15	Teichmann	0	0	0	½	0	½	0	0	0	0	0	0	0	1	×	2

After four rounds Teichmann retired, having beaten Tinsley, drawn with Pillsbury and Blackburne and lost to Tchigorin.

PARIS 1900

	1	2	3	4	5	6	7	8	9	10	11	12	13	14	15	16	17	
1 Lasker	X	1	1	0	1	1½	½1	1	1	1	1	1	1	1	1	1	1	14½
2 Pillsbury . . .	0	X	1	0	0	1	1	½1	1	1	1½	1	1	1	1	1	1	12½
3 Maroczy . . .	0	0	X	1	0	1½	1	1	1½	1	1	1	½1	½1	1	1	1	12
4 Marshall. . .	1	1	0	X	1	1½	1	1	1½	0	1	1	½1	1	1	1	1	12
5 Burn	0	1	1	0	X	½1	½0	1	1	1	0	½0	1	1	1	1	1	11
6 Tchigorin . .	½1	0	½1	½1	½1	X	1	1	1	1	1	½1	1	1	1	1	1	10½
7 Marco. . . .	½0	0	0	0	½1	0	X	1	0	0	1	1	1	1	1	1	1	10
8 Mieses . . .	0	½0	0	0	0	0	0	X	½1	1	1	1	1	½0	½1	1	½1	10
9 Schlechter . .	0	0	½0	½0	0	0	1	½0	X	1	½1	1	½1	1	½1	1	1	10
10 Janowski . .	0	0	0	1	0	0	1	0	0	X	1	½0	1	1	1	1	1	9
11 Showalter . .	0	½0	0	0	1	0	0	0	½0	0	X	½0	1	1	½1	1	1	9
12 Mason . . .	0	0	0	0	½0	½0	0	0	0	½1	½0	X	0	½0	½1	½1	1	4½
13 Brody. . . .	0	0	½0	½0	0	0	0	0	0	0	0	1	X	1	½0	1	½1	4
14 Rosen . . .	0	0	½0	0	0	0	0	½1	0	0	0	½1	0	X	0	½1	1	3
15 Mortimer . .	0	0	0	0	0	0	0	½0	½0	0	½0	½0	½1	1	X	1	0	2
16 Didier . . .	0	0	0	0	0	0	0	0	0	0	0	½0	0	½0	0	X	1	1
17 Sterling . . .	0	0	0	0	0	0	0	½0	0	0	0	0	½0	0	1	0	X	1

Drawn games were replayed once. The result of the second game counted.

There was a newcomer too, Frank Marshall, a young star from America whose rise to fame was to be no less fast and brilliant (and rather more lasting) than that of his equally young compatriot Pillsbury. Indeed, it was young Marshall who at the Paris tournament was the only one to score against Lasker, and in a very pretty game too. Apart from that one loss, Lasker yielded only ½ point, and that draw (against Tchigorin) occurred in the last round when Lasker's victory was already assured; for he had won all the other fourteen games, an almost unbelievable achievement in so strong a field. The result: Lasker 14½, Pillsbury 12½, Maroczy and Marshall 12 each, Burn 11, Tchigorin 10½, etc. A particularly elegant game was the victor's triumph over Maroczy—see p. 95—,but no less noteworthy—see pp. 94 and 97.—were his games against Burn and Pillsbury who, having put up tenacious resistance in a 'marathon' of 85 moves, could not prevail against Lasker's flawless endgame technique.

No world champion—not even Steinitz in his prime—had ever demonstrated his supremacy quite so convincingly. Emanuel Lasker had certainly gone far in the mere ten years that had elapsed since he was a young pauper going to Breslau to try his luck in the qualifying tournament.

For anyone who knew Lasker it was no surprise that, once again, he should feel bored by success and tired of that narrow realm of chess in which he could rule so undisputedly. He had no desire to rule, no taste for sitting back on his laurels; he was pining to tackle new tasks, to wrestle with new ideas, to get away from chess. So he retired from the arena to return to his true love. Naturally he preferred the lure of mathematics and philosophy, but he also felt an almost moral obligation to conclude his studies at the university. More than a decade had passed since he had had to leave for economic reasons. Now he was going to go back to school and take his degree.

GAME 16

CARO-KANN

LASKER–LEE

3rd round London 1899

1) P—K4	P—QB3
2) P—Q4	P—Q4
3) Kt—QB3	P×P
4) Kt×P	B—B4
5) Kt—Kt3	B—Kt3
6) Kt—B3	Kt—Q2
7) P—KR4	P—KR3
8) B—Q3	B×B
9) Q×B	KKt—B3
10) B—Q2	P—K3
11) O—O—O	Q—B2
12) KR—K1	O—O—O
13) Q—Kt3	B—Q3
14) Kt—K2	Kt—Kt5

Black ought to play 14) ...Kt—K5 so as to exchange the White QB; should White

Position after Black's 24th move

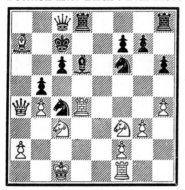

counter by 15) B—K3 Black could usefully answer ...QKt—B3 followed by ...Kt—Kt5.

15) R—B1   Kt(2)—B3
16) Q—R4   K—Kt1
17) P—B4   Q—K2

So as to vacate the square QB2 for the Bishop; it might have been even more useful though to play ...P—QB4.

18) Kt—B3   Q—B2

Threatening 19) ...B—KB5.

19) P—KKt3   Q—B1

Now ...P—QB4 would be refuted by 20) Kt—QKt5.

20) P—QKt4   P—K4
21) P×P   Kt×KP

22) B—K3

White now threatens to win a piece by 23) R×B.

22) .....   Kt×P

If 22) ...Kt×Kt; White would win by Q×P ch, K—B2; 24) B—Kt6 ch, K—Q2; 25) P—B5 etc.

23) B×P ch   K—B2
24) R—Q4   P—QKt4
25) Kt×P ch

This fairly obvious sacrifice is the quickest way to win.

25) .....   P×Kt
26) Q×P   Kt—R6
27) Q—R5 ch   K—Kt2 ch
28) B—B5   B×B
29) P×B   R×R
30) Kt×R   Q—Q1
31) P—B6 ch   K—B1
32) Q—R8 ch   K—B2
33) Q—R7 ch   K—Q3
34) Q×Kt ch   K—Q4
35) R—Q1   Q—Kt3
36) Kt—B3 ch   K—K3
37) Q—Q6 ch   K—B4
38) Q—Q3 ch   K—Kt5
39) Kt—K5 ch   Resigns

(Notes by LUDWIG BACHMANN: *Schachjahrbuch 1899*)

GAME 17

QUEENS PAWN GAME

(which may well be styled 'Colle System', even though Edgar Colle himself, when this game was played, was barely two years old)

BLACKBURNE–LASKER

London Tournament, 16th round, 30. June 1899

1) P—Q4   P—Q4
2) Kt—KB3   Kt—KB3
3) P—K3   P—K3
4) B—Q3   QKt—Q2
5) QKt—Q2   B—Q3
6) P—K4

Otherwise Black would push his KP

6) .....   P×P
7) Kt×P   P—QKt3

8) 0—0	B—Kt2
9) Kt × B ch	P × Kt
10) R—K1	0—0
11) B—KKt5	Q—B2
12) P—B3	KR—K1

Intending to strengthen his position by ...P—K4.

13) B—Kt5	B—B3

So as to avoid a double Pawn on the KB file after B × Kt.

14) B × B	Q × B
15) Q—Q3	P—KR3
16) B—R4	

Simplification by B × Kt would have been preferable. As it happens the B will be practically immobilised.

16)	QR—B1
17) QR—Q1	Kt—Q4
18) B—Kt3	P—QKt4
19) Kt—Q2	Kt(2)—Kt3
20) P—QR3	P—QR4
21) R—QB1	P—R5
22) P—R4	

If White was afraid of Black pushing his KKtP and KBP 22) P—KB4 would have been a more natural move.

22)	P—B4!
23) B—R2	

23) P—KB4 would now have created dangerous 'holes' for the Black Kt while hardly improving the mobility of the White B.

23)	Q—Q2
24) Q—Kt3	P—B5
25) Q—Q3	P—K4
26) P—B4	

A brave attempt thwarted by Black's fine play.

26)	KtP × P
27) Kt × P	P—K5!

Position after White's 27th move

Tempting was 27) ...Q—B3, since it seemed to force White either to lose a piece or to give both Rs for the Q in unfavourable circumstances. But Lasker's text-move was much stronger, since after 27) ...Q—B3 White could have put up some defence by the subtle manoeuvre 28) Kt × Kt, Q × R 29) Q—B1!

28) Q—B1

Not, of course, 28) Kt × Kt??, on account of ...R × R 29) R × R, P × Q 30) Kt × Q, P—Q7! etc.

28)	Kt × Kt
29) R × Kt	R—Kt1
30) R—B2	K—R1
31) R(1)—B1	Q—Kt5
32) P—B3	Q × RP
33) P × P	R × KP
34) R—B8 ch	R × R
35) R × R ch	K—R 2
36) Q—Kt1	Kt—B3
37) P—Q5!	

Threatens to win the game by R—K8

37)	P—Kt3

38) R—B7 ch   K—R1!
K—Kt1 would be a mistake since the Black R would be unable to push to the 7th rank
39) R—B1   R—K7
40) K—R1   Kt—Kt5

41) R—B8 ch   K—Kt2
42) R—B7 ch   K—B3
Resigns

(Notes by G. MARCO in the *Wiener Schachzeitung*, 1899)

GAME 18

FRENCH DEFENCE

TCHIGORIN–LASKER

London, 17th round, 1899

1) P—K4   P—K3
2) Q—K2

This was Tchigorin's very own way of dealing with the French defence (Translator's note).

2) .....   Kt—QB3

In his match against Tchigorin Dr. Tarrasch here used to play ...P—QB4 or ...B—K2. The text move was first used by Teichmann and, according to Schlechter, it would best be countered by 3) P—KB4.

3) Kt—QB3   P—K4
4) P—KKt3

With all these transitions what has now been reached is a certain variation of the 'Vienna' with White having the additional move of Q—K2; but this is hardly an advantage since the Q here hampers the usual development of the KKt.

4) .....   Kt—B3
5) B—Kt2   B—B4
6) P—Q3   P—Q3
7) B—Kt5   P—KR3
8) B × Kt

So far honours were fairly equal but now White allows the opponent the advantage of the two Bishops. 8) B—K3 was preferable.

8) .....   Q × B
9) Kt—Q5   Q—Q1
10) P—QB3   Kt—K2
11) Kt × Kt   Q × Kt

If anyone could win this game it must be Black. The White Bishop is somewhat awkwardly posted and moreover Black has a definite advantage in development.

12) 0—0—0   B—Q2
13) P—KB4   0—0—0
14) Kt—B3   B—Kt3
15) KR—B1   P—KB3
16) K—Kt1   KR—K1!
17) P—B5

When two moves ago White put his KR on B1 he would have thought of opening the file rather than pushing the pawn. In the circumstances, however, it seems reasonable enough; Black was threatening to get the better Pawn position by means of ...P × BP coupled with ...P—Q4, and so as to avoid this by means of 17) P × KP White would have had to saddle himself with a backward QP.

17) .....   B—R5
18) R—B1   K—Kt1

19)	Kt—Q2	P—R3
20)	B—B3	B—R2
21)	P—KR4?	

In lieu of this White should have played 21) Q—K1 with the idea of playing his B over to the Q-wing via Q1.

21)	.....	R—QB1
22)	Kt—B4	KR—Q1
23)	Kt—K3	B—K1!
24)	KR—Q1	

But now White really ought to do something such as R—KKt1 followed by the push of the KtP.

24)	.....	B—B2
25)	P—B4	

Since anyway this will not stop ...P—Q4 this move merely means a weakening of his position, as is well emphasised by Black's 26th and 29th moves.

25)	.....	P—B3
26)	R—B2	B—Q5
27)	R(1)—QB1	Q—B2
28)	Kt—Q1	Q—R4
29)	Kt—B3	P—QKt4!
30)	P—Kt3	R—Q2
31)	P×P	

Schlechter here recommended 31) Q—K1 coupled with Kt—K2. Certainly the text move gives the opponent a chance of attacking on the QR-file.

31)	.....	RP×P
32)	Kt—Q5	K—Kt2
33)	P—KKt4	R(2)—Q1

Position after White's 34th move

34)	Kt—K7?	B×P!
35)	Kt×R	

35) Kt × BP would be countered by ...R×Kt, followed by ...Q—Kt5 and an easy win for Black.

35)	.....	R×Kt!
36)	Q—Q2	Q—R6
37)	R—R1	R—QR1
38)	R—R2	B×P ch!!
39)	R×B	Q—Kt6 ch
40)	K—B1	R×R
41)	Q×R	B—K6 ch
42)	Q—Q2	Q×P
	Resigns	

(Notes by GEORG MARCO in the *Wiener Schachzeitung* of 1899)

GAME 19

FRENCH DEFENCE

LASKER–SHOWAKTER

London Tournament, 25th round, July 3rd 1899

1)	P—K4	P—K3
2)	P—Q4	P—Q4
3)	Kt—QB3	Kt—KB3
4)	B—KKt5	B—Kt5
5)	P—K5	P—KR3
6)	B—Q2	B×Kt

7) P×B   Kt—K5
8) B—Q3

In the light of modern theory 8) Q—Kt4, P—KKt3 9) B—B1! is considered more incisive. R.T.

8) .....   Kt×B
9) Q×Kt   P—QB4
10) P—KB4   Q—R4

10) ...P—QB5 was preferable. The text-move gives White the chance of achieving the superior endgame by means of a very subtle and long-term combination.

Position after Black's 10th move

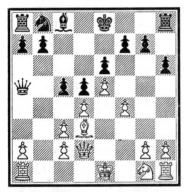

11) P—B4   Q×Q ch
12) K×Q   QP×P
13) B×P   P×P
14) Kt—B3   Kt—B3
15) B—Kt5   B—Q2
16) B×Kt   B×B
17) Kt×P   B×P

This will soon turn out to be a mistake as the hope of immuring the R at g7 proves to be a fallacy. The R will prove to be a nuisance rather than a captive.

18) KR—KKt1   B—K5
19) R×P   K—K2

...B—Kt3 would be countered by R(1)—KKt1 which, (what with the threat Kt×P) would force the B to R4, whereupon White would get a much superior game by Kt—Kt5—Q6 etc.

20) K—K3   B—R2
21) QR—KKt1!   QR—QB1

21) ...QR—KKt1 would have been refuted by R×B; but KR—KKt1 was playable

22) Kt—Kt5!   P—Kt3

The Black position is indefensible. 22) ...B×P would be countered by 23) Kt—Q6, QR—KB1 24) R—QB1, followed by R—B7 ch etc.

23) Kt—Q6   QR—B1
24) P—B4   KR—Kt1
25) R×R   B×R
26) P—KR4   R—Q1
27) P—R5

Lasker plays the ending as flawlessly as the whole game. His last two moves served the purpose of depriving the B of g6.

27) .....   K—B1
28) P—R4   B—R2
29) P—R5!   R—Kt1
30) P×P   R×P

if 30) ...P×P White completely bottles up his opponent by R—QR1—R7.

31) P—QB5   R—B3
32) K—Q4   B—B7
33) R—QB1   B—Kt6

The anticipated new B-perch at d5 doesn't turn out to be comfortable either, but one can readily understand that

Black didn't fancy going back
to R2 again.

34)	R—QKt1	B—Q4
35)	P—B5	B—B6
36)	P×P	B×P

37)	P×P	B×P
38)	R—KB1	Resigns

(Notes by G. MARCO,
Wiener Schachzeitung 1899)

GAME 20

RUY LOPEZ

LEE–LASKER

London Tournament, 26th round,
July 4th 1899

1)	P—K4	P—K4
2)	Kt—KB3	Kt—QB3
3)	B—Kt5	P—QR3
4)	B—R4	Kt—B3
5)	P—Q3	P—Q3
6)	P—B3	P—QKt4
7)	B—B2	P—Kt3
8)	P—QR4	B—QKt2!

'As a rule this move is not
good because it allows White
to plant at Kt at KB5; in the
present instance however it is
unobjectionable because White
does not have access to this
square'. (F. Reinfeld)

9)	QKt—Q2	B—Kt2
10)	Kt—B1	P—Q4
11)	Q—K2	0—0
12)	Kt—Kt3	Q—Q3
13)	0—0	KR—K1
14)	P—R3	Kt—QR4!
15)	B—Q2	

15) P—Kt4 would, of course,
be countered by ...P×KP
16) QP×P, Kt—B5

15)	.....	P—B4
16)	KR—Q1	Q—B2
17)	Q—K1	P—B5!
18)	P—Q4	Kt×P
19)	Kt×Kt	P×Kt

20)	Kt×P	B×Kt
21)	P×B	Q×P
22)	B—K3	Kt—B3
23)	P—QKt3	Kt—R4
24)	P—QKt4	Kt—B3
25)	R—Q7?	R—K2
26)	R(7)—Q1	R—Q1
27)	R×R ch	Kt×R
28)	P×P	P×P
29)	Q—Q2	Kt—K3
30)	P—R4?	B—B3
31)	R—R6	R—Q2
32)	Q—K1	B—Kt2
33)	R—R5	P—B4
34)	P—Kt3	P—B5
35)	P×P	Kt×P
36)	B—Q4	Q—KB4

Position after White's 37th move

| 37) | Q—K3 | R×B! |

A very beautiful combination,
ten moves deep; but an even
quicker decision, according to
Dr. Tarrasch, could be forced

by ...Q—Kt5 ch 38) K—B1,
Q—Kt7 ch 39) K—K1, Q—
Kt8 ch 40) K—Q2, Kt—Kt7!
41) Q—K2!, P—K6 ch 42)
P×P, B—B6!!

38)	P×R	Q—Kt5 ch
39)	K—B1	Q—Kt7 ch
40)	K—K1	Q—Kt8 ch
41)	K—Q2	P—B6 ch!
42)	Q×P	Q×P ch
43)	K—Q1	P—K6

44)	B—Kt3 ch	K—Kt2
45)	P—Q5 ch	K—R3
46)	Q—K1	B—B1!

Resigns

After the end of the game
Lasker claimed to have fore-
seen his 46th move when
sacrificing the exchange on the
37th.

(Notes by G. MARCO,
Wiener Schachzeitung, 1899)

GAME 21

VIENNA GAME

STEINITZ–LASKER

27th round London Tournament
July 5th 1899
(First brilliancy prize)

1)	P—K4	P—K4
2)	Kt—QB3	Kt—KB3
3)	P—B4	P—Q4
4)	P—Q3	Kt—B3

This move, first played in 1871
by Fenton (against Black-
burne), seems to be quite as
good as the more usual continuations.

5)	BP×P	QKt×P
6)	P—Q4	Kt—Kt3
7)	P×P	

After 7) P—K5, according to
Bilguer, Black should get the
advantage by ...Kt—K5 8)
Kt×Kt, P×Kt 9) B—QB4,
P—QB4!. The text leaves Black
with superior development,
due to White's timewasting
second push of the QP. He
should have played 6) Kt—
KB3.

7)	.....	Kt×P

8)	Kt×Kt	

Here too, development by
Kt—KB3 was preferable

8)	.....	Q×Kt
9)	Kt—B3	B—KKt5
10)	B—K2	0—0—0
11)	P—B3	B—Q3
12)	0—0	KR—K1
13)	P—KR3	B—Q2
14)	Kt—Kt5	

White may have expected
...P—KB3 15) B—B3, Q—
Kt1 16) Kt—K4, which indeed
would have considerably improved his position

14)	.....	Kt—R5!

Position after White's 15th move

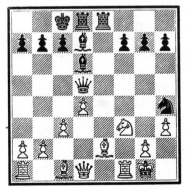

15) Kt—B3
    15) B—B3 was ruled out by
    ...Kt×B ch 16) Kt×Kt, B—
    Kt6. The R obviously mustn't
    retake the Kt on account of
    ...P—KB3.
15) .....   Kt×P!!
16) K×Kt   B×P ch
17) K—B2
    17) K×B is defeated by
    ...Q—KB4 ch, followed by
    Q—Kt5—R6—Kt6 ch and
    R—K5
17) .....   P—KB3!
    Very subtle, and certainly
    stronger than ...B×R
18) R—KKt1   P—KKt4
19) B×P
    Relatively best.
19) .....   P×B
20) R×P   Q—K3

21) Q—Q3   B—B5
22) R—R1
    22) R—Kt7 was ruled out by
    ...B—B4 and R—Kt1 by
    ...B—K6 ch; and if the R
    goes somewhere in the 5th
    rank Black wins very quickly
    by ...B—K6 ch, followed by
    ...Q—Kt5.
22) .....   B×R
23) Kt×B   Q—B3 ch
24) B—B3   B—B4
25) Kt×P   Q—KKt3
26) Q—Kt5   P—B3
27) Q—R5   R—K2
28) R—R5   B—Kt5
29) R—Kt5   Q—B7 ch
30) K—Kt3   B×B
    Resigns

(Notes by G. MARCO,
Wiener Schachzeitung 1899)

GAME 22

QUEEN'S GAMBIT DECLINED

BURN–LASKER

Paris Tournament, 4th round,
May 22nd 1900

1) P—Q4   P—Q4
2) P—QB4   P—K3
3) Kt—QB3   Kt—KB3
4) Kt—B3   P—B4
5) P×QP   BP×P
6) Q×P   Kt×P
7) P—K4
    *By 7) Kt×Kt White could have
    saddled Black with an isolated
    pawn. R.T.*
7) .....   Kt×Kt
8) Q×Q ch   K×Q
9) P×Kt   B—B4
    Black, even though temporarily

behind in development, has
the better P-position.
10) Kt—K5   K—K2
11) Kt—Q3   B—Kt3
12) B—R3 ch   K—K1
13) Kt—K5   Kt—Q2
14) B—Kt5   B—B2
15) Kt—Q3
    White could get no advantage
    by swopping pieces on d7.
15) .....   P—QR3
16) B—R4   P—QKt4
17) B—Kt3   B—Kt2
18) P—B3   R—QB1
    Black now goes to the attack,
    with the isolated P as the
    obvious target
19) K—Q2   P—QR4
20) QR—QKt1   B—B3
21) B—B2   P—B3!

Position after White's 31st move

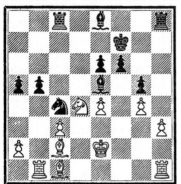

22)	P—Kt3	K—B2
23)	K—K2	P—Kt4

Depriving the White Kt of any aggressive outpost. On c5, of course, the Kt, would get lost after ...B—Q3 25) Kt×Kt, B×B 26) Kt—Kt6, R—QKt1

24)	P—Kt4	P—R4!
25)	P—R3	B—Kt1
26)	B—Kt2	Kt—Kt3
27)	Kt—B5	B—K1
28)	Kt—Kt3	Kt—B5

Black exploits his positional superiority with consummate mastership

29) B—B1

If the B retreated to R1 the Black KB would get planted at his B5

29)	.....	P×P!
30)	BP×P	B—K4
31)	Kt—Q4	B×Kt
32)	P×B	Kt—R6!

The decisive move. The invasion of the rooks makes White's game untenable.

33)	B×Kt	R×B ch
34)	K—Q3	QR×P
35)	B—Q6	P—Kt5
36)	QR—QB1	B—Kt4 ch
37)	K—K3	K—Kt3
38)	R—B5	R—R6 ch
39)	K—B2	B—Q6
40)	R—K1	R×P
41)	R—B7	R—QR7 ch
42)	K—Kt1	R—KR5
43)	P—K5	R×P ch
44)	K—R1	B—K5 ch
	Resigns	

(Notes from *Deutsches Wochen-schach*, 1900)

GAME 23

QUEEN'S GAMBIT DECLINED

LASKER–MAROCZY

Paris Tournament, May 25th 1900

1)	P—Q4	P—Q4
2)	P—QB4	P—K3
3)	Kt—QB3	Kt—KB3
4)	Kt—B3	P×P
5)	P—K3	

If 5) P—K4, B—Kt5! gives Black a good game

5)	.....	P—B4
6)	B×P	P—QR3
7)	P—QR4	

Creating a 'hole' at QKt4, but cramping Black's position.

7)	.....	Kt—B3
8)	0—0	P×P
9)	P×P	B—K2
10)	B—K3	0—0
11)	Q—K2	Q—R4

Steinitz's manoeuvre

12)	KR—Q1	R—Q1
13)	QR—B1	Kt—QKt5
14)	Kt—K5	Kt(3)—Q4?

Black's next few moves are incomprehensible. 14) ...B—Q2, followed by ...B—K1 would have equalised.

15) B—Kt3   R—B1?
...B—Q2 was still the move, for the possible reply 16) Kt—B4, Q—B2 17) Kt×Kt, Kt×Kt leads to nothing.

16) Kt—K4!
Now White is able to avoid exchanges and thus build up a promising attack.

16) .....   Q—Q1
17) P—B4   P—QKt3
Inferior to ...B—Q2-QB3.

18) B—Q2   B—Kt2
19) Kt—Kt3   R—B1
20) P—B5
Undermining the position of the blockader on Black's Q4

20) .....   R×R
Not good because it relinquishes control of the QB file; but Black has no really good moves.

21) R×R   P×P
If 21) ...B—Kt4; 22) QB×Kt,

Position after White's 22nd move

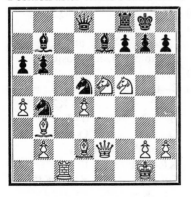

B×R 23) B×R, Q×B 24) Kt—Q3, Kt—B5 25) Kt×Kt, B×Kt 26) P×P with a winning game.

22) Kt(3)×P   B—KB3
A mistake in a bad position. The tournament book recommends 22) ...B—B1 23) QB×Kt, B×B 24) Kt—B6, Q—Kt4 'with a defensible position'. But Lasker would have refuted 22) ...B—B1 with 23) Kt×BP!, (see the note to White's 20th move), which leads to some charming positions, such as 23) ...K×Kt 24) R×B!! etc.; or 23) ...R×Kt 24) Q×B!! etc.

23) QB×Kt   Kt×B
24) Kt×BP!   R×Kt
25) Q—K6   K—R1
There is no defence. If 25) ...Q—KB1, 26) R—B7 wins; or if 25) ...B—Q4 26) B×B, Kt×B 27) R—B8; while if 25) ...Kt—Q4 26) Kt—Q6, Q—K2 27) B×Kt!, B×P ch 28) K—R1, winning easily.

26) Q×R   B×P ch
27) K—R1   Kt—Q6
28) R—B1   B×P ch
Not bad because the position is beyond good and evil!

29) K×B   Q—Kt4 ch
30) K—R3   Resigns
An elegant game. It is, incidentally, one of those rare encounters where Lasker wins by a direct attack on his adversary's King.

(Notes by FRED REINFELD in *Dr. Lasker's Chess Career.*

GAME 24

DUTCH DEFENCE

LASKER–PILLSBURY

Paris Tournament 15th round,
June 14th 1900

1) P—Q4   P—KB4
2) P—K4

The 'Staunton Gambit', already tried by Lasker in the London Tournament. R.T.

2) .....   P×P
3) Kt—QB3   Kt—KB3
4) B—Kt5   P—B3

If ...P—Q4 White regains the P by B×Kt, followed by Q—R5 ch.

5) P—B3

But now White plays for quick development rather than regaining the P.

5) .....   P×P
6) Kt×P   P—K3
7) B—Q3   B—K2
8) Kt—K5   0—0
9) B×Kt   R×B
10) Q—R5   P–KKt3
11) Kt×KtP!   Q—K1

If ...P×Kt, 12) B×P wins

12) Kt×B ch   Q×Kt
13) 0—0—0   P—Q4
14) QR—K1   Kt—Q2
15) R—K3

The advance of the KKtP and the occupation of the KKt file by the Rooks would have been still stronger

15) .....   R—B2
16) R—Kt3 ch   K—R1
17) B—Kt6   R—Kt2
18) R—B1   Kt—B3
19) Q—R4   Kt—Kt1
20) Q×Q   R×Q

21) B—Q3

The backward KP is Black's weakness and will seal his doom.

21) .....   B—Q2

Position after Black's 21st move

22) Kt—Kt1

A subtle manoeuvre aiming at the capture of the QKtP

22) .....   R(1)—K1

Black must try to free his game by pushing the KP, but he can't do it at once, on account of 23) P×P, R×P 24) R—B7

23) Kt—Q2   P—K4
24) P×P   R×P
25) Kt—B3   R—K6
26) Kt—Kt5   R×R
27) P×R   P—KR3
28) Kt—B7 ch   K—Kt2
29) Kt—Q6   R—K2
30) Kt×P   Kt—B3
31) Kt—B5   B—Kt5

At once ...B—B1 would have been preferable.

32) R—B4   B—B1
33) R—QR4   Kt—Kt5
34) B—R6   B—B4
35) R—KB4   Kt—K6
36) P—B3   K—Kt3

37)	R—B2	B—K5	
38)	P—Kt3		

So as to give the K access to the Q-wing pawns.

38)	.....	B×P	
39)	B—Q3 ch	K—Kt4?	

'Up to this point Pillsbury's defence has been exemplary, but here he goes astray. 39) ...B—K5 would have equalised' (F. Reinfeld)

40)	R—B8	K—Kt5
41)	R—Kt8 ch	K—B6
42)	R—Kt6	Kt—Kt5
43)	B—B5	P—KR4
44)	R—Kt5	R—K8 ch
45)	K—Kt2	R—KR8
46)	B—Kt6	K×P
47)	B×P	B—B6
48)	B×Kt	B×B
49)	R—Kt6	

What with the K-wing safely liquidated White's Q-wing superiority can no longer be denied

49)	.....	R—R7 ch
50)	K—R3	R—QB7
51)	Kt—Q3	

'Avoiding the trap 51) R×P?, R×P! (52) Kt—K4 ch, P×Kt 53) R×R ch, K—B7 54) R—B7, P—K6 and draws' (F. Reinfeld)

51)	.....	K—R5
52)	Kt—K5	B—B4
53)	R×P	K—Kt6
54)	R—B5	R—Q7
55)	Kt—B6	K—B5
56)	Kt—Kt4	P—Q5
57)	P×P	R×P
58)	R—R5	R—Q2

59)	Kt—B6

White overlooked that Kt—Q5 ch would have won at once. The text leads to an interesting but none too easy ending.

59)	.....	B—K5
60)	Kt×P	R—Q7

Not so long ago Lasker had won a similar ending against Marco; the difficulty being to deprive the opponent of an opportunity to sacrifice his B for the two Pawns.

61)	Kt—Kt5	R—Q4
62)	K—Kt4	B—Q6
63)	Kt—B7	R×R
64)	K×R	K—K4
65)	K—Kt4	K—Q3
66)	Kt—Kt5 ch	K—B3
67)	P—R4	K—Kt3
68)	Kt—R3	B—K7
69)	Kt—B4 ch	K—R3
70)	K—B3	B—Q8
71)	Kt—Kt2	B—R4
72)	P—Kt4	B—K1
73)	K—Kt3	B—B3
74)	K—B4	B—Q2
75)	K—B5	B—Kt5
76)	Kt—B4	B—Q8
77)	P—Kt5 ch	K—R2
78)	P—R5	B—B6
79)	Kt—K5	B—Kt2
80)	Kt—B6 ch	K—R1
81)	K—Kt6	B—R3
82)	Kt—Kt4	B—Kt2
83)	Kt—R6	B—B6
84)	Kt—B7 ch	K—Kt1
85)	P—R6	Resigns

(Notes from *Deutsches Wochenschach*, 1900)

CHAPTER TWELVE

Back to School and Meeting Martha

Victory at the London and Paris tournaments had provided a useful nest-egg, and Lasker could well afford now to study at leisure and in reasonable comfort. He went to Erlangen University where, in January 1902, he took his doctorate with high honours. Here is an extract from a letter he wrote to a friend soon after the event.

'My thesis seems to have impressed Professor Nöther considerably, and neither he nor his colleagues made any difficulties at all in the oral examination. They were all uncommonly friendly and the Dean almost made me blush by telling me that he considered it an honour for the University to give me its degree . . .'

Since German university professors have never been known to flatter students excessively, the explanation is simply that Lasker did exceptionally well; as a matter of fact, his thesis was later expanded in book-form; it dealt with an uncommonly complex mathematical problem, and some further research was based on it.

The above-mentioned letter, incidentally, was addressed to a young actress who seems to have been a great friend of Lasker's in those early years of the new century. Some forty years later she kindly provided these notes which give a vivid impression of Emanuel's private life at the time when, a man in his early thirties and world-famous in his own profession, he chose to lead the life of a carefree undergraduate in a small German university town.

'He loved to go to the theatre and he used to come back-stage almost every evening. Our manager happened to be a keen chess-player and he was delighted whenever Lasker gave him a game. Emanuel had a great sense of humour and willingly lent himself to a practical joke the manager wanted to play on a certain pompous old fool who rather fancied himself as a chess-player. Perhaps he had never seen the world champion's picture in the papers, anyway he did not recognise Emanuel when one evening, at a party in our manager's house, he was introduced to him as a young man, supposed to be quite good at chess and certainly most eager to play someone reputed to be so much better. The conceited old fool consented to play, and we all stood around watching the contest. Lasker deliberately opened the game very queerly, and as his opponent, move after move, persisted in lecturing him on the poor standard of his play it wasn't easy for us to keep a straight face while watching Emanuel's demure expression and respectful demeanour. When the old boy said: 'You are going to lose a piece, young man: I am afraid you have a good deal to learn yet', Lasker scratched his head with a worried expression so well acted that we were almost taken in. 'Good gracious', he said, 'I seem to be losing yet another piece after this one.' As his opponent triumphantly took both pieces, Emanuel shook his head sadly and said with mock modesty: 'What an extraordinary fluke for me! Look! It just so happens you'll be mate in three moves.' As he proceeded to demonstrate it to his nonplussed opponent we all burst out laughing; but the old fool, when told that he had been playing the world champion, did not see the joke. He left in a huff.

Emanuel had little time for chess those days. He worked very hard at his studies, and in the evening he came to the theatre, either sitting in the pit or actually getting himself a job as an 'extra' in crowd scenes. Even on our Sunday outings as we were roaming through the near-by woods he would ask me to play scenes from his favourite plays.'

Having taken his degree Lasker went back to Berlin for some time, and here it may be apt to quote from the notes of Frau Martha Kohn, so as to give an impression of Lasker's private life at that period. For Martha, many years later, was to become Mrs Lasker and his devoted companion from his early middle age up to the end. Here then are some of her notes about that early Berlin period when she first met Lasker.

'At the home of Ludwig Metzger, City Editor of the *Berliner Lokalanzeiger*, a gay crowd used to assemble every Sunday, most of them authors, artists, actors and particularly musicians; for Frau Metzger, a charming hostess, was very musical and her eldest daughter—at that time still a student at the Academy— was soon to become a famous opera star.

My mother had met the Metzgers on a holiday at the seaside, and soon I came to know them too and to be a fairly regular Sunday guest. One day Frau Metzger told me that they had a rather unusual guest that afternoon and I might be particularly interested to meet him. He was a young professor of mathematics and, incidentally, the world champion at chess.

"How horribly dull!" I said, "I know practically nothing about mathematics, and even less about chess."

At that moment Lasker approached and was duly introduced. He seemed to be very shy. When I was about to leave the party he asked if he could see me again.

"Come to tea any Monday you like", I said; "my husband should be pleased to meet you."

"You are married?" he asked in some astonishment; whereupon I told him that my husband had been very ill and was now a permanent invalid. "But he likes people who have got around a bit", I said; "I am sure he'll be glad to meet you."

A week later Lasker did come to tea. Among those present I remember the Socialist Reichstag Deputy Dr Stadthagen, a great friend of mine who wrote popular books under the pen-name Ernst Georgy. There was also Josepha Metz([1]) and a number of other interesting people. Emanuel knew none of them, but we all got to like him and soon he came to be a regular member of our circle and a very frequent guest. His interests ranged far beyond his own special fields and he seemed much at home among artists.

One day we had arranged to go for a walk in the *Tiergarten*. As I came to meet him at the *Brandenburger Tor*, Lasker was already waiting and evidently quite delighted to see me. But we had hardly been gone five minutes, chatting pleasantly, when he suddenly stopped and said he must go home at once. He would explain it all later. And he went forthwith, almost at a run. I was rather annoyed at being left like that in the middle of the park, and when I complained to my husband about such unseemly behaviour he consoled me with a smile: "You can't apply the ordinary yardstick to people like Lasker. No doubt, he'll give you some reasonable explanation."

But I was still angry and more or less determined to let him know that I did not wish to see him again. A few days later, though, he suddenly appeared, carrying a bulky mathematical manuscript and plonking it on the table.

"There", he said, "that's your work."

"Mine? What on earth do you mean?"

"Yes, it is yours and yours alone! When we met the other day I was so happy that, all of a sudden, I solved a mathematical problem that had been bothering me for years. The inspiration came upon me like a flash. I simply had to rush home and put it on paper lest it escape me again. I know it must have seemed rude to run away like that. Please, please, don't be angry any more!"

Well, what could I do? Even though I don't know a thing about

([1]) In the Germany of those days Josepha Metz was as popular as Enid Blyton now is in the English-speaking world. Most of her delightful stories for children, incidentally, were in verse.

mathematics, I could not but feel flattered at having enriched that mysterious science by a mere rendezvous in the Park.

Emanuel remained a frequent and ever welcome guest in our house till, one day, he said that he was going to America shortly.

"But before I go", he said, "I want you to meet my mother. I have told her so much about you."

I was glad to meet her and she was most kind to me. When he introduced me, Emanuel said: "I want the two persons I love more than anybody else to be real friends."

Never before had he revealed his feelings so clearly, and being a little disconcerted by it I tried to pass if off by turning to the old lady with a joke: "If he really knew me he would send me to the devil rather than take me to his mother."

"Oh no", she said without a smile and answering me very seriously; "Emanuel knows exactly what he says; and when he says it he means it."

A week later Emanuel sailed for New York, and four months after his departure his brother Berthold came to tell us that their mother had just passed away . . . . .'

Let us interrupt Martha's notes to fill in a few details about her own life and background. She was just over a year older than Emanuel, having been born in November 1867. Her father, Jacob Bamberger, was the chief of L.M. Bamberger & Sons, one of the oldest and most highly respected banking firms in the City of Berlin. Does the name strike a chord of memory? Yes, it was the very same Herr Bamberger whose monthly donation helped to keep the struggling schoolboy and student Emanuel Lasker from utter starvation. He never met his benefactor's daughter in those days. Martha was a young lady getting on for twenty and just engaged to be married. She little knew that of the innumerable half-sovereigns collected by deserving youngsters in her father's office, one went to the man she was going to marry some twenty years later.

Herr Bamberger's banking house had been founded by Jacob Moses (1724–1802) who was the recognised 'Elder' of German Jewry and, incidentally, a friend and benefactor of Moses Mendelssohn, the great philosopher. Martha's grandfather on her mother's side was Giacomo Meyerbeer, the composer famous for his operas and his life-long feud with Richard Wagner.

So much about Martha's antecedents. In 1886 she married Emil Kohn, proprietor of a well-known piano factory. Stricken by illness soon after the marriage, he bore the fate of a doomed man with stoic equanimity, seeking diversion in his manifold cultural interests. In the first year of marriage they had a daughter, Lotte, who married in 1908 and who, thirty years later, came back to look after the Laskers in their declining years. Lotte's own daughter is married to a well known Chicago physician.

It was a long time before Martha became Mrs Lasker. All through those early years of the century she was merely his friend and confidante, and most of the time over a distance of some three thousand miles. For, once again, he moved to the USA. He had decided to take residence there and to settle down as a scholar mainly occupied with certain scientific and scholastic projects.

Chess was to be only an additional means of livelihood. As a matter of fact he was going to start and to edit a chess magazine, all his own and on lines rather different from the established type of chess journalism. He hoped that this venture, while keeping him in constant touch with the chess world and providing a regular income, would leave him enough time to serve his real interests.

CHAPTER THIRTEEN

Editorial Interlude in New York

A chess magazine certainly isn't the easiest way to make money, though it may be a fairly easy way to lose it. To 'break even' is usually something devoutly to be hoped for, but no chess magazine can ever be a lucrative undertaking. The only thing certain about it is that it involves a great deal of work and trouble, and even if it is a mere monthly it usually means a full time job for a much harrassed editor, burdened by a great deal of research, proof-reading, and correspondence. As for the number of paying subscribers it is usually not very much in excess of the number of copies given away to other editorial offices, to contributors and to impecunious friends. For the international chess fraternity, though very rich in numbers and in enthusiasm, has never been blessed with pecuniary wealth.

If one were to tot up the number of chess-magazines founded within the last hundred years one would reach a most respectable figure, but it would be no exaggeration to say that nine out of ten did not very long survive their first birthday. Most of them, sooner or later, had to fold up for lack of subscribers and advertisers. One of the few worthy exceptions to the rule is the *British Chess Magazine* which, after a sound and relatively untroubled life of seventy-eight years, is doing as well as ever. An even older magazine is the *Deutsche Schachzeitung* which, after over a hundred years of existence had to be discontinued in 1944, but got a new lease of life a few years ago, as did the venerable *Magyar Sakkélet*, also resuscitated after a few years' interruption. As for more recent and fairly sound publications, mention should be made of the American *Chess Review* and the British *Chess*, both of which have been doing well for some twenty years.

But the casualities on the field of chess journalism are far too many to be listed. It is a battlefield littered with disappointed hopes and destroyed illusions. Even the great Steinitz was among the victims, for his *International Chess Magazine*, founded in New York in 1885, had to fold up after only six years, although it was certainly the most readable and instructive chess periodical of its time; nor indeed had Lasker's own chess magazine a long life, for after two or three years of editorship Lasker realised that he could no longer cope with the burden of financial and administrative worries which interfered with his other work.

While it lasted, *Lasker's Chess Magazine* was a unique piece of chess literature and certainly as personal as its title implied. It avoided the dry tone and unimaginative style of almost all its contemporaries. It didn't just contain the usual collection of games and problems, coupled with a few news items; it went much deeper, revealing more of the meaning and the background of chess than any previous chess editor had attempted.

Lasker had a very readable personal column in most issues, and so far as the problem section of the magazine was concerned he was fortunate enough to secure the collaboration of none less than Sam Loyd, one of the greatest problemists of all times, a prolific composer and a great expert. Loyd was a very old man at that time, but he had lost none of his charm and certainly none of his sense of humour; it may be fitting perhaps to call him the Mark Twain of chess literature, and his addition to the editorial board of Lasker's magazine certainly helped to make these few volumes unique in quality as well as in style. Even now, fifty years after their publication, these volumes are prized possessions of anyone who has a collection of chess-books, and are becoming a bibliophile rarity.

Among the men who helped Lasker to finance and organise the magazine was his old friend Harold M. Phillips, a prominent lawyer, a devoted chess player and for many years President of the Manhattan Chess Club. Another friend who helped Lasker in his administrative problems and in many other ways was Professor Rice, also a devoted chess player and, incidentally, a wealthy man who, over the years, spent many thousands of dollars promoting a thorough analysis of his own gambit, (an enterprising form of the King's Gambit which, for a long time now, has been considered too unsound for modern tournament practice).

Lasker enjoyed his few years of editorship, particularly because it gave him a welcome chance to keep in close touch with the chess world, without having to stir much from his study. For at that time —and this was one of his main reasons for relinquishing the cares of editorship—he was deeply engrossed in elaborate preparatory work for his first philosophical treatise; he was indeed 'in labour', for he was about to develop his own philosophy of 'machology', which will be discussed more fully in a later chapter.

CHAPTER FOURTEEN

Cambridge Springs 1904

Once again, a major chess-event was to interrupt the kind of work that Lasker preferred. There had been no U.S.A. competition since the great New York Tournament of 1889 comparable to the one now projected at the Pennsylvanian resort, Cambridge Springs.

The only fly in the ointment was that Maroczy could not come and that, once again, Tarrasch had declined the invitation to compete in a tournament likely to be entered by Lasker; this seemed all the more deplorable as only the year before, at Monte Carlo 1903, Tarrasch had scored yet another great triumph, ahead of Maroczy, Pillsbury, Schlechter, Teichmann, Marco, Wolf, Mieses, Marshall and other famous masters. Still, apart from Tarrasch and Maroczy, practically all the leading masters of the day were duly booked for Cambridge Springs.

The tournament came most inconveniently for Lasker, who had been out of practice for four years and was deeply preoccupied with other matters. He rightly felt that after all the courtesy shown him in the USA for so many years he was in honour bound not to disappoint his friends by ignoring the first really great tournament held on American soil in fifteen years. So he accepted the challenge, and of course he was considered 'hot favourite'.

But his innumerable backers and well-wishers were to be disappointed; not that Lasker, in spite of his preoccupations, did not do his best. He was always conscientious, once he had accepted a responsibility. But this time the lack of practice proved too much of a handicap, and even though his 'best' was still very good indeed and quite worthy of a great master it wasn't, this time, up to the sovereign supremacy of Nuremberg 1896, London 1899 or Paris 1900.

In the first few rounds he lost to Schlechter, and then to Pillsbury. He was used to being a bad starter, and once he got into his stride he did begin, quickly enough, to make up for the ground initially lost; he did it as rapidly as usual and in normal circumstances it might have been good enough for him to climb to the very top. But circumstances weren't normal; for this was another tournament where an American carried all before him.

It seemed to be Hastings all over again, but it wasn't Pillsbury this time who won, though he did play in the tournament and was generally expected to be Lasker's most dangerous rival. Few of his admirers knew that Pillsbury was already in the grip of the disease which, a year later, was to cause his untimely death. At Cambridge Springs he was a complete failure and did not even qualify for one of the minor prizes. In the whole of that tournament he achieved only one remarkable feat, his triumph over Lasker.

And thereby hangs a tale which chess players all over the world have been enjoying for half a century. Remember Lasker's sensational triumph over Pillsbury in the St. Petersburg 'Grand-Master Tournament' of 1895-6, the game that won the brilliancy prize and turned the tables of the tournament in Lasker's favour. (See pp. 66 and 115). Now in that game, as soon as Pillsbury had made his 7th move (which turned out to be the source of all his subsequent troubles) he felt that he should have made another move, never tried in that variation and yet—so it seemed to Pillsbury—likely to lead to a rather more advantageous line. That very night, after his shattering defeat, Pillsbury sat down for many hours, analysing his new idea and satisfying himself that indeed it would have given him the advantage. During the next weeks and months he burned a good deal more midnight oil in the privacy of his room, analysing his new variation as thoroughly as he knew how; but he did not tell anybody about it. Since the opening concerned was a variation of the Queen's Gambit very popular in those days, Pillsbury had countless opportunities to give his new line the practical test; but he would not waste his precious discovery on any of the small fry, thereby divulging his great secret; he would spring that surprise on no one less than Lasker.

It had become almost an obsession with Pillsbury, yet the years rolled by and the opportunity never arose. Whenever he did play Lasker, Pillsbury either did not have the White pieces or it so happened that he could not steer the opening into that particular variation. At long last, already a doomed man and playing in what was to be his last major tournament, Pillsbury got the chance he had worked for, yearned for, and dreamed about for eight long years and four months to a day. He did play White against Lasker, and up to the sixth move it did turn out to be a repetition of their Petersburg game in 1896. Then Pillsbury made his new move and steered the game into one of the many lines he had so patiently and so thoroughly analysed night after night, year after year. He soon got Lasker into trouble, and he played and won one of the finest games in his career. Alas, it was to be almost the last game and certainly the last brilliant one he ever played in the brief span of life still left to him. Yet, it seems an odd coincidence that at the very beginning and the very end of his meteoric carreer, at Hastings 1895 and at Cambridge Springs 1904 Pillsbury, succeeded in queering the world champion's pitch. At Hastings Pillsbury lost his individual game to Lasker and yet he ran away with the tournament; at Cambridge Springs Pillsbury was 'nowhere' in the tournament and yet, by beating Lasker, he helped a young fellow-American to run away with the tournament.

It was Frank Marshall who achieved this feat. Marshall was probably the most assiduous of all chess masters in the first decade of the century, never missing a chance to play on any occasion, big or small. He was also one of the most brilliant and certainly the most erratic one; he was capable of losing a dismal game against the weakest competitor in the tournament and on the next day or two to topple grandmasters like ninepins. At Monte Carlo 1903 he had been among the 'also-rans', and a few months later at Cambridge Springs there was no stopping him. He simply won game after game. When the last round had been reached, Marshall, without the loss of a single game, had conceded draws to Lasker, Marco, and Napier, having won all the other games. Thus, with a score of 12½ and 1½ points ahead of his nearest rival he was already certain of the first prize and in the last round he played a quick *remis de convéniance* against Tchigorin who was out of the running anyway.

It was the struggle for the second prize which gave a dramatic turn to the last round of that tournament. Janowski had reached 11 points, Lasker's score was only 10, but the two had to play one another in that last round. For Janowski a draw was quite sufficient to give him the undivided second prize. As for Lasker, what with the other field well behind, he was certain of the third prize even if he lost, but he had to win in order to share the second prize.

It wasn't the first nor the last time that Lasker found himself in so unenviable a position. Yet, it seems significant that whenever he *had* to win a game, he invariably won it. It happened again at St. Petersburg 1909 (when, in the last round, he had to beat Teichmann so as to share first prize with Rubinstein) and it happened in what was, without a doubt, the most sensational game he ever played, the last (and decisive) one against Capablanca at St. Petersburg 1914.

To revert to Cambridge Springs, it was certainly no mean task to *have* to beat as erudite and aggressive a player as Janowski, and with the Black pieces too. Yet, Lasker did it with what seemed to be the greatest of ease, almost nonchalantly. (See p. 116). Again

CAMBRIDGE SPRINGS 1904

		1	2	3	4	5	6	7	8	9	10	11	12	13	14	15	16	
1	Marshall	×	1	½	½	1	1	½	1	1	1	1	1	½	1	1	1	13
2	Janowski	0	×	0	½	½	1	1	1	1	0	1	1	1	1	1	1	11
3	Lasker	½	1	×	½	½	0	1	1	0	1	1	1	1	½	1	1	11
4	Marco	½	½	½	×	½	½	1	0	½	1	0	1	½	½	1	1	9
5	Showalter	0	½	½	½	×	½	1	1	1	½	0	½	½	½	½	1	8½
6	Schlechter	0	0	1	½	½	×	0	½	½	0	½	1	1	½	1	½	7½
7	Tchigorin	½	0	0	0	0	1	×	1	½	0	1	½	1	1	0	1	7½
8	Mieses	0	0	0	1	0	½	0	×	1	1	1	0	1	½	1	0	7
9	Pillsbury	0	0	1	½	0	½	½	0	×	1	½	0	½	1	½	1	7
10	Fox	0	1	0	0	½	1	1	0	0	×	1	1	0	1	0	0	6½
11	Teichmann	0	0	0	1	1	½	0	0	½	0	×	½	1	0	1	1	6½
12	Lawrence	0	0	0	0	½	0	½	1	1	0	½	×	1	½	0	½	5½
13	Napier	½	0	0	½	½	0	0	0	½	1	0	0	×	1	1	½	5½
14	Barry	0	0	½	½	½	½	0	½	0	0	1	½	0	×	0	1	5
15	Hodges	0	0	0	0	½	0	1	0	½	1	0	1	0	1	×	0	5
16	Delmar	0	0	0	0	0	½	0	1	0	1	0	½	½	0	1	×	4½

it was the psychologist rather than the chess player at work when Lasker, out of a humdrum opening, steered the game into complications where Janowski lost his way and felt almost 'bewitched' to overreach himself by venturing into an unsound combination.

A few days earlier Lasker had played an even more fascinating 'psychological' game against Napier, yet another one of those typical Lasker-games hovering near (and almost beyond) the abyss. It was a game of which Napier used to say that, although he lost it, he was proud to consider it the best he had ever played.

Thus, even though Cambridge Springs was not one of Lasker's triumphs he had not quite failed to show his mettle. Moreover, whatever disappointment he may have felt about his failure to win the tournament was amply assuaged by some splendid news from England. While still at Cambridge Springs he was informed that the Royal Society had decided to publish a substantial mathematical essay of Lasker's. Such recognition on so exalted a plane meant more to him than any success in a chess tournament.

Nor did he feel the urge—as he had after Hastings—to take immediate steps in re-emphasizing his supremacy as a chess master. After all, *Lasker's Chess Magazine* had put in its appearance, and he gave it all the time he could possibly spare for chess. He would not neglect his other work and his many other interests. And far away, on the other side of the ocean, there was a woman to whom he wrote from time to time, telling her about all his problems and ideas, and about the work he was doing, but also telling her something personal in every letter, something like this: 'Whenever I think of Europe I think of you!'

CHAPTER FIFTEEN

The Match against Marshall

While Lasker cared little or nothing about the tourneys and matches contested in Europe, the chess world cared all the more about him and his position in the scheme of events.

For meanwhile, some major chess events *had* taken place in Europe. At Monte Carlo 1904, Ostend 1905, and Barmen 1905 Maroczy had scored three great triumphs in succession, and Tarrasch had convincingly beaten Marshall in a match (8 : 1, with eight draws). Surely, people said, it was about time for Lasker to defend his title against either Maroczy or Tarrasch, or both. Lasker was not unwilling, and negotiations were first started with Tarrasch, a provisional agreement was reached and the time actually fixed for the match. But Tarrasch suddenly decided to withdraw. Once again he had missed a chance to face that crucial test.

The obvious alternative was to defend the title against Maroczy. Once again negotiations were started, and an agreement was reached and published in the 1905 volume of *Lasker's Chess Magazine*. All the chess world was eagerly looking forward to an exciting struggle between Lasker and the Hungarian grandmaster; and there was widespread disappointment when Maroczy cancelled the arrangement at the last moment.

It had not been Lasker's fault that the projected contests against the two most worthy opponents of the day came to nought. Yet, so widespread was the general discontent about all those fruitless negotiations and disappointed hopes that public opinion demanded that Lasker play some match òr other in defence of his title. In the circumstances, Tarrasch having evaded the direct challenge, Lasker thought of demonstrating his superiority indirectly by picking Tarrasch's opponent of the year before and by trying to beat Marshall even more convincingly than Tarrasch had done. There were some practical advantages too in choosing Marshall as an opponent. Since both contenders were resident in the USA no transatlantic travelling expenses were involved: moreover, with an American as the challenger for the title it was relatively easy to finance the match.

The contest began in January 1907, starting in New York and then moving on to other cities. For more than ten years, ever since the return match with Steinitz, it was the first time that the world championship was at stake; but there were very few who seriously considered the possibility of Marshall wresting the title from Lasker. Marshall was far too erratic to be a reliable match-player. Everybody expected some fireworks from him but hardly anyone expected him to win the match. The main point of interest was whether Lasker would defeat him at least as convincingly as Tarrasch had done.

Lasker certainly did not fail to live up to these expectations; nor could he afford this time to be a 'bad starter'. As a matter of fact, he won the first three games running, the third one being yet another of those shrewd psychological masterpieces fought out on the very brink of the abyss. (See p. 119). Marshall managed to draw every one of the next four games. Number eight was once again a win for Lasker, and then followed three further draws. Thus, with a score of 4 : 0, with seven draws, there seemed to be no end in sight yet; for the contest was to be decided by eight wins, draws not counting. It was now generally assumed that, to win the match, Lasker would have to play a good many more games than the seventeen Tarrasch had required against the same opponent and under the same conditions. But Lasker realised that he was facing an important test and that he had to race time no less than his opponent. He was determined to improve on Tarrasch's record of 8 : 1, with eight draws; and once again—as in the vital game against Janowski at Cambridge Springs—Lasker summoned his uncanny powers of safely winning games whenever he had to: he won the next four games in succession, thereby concluding the match in a mere fifteen rounds and with a score of 8 : 0 with seven draws.

GAME 25

SICILIAN DEFENCE

LASKER–NAPIER

3rd round at Cambridge Springs, 28th April 1904

1)	P—K4	P—QB4
2)	Kt—QB3	Kt—QB3
3)	Kt—B3	P—KKt3
4)	P—Q4	P×P
5)	Kt×P	B—Kt2
6)	B—K3	P—Q3
7)	P—KR3	

The more usual and more natural move is 7) B—K2. With the text, Lasker prepares for a P-attack on the K-wing, such as he has repeatedly carried to success in this opening

| 7) | ..... | Kt—B3 |
| 8) | P—KKt4 | 0—0 |

Black is wise not to be deterred from castling by the coming storm. His only chance is a counter-attack in the centre, which is one more reason for first removing the K.

9) P—Kt5   Kt—K1
10) P—KR4   Kt—B2
11) P—B4   P—K4
12) Kt(4)—K2   P—Q4

Rather than consolidate his position by B—Kt5 Napier, by means of this P-sacrifice aims at a quick break-through in the centre. We will soon see that Napier has worked it all out as far as seems humanly possible, and yet not quite far enough.

13) KP×P   Kt—Q5
14) Kt×Kt

After 14) B×Kt, P×B 15) Kt×P, Kt×P the White position would, obviously, be demolished.

14) .....   Kt×P!

A nasty surprise. After 15) Kt×Kt Black would grab the advantage by P×Kt

15) Kt—B5!

Lasker paries with an equally surprising move; but Napier must have seen it since, otherwise, he would lose a piece.

15) .....   Kt×Kt
16) Q×Q   R×Q
17) Kt—K7 ch

How far Black has seen is evident from the fact that neither this move nor 17) Kt×B would gain material for White. The latter move would be countered by ...Kt—Q4 18) 0—0—0, B—Kt5! with advantage for Black.

17) .....   K—R1

The Black Kt is still taboo, for 18) P×Kt would be advantageously countered by ...P×P

19) B—Q4, B×B 20) P×B, R—K1. If however White plays Kt×B first so as to capture the Kt later, 18) ...Kt—Q4 would thwart the plan.

18) P—R5!

In such positions precariously balanced on a razor's edge, Lasker feels in his very own element. The Black Kt is allowed to remain *en prise*, while White concentrates on his K-side attack, the immediate threat being 19) P× KtP, P×KtP 20) Kt×P ch, K—Kt1 21) B—B4 ch, Kt—Q4 22) B×Kt ch, R×B 23) Kt— K7 ch etc.

18) .....   R—K1!
19) B—B5

Maintaining the same threat

19) .....   KtP×P

A surprising, but well considered move. The more obvious move ...P×BP would be refuted by 20) P×KtP, P×KtP 21) B—B4 with the threat of B—B7. Now however, White is faced by more difficult problems; he still cannot take the Kt, since after 20) P×Kt, B—B1! 21) B—Kt5, R×Kt 22) B×R, B×B Black would have the better of it, in spite of being the exchange down. Hence, Lasker consistently continues his K-side attack

20) B—B4   P×P

Napier too tries to force his counter-attack *à tout prix*, and very wisely too, for defensive manoeuvres such as ...B—K3 would end up in White's favour

21) B×BP   Kt—K5!

This ingenious sacrifice was certainly Napier's best chance, and against any less brilliant tactician than Lasker it might well have saved the game

22) B×R   B×P
23) QR—Kt1   B—B6 ch
24) K—B1   B—KKt5

White is a whole R up, but his position is far from pleasant. He has to face as many as four immediate threats: R × B, Kt×B, Kt—Q7 ch, and Kt—Kt6 ch. Moreover, the White K is dangerously exposed, and while White's attack seems dead and forgotten all Black's pieces are poised most aggressively. At this juncture it would seem to be unbelievable that White will yet win the

Position after Black's 24th move

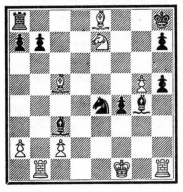

game by continuing the very attack started in the opening stage

25) B×KRP

By relinquishing all his material advantage White grasps the attack once again, and in spite of the reduced forces it will just suffice to ensure victory

25) .....   B×B
26) R×B   Kt—Kt6 ch
27) K—Kt2   Kt×R
28) R×P   P—R4
29) R—Kt3   B—Kt2
30) R—KR3   Kt—Kt6
31) K—B3

The first tangible success. The Black KBP is doomed, since ...B—K4 is ruled out by Kt—Kt6 ch, the very same move (or threat) which has been a sort of *leitmotiv* all through White's attack.

31) .....   R—R3
32) K×P   Kt—K7 ch
33) K—B5   Kt—B6
34) P—R3   Kt—R5
35) B—K3   Resigns

Black has no defence against the threat of P—Kt6.

(Notes by RICHARD RETI in *Die Meister des Schachbretts*

(*This is the game of which Napier said that, in spite of having lost it he would be for ever prouder of it than of any game he won*)

GAME 26

QUEEN'S GAMBIT DECLINED

PILLSBURY–LASKER

6th round at Cambridge Springs, May 3rd 1904

1)	P—Q4	P—Q4
2)	P—QB4	P—K3
3)	Kt—QB3	Kt—KB3
4)	Kt—B3	P—B4
5)	B—Kt5	BP×P
6)	Q×P	Kt—B3
7)	B×Kt!	

That was Pillsbury's 'secret weapon' which he had patiently forged for seven years to use it against Lasker and no one else! (See game 8 as well as p. 107)

7)	.....	P×Kt

Black mustn't play ...Kt×Q 8) B×Q, Kt—B7 ch 9) K—Q1, Kt×R, as the Kt would get lost

8)	Q—R4	P×P

...P—Q5 would be countered by 9) 0—0—0

9)	R—Q1	B—Q2
10)	P—K3	Kt—K4

Black should have played ...P—B4 11) Q×P, B—Kt2 12) Q—Kt3, B×Kt ch 13) Q×B, Q—R4, with a good game. R.T.

11)	Kt×Kt	P×Kt
12)	Q×BP	Q—Kt3
13)	B—K2!	

A fine positional sacrifice yielding a lasting attack

13)	.....	Q×KtP
14)	0—0	R—B1
15)	Q—Q3	R—B2
16)	Kt—K4	B—K2

17)	Kt—Q6 ch	K—B1

After ...B×Kt 18) Q×B, Q—Kt3 19) Q×P, 0—0 20) Q—Kt5 ch White also has much the superior game

18)	Kt—B4	Q—Kt4
19)	P—B4	P×P
20)	Q—Q4	

Very well played. Black now gets into a hopeless position.

20)	.....	P—B3
21)	Q×BP	Q—QB4
22)	Kt—K5	B—K1
23)	Kt—Kt4	P—B4
24)	Q—R6 ch	K—B2

Position after Black's 24th move

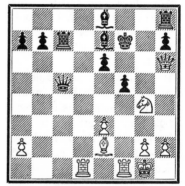

25)	B—B4!	R—B3
26)	R×P ch	Q×R
27)	R—KB1	Q×R ch
28)	K×Q	B—Q2
29)	Q—R5 ch	K—Kt1
30)	Kt—K5	Resigns

With this fine combination, initiating the swop of both Rooks for the Q, White concludes the game as brilliantly as he played it in all its phases.

(Notes from *Deutsches Wochenschach* 1904)

GAME 27

FOUR KNIGHTS' GAME

JANOWSKI–LASKER

Last round at Cambridge Springs,
19th May 1904

1) P—K4	P—K4
2) Kt—KB3	Kt—QB3
3) Kt—B3	Kt—B3
4) B—Kt5	B—B4
5) Kt × P	

A move more customary after
both sides have castled

5)	Kt × Kt
6) P—Q4	B—Q3
7) P—B4	Kt—Kt3

This move and the next one
constitute a novelty. The book-
move is 7) ...Kt—B3

8) P—K5	P—B3
9) B—B4	

It would be preferable to
retreat the B to R4. Another
possibility would be the sacrificial line suggested by Dr.
Tarrasch: 9) P × B, P × B 10)
Q—K2 ch, K—B1 11) P—B5,
Kt—R5 12) 0—0

9)	B—B2

Position after Black's 11th move

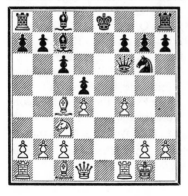

10) P × Kt	Q × P
11) 0—0	P—Q4
12) B × P	

The sacrifice can hardly be
correct, but the alternative for
White would be the loss of yet
another tempo, leaving Black
with an excellent position.

12)	P × B
13) Kt × P	Q—Q3
14) Q—K2 ch	Kt—K2
15) R—K1	B—Q1
16) P—B4	P—B3

Tarrasch suggests ...B—K3
which would seem to give
Black an equally satisfactory
defence

17) B—Q2	P—QR4
18) Q—R5 ch	P—Kt3

The more 'correct' move was
K—B1.

19) P—QB5!	Q—R3

After ...Q—B3 Janowski
claims to have had a win by
20) Kt × Kt, B × Kt 21) Q—K2,
Q—B2 22) P—B5!, K—Q1
23) B—B4, Q—Q2 24) Q—K3,
R—K1 25) P—Q5.

20) Q—R6	B—K3
21) Kt × P ch	

A mistake. White might have
advantageously played 21)
Kt × Kt, B × Kt 22) P—Q5.
Janowski himself, after the
game, suggested 21) Q—Kt7

21)	K—B2
22) Kt—K4	Kt—B4
23) Q—R3	B—K2
24) B—B3	B—Q4
25) P—KKt4	Kt—R5
26) Kt—Q6 ch	K—B1
27) R × B	

The Q-sacrifice herewith initiated is a counsel of despair. But there is nothing else that White could invent against Black's solid defence.

27)	Kt—B6 ch
28) Q×Kt	B×Q
29) R—B7 ch	K—Kt1
30) P—Q5	B×QP
31) R—Kt7 ch	K—B1
32) R—K1	Q—B3
33) P—Kt4	R—Q1
34) B—Q4	R×Kt
35) P×R	B—R8
	Resigns

Deprives White of his very last chance. After 35) ...Q—B7 White would have actually won by 36) R—K8 ch, K×R 37) P—Q7 ch etc.

(Notes by *Deutsches Wochenschach,* 1904

GAME 28
RUY LOPEZ
MARSHALL–LASKER

1st game of the match (played at New York, Jan.. 26th 1907)

1) P—K4	P—K4
2) Kt—KB3	Kt—QB3
3) B—Kt5	Kt—B3
4) P—Q4	

The idea of this move is to ease White's game but that is only feasible if Black already played ...P—Q3. By playing P—Q4 prematurely White gives Black a chance of freeing his own game by ...P—Q4.

4)	P×P
5) 0—0	B—K2
6) P—K5	

The advance of this pawn should have been more carefully considered.

6)	Kt—K5
7) Kt×P	0—0
8) Kt—B5	P—Q4
9) B×Kt	

This exchange proves that Marshall evidently considered his advanced KP as a source of weakness rather than of strength.

9)	P×B
10) Kt×B ch	Q×Kt
11) R—K1	Q—R5

The position clearly calls for 11) ...P—KB3 and it might be simplest and best to make the move at once; But Lasker always likes to create complications so far as they are consistent with the positional requirements of the game. In the present position, the great tactician decides to exploit the fact that by using his KR for supporting the Pawn White has weakened his KB2. This fact coupled with the forthcoming opening of the KB file is to support his own attack against White's weak spot.

12) B—K3	P—B3
13) P—KB3	

(See diagram on following page)

13)	P×P!
14) P×Kt	P—Q5

The White Bishop is now unable to move for obviously B—Q2 would give Black an

Position after White's 13th move

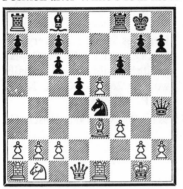

immediate win by ...B—Kt5;
16) Q—B1 and then R—B7!
etc.; hence Marshall first drives
away the Black Queen but he
hasn't grasped the full depth
of Lasker's combination. Since
he cannot save his Bishop
anyway he might have done
better to return it at once.

15) P—KKt3   Q—B3
16) B×P
Now White must return the
piece after all since 16) B—Q2
would be countered by ...Q—
B7 ch; 17) K—R1, B—R6;
18) R—KKt1, P—KR4!; this
being the subtle point of the
combination with White absolutely defenceless against the
threat of ...B—Kt5.

16) .....   P×B
17) R—B1   Q×R ch
18) Q×Q   R×Q ch
19) K×R   R—Kt1
The obvious move here would
seem to have been ...B—R3ch
followed by ...R—KB1. Since
however, in its present position,
Black's QB is doubly effective

(aiming at R3 as well as R6)
Lasker very wisely omits that
obvious check.

20) P—Kt3   R—Kt4
Here the R completely dominates the 5th line.

21) P—B4
Now the Black QP has become
a passed Pawn but then the
more obvious 21) Kt—Q2
would have been countered by
...R—R4; 22) K—Kt2,R —
QB4; 23) R—QB1, B—R3;
with the threat of ...B—Q6.
It can now be seen how wise
Lasker was to utilise every
possibility of that Bishop for
it was his omission of the
obvious B-check on his 19th
move which has forced White
to play P—QB4, thereby giving
Black the passed Pawn which
will finally decide the game.

21) .....   R—KR4
22) K—Kt1   P—B4
Covering the passed Pawn, and
while that blocks the 5th line
for the R, it opens up the 6th.

23) Kt—Q2   K—B2
Developing his K before White
has a chance of R—KB1.

24) R—B1 ch   K—K2
25) P—QR3   R—R3
26) P—KR4   R—R3
27) R—R1   B—Kt5
28) K—B2   K—K3
29) K—Kt2   K—K4
30) P—R4   R—KB3
31) R—K1   P—Q6
The Passed pawn supported by
the K will now bring about the
decision.

32) R—KB1   K—Q5

33) R×R   P×R
34) K—B2

White is getting into Zugzwang since any move of the Kt would allow the Black K to penetrate.

34) .....   P—B3
35) P—QR5   P—QR3
36) Kt—B1   K×P
37) K—K1   B—K7
38) Kt—Q2 ch

Now the Zugzwang is complete. The Kt must move and the Black K will be able to penetrate at B6 but Black can even take his time about it.

38) .....   K—K6
39) Kt—Kt1   P—B4
40) Kt—Q2   P—R4
41) Kt—Kt1   K—B6
42) Kt—B3   K×P
43) Kt—R4   P—B5
44) Kt×P   P—B6
45) Kt—K4 ch   K—B5
46) Kt—Q6   P—B4
47) P—Kt4   P×P
48) P—B5   P—Kt6
49) Kt—B4   K—Kt6
50) Kt—K3   P—Kt7
Resigns

(Notes by RICHARD RETI in *Die Meister des Schachbretts*)

GAME 29

QUEE'NS GAMBIT DECLINED

MARSHALL–LASKER

3rd game of the match, played in New York, January 31st 1907

1) P—Q4   P—Q4
2) P—QB4   P—K3
3) Kt—QB3   Kt—KB3
4) B—Kt5   B—K2
5) P—K3   Kt—K5
6) B×B   Q×B
7) B—Q3   Kt×Kt
8) P×Kt   Kt—Q2
9) Kt—B3   0—0
10) 0—0   R—Q1
11) Q—B2   Kt—B1
12) Kt—K5   P—QB4
13) QR—Kt1   Q—B2

So as to play ...P—QKt3, (now impossible on account of Kt—B6)

14) Q—Kt3   P—QKt3
15) P×QP   KP×P
16) Q—R4?

Here was White's last chance to make sure of a superior game by means of 16) P—QB4.

16) .....   B—Kt2
17) Q—Q1   R—Q3

So as to develop the QR which, on account of B—B5, cannot find a perch at QB1. Moreover, the R keeps a defensive watch on h6 and f6, if and when necessary.

18) Q—Kt4   R—K1
19) Q—Kt3

Preparing for Kt—Kt4, but Lasker immediately unpins his R.

19) .....   R(3)—K3
20) B—B5   R(3)—K2

Even though the White pieces are, all of them, posted rather more aggressively, the Black ones are lurking menacingly in the background, and the Black position offers no weakness for White to attack.

Superficially the position might be considered equalised, but I prefer Black, largely on account of his QBP.

21) P—KB4?

Making the KP backward, weakening the square e4, and thus seriously compromising the White position

21) .....   B—B1

Marshall expected ...P—B3 which he meant to counter by the menacing Kt—Kt4. The excellent text-move forces the exchange of Bs, for if the White B moves Black, of course, wins the KP after ...P—B3.

22) B×B   R×B

Not with the Q, whereafter White could have restricted Black's position by P—B5. Now this is impossible because ...P—B3 would lead to the exchange of Qs and the win of the KP.

23) Q—B3   Q—Q3
24) KR—B1   R(2)—B2
25) P—KR3

Marshall would like to get his K to R2, regardless of the Black Q's dangerous *vis-à-vis*.

25) .....   P—KR3

Making room for the Kt, *en route* to K5.

26) K—R2   Kt—R2
27) Q—R5

Since the K has left the 1st rank White could now recapture on Q4 with the BP, since ...R×R could be countered by Q×BP ch.

27) .....   Kt—B3

28) Q—B5

A typical Marshall trap which Lasker evidently didn't spot at once; for otherwise, (since it isn't immediately effective) he would not have played ...P×P at once.

Position after White's 28th move

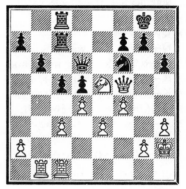

28) .....   P×P
29) KP×P

Black must not now take the QBP because White would swop his Q for the two Rs and then win the Black Q by ...R—R8 ch, followed by ...Kt×P ch

29) .....   Kt—K5

Most commentators have adorned this move with one or two exclamation marks of praise. In point of fact it was a mistake jeopardising a well earned victory. The proper way to win was ...P—Kt3 30) Q—Q3, Kt—K5 31) R—Kt3, P—B3 32) Kt×P, K—Kt2, and the Kt gets lost, since it can't move owing to the threat of ...Q×P ch. After 31) P—B4, K—Kt2 Black would also have much the better of it.

30) Kt×P!   R×Kt!

Nothing daunted, Lasker makes a virtue of necessity. The sacrifice of the exchange, at any rate, gives him some attack; but against correct defence it should have yielded a draw at most.

31)	Q×QR ch	R—B1
32)	Q—Kt7	Q×P ch
33)	K—Kt1	Q—K6 ch
34)	K—R2!	Q—Kt6 ch
35)	K—Kt1	Kt—Q7
36)	Q×QP ch	K—R1
37)	K—R1	Kt—B6!
38)	P×Kt	Q×RP ch
39)	K—Kt1	Q—Kt6 ch

40)	K—R1	R—B5
41)	Q—Q8 ch	

By this and the following move Marshall evidently hoped not merely to save the game but even to win it. A grievous error. His only chance was Q—KR5 whereupon Black had nothing better than forcing the draw by ...R—R5 ch

41)	.....	K—R2
42)	R—B1	R—B4
43)	Q—K8	Q—R5 ch
	resigns	

For the R mates next move. A neat finish.

(Notes by Dr. TARRASCH in the Book of the Match)

CHAPTER SIXTEEN

First Philosophical Essay

Thus the first man of the younger generation who had dared to reach out for the crown had been rapped over the knuckles in no uncertain manner. Not that Marshall was much depressed by his failure. He went to Europe again in the spring of 1907 and did extremely well in the great Ostend tournament. But then, behind that 'younger' generation of Maroczy, Marshall and Janowski, there already stood the 'youngest' generation, coming to the fore and soon to dominate the stage.

It was in that summer of 1907 in the great Karlsbad tournament, that the leader of the 'youngest' generation, Akiba Rubinstein, wrested the first prize from Maroczy, thereby breaking the monopoly of triumph long enjoyed by the galaxy of grandmasters who, in Tarrasch's opinion, could be considered 'top-class'. But even apart from Rubinstein, soon to go from success to success, there were others of the 'youngest' generation who were not to be denied: Bernstein, Duras, Nimzowitsch, Spielmann, Tartakower, Vidmar. They were all coming into Tarrasch's 'top-class'; they were, in fact, the new top-class and living evidence for the fact that the future belonged to the new generation rather than to the contemporaries of Tarrasch.

Was not the advent of Rubinstein and his contemporaries a warning signal for Lasker too? If it was, he certainly did not seem to take much notice of it, for while the great challenge of young Rubinstein came to its dramatic climax at Karlsbad, Lasker sat in New York, busy with the proofs of his first published work on a subject other than chess. It was only a slim volume, but it contained the essence of many years of hard thinking; it was Emanuel Lasker's first philosophical essay, significantly entitled *Kampf*. For just as chess to him was always a struggle, a fight rather than the implementation of some theoretical abstractions, so had he now attempted to apply the same idea to wider fields. He had even coined a new word for his own philosophy, he called it *machology*, derived from the Greek word for fight, *machos*.

To say that *Kampf* is not a chess book is true in the ordinary meaning of the term; yet the statement should be qualified since, to a certain extent, like most of Lasker's thinking, his philosophy is derived from what we might call the essence of chess. He was inevitably impressed by this observation of Goethe's:

".... at the chess-board we cannot go beyond it nor do we want to. We have got our chess men and we know their every value, and movement and power, so it is up to us to make the moves which we hope will give us victory .... yet all the time, just as in life, we have to face problems. We have to watch out for them, and particularly for those that appear to us objectionable, obnoxious and unfavourable. Thus only can we notice and master the problems we encounter in the objects we come across and even more so in the persons we have to deal with."

This quotation, (somewhat freely translated) sums up the essence of Lasker's style in chess (and in life). All his life he was impressed, and also exasperated, by the first sentence. 'At the chess-board we cannot go beyond it, nor do we want to'. But he wanted it very badly. To 'go beyond it' was precisely what Lasker was trying to do. As his life and thinking matured, he was inevitably driven from *Kampf* to *Unvollendbar* and *Unvollendlich*, to the notion of the 'unattainable' which was to provide the title as well as the basic ideas of his later philosophical work.

But meanwhile, he had to tear himself away again from the desk in his quiet study to his professional work at the chess-table. He had to make the major part of his living from chess, and also felt a moral obligation to justify his right to his proud title. Marshall, after all, was merely a 'lightweight'. A more convincing test was demanded from Lasker. He had yet to show that he was strong enough to hold his title against the strongest possible challenge.

CHAPTER SEVENTEEN

At long last, the Tarrasch Match

Thus, Lasker embarked on yet another period of intensive chess activities. One after another, he was to measure his strength against the leading masters of his own generation. Tarrasch, at 46, was the oldest of these. It was to be his turn first. First and yet too late. He had evaded the ultimate decision too long, but now the issue had to be faced. Pressure of public opinion had become so strong that any further evasion would be tantamount to final resignation. The match was to be arranged at last.

Lasker's financial demands were high by the modest standards usually applied to chess events; it was one of his principles to protest against the parsimonious treatment of chess masters. The difficulties in financing the match were considerable and the negotiations were protracted and not without friction and some acrimony on all sides.

The match was to be sponsored by the German Chess Federation and at one time its President, Professor Gebhardt was on the point of dropping the whole matter. It looked as if the chess world was once again to be deprived of the eagerly awaited spectacle. But at long last the financial arrangements were satisfactorily settled, and a triumphant telegram went round the world from Coburg where the final negotiations had taken place. The funds required to meet Lasker's demands had been found. The winner was to receive M. 4000 (£200), the loser M. 2500 (£125); moreover Dr Lasker was to receive a lump sum of M. 7500 (£375), for which fee he was obliged to stake his title in the match. It was only by winning or drawing the match that he could retain the world championship. The match was to begin at Düsseldorf on 17 August 1908, and in September it was to be continued and concluded at Munich; victory to go to the first player to win eight games, draws not counting.

No chess match ever caused anything like the excitement roused by the Lasker–Tarrasch match of 1908. Public interest had been keyed up by those long protracted negotiations, and the legendary fame of both contenders had caught the imagination of the masses, far beyond the relatively few chess players expert enough to understood that this was a contest of two diametrically opposed styles, principles and characters, truly a most exciting event for the connoisseur.

As for the masses, their excitement was less subtle but none the less feverish; for them it was just a particularly sensational sporting event, and oddly enough—the first time in the history of chess—the thrill of it had gripped millions of people who knew little or nothing about the game. For them the names of Lasker and Tarrasch seemed to have achieved some magic significance. Certainly these names 'made news', and for many weeks before the start of the match the Press was full of reports, paragraphs, and essays on chess generally and the two contenders in particular. The advance publicity resembled the ballyhoo let loose by a particularly sensational boxing match for the heavy-weight title, the only difference being that the financial stakes were on a relatively infinitesimal scale.

* * *

One evening that spring there was one of those informal little dinner parties which Frau Martha Kohn, née Bamberger, liked to arrange in her Berlin town house. She was now even better known as Martha Marco, this being the pen-name under which she contributed regularly to various literary magazines, such as the famous Munich *Simplicissimus*, at that time the German equivalent of *Punch* and continually at loggerheads with the Kaiser whose sense of humour failed him when his own person was made an object of satire. Martha Marco's essays were not bitterly political, but they were none the less witty, and some of them had been successfully collected in book form. It cannot have been easy for her at that time to preserve her vivacity and her sense of humour; for her invalid husband's condition was steadily worsening, and his doctors gave no hope of recovery. He was bearing his agony with infinite patience and fortitude, and since he was fully aware of the end being near he had banished all thoughts of doom and insisted, more than ever, on being surrounded by gay and carefree people. It was he who encouraged his wife in her professional and social activities and in her friendship with men such as Berthold and Emanuel Lasker and with that congenial company of artists, journalists and authors who used to frequent her drawing-room and her dinner-parties.

That particular evening, soon after dinner, the maid announced that 'a visitor from America' was waiting in the hall and wished to call on madam. It turned out to be Emanuel who had arrived in Berlin an hour ago, put up at an hotel and made straight for the home of the friends he had not seen in five years.

Everybody was delighted as well as surprised; for though it was common knowledge that the match with Tarrasch was to take place some time later that year, Lasker was not yet expected; as usual, he had come on the spur of the moment and unannounced.

After five years in the USA he was anxious to come to Europe, even more anxious to see the woman he loved; for while he couldn't say it to anybody else, least of all to her, he was now convinced in his own mind that he was deeply in love with Martha. He wanted to be near her as much as possible during the few months still left for him to prepare for the match.

It started promptly on 17 August, and as contractually arranged the first four games were to be played in Düsseldorf. Lasker won the toss, which meant that he had the White pieces in the first game. He chose the Ruy Lopez, the 'fashionable' opening of the time, the very one which Tarrasch was known to have studied more thoroughly than any master on earth. It seemed absurd to impress the *praeceptor Germaniae* with this of all openings. Yet, even on the fourth move Lasker sprang a surprise. He chose the 'exchange variation', a fairly unusual line, but the one he had employed to beat Tarrasch at Nuremberg 1896. In his own notes Tarrasch tartly commented: 'A rather dull line, but not without some difficulties for Black.' Exactly! For after the early exchange of Queens Black, what with his two Bishops and a slight positional advantage, is virtually forced to attack; if he fails to avail himself of that chance he is left with the inferior pawn-skeleton for the ending. That was precisely what Lasker brought about by his solid if unspectacular play. In the middle-game Tarrasch never succeeded in getting that vital attack going and so, almost imperceptibly, he drifted into a lost ending.

But the second game (see p. 130) was even more remarkable, it was indeed one of the most remarkable of Lasker's many demonstrations of 'psychological warfare' on the chess-board. It was again a Ruy Lopez and, playing White in one of his favourite variations Tarrasch was very much in his element and soon reached a distinctly superior position. Presently Lasker made a move (his fourteenth) which Tarrasch in his own notes significantly calls ' . . . evidently an oversight, such as is apt to occur in inferior positions'.

How little he knew his wily opponent! It was anything but an oversight, it was Lasker, the psychologist at his best. The move put his opponent in the quandary of having to choose between either winning a pawn immediately or continuing a promising attack. It seemed a delectable choice, and Tarrasch, as conscentiously and thoroughly as ever, spent a lot of time and nervous energy in deciding the course to take. But Lasker was never in any doubt as to what that decision would be; he knew his opponent's mind rather better than Tarrasch did himself; he knew that, having lost the first game, Tarrasch would grasp the tangible advantage of the pawn rather than the speculative one of the attack; and Lasker also knew that this would not be the wiser choice for him to take. Yet, he took it, and once again a deliberately poor move made by Lasker, the chess player, was justified by Lasker, the psychologist. By grabbing that pawn Tarrasch saw his own attack come to a standstill, and soon Lasker's counter-attack got going. Tarrasch still might have drawn the game, but having spent so much thought on that previous decision he was getting into serious time-trouble and increasingly worried by seeing an apparently certain win slip through his fingers. A few indifferent moves worsened his position, and Lasker really began to get the better of it. Tarrasch, by now, was completely flustered, and very soon his game went to pieces.

'I am thoroughly ashamed of that game' was Tarrasch's own comment, and to the end of his days he could never understand why he had lost, why, indeed, he had to lose a game that to his dogmatic mind was a 'theoretical win'; to the end of his days he ascribed the result of that game to 'Lasker's incredible luck'. Now let us see how clearly Lasker was aware of his own as well as his opponent's style and character. This is what he wrote on the eve of the match:

'Dr Tarrasch is a thinker, fond of deep and complex speculation. He will accept the efficacy and usefulness of a move if at the same time he considers it beautiful and theoretically right. But I accept that sort of beauty only if and when it happens to be useful. He admires an idea for its depth, I admire it for its efficacy. My opponent believes in beauty, I believe in strength. I think that by being strong a move is beautiful too.'

Tarrasch was deeply depressed by the unexpected outcome of the second game, so utterly incomprehensible to his own methodical mind. But he was far from being demoralised, he fought back bravely and he promptly grasped his chance when his wily opponent rather overreached himself in the third game. It was a well deserved victory for Tarrasch. But the fourth game saw Tarrasch once again enmeshed by Lasker, the psychologist. In the middle-game Lasker had got himself into trouble; but instead of doing the obvious thing and simplifying the position he did something absolutely abhorrent to Tarrasch's tidy mind: he complicated things even more, and in doing so he made a virtue of necessity. Lasker had allowed one of his rooks to be lured right into the middle of the board where it seemed to be in jeopardy; but in the ensuing complications Tarrasch went astray and gave Lasker the chance of a magnificent counter-coup. Once again he had managed to turn a 'theoretical loss' into victory.

Thus, at the end of the Düsseldorf phase Lasker had established a useful lead of 3 : 1 when, after a week's rest, the match was continued at Munich. By now public interest had been roused to fever-pitch, the match had become front-page news, and a daily average of 1,400 spectators —on some days well over 2,000—crowded the hall. A multitude of people who knew little or nothing about the game had been caught by the thrill of a great sporting event, and in those weeks a single Munich bookshop sold nearly a hundred copies of a popular chess-primer every day.

In the fifth game too Lasker won by shrewd psychology. (See p. 134). It was, once again, a Ruy Lopez, and Tarrasch was amazed to see his opponent adopt precisely the same variation that had led to his only loss in the third game. Move by move Lasker followed the course of that ill-fated game, and Tarrasch was getting more and more nervous about the danger of falling into some 'prepared variation'. When, he was wondering, would his opponent finally deviate to avoid the fatal development of that other game? It happened when he least expected it, (on the 16th move), and very soon Tarrasch went astray and lost yet another game.

With a score of 4 : 1 against him Tarrasch was obviously depressed, but he was far from deprived of his considerable courage and self-confidence; he fought on doggedly, and the sixth game, after manifold complications, led to a draw, the first in the match. But in the seventh game Tarrasch, for once, got into a bad position at an early stage; he put up tenacious resistance, but after more than seventy moves he had to capitulate again.

5 : 1, and only one draw! It looked like a landslide. But experience has proved that at just such a stage of a match a reaction can usually be expected. The one who seems to have victory already in his grasp will relax and show signs of nervousness, and the one who seems no longer to have anything to lose but everything to gain will show unexpected powers of resistance and, indeed, of attack. It happened in the Lasker-Steinitz match and on a good many similar occasions; and it happened again when Tarrasch, just as his position seemed to be quite hopeless, began to fight back more vigorously than ever. With his back to the wall, he was no longer so easily cowed by Lasker's shrewd psychology and surprise tactics. Moreover, Lasker seemed nervous and listless, as he had never been before in the course of an important match. All of a sudden, he seemed to have lost that self-assurance and mental agility and elasticity that used to give the impetus to his 'psychological warfare'. The eighth and ninth game were drawn, and in the tenth game Tarrasch scored a brilliant victory, one of the most magnificent games in his career.

The score was still 5 : 2 in Lasker favour; but in the last three games he had not scored a single win. Obviously, there was something wrong with him.

It seemed inexplicable at the time to all except the very few who knew Lasker intimately. The real reason, of course, was Martha. A string of letters and telegrams went from Munich to Berlin, beseeching her: 'Do come at once, come as my guardian angel, or I might lose the whole match!' But Martha had many duties and responsibilities, and much though she would have liked to help Lasker she felt that she could not leave her invalid husband for any length of time.

It was her husband who decided the issue: 'We can't leave him in the lurch, Martha. You get on the next train to Munich, and Berthold had better go too. It'll make all the difference for Emanuel.'

Martha yielded. Next day she was in Munich, and Emanuel met her at the station. He was blissfully happy now.

There is no telling if Lasker would not have won the match anyway, even if Martha had let him down. But it seems quite probable that this dominating personality, if he had not had his will in the sphere that mattered most to him, would have lost his uncanny faculty of exercising his will power over the chess-board. It is a purely academic question since the contingency did not arise; yet, it seems highly probable that a woman who never played a game of chess all her life, may well have decisively influenced the history of chess.

Martha was sitting in the audience when the eleventh game came to be played, and it was soon obvious to everybody that the real Lasker was back again, as sure of himself as ever. He got the advantage in the opening and won the game with what seemed to be the greatest of ease. The score was now 6 : 2; the spell was broken, and from now on Tarrasch didn't have a chance, even though he managed to win one more game and to draw two. The end came in the sixteenth game, when, in a difficult position and under great time pressure Tarrasch made a crude mistake, an oversight that cost him a piece. He resigned at once.

The great match was over, with a score of 8 : 3 and five draws. It wasn't really as great a match as it might have been if Tarrasch had been able to do himself justice. But he had waited too long. He had missed the great chances of his life: against Steinitz in the early nineties, and now against Lasker (if indeed he ever had a chance against him). The match of 1908 did not mark the end of Tarrasch's career—he still had twenty-five years before him, as a teacher and author rather more than as a practising grandmaster—, but it did mark the end of Tarrasch's consuming ambition for absolute supremacy in chess. Eight years later he was to get the chance of another match against Lasker, and as we shall see he lost it even more convincingly.

The one unpleasant aspect of the great match of 1908 was the fact that the two contenders did not happen to be on speaking terms. Tarrasch was not a very conciliatory man, and his animosity against his great adversary had been embittered by the lengthy negotiations due to Lasker's insistence on holding out for his financial terms. At the beginning of the match mutual friends among the members of the organising committee hoped to bring about a reconciliation of the two masters or at least their readiness to observe the conventional social civilities in the course of the match.

Lasker was quite willing, and it was arranged for him to wait in a private room while the kindly committee member went to fetch Dr Tarrasch. But the Doctor only came as far as the door. There he made a stiff little bow and exclaimed: 'To you, Herr Lasker, I have only three words to say: Check and Mate!' He made another bow and turned on his heels. Lasker merely shrugged his shoulders. As for Tarrasch, he was not to have many opportunities of speaking the three ominous words.

GAME 30

RUY LOPEZ

TARRASCH–LASKER

2nd game of the match, Düsseldorf
August 19th 1908

1)	P—K4	P—K4
2)	Kt—KB3	Kt—QB3
3)	B—Kt5	Kt—B3
4)	0—0	P—Q3
5)	P—Q4	B—Q2
6)	Kt—B3	B—K2
7)	R—K1	P×P
8)	Kt×P	0—0
9)	Kt×Kt	

With the variation he chose to play here Tarrasch had achieved a magnificent victory against Steinitz at Vienna, 1898. Ever since, and until Lasker refuted it in the present game in apparently so simple a manner, this variation was considered particularly good for White. To say that he 'refuted' it does not imply, of course, an actual advantage for Black, it just means that the natural problem of surviving the opening unscathed, could be solved with relative ease.

9)	.....	B×Kt

In the above-mentioned game Steinitz played ...P×Kt. After the text, White cannot in the long run stop his opponent from easing his game by ...P—Q4.

10)	B×B	P×B
11)	Kt—K2	

Since Black's ...P—Q4 could not be stopped anyway White indulges in a bit of finessing. Of course, Black mustn't take the KP, on account of 12) Kt—Q4, followed by Kt × P.

11) .....   Q—Q2

It was simpler to push the QP at once. But true to his complicating style Lasker wanted to develop his rooks first, so as to put more power behind ...P—Q4. A good idea, but in executing it Lasker, somewhat inaccurately, posts his rooks at Q1 and K1; he should have put them at Q1 and QKt1, so as to reserve K1 as a retreat for his Kt.

12) Kt—Kt3   KR—K1?
13) P—Kt3   QR—Q1
14) B—Kt2

The disadvantage of Black's careless 12th is now plainly evident. Black has gratuitously deprived himself of the opportunity of liberating his position by ...P—Q4, since White could exploit the lack of a retreat for the Kt by pushing his KP. Hence, Black is in a hopelessly restricted position, and since there was no one to equal Tarrasch in his consummate mastership of dealing with precisely that type of position, he should have won almost automatically, against anybody in the world—anybody but Lasker. For that great psychologist choses the right moment for mixing things up. His next move looks like

Position after White's 14th move

an oversight, but in point of fact it is a very shrewd sacrifice of a P, aiming at the isolation of the White KP. But, as we shall see, it is a credit to Lasker, the psychologist rather than Lasker, the chess-master.

14) .....   Kt—Kt5
15) B × P   Kt × BP!

Obviously, ...K × B would have been countered by 16) Kt—B5 ch.

16) K × Kt

Instead of winning the P, Tarrasch, by 16) Q—Q4 could have gone in for a very strong and probably irresistible attack. Against an attacking player Lasker would almost certainly have lost this game; but then, against an attacking player Lasker, the psychologist just would not have played 14) ...Kt—Kt5.

16) .....   K × B
17) Kt—B5 ch   K—R1
18) Q—Q4 ch   P—B3
19) Q × RP

Tarrasch may well be pardoned

for having flattered himself at this juncture for being not merely a very healthy P up but for having a promising attack as well against Black's dangerously exposed K. But this soon turns out to be a fallacy. Owing to the isolation of the KP, Black's K4 has become a very strong square whence the White attack will soon be brought to a standstill.

19) .....   B—B1!
20) Q—Q4   R—K4!

A sort of deadlock has already been reached. True, White still has his dangerous passed P on the Q-wing, but in the centre Black has the superior position. When assessing the position objectively it is still undeniable that White has the better of it, but it is the very type of highly dynamic position in which Lasker was for ever at his best, pulling out reserves of energy which as dogmatic a player as Tarrasch was ill equipped to cope with.

21) QR—Q1   R(1)—K1
22) Q—B3   Q—B2
23) Kt—Kt3

The aggressive White Kt retreats to a defensive role while the Black B, heretofore restricted, joins in the attack. Note that all this is caused by the isolation of the White KP

23) .....   B—R3
24) Q—B3   P—Q4
25) P×P   B—K6 ch
26) K—B1   P×P

27) R—Q3

Tarrasch suggested after the game that here was his last chance, by means of 27) Kt—B5, to convert White's material superiority to victory.

27) .....   Q—K3
28) R—K2   P—KB4
29) R—Q1   P—B5
30) Kt—R1   P—Q5
31) Kt—B2

Now, by means of two fine and deeply considered moves (31st and 33rd) Lasker forces the decision

31) .....   Q—QR3!
32) Kt—Q3   R—KKt4
33) R—R1   Q—R3!

The White KRP can no longer be defended. If 34) P—KR3 Black plays ...R—Kt6 with the unanswerable threat of ...Q×P.

34) K—K1   Q×P
35) K—Q1   Q—Kt8 ch
36) Kt—K1   R(4)—K4
37) Q—B6

So as to counter ...B—B7 by Q×R ch

37) .....   R(4)—K3
38) Q×P   R(1)—K2
39) Q—Q8 ch   K—Kt2
40) P—R4   P—B6!

So as to be able to play the B to Kt4, thereby depriving White of the chance of giving his Q for the two Rooks.

41) P×P   B—Kt4
Resigns

Notes, (slightly elaborated by the translator) from RICHARD RETI'S *Die Meister des Schachbretts*

GAME 31
RUY LOPEZ

TARRASCH–LASKER

4th match game, Düsseldorf
August 24th 1908

1)	P—K4	P—K4
2)	Kt—KB3	Kt—QB3
3)	B—Kt5	Kt—B3
4)	0—0	P—Q3
5)	P—Q4	B—Q2
6)	Kt—B3	B—K2
7)	R—K1	P×P
8)	Kt×P	Kt×Kt
9)	Q×Kt	B×B
10)	Kt×B	0—0

This way of treating the opening is by no means easy for the defence. Black is cramped for space while White enjoys a very comfortable and aggressive development. The one advantage for Black is to be able to avoid any loosening of the Q-wing.

11)	B—Kt5	P—KR3
12)	B—R4	R—K1
13)	QR—Q1	

White is fully developed and threatens to win by 14) P—K5.

13)	.....	Kt—Q2

The only move, serving the double purpose of unpinning the QP as well as mobilising the Kt for taking up a strong defensive position either on K3 or on QKt3

14)	B×B	R×B
15)	Q—B3	

Immediately threatening the QBP, to say nothing of the menacing push of the KP as well as of very aggressive Kt-

manoeuvres such as Kt—Q4—B5.

15)	.....	R—K4!

The saving grace

16)	Kt—Q4	R—QB4

The R must be dangerously exposed so as to draw the brunt of the attack.

17)	Q—QKt3	Kt—Kt3

Again the only move, for 18) R—K3 could now be countered by ...Q—K1, and if then 19) Kt—B5, ...K—R2 would be an adequate defence.

18)	P—KB4	

Useful in laying siege to the Black R, but the move has the drawbacks of weakening K4 and blocking the KB file for the White Rooks.

18)	.....	Q—B3
19)	Q—KB3	R—K1

It may have been safer to play ...P—QR4. But as we shall see the defence of the R could be delayed by one move; and the more one delays a defensive manoeuvre—provided one can afford delay—the more effective it usually is.

20)	P—B3	P—QR4
21)	P—QKt3	P—R5!
22)	P—QKt4	R—B5
23)	P—Kt3	

Wishing to keep the KBP covered in anticipation of the push of the Black QBP

23)	.....	R—Q1!
24)	R—K3	P—B4!
25)	Kt—Kt5	

(See diagram on following page)

25)	.....	P×P
26)	R×P	R×R

Position after White's 25th move

27) P—K5

This was the point of Tarrasch's combination, *(but evidently, he hadn't bargained for Black's counterstroke. R.T.)*

27)	.....	R × KBP!
28)	KtP × R	Q—Kt3 ch
29)	K—R1?	Q—QKt8 ch
30)	K—Kt2	R—Q7 ch
31)	R—K2	Q × P
32)	R × R	Q × R ch
33)	K—Kt3	P—R6!
34)	P—K6?	Q—K8 ch
35)	K—Kt4	Q × P ch
36)	P—B5	Q—B5 ch
37)	Kt—Q4	P—R7
38)	Q—Q1	Kt—Q4
39)	Q—R4	Kt × P
40)	Q—K8 ch	K—R2
41)	K—R5	P—R8(=Q)

Resigns

LASKER's own notes in *Pester Lloyd* of 2nd Sept. 1908

GAME 32

RUY LOPEZ

LASKER–TARRASCH

5th match game Munich, 1st Sept. 1908

1)	P—K4	P—K4
2)	Kt—KB3	Kt—QB3
3)	B—Kt5	P—QR3
4)	B—R4	Kt—B3
5)	0—0	B—K2
6)	R—K1	P—QKt4
7)	B—Kt3	P—Q3
8)	P—B3	Kt—QR4
9)	B—B2	P—B4
10)	P—Q4	Q—B2
11)	QKt—Q2	Kt—B3
12)	P—KR3	0—0
13)	Kt—B1	BP × P
14)	P × P	Kt × QP
15)	Kt × Kt	P × Kt

So far it's exactly like the third game of the match when I continued 16) Kt—Kt3.

16) B—Kt5

The idea being either to get rid of Black's important KB or to hamper its development. The position is now getting very complicated.

16) .....   P—R3

17) B—KR4   Q—Kt3

This is much too passive a move and Black will almost immediately get into trouble.

18) Q—Q3

The threat being 19) B × Kt, followed by P—K5. Black can't parry this by 18) ...B—K3 on account of 19) B × Kt, B—B4; 20) Q × QP; hence the loosening of Black's K-wing is practically forced.

18) .....   P—Kt4

Position after Black's 27th move

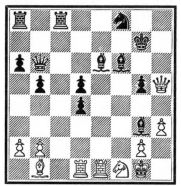

19) B—KKt3   B—K3
20) QR—Q1!   KR—B1
21) B—Kt1   Kt—Q2
22) P—K5!   Kt—B1
23) Q—KB3
    Threatening P × P followed by
    Q—KB6.
23) .....   P—Q4
24) Q—R5   K—Kt2
25) P—B4
    Threatening P—B5.

25) .....   P—B4
Like an ancient Roman hero Tarrasch throws himself on his own sword! Evidently he did not feel like offering some prolonged but hopeless resistance by 25) ...Kt—Kt3.

26) P × P e.p. ch   B × P
27) P × P   P × P
28) B—K5!   P—Q6 ch
29) K—R1   Kt—Kt3
30) Q × P   B—B2
31) Kt—Kt3   B × B
32) R × B   R—R1
    ...Q—Q1 would have been countered by 33) R—K7.
33) B × P   R—QR2
34) R(1)—K1   K—B1
35) B × Kt   Q × B
36) Q—K3   R—B2
37) Kt—B5   Q—QB3
38) Q—Kt5!   Resigns

(Notes by Dr. LASKER in *Pester Lloyd* of 9th September 1908

CHAPTER EIGHTEEN

St. Petersburg 1909

No doubt, the Lasker-Tarrasch match had given a tremendous impetus to chess all over the world, and even the most parsimonious club secretaries and the most conservative Federation-treasurers began to see that the 'staggering' expense of the match—£875, all told—was not such a bad investment after all. New clubs sprang up everywhere, more and more papers all over the world began to feature regular chess columns, more tournaments, matches and local championships were being organised in places big and small, and a growing demand for simultaneous performances and lectures provided more employment and a less precarious and less penurious standard of living for a steadily increasing number of masters. Such, unquestionably, were the economic consequences of the match, thereby justifying Lasker in his insistant demands that chess masters should claim their right to decent remuneration.

Lasker himself was caught up by the new wave of enthusiasm which had been largely caused by his own efforts. He seemed more keen on chess than ever and more willing to give public exhibitions and to enter some great international competition. An opportunity arose soon enough. Tchigorin, the veteran Russian master, had died in 1908, and just as in the zenith of his career he had been the initiator of the great Petersburg Tournament of 1895–6, so his death inspired that city's enthusiastic and wealthy chess-fraternity to stage a great Tchigorin Memorial Tournament.

It was held in 1909, and only Maroczy, Marshall, and Tarrasch were missing in an otherwise almost complete array of all the greatest masters of the time. Lasker, of course, was 'hot favourite', but no mean chances either were conceded to Schlechter and Duras who had shared first and second prize in the two greatest international tournaments of 1908, at Vienna and at Prague. There were also Burn, Mieses, and Teichmann to represent the older generation, but even more was expected of Bernstein, Rubinstein, Spielmann, Tartakover, Vidmar and other younger players. It was a stiff test for Lasker to measure his strength not only against some of the élite of his own contemporaries, but also against those dangerous 'youngsters' most of whom he had never met. For in the five years since Cambridge Springs he had had no tournament practice and, apart from the Tarrasch match the year before, he had played hardly any serious chess at all for years.

This time, indeed, Lasker had good cause to be worried about his lack of preparation for so severe a test of strength; so he decided, immediately prior to the tournament, to stop over in Amsterdam for a small practice match arranged with the Dutch master Speyer. Lasker won it convincingly enough with 2 : 0 and one draw, but he was yet far from running to his top-form.

Drawn against the redoubtable Schlechter in the first round at Petersburg, Lasker failed to exploit a winning chance and had to be content with a draw. In the second round he won a beautiful game against the young Hungarian Forgacz (see p. 140), a relatively 'easy' customer in such exalted company; but in the third round he came up against the stiffest test of all: Akiba Rubinstein, the most dangerous representative of the young generation. Here was an opponent with whom 'psychological warfare' would cut less ice than with anybody else, and there was indeed a great deal of ice to be cut; for one could aptly compare that modest young man to an iceberg: not only on account of his cool and quiet demeanour, but also because, however little of him appeared superficially, there was a great deal more below the surface, (and that applies to the man no less than to his style in chess). Hailing from the humble background of a Polish ghetto and educated in the stern sophistry of a Talmud school, Rubinstein was by tradition, circumstances and character an introvert devoting all his immense powers of reasoning to chess; he lived for chess, studied chess and thought of chess all his waking hours (and, as likely as not, in his dreams). His style was of the utmost lucidity and almost crystal clarity, his knowledge of opening theory stupendous, and his end-game technique unequalled by anybody except, perhaps, Lasker.

This was the man Emanuel was up against in the third round, and young Rubinstein, fully conscious of the great occasion, played what was probably the greatest of the many great games he was yet to play (See p. 141). Lasker was a good loser (on the few occasions he had a chance to prove it), and he was the first to recognise a great achievement even if he happened to be the victim. Yet, this defeat gave him a jolt. Used though he was to being a bad starter in tournaments, he had never yet started quite so badly. One and a half points out of three games just wasn't good enough. In the fourth round Lasker was drawn against the young and inexperienced von Freymann, one of the few 'outsiders' in that tourney of giants, and lo and behold, Lasker all but lost the game. Indeed he ought to have lost it, though by shrewd tactics he managed to wriggle out of the lost position and finally even to win. But that narrow escape gave Lasker even more of a jolt, and in the fifth round he could do no better against young Spielmann—another one of the budding grandmasters—than holding him to a draw.

By now, Rubinstein was one and a half points ahead, but Lasker had found his feet, and soon he was in his stride, running to truly magnificent form. Out of the next ten games he scored 9½ points, a stupendous achievement, considering that his victims included such famous masters as Salwe, Tartakover, Mieses, Vidmar and that some of these games (see p. 142 *et seq*) are veritable gems of chess literature. In the ninth round Lasker had caught up with Rubinstein who suffered an unexpected defeat against Dus-Chotimirski; in the eleventh round Lasker was half a point ahead, and he maintained that lead up to the fifteenth round.

Then came the momentous sixteenth round in which Lasker was drawn against Dus-Chotimirski who was by no means quite in the class of the great masters whose scalps the world-champion had taken in his stride. But had not Dus-Chotimirski beaten the invincible Rubinstein? Like many artists, Lasker was not free from superstition; he was distinctly nervous when he sat down to play that game, he made a poor move in the opening, and soon got himself into such a mess that all his tactical ingenuity could not stave off defeat. Thus, one of the 'outsiders' of that great tournament could score the sensational triumph of beating both the first prize-winners.

Now Rubinstein had regained the lead, and when the last round came to be played the score was: Rubinstein 14, Lasker 13½. Rubinstein had to play Tartakover and could only just manage to draw. Even so, to equalise with him, Lasker had to win his own last round game. It was neither the first nor the last time that he found himself in such a predicament; yet, whenever he *had* to win a game, somehow he always pulled it off. It had happened in that last-round game against Janowski at Cambridge Springs, and, as we shall see, it was to happen again in the last match-game against Schlechter which saved him the title in 1910 and in that famous game against Capablanca which would decide his victory at Petersburg 1914. In that last-round game in 1909 he also produced that extra ounce of will-power that never failed him in an emergency; nor was his opponent a 'push-over'; he was none other than the redoubtable Teichmann for whom an extra half point made all the difference of sharing a higher prize. Yet, Lasker floored him in a mere 27 moves, having first disconcerted him by a novelty introduced in one of the standard variations of the Ruy Lopez. (See p. 148).

Thus, Lasker and Rubinstein shared the victory with 14½ points, their nearest rivals trailing as much as 3½ points behind. Oddly enough, Lasker won every single one of the nine games in which

ST. PETERSBURG 1909

		1	2	3	4	5	6	7	8	9	10	11	12	13	14	15	16	17	18	19	
{1	Rubinstein	×	1	1	1	½	½	½	1	1	1	1	½	0	1	½	1	1	1	1	14½
{2	Lasker	0	×	1	½	½	1	1	1	1	½	1	1	0	1	1	1	1	1	1	14½
3	Duras	0	0	×	0	0	1	½	0	1	½	1	0	1	1	1	1	1	1	1	11
4	Spielmann	0	½	1	×	0	1	1	½	½	1	½	½	1	0	½	1	½	½	1	11
5	Bernstein	½	½	1	1	×	0	1	0	1	1	1	1	½	0	0	0	½	½	1	10½
6	Teichmann	½	0	0	0	1	×	0	½	½	½	1	½	1	½	1	½	1	1	½	10
7	Perlis	½	0	½	0	0	1	×	½	1	½	1	½	1	½	1	½	0	0	1	9½
8	Cohn (E)	0	0	1	½	1	½	½	×	0	0	½	1	½	0	½	½	½	1	1	9
9	Salwe	0	0	0	½	0	½	0	1	×	0	1	½	1	1	½	0	1	1	1	9
10	Schlechter	0	½	½	0	0	½	½	1	1	×	0	0	1	1	½	0	1	½	1	9
11	Mieses	0	0	0	½	0	0	0	½	0	1	×	1	½	1	1	1	0	1	1	8½
12	Tartakover	½	0	1	½	0	½	½	0	½	1	0	×	0	0	½	1	1	1	½	8½
13	Dus-Chotimirsky	1	1	0	0	½	0	0	½	0	0	½	1	×	½	½	½	1	0	1	8
14	Forgacs	0	0	0	1	1	½	½	1	0	0	0	1	½	×	½	½	½	0	½	7½
15	Burn	½	0	0	½	1	0	0	½	½	½	0	½	½	½	×	1	½	½	0	7
16	Vidmar	0	0	0	0	1	½	½	½	1	1	0	0	½	½	0	×	½	1	0	7
17	Speijer	0	0	0	½	½	0	1	½	0	0	1	0	0	½	½	½	×	½	½	6
18	von Freymann	0	0	0	½	½	0	1	0	0	½	0	0	1	1	½	0	½	×	0	5½
19	Znosko-Borovsky	0	0	0	0	0	½	0	0	0	0	0	½	0	½	1	1	½	1	×	5

he had the White pieces; but more significant is the fact that, just as he lost to Rubinstein on this their first encounter, so he had lost to Tarrasch as well as to Marshall in the first games ever played against them, whereas not one of those three great masters ever managed to repeat his initial triumph; Lasker never lost another important tournament game to any of them.

After the great event the Petersburg committee commissioned Lasker to edit the book and to annotate all the games. It is probably no exaggeration to say that, to this day, that particular tournament book remains the most lucid and erudite of its kind; and Alekhine —himself one of the greatest annotators of all times—proclaimed more than once that as a young student of chess on his own way to mastership he learned more from that book than from all the others he studied.

GAME 33

RUY LOPEZ

LASKER–FORGACZ

2nd round, St. Petersburg 1909

1) P—K4	P—K4
2) Kt—KB3	Kt—QB3
3) B—Kt5	P—Q3
4) P—Q4	B—Q2
5) Kt—B3	Kt—B3
6) P×P	

Here I felt like opening up the game.

6)	P×P
7) B—Kt5	B—QKt5
8) 0—0	B×Kt
9) P×B	P—KR3
10) B—KR4	Q—K2

If ...P—KKt4; 11) B—Kt3, Kt×P 12) Kt×P and Black's game will be far from satisfactory.

11) Q—Q3	P—R3
12) B—R4	R—Q1
13) Q—K3	P—KKt4
14) B—KKt3	P—Kt4

Now Black's QB4 is very weak and there indeed he has planted the roots of his subsequent downfall.

15) B—Kt3	Kt—KR4
16) Kt—K1	Kt—R4
17) Kt—Q3	Kt—KB5
18) P—B3	R—KKt1

After ...Kt×Kt 19) P×Kt, P—QB4 20) P—Q4, and after the exchange of Pawns the Black K would be dangerously exposed.

19) KR—Q1	R—Kt3
20) B—B2	B—B1
21) Q—K1	Kt×Kt

He is trying to keep the White B off his QB5. 21) ...Kt—Kt2 would have been strongly countered by 22) P—QR4.

22) P×Kt	Kt×B
23) P×Kt	P—QB4
24) P—QKt4!	P×P
25) P×P	P—Kt5
26) B—B5	Q—Kt4
27) P×P	Q×P
28) R—R2	B—K3
29) R—KB2	B—B5
30) Q—KB1	B—Kt6
31) R—R1	Q—Q2

Position after Black's 33rd move

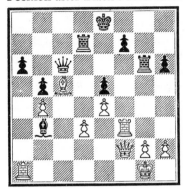

So as to parry the threatened
R—KB5 by Q—QB2.

| | 32) R—B3 | Q—B3 |
| | 33) Q—B2 | R—Q2 |

The B at QKt3 is in jeopardy
hence he ought to have retreated it to K3 but even then
White would have obtained a
decisive attack by 34) R—KB1
followed by R—B6.

	34) Q—Kt2	Q—K3
	35) P—Q4	P×P
	36) Q×B	Q×P
	37) Q—Q3	Q—Q4
	38) Q×R	Resigns

(Notes by Dr. LASKER in the Book
of the Tournament)

GAME 34

QUEEN'S GAMBIT DECLINED

RUBINSTEIN–LASKER

St. Petersburg 1909

1) P—Q4	P—Q4
2) Kt—KB3	Kt—KB3
3) P—B4	P—K3
4) B—Kt5	P—B4
5) P×QP	KP×P
6) Kt—B3	P×P
7) Kt×P	Kt—B3

The cause for subsequent
embarrassement. 7) ...B—K2
was preferable

| 8) P—K3 | B—K2 |
| 9) B—Kt5 | |

Showing up the weakness of
Black's 7th move

9)	B—Q2
10) B×KKt	B×B
11) Kt×P	B×Kt
12) P×B	Q—Kt4
13) B×Kt	B×B
14) Kt—K3	0—0—0

A careless move. There was
no reason for Black to desist
from his intention of capturing the KKtP simply because White had omitted
Q—K2 ch. As a matter of
fact, after ...B×KtP; 15)
R—KKt1, Q—R4 ch; 16) Q—
Q2, Q×Q ch 17) K×Q, B—K5
Black would have been quite
comfortable.

| 15) 0—0 | KR—K1 |

Position after Black's 15th move

16) R—B1!

A very subtle move. What with the threat of R—B5 and P—Q5, White retains his advantage, and he can certainly cope with Black's threat of ...R×Kt.

16) .....   R×Kt
17) R×B ch   P×R
18) Q—B1!   R×P
19) P×R   R—Q2
20) Q×P ch   K—Q1
21) R—B4!

A splendid idea, threatening to decide the game at once by Q—QR8 ch, followed by a R-check on K4 or QB4; hence, Black is forced to swap Queens and to face a lost ending.

21) .....   P—B4
22) Q—B5   Q—K2

After 22) ...R—Q8 ch; 23) K—B2, R—Q7 ch; 24) K—K1,

Q×P White would win the R by 25) Q—R5 ch

23)	Q×Q ch	K×Q
24)	R×P	R—Q8 ch
25)	K—B2	R—Q7 ch
26)	K—B3	R×QKtP
27)	R—QR5	R—Kt2
28)	R—R6	K—B1
29)	P—K4	R—QB2
30)	P—KR4	K—B2
31)	P—Kt4	K—B1
32)	K—B4	K—K2
33)	P—R5	P—R3
34)	K—B5	K—B2
35)	P—K5	R—Kt2
36)	R—Q6	K—K2
37)	R—R6	K—B2
38)	R—Q6	K—B1
39)	R—B6	K—B2
40)	P—R3	Resigns

(Notes by Dr. LASKER in the Book of the Tournament)

GAME 35

RUY LOPEZ

LASKER–SALWE

St. Petersburg 1909 (6th round)

1) P—K4   P—K4
2) Kt—KB3   Kt—QB3
3) B—Kt5   P—Q3
4) P—Q4   B—Q2
5) Kt—B3   Kt—B3
6) 0—0

6) B×Kt, B×B; 7) Q—Q3 is considered preferable. (R.T.)

6) .....   B—K2
7) B—Kt5

This seems stronger than the customary 7) R—K1

7) .....   P×P

8) Kt×P   0—0
9) B×QKt   P×B
10) Q—Q3   R—K1
11) QR—K1   P—B4
12) Kt—Kt3   Kt—Kt5

12) ...R—QKt1 (with the idea of embarrassing the Kt by the attack on the KtP) could be countered by 13) B—B1, and White will still be able to fortify his centre by P—KB4.

13) B×B   R×B
14) P—B4   R—Kt1
15) P—KR3   Kt—R3
16) P—B5

White could have achieved more by 16) P—KKt4 which

would have avoided yielding e5 and g5 to Black. The text-move seemed to have the advantage of getting the KR into play via KB4 and of keeping the KKt file open for the Q.

16)	P—KB3
17) Kt—Q5	R—K1
18) P—B4	Kt—B2
19) Q—QB3	R—K4
20) Kt—Q2	P—B3
21) Kt—B4	Q—Kt3
22) P—QKt3	R(1)—K1
23) Q—Kt3	K—R1
24) Kt—R5	R—KKt1
25) R—B4	Q—Q1
26) Kt—B3	R—K2
27) R—R4	

27) R—Kt4 could have been adequately countered by ...Q—KB1.

27)	Q—K1
28) Q—B2	

Even though Black suffers from a cramped position there is no immediate winning combination available for White. Hence, the Black pieces must be disorganised by tactical manoeuvres before the attack can be resumed.

28)	R—B1
29) Q—Q2	Q—Kt1
30) K—R1	R(1)—K1
31) R—Kt4	R—Kt1
32) R—Q1	Q—Kt5
33) Q—KB2	Q—B6
34) Q—R4	Kt—R3
35) R—B4	Kt—B2
36) K—R2	R(1)—K1
37) Q—Kt3	R—KKt1
38) R—R4	P—Kt4

The threat was 39) Kt—B4, Kt—R3; 40) R×QP

39) P×P e.p.
R—Kt4 could have been countered by B—K1.

39)	R×KtP
40) Q—B2	P—B4
41) Kt—B4	R—B3
42) Kt—K2	Q—Kt7
43) R—Q2	Q—R8
44) Kt—Kt3	K—Kt1

The threat was 45) P×P, B×P; 46) Kt×B, R×Kt; 47) R×P ch

45) P×P	B×P
46) Kt—Q4!	

Decisive.

Position after White's 46th move

46)	P×Kt
47) Kt×B	K—B1
48) Q×P	Q×Q
49) Kt×Q	Kt—K4
50) R—R5	R(2)—KB2
51) P—B5	P×P
52) R×Kt	P×Kt
53) R×P	R—B7
54) R—Q8 ch	K—Kt2
55) R—QR5	R—B7
56) P—R3	

Necessary since ...R—B7

would have won the important QRP

56) .....   P—B4
57) R—QB8 R—Kt7
58) R—Kt5 R(2)—B7
59) R—Kt7 ch K—Kt3
60) R—B6 ch R—B3
61) R×BP R—R3
62) P—QR4 R—KB3

62) ...R×RP would be refuted by 63) R—B6 ch, followed by R—Kt5 ch and P×R.

63) R—B3 P—QR3
64) R—Kt3 ch K—R3
65) R(3)—Kt7 Resigns

(Notes by Dr. LASKER in the Book of the Tournament)

GAME 36

FRENCH DEFENCE

LASKER–ZNOSKO–BOROVSKY

St. Petersburg 1909 (8th round)

1) P—K4 P—K3
2) P—Q4 P—Q4
3) Kt—QB3 Kt—KB3
4) B—Kt5 B—Kt5
5) P×P Q×P
6) Kt—B3

There is nothing better for White than 6) B×Kt, P×B; 7) Kt—KB3

6) ..... Kt—K5
7) B—Q2 B×Kt
8) P×B Kt×B
9) Q×Kt Kt—Q2
10) B—Q3 P—QB4
11) P—B4 Q—Q3
12) P—B3 P—QKt3
13) 0—0 B—Kt2
14) Q—K3 0—0
15) QR—Q1

White should force the exchange of the Black QB by 15) B—K4, B×B; 16) Q×B, QR—QB1; 17) QR—QB1. White should hardly get more than a draw out of this position

15) ..... QR—Q1
16) KR—K1 Q—B2

17) B—B1 P—QR3?

This gives White some chances, since it not merely weakens the Black QKtP, but also stops the Black QB from attacking White's weak c4 via QR3. Black should have played 17) ...B×Kt; 18) Q×B, P—K4.

18) Kt—Q2 Kt—B3
19) Kt—Kt3 R—B1
20) R—Kt1 KR—Q1

The QKtP being weak anyhow Black sacrifices it so as to seek some compensation in open files.

21) P×P P×P
22) Q×P Q×Q
23) Kt×Q R×Kt

23) ...B×KtP would have been countered by 24) Kt×KP, P×Kt; 25) K×B.

24) R×B R—QR4
25) R—Q1 R—QB1
26) R—B7 R—Kt1
27) P—B5 Kt—Q4

27) ...R×RP was ruled out on account of 28) P—B6, followed by R—Kt7 and P—B7.

(See diagram on following page)

28) R—Q7

The threat being P—QB4

Position after Black's 27th move

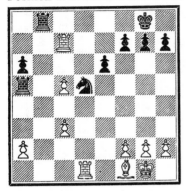

28)	.....	K—B1
29)	P—B6	R—B4
30)	P—QB4	Kt—B3
31)	P—B7	R—K1
32)	R(7)—Q6	P—QR4

33)	R—R6	K—K2
34)	R—Kt1	R × P(B2)
35)	R × P	Kt—K5
36)	R—B1	R—Q1
37)	P—B3	Kt—Q7
38)	B—K2	R—Q5
39)	K—B2	P—K4

A desperate attempt to rescue the Kt. 39) ...Kt × QBP would have been refuted by R—R4

40)	R × P ch	K—B3
41)	R—QKt5	Kt × P
42)	R—Kt4	Resigns

42) ...Kt—Q3 would be refuted by R × R(d4); any other Kt-move by R—Kt6 ch.

(Notes by Dr. LASKER in the Book of the Tournament)

GAME 37

RUY LOPEZ

LASKER–VIDMAR

11th round Petersburg 1909

1)	P—K4	P—K4
2)	Kt—KB3	Kt—QB3
3)	B—Kt5	P—Q3
4)	P—Q4	B—Q2
5)	Kt—B3	P × P
6)	Kt × P	P—KKt3

A new attempt to shorten the usual manoeuvre B—K2—B1, P—KKt3, B—Kt2 by the seemingly wasted couple of moves but this doesn't turn out too well since White now adopts an entirely different set-up enabling him to exploit the weakness of Black's KB3 and Kt3 rather more decisively than in the normal variation.

| 7) | B—K3 | B—Kt2 |
| 8) | Q—Q2 | Kt—B3 |

If 8) ...KKt—K2 the White P would march to KR4 and KR5 forthwith.

9)	P—B3	0—0
10)	0—0—0	P—QR3
11)	B—K2	P—QKt4
12)	P—KR4	Kt—K4
13)	B—R6	Kt—B5

Black would seem to obtain a lively and promising attack by pawn attacks of the Kt at QB4 and QB5 as well as at QKt4 and QB6. But that is not so since the Pawns will fall by the wayside.

(See diagram on following page)

| 14) | B × Kt | P × B |
| 15) | P—R5 | P—B3 |

If 15) ...Kt—KRP then 16) B × B, K × B 17) P—Kt4,

Kt—B3; 18) Q—R6 ch, K—
Kt1; 19) Kt—Q5; or even
stronger perhaps 19) P—KKt5,
Kt—KR4 20) Kt—Q5, etc.

Position after Black's 13th move

16)	B×B	K×B
17)	P×P	BP×P
18)	Kt(4)—K2	R—B2
19)	Q×QP	Q—Kt3
20)	Q—Q4	P—B4
21)	Kt—Q5	Q—Kt2
22)	Q—B3	QR—KB1
23)	Kt×Kt	R×Kt
24)	R—Q6	Resigns

(Notes by Dr. LASKER in the Book of the Tournament)

GAME 38

SCOTTISH

MIESES–LASKER

St. Petersburg 1909 (14th round)

1)	P—K4	P—K4
2)	Kt—KB3	Kt—QB3
3)	P—Q4	P×P
4)	Kt×P	B—B4
5)	B—K3	B—Kt3
6)	Kt—QB3	P—Q3
7)	Kt—Q5	

What with White having to
forfeit a tempo so as to get rid
of the Bishop. Black has
quickly managed to equalise.

7)	.....	Kt—B3
8)	Kt×B	RP×Kt
9)	Kt×Kt	

This exchange is quite unnecessary and merely strengthens Black's centre, giving him
the initiative.

9)	.....	P×Kt
10)	B—Q3	Q—K2
11)	0—0	Q—K4
12)	Q—B1	0—0

13)	R—K1	R—K1
14)	P—KB3	Kt—Q2
15)	P—B3	Kt—B1
16)	Q—Q2	Q—KR4
17)	B—KB4	P—B3

White must not be allowed to
open up diagonals for his
Bishops by P—K5.

18)	P—QR3	B—K3
19)	B—Kt3	Kt—Q2
20)	R—K3	Q—B2
21)	QR—K1	B—B5
22)	B—QB2	R—R4
23)	Q—B1	K—R1
24)	Q—Q1	R—K2
25)	Q—Q2	B—Kt6
26)	B×B	

This exchange is forced for if
he retreated B—Kt1 Black
would get an overwhelming
position by advancing his QBP
and later playing his Kt to Q6
via B4.

26)	.....	Q×B
27)	R—QB1	Q—B2
28)	R—Q1	

Better would be P—QB4.

28) .....   K—Kt1
29) Q—QB2   R—R1
30) R(3)—K1   P—QKt4
31) R—R1   Kt—B4
    Parrying the counter-thrust of
    the QRP just in time.
32) B—B2   Kt—Kt6
33) R(R1)—Q1   R(2)—K1
34) B—K3   Q—B5
35) Q—K2   R—K2
36) Q—QB2
    If he swapped Queens, the
    QKtP would prove untenable
    in the long run.
36) .....   QR—K1
37) B—B2   R—K3
    Black is about to move his K
    over to the Q-Wing and there
    is little that White can do
    about it.
38) Q—Kt1   P—R4
    To forestall an attack on the
    pawn by P—K5, once the
    Black K has moved.

Position after Black's 41st move

39) P—R3   K—B2
40) P—Kt4
    White must needs weaken his
    own position in the attempt to
    disturb Black's plan by an
    attack.
40) .....   P × P
41) RP × P   P—Q4
42) P × P   R × R ch
43) B × R
    R × R is ruled out by ... Kt—Q7
    etc.
43) .....   Q—K7
44) P × P   Q × BP
45) R—Q7 ch   K—Kt1
46) Q—Q1   R—K7
47) Q—Q5 ch   Q × Q
48) R × Q   R × B ch
49) K—B2   R—K3
50) R × P   Kt—Q7
51) P—R4   Kt—K5 ch
52) K—Kt2   R × P
53) P—R5   K—B2
54) P—Kt4   Kt—Q3
55) R—Kt8   R × P
56) P—R6   R—QR6
57) R—QR8   K—Kt3
58) R—R7   Kt—Kt4
59) R—Kt7   P—B3
60) R—Kt6   Kt—Q5
61) K—B2   K—Kt4
62) K—K1   K × P
63) K—Q2   P—KB4
64) K—B1   P—B5
65) K—Kt2   P—B6
    Resigns

(Notes by Dr. LASKER in The Book
of the Tournament)

GAME 39

RUY LOPEZ

LASKER–TEICHMANN

Last round St. Petersburg 1909

1)	P—K4	P—K4
2)	Kt—KB3	Kt—QB3
3)	B—Kt5	P—QR3
4)	B—R4	Kt—B3
5)	0—0	B—K2
6)	Q—K2	P—QKt4
7)	B—Kt3	P—Q3
8)	P—B3	0—0
9)	P—Q4	P×P
10)	P×P	B—Kt5
11)	R—Q1	P—Q4

White was threatening P—K5, followed by B—Q5.

12)	P—K5	Kt—K5
13)	Kt—B3	Kt×Kt
14)	P×Kt	P—B3

Premature. He should have played ...Kt—R4 first

Position after Black's 14th move

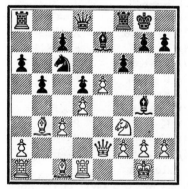

15)	P—KR3	B—R4

Obviously ...B—K3 was ruled out by 16) P×P, R×P; 17) B—Kt5, R—Kt3; 18) B—B2.

As for ...B—B4, 16) P—Kt4!, this was just as unpleasant for Black as ...B—B1; 16) P—QR4 with numerous threats, such as Q—QR2.

16)	P—Kt4	B—B2
17)	P—K6	

This had to be very carefully considered. It was risky to give Black his Q3-square and to face the possibility of the advanced P being cut off from his fellows by ...P—KB4.

17)	.....	B—Kt3
18)	Kt—R4	Kt—R4
19)	Kt×B	

This exchange was necessary since, after 19) B—B2, B×B; 20) Q×B, Kt—B5; 21) P—KB4, Kt—Q3; 22) P—B5, Kt—K5 White would have bottled up his lines of attack.

19)	.....	P×Kt
20)	B—B2	P—KB4
21)	K—R1	B—Q3
22)	P×P	Q—R5
23)	Q—B3	P×P
24)	R—KKt1	

Threatening B—Kt5, as well as 25) B×BP, Q—B3; 26) Q—Kt2

24)	.....	P—B5
25)	R—Kt4	Q—R3
26)	P—K7	B×P
27)	B×P	Q—K3

Seeing that 28) R × P ch would be immediately decisive Black resigned even before White had moved.

(Notes by Dr. LASKER in the Book of the Tournament)

CHAPTER NINETEEN

Narrow Escape in the Schlechter Match

From the East of Europe Lasker now moved to the West, pitching his tent in Paris for the better part of 1909. It so happened that a wealthy French 'patron' of chess, Pierre Nardus, was an ardent admirer of Janowski, having backed him in several matches against Marshall and others. He was now prepared to finance his protégé's burning ambition to match his wits against the world champion. It was arranged first to play a series of four games and then, if Janowski stood up well to his great adversary, to stage a proper match for the title.

In the first trial of strength Janowski did very well indeed. Having lost the first game he won the second and third, and once again Lasker found himself in the predicament of being forced to play for a win; and as usual when he *had* to win, he did win; it was indeed one of his finest combinative games. (See p.. 153).

Now the 'big' match was organised; it was to be limited to ten games, and by now Lasker clearly had the measure of his fiery opponent. He just let him 'come on', provoking his fierce offensive in almost every game, and every time knowing full well that his own subtle defence would be more than adequate to cope with the attack and finally to turn the tables on his dashing opponent. The result: 7 : 1, and two draws.

A couple of years later Janowski was to get another chance against Lasker, and this time he was defeated even more convincingly by 8 : 0 and three draws. But in between these two matches against an opponent who, however brilliant, was no real 'match' for him, Lasker was to face the stiffest test in all his long career as a match-player: his contest with Schlechter in 1910.

Carl Schlechter was then at the peak of his fame and his immense prowess. True, he wasn't as dashing as Janowski, he was indeed anything but dashing, as a person as well as on the chess-board. He had all the amiable charm and nonchalance of a Viennese, he was extremely frail and slight, and so gentle that even on the chess-board where he could muster the strength of a giant he seemed loath to hurt anybody; indeed, he must have drawn many a game which with a little more dash and enterprise he might have won. Yet, while his magnificent tournament record shows a great many half points—perhaps more than necessary—one seldom finds a

0 next to his name. He was, for many years, considered almost invincible, and what with his flawless end-game technique and his stupendous knowledge of opening theory he was the one grandmaster relatively easy to draw against, but almost impossible to beat.

Against this opponent Lasker was to stake his title in a match limited to ten games, five of which were to be played in Vienna and five in Berlin. Lasker soon had cause to regret that he had not insisted on what had heretofore been the usual procedure in title matches: victory to be decided by a given number of wins, draws not counting. It was mainly for financial reasons that so sensible a scheme could not be entertained on this occasion. To play for eight or ten wins (as against Tarrasch or Steinitz) might have involved dozens or even scores of games where a 'draw-wizard' such as Schlechter was concerned, and although the backers of the match included the Viennese Baron Rothschild and other wealthy 'patrons' there just wasn't enough money to finance a match of such incalculable duration. Hence the numerical limitation, even though there seemed to be little doubt that, with a Schlechter on one side of the board, a match of merely ten games would be decided by one or at most two wins. Such predictions proved to be not far off the mark, but no one could possibly foresee how that very limitation, however unsatisfactory, would yet provide one of the greatest sporting thrills in the history of chess.

As usual, Lasker started unconvincingly, and in the first game he had to work very hard to secure a draw. In the second game too, his position for a while looked precarious, and it was he who had to fight for the draw. Then he began to get the hang of Schlechter's defensive tactics and he started to mix things up a bit, getting a little edge on his game here and there. But Schlechter would carefully evade complications and shrewdly dodge every snare; he was not to be taken out of his depth. Thus the third and fourth game too led to a draw, and Lasker publicly admitted that he was beginning to feel seriously concerned about his chances of 'solving the Schlechter-problem' within the narrow compass of the six games left to play.

But things were to get even worse for Lasker. In the fifth game —the last to be played in Vienna—Lasker (playing Black) went all out for a win, and he did it in his own way by tempting Schlechter to attack the Black King who had wandered all across the board to the Queen's wing. Schlechter sacrificed one pawn, then another, but Lasker held the position safely, and round about the fiftieth move, with his own plus-pawns about to get going, he could relax in the comfortable feeling that for the first time in this gruelling match he had achieved a 'clear win' which merely required some careful routine to be materialised. Did I say, 'he could relax'? Well, he did, but he shouldn't have, just yet; as it happened he made one careless move, and for once Lasker found himself in the same plight he had so often conjured up for others: to see a 'theoretical win' suddenly transformed into an impending loss. Having carelessly allowed Schlechter's Queen to penetrate the position the world-champion, all of a sudden, found himself in a mating net, and there was no way out.

Being one game down with only five more to be played he was in mortal danger of losing the title. To most of the experts it seemed almost a certainty that Schlechter would manage to draw every one of those five games, and such expert opinion seemed fully justified by the progress of the match in Berlin.

It wasn't for lack of trying on Lasker's part; he did bring up his light artillery and the heavy guns, he emptied his whole bag of tricks, he kept worrying his opponent by deep strategic conceptions and by clever tactical finessing, by frightful complications and appallingly risky manoeuvres; but Schlechter was not to be flustered, he stood fast, and as often as not it was he who had the better of it and Lasker who in the end had to seek the draw.

Thus, the sixth game was drawn, and so was the seventh and the eighth. In the ninth, for once, Lasker had a legitimate winning chance, but he could not bring it off; this time it was Schlechter who wriggled out of danger, and most efficiently too. So this was also a draw, and everything now depended on the last game. Schlechter only had to draw that one too to gain the coveted crown, and all over the world the chess-fraternity was agog with excitement. Would Lasker pull it off again, just as he had at Cambridge Springs and Petersburg where he also *had* to win his last-round game? But then it was merely to decide a place in a tournament; this time the proud title of the world-championship depended on that one game, the title he had held for sixteen years! And this time the opponent was not a nervous firebrand like Janowski, not a lackadaisical giant like Teichmann, this time it was Schlechter, the draw-wizard, the most difficult man to beat, the man who, having once upset that great psychologist and champion, had stood fast against him, game after gruelling game.

No doubt, this was the grimmest test Lasker had ever had to face, and he faced it at a time when he was least prepared to show his usual composure. He was deeply worried in his private no less than in his professional life. In vain he had implored Martha to come to Vienna and, once again, to act as his 'guardian angel'; for in his deeply superstitious mind—most peculiar for so sober and clear-minded a rationalist—he was convinced that, so long as Martha was sitting within sight he could not lose a game (and indeed he never had).

Martha had not come to Vienna, and she could not even attend one of the Berlin sessions which took place merely a mile or two from her own house. For in that house, just at that time, her husband lay dying. Had he still been conscious, his kindly smile and chivalrous banter might well have persuaded her to come to their friend's rescue again; but he was in his last agony, and while his widow mourned the death of the man who had borne his burden so nobly, Emanuel Lasker sat in the crowded hall a couple of miles away, facing the greatest test of his career and feeling more wretched and lonely than ever.

That last and truly sensational game (see p. 157) certainly was uncommonly 'wild' in many ways and on both sides. It is all very well to say that Lasker, by dint of his dominating personality and shrewd psychology, forced his opponent to step out of character, as it were, and for once to throw caution to the winds and to wrestle with him on that narrow edge of the precipice where ultimately the stronger character, the harder will-power, the steadier nerves would prevail. To some extent, all this is quite true; but in fairness to Schlechter's noble character it should be added that in that one game he was not unwilling to be dragged into adventures uncongenial to his character and style. He too wanted to avoid a draw. He did not want to win the match on the strength of Lasker's unlucky slip in the fifth game. He was loath to win the World Championship 'by a fluke'. He wished to earn the title the hard way, and in trying his hardest to do so, this frail and amiable Viennese put up a truly heroic fight.

Even in the opening—by making a 4th move which was then practically a novelty, though twenty or thirty years later it would be of the common-or-garden variety—Schlechter deviated from the beaten track, and a few moves later the world-champion had a most promising game, almost a 'theoretical win'; but Lasker overreached himself, his positional advantage was frittered away in a premature, erratic and far too risky attack, and soon it was Schlechter who had the advantage. At the very least, at that stage, he could have made sure of a safe draw, and had this been a normal game and Schlechter in his usual frame of mind, no power on earth could have robbed him of that draw.

But it was anything but a normal game and Schlechter, the 'draw-wizard' was determined to win; while Lasker just kept on mixing things and adding fuel to the flames. Now these two were truly wrestling on the edge of the precipice, but it was Lasker who was most precariously dangling over the abyss. For a while, at any rate, he clearly had the worst of it and should have lost; but in the midst of that ferocious battle Schlechter missed his way, and presently Lasker wriggled out of trouble. From now on there was no stopping him, and having scotched his opponent's last chance to win he soon robbed him of any drawing chance too and went on, with clockwork precision, to materialise his advantage and to win the game. It had lasted three days, and 71 moves had been played when Schlechter laid down his King and rose to shake hands with the man who was still Champion of the World.

How could Lasker dare to tempt fate so recklessly and to take such appalling risks? Well, it wasn't quite so reckless; to 'dare' was indeed the very essence of Lasker's philosophy, and thoroughly in keeping with his favourite lines:

Besides this fear of danger
There is no danger here;
And he who fears danger
Does deserve his fear.

GAME 40
RUY LOPEZ
LASKER–JANOWSKI

Last game of 1st Paris match
20th and 21st May 1909

1) P—K4   P—K4
2) Kt—KB3   Kt—QB3
3) B—Kt5   P—QR3
4) B×Kt
   At all times one of Lasker's favourite variations.
4) .....   QP×B
5) Kt—B3
   To obtain the tangible advantage of a Pawn majority on the K-Wing 5) P—Q4 followed by an exchange of Queens is preferable.
5) .....   B—QB4
6) P—Q3   Q—K2
7) B—K3   B×B

Not so good because it opens the KB file for White.

8) P×B   B—Kt5
9) Q—K2   Kt—R3
10) 0—0—0   0—0—0
11) P—KR3   B—R4
12) P—Q4   P×P
   12) ...P—KB3 would have been preferable so as to keep White saddled with his double-pawn.
13) P×P   KR—K1
14) KR—K1   P—B3
   It has been suggested that 14) ...P—KB4 was preferable, the more so since Janowski merely needed a draw to win the match. However, this may well be a moot point.
15) P—KKt4   B—B2
   15) ...B—Kt3 would have been preferable so as not to

rob the Kt of a vital square to get back into action.

16) Q—B2   K—Kt1
17) K—Kt1   B—Kt1
18) Kt—KR4   Kt—B2
19) Kt—B5   Q—B1

The consequences of his weak 15th move. Even though he is not seriously threatened yet, Black has got into a very cramped position.

20) P—Kt3   Kt—Q3
21) R—Q3   Kt—Kt4
22) Kt—QR4   P—QKt3
23) P—B4

It is evident that the Kt cannot easily return to Q3. With his 21st move Janowski obviously burnt his boats, conceiving the courageous plan of sacrificing the Kt.

23) .....   Kt—R6 ch
24) K—B1

Of course not 24) K—Kt2 on account of ...Kt×P ch; 25) P×Kt, Q—Kt5 ch etc.

24) .....   P—Kt3

Creating yet another weakness in the Black camp. Preferable would be 24) ...P—QR4.

25) Kt—Kt3   Q—K2
26) Q—Q2   K—Kt2?
                (P—QR4!)
27) Q—B3   P—QR4

Too late. The Black Kt remains locked out and White increases his advantage by pressure on the KB file.

28) R—B3   R—KB1

29) R(1)—B1   P—R4
30) P×P   P×P

Position after Black's 30th move

31) Kt—KB5?

A very strong move, maintaining the positional advantage; and certainly much stronger than 31) Kt×RP which would give the opponent some counterchances.

31) .....   Q—Kt5

Now 31) ...Q×P would be simply countered by 32) K—Kt2.

32) P—Q5   B—R2
33) Kt—Q4   B×P
34) Kt×BP   Q×Q ch
35) Kt×Q   B×R
36) Kt×R ch   R×Kt
37) R×B   P—Kt4
38) P×P   K—Kt3
39) R×P ch   R—Q3
40) R—B8   Resigns

(Notes by GEORG MARCO in the *Wiener Schachzeitung* 1909)

GAME 41

FOUR KNIGHTS

JANOWSKI–LASKER

2nd game of the 2nd Paris match
21st Oct. 1909

1)	P—K4	P—K4
2)	Kt—KB3	Kt—QB3
3)	Kt—B3	Kt—B3
4)	B—Kt5	B—Kt5
5)	0—0	0—0
6)	P—Q3	P—Q3
7)	B—Kt5	B×Kt
8)	P×B	Kt—K2

This is the usual move introduced by Pillsbury, the alternative 8) ...Q—K2 is not very attractive. [*As a matter of fact it is that very line, the so-called Metger vatiation, which is almost exclusively used these days, eg. ...Q—K2 9) R—K1, Kt—Q1 10) P—Q4, Kt—K3 11) B—B1, P—QB4! etc. R.T.*]

9) B—QB4

The usual B×Kt is better, but Janowski had a predilection for preserving his 2 Bishops.

9)	.....	Kt—Kt3
10)	Kt—R4?	Kt—B5!

This very strong move was first made by Pillsbury.

11)	B×QKt	P×B
12)	Kt—B3	

Loss of time; 12) P—KKt3 followed by Kt—Kt2 was preferable.

12)	.....	B—Kt5
13)	P—KR3	B—R4
14)	R—Kt1	P—QKt3
15)	Q—Q2	

Unnecessary, but Janowski evidently hoped for attacking chances on the open Kt-file.

15)	.....	B×Kt
16)	P×B	Kt—R4
17)	K—R2	Q—B3
18)	R—Kt1	QR—K1
19)	P—Q4	K—R1
20)	R—QKt5	Q—R3
21)	R(5)—Kt5	P—KB3
22)	R(5)—Kt4	P—Kt3
23)	B—Q3	

So as to stop ...P—KB4.

23)	.....	R—K2
24)	P—B4	

A careless move: White might have tried something more passive such as Q—B1 or R—Kt2, but he was under great time pressure.

24)	.....–	Kt—Kt2!
25)	P—B3?(P—Q5!)	Kt—K3
26)	B—B1	P—KB4!
27)	R(4)—Kt2	R—B3!

Position after White's 28th move

28)	B—Q3	P—KKt4!
29)	R—KR1	

Only now White sees the terrible threat of the Q sacrifice, but there is no defence anyway.

29)	.....	P—Kt5

| 30) B—K2 | Kt—Kt4 |
| 31) BP×P | P—B6 |

| 32) R—Kt3 | P×B |
| | Resigns |

(Notes by SIMON ALAPIN in the *Wiener Schachzeitung* 1910)

GAME 42

RUY LOPEZ

SCHLECHTER–LASKER

Fifth game of the match, Vienna January 21st and 24th 1910

1) P—K4	P—K4
2) Kt—KB3	Kt—QB3
3) B—Kt5	Kt—B3
4) 0—0	P—Q3
5) P—Q4	B—Q2
6) Kt—B3	

For the suggestive power exercised by the world-champion over his contemporaries it seems rather significant that even his opponent chooses Lasker's favourite line rather than Tarrasch's 6) R—K1 which, after all, forces Black to play ...P×P.

6)	B—K2
7) B—Kt5	0—0
8) P×P	QKt×P
9) B×B	KKt×B
10) B×B	Kt×Kt ch
11) Q×Kt	Q×B
12) Kt—Q5	

White has maintained his positional opening advantage, but Black has got conveniently rid of his hemmed-in KB.

12)	Q—Q1
13) QR—Q1	R—K1
14) KR—K1	Kt—Kt3
15) Q—B3	Kt×Kt
16) R×Kt	R—K3
17) R—Q3	Q—K2

| 18) R—Kt3 | R—Kt3 |

Of course not 18) ...P—KB4, on account of 19) Q—Kt3!

19) R(1)—K3	R—K1
20) P—KR3	K—B1
21) R×R	RP×R
22) Q—Kt4	P—QB3
23) Q—R3	P—R3
24) Q—Kt3	R—Q1
25) P—QB4	

White has systematically weakened the P-formation of the Black Q-wing, and the backward Black QP is a permanent weakness.

25)	R—Q2
26) Q—Q1	Q—K4
27) Q—Kt4	K—K1
28) Q—K2	K—Q1
29) Q—Q2	K—B2
30) P—R3	R—K2
31) P—QKt4	P—QKt4

Black is energetically playing for a win, and all he now wants is to swap Queens.

32) P×P	RP×P
33) P—Kt3	P—Kt4
34) K—Kt2	R—K1
35) Q—Q1	P—B3
36) Q—Kt3	

Lipke here suggested 36) P—QR4

36)	Q—K3
37) Q—Q1	R—KR1
38) P—Kt4	Q—B5

By means of ...R—QR1 Black could easily avoid the complications involved in the sacrificial attack now launched by White

39) P—QR4

What with his useful knack for throwing his customary caution to the winds whenever he feels like being outplayed, Schlechter grasps the opportunity for playing *va banque*.

39)	Q×P
40) P×P	Q×P
41) R—QKt3	Q—R3
42) Q—Q4	R—K1
43) R—Kt1	R—K4
44) Q—Kt4	Q—Kt4

Obviously, ...R—Kt4 was ruled out by 45) Q—B4!

45) Q—K1	Q—Q6

Position after White's 46th move

46) R—Kt4!	P—QB4

47) R—R4	P—B5
48) Q—QR1	Q×KP ch
49) K—R2	R—Kt4
50) Q—R2!	

The threat was ...Q—K4 ch, swapping Queens.

50)	Q—K4 ch
51) K—Kt1	Q—K8 ch
52) K—R2	P—Q4
53) R—R8	Q—Kt5
54) K—Kt2	Q—B4?

A grievous mistake under time pressure. Lasker thinks he should have played 54) ...R—Kt1. Schlechter considered ...R—Kt2 to be best.

55) Q—R6!

Now ...R—Kt2 would be defeated by 56) Q—K6!. Lasker thinks that even now he could still achieve a draw by ...P—B6, giving up the Queen.

55)	R—Kt1
56) R—R7 ch	K—Q1
57) R×P	Q—Kt3
58) Q—R3	K—B1

58) ...Q—Kt5 would be defeated by 59) Q—R7! etc.

59) Q—B8 ch	Q—Q1
60) Q—B5 ch	Q—B2
61) Q×Q	Mate

(Notes by W. THERKATZ in the *Krefelder Zeitung* of Feb. 13th, 1910

GAME 43

QUEEN'S GAMBIT DECLINED

LASKER–SCHLECHTER

Final game of the match, played in Berlin on 8th, 9th, and 10th February 1910

1) P—Q4	P—Q4
2) P—QB4	P—QB3
3) Kt—KB3	Kt—B3
4) P—K3	P—KKt3
5) Kt—B3	B—Kt2
6) B—Q3	0—0
7) Q—B2	Kt—R3
8) P—QR3	P×P
9) B×BP	P—QKt4

10) B—Q3   P—Kt5
A brilliantly enterprising continuation, all the more surprising since Schlechter merely required a draw to win the match; and all the more significant for his truly sportsmanlike attitude. Evidently, he did not wish to owe the world-championship to the mere chance-victory of the 5th game.

11) Kt—QR4   P×P
12) P×P   B—Kt2
13) R—QKt1   Q—B2
14) Kt—K5
Fishing for trouble. By 14) 0—0, followed by B—Q2 and KR—QB1 White could have obtained considerable positional advantage.

14) .....   Kt—R4
Looks queer, but it is part of Black's ingenious conception. Obviously, 14) ...Kt—Q2 would be refuted by 15) R×B, Q×R; 16) B×Kt etc.

15) P—Kt4
Fishing for more trouble and compromising White's position considerably. By 15) P—KB4 he could have still maintained his positional advantage.

15) .....   B×Kt
16) P×Kt   B—Kt2
17) P×P   RP×P
18) Q—B4
With the double threat of R×B and B×KtP.

18) .....   B—B1
19) R—Kt1
Lasker considered 19) B×P, B—K3; 20) Q×Kt, P×B inadvisable

19) .....   Q—R4 ch
20) B—Q2   Q—Q4
21) R—QB1   B—Kt2
22) Q—B2   Q—KR4
23) B×P   Q×P
24) R—B1   P×B
25) Q—Kt3 ch   R—B2
26) Q×B   QR—KB1
The point of Schlechter's deep conception. Now if White took the Kt he would be annihilated by ...R×P etc.

27) Q—Kt3
Very feeble. Evidently the world-champion was flustered by the force of the challenger's last move. Much better was 27) P—B4, forcing Black first to salvage his Kt. Thereafter 28) Q—Kt3 would have been much stronger.

27) .....   K—R1
28) P—B4   P—Kt4
29) Q—Q3   P×P
30) P×P   Q—R5 ch
31) K—K2   Q—R7 ch
32) R—B2   Q—R4 ch
33) R—B3   Kt—B2
34) R×P   Kt—Kt4
Schlechter's courageous attack is as admirable as the champion's imperturbably cool defence. Centralising the Kt by 34) ...Kt—Q4 seemed more obvious, and at the very least it would have sufficed to secure the draw required to win the title. But Schlechter's actual move was even stronger.

35) R—B4!
Not, of course, 35) R—B5, on account of ...Kt×P ch

35) .....   R×P

An hallucination. By 35) ...R—Q1 Schlechter could have won without fail, but now the seemingly strong Black attack is refuted by Lasker with surprising ease

36) B×R   R×B
37) R—B8 ch   B—B1
38) K—B2!   Q—R7 ch

Position after White's 39th move

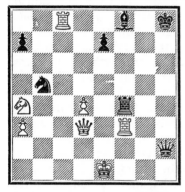

39) K—K1   Q—R8 ch?

The decisive mistake. By 39) ...Q—R4 ch; 40) K—Q2!, Q—R7 ch etc. Black could still have forced the draw, since both 40) K—Q1 or 40) R—Kt3 would obviously lose for White.

40) R—B1   Q—R5 ch
41) K—Q2   R×R

The only chance of continuing the attack, since obviously 41) ...R×P is ruled out by 42) R×B ch, K—Kt2; 43) R(1)—B7 ch etc.

42) Q×R   Q×P ch
43) Q—Q3   Q—B7 ch
44) K—Q1   Kt—Q3
45) R—B5   B—R3
46) R—Q5   K—Kt1
47) Kt—B5   Q—Kt8 ch
48) K—B2   Q—B7 ch
49) K—Kt3   B—Kt2
50) Kt—K6   Q—Kt7 ch
51) K—R4   K—B2
52) Kt×B   Q×Kt
53) Q—QKt3   K—K1
54) Q—Kt8 ch   K—B2
55) Q×P   Q—Kt5 ch
56) Q—Q4   Q—Q2 ch
57) K—Kt3   Q—Kt2 ch
58) K—R2   Q—B3
59) Q—Q3   K—K3
60) R—KKt5   K—Q2
61) R—K5   Q—Kt7 ch
62) R—K2   Q—Kt5
63) R—Q2   Q—QR5
64) Q—B5 ch   K—B2
65) Q—B2 ch   Q×Q ch
66) R×Q ch   K—Kt2
67) R—K2   Kt—B1
68) K—Kt3   K—B3
69) R—B2 ch   K—Kt2
70) K—Kt4   Kt—R2
71) K—B5   Resigns

(Notes by GEORG MARCO in the *Wiener Schachzeitung*

CHAPTER TWENTY

Happily Married

It had been quite a wrench, and no match had ever exhausted Lasker as much as that one. It wasn't only that he had hardly expected Schlechter to put up quite so stiff a fight, but more the nervous strain due to his private thoughts and worries. Before the start of the match he had been keenly looking forward to a repetition of the happy Munich days of 1908: to see Martha every day, to take her for long walks in the delightful surroundings of Vienna, to glance at her as his 'guardian angel' in the match-hall, to have the joy of her company and her conversation on anything but chess. (Martha hardly knew the moves and never really cared to learn the game).

But such happiness was not to be. Instead, there was much worry and grief; and just now, after the exhausting match, Martha was in deep mourning. He had called on her once, but he could not intrude any further. Besides, she left Berlin a few days later; accompanied by her young daughter she went to Italy and North Africa for many months. Lasker remained in Berlin, and he had never felt quite so lonely. Women—other than Martha—had never meant much in his life. By nature as well as by the demands of his profession he had been too much of a vagabond to contemplate a permanent union with any woman, and perhaps this was the deepest reason why he had lost his heart to the one he could not reasonably hope ever to win for himself.

But now death had taken a hand in his affairs. Soon now Martha would be free to marry. Lasker knew that he stood on the brink of a vital decision. There was, of course, the customary year of mourning. He would have one year to consider this important move; but deep down in his heart Emanuel knew that here was a move that required no further consideration on his part. He had not mentioned it to anybody, let alone the person most concerned; but he knew that after a year it would be Martha or none other.

Somehow, during that year of waiting, he felt embarrassed by the proximity of the woman he loved. True, she was in Italy, and he was in Berlin. But such places as Florence, Rome, Naples seemed altogether too near; he did not wish to yield to the ever present temptation of catching the next train and being with her a day or two later. Thus, the invitation from the South American Chess

Federation could not have reached him at a more opportune moment.

Chess was flourishing in South America. There were many keen young students of the game, some budding masters, and quite a few wealthy patrons. Some time ago they had invited Teichmann to tour their clubs, and now they wanted some exhibitions and even more lectures from the world-champion. They were particularly gratified that, in so many of his match games, Lasker had employed the Rio de Janeiro variation of the Ruy Lopez so named because Brazilian chess masters had devoted much time and ingenuity to its analysis.

For just over a year Lasker toured the chess clubs of the Argentine, Brazil and other South American states. It was to be a period full of pleasant memories for him, and it was also most useful for South American chess. Directly or indirectly, an entire generation of South American chess-masters owed much to the world-champion's visit, and in many subsequent international events they proved to be excellent pupils of an excellent teacher.

In March 1911 Lasker returned to Europe. He went straight to Berlin, straight to Martha Marco's house and, forthwith, asked her to marry him. Even though she was fond of him she hesitated for a little while, but hardly on account of the 'vagabond' life she would have to share; for despite her thoroughly 'bourgeois' background she rather enjoyed such mental and physical mobility. Was it that she feared having to share that man's love with his devotion to Caissa, Goddess of Chess? However, she soon accepted him, and in July they were married. The intervening few months were usefully employed by Lasker in providing his own wedding present by dint of his 8 : 0 victory in the return match against Janowski.

Thus, nearly ten years of secret yearning and devoted friendship had led to a 'happy ending' which, in fact, was a happy beginning for thirty years of endless happiness. If ever a mature man chose the right woman, that man was Emanuel Lasker. While the two of them proved it every day of their long and happy companionship, it was just as clearly evident to anyone who came to know them at all well; and if any proof were needed of the possibility of a harmonious match between 'difficult' and highly independent individuals, it was furnished by the model marriage of Emanuel and Martha Lasker.

No doubt, Emanuel was 'difficult'. He knew it well enough himself, but no one knew better than his wife how to cope with these very 'difficulties', and how to handle that queer and yet lovable person with charm and wisdom, with energy and great good humour. She knew better than to try to change that inveterate bachelor and bohemian into a 'respectable' family man overnight. She effected the metamorphosis in easy stages and almost imperceptibly to its object. Strictly speaking, it was no metamorphosis at all: she did not even try to change some of his bohemian habits, she merely gave him the useful background of a solid and well organised household.

Lasker could certainly do with a deal of domestic care; even though world-famous and fairly well off for a long time now, he was frequently seen about in shabby clothes, simply because it never occurred to him to do anything about his sartorial requirements. Martha saw to it that, in due time, he came to be a reasonably well dressed man. But it wasn't an easy task, and there were some setbacks. One day, for instance, being expected to attend some official reception, she had persuaded Emanuel to buy a pair of shoes. She took him to the best shop in town, and Lasker tried on a pair that looked very nice. But one shoe pinched his toes a bit. 'I wouldn't worry, sir', said the attendant, 'all new shoes pinch a bit.' That was the very cue Lasker wanted. 'You see', he said to his wife, 'he admits that all new shoes pinch. So I had better stick to the old ones.' And in a jiffy he had them on again and was out of the shop.

Lasker had all sorts of queer fads, but some of them, such as his horror of bad time-keepers, were eminently logical. He would argue that a clock that wasn't precise was worse than no clock at all. One day, annoyed at being late for an appointment owing to Martha's slow desk-clock, he threw the ancient thing into the dustbin. 'I will not suffer liars in my house', he said, 'it is a clock's business to tell the time.'

One of Emanuel's pet aversions were perfumes and strongly scented soap. One day Martha had managed, with considerable difficulties, to get seats for the opera. It was a gala performance of 'Lohengrin', and they had both been looking forward to it. Yet, quite early in the first act Lasker suddenly rose from his seat, squeezed through a row of irritated spectators, and rushed to the exit. Martha followed him in some perturbation; she thought he was feeling sick and asked him what on earth was the matter. But it was not until they had reached the street that he answered, growling furiously: 'It was absolutely impossible to stand the perfume of that woman on my other side. I'd rather go without Lohengrin than suffer such a stench!'

Significantly, it was only artificial scent to which he was so violently allergic; but he was rather fond of the smell of flowers. One day in Paris, walking along one of the boulevards, he noticed that Martha was wearing a small bunch of artificial violets. He took it away from her reproachfully: 'Why don't you wear real flowers

instead of this artificial trash? Such deception is not like you at all!'
And at the next street-corner he bought her a living red rose.

His deeply rooted aversion to anything 'unnatural' applied also
to such harmless things as aspirins and bicarbonate of soda and,
oddly enough, even to shaving creams. He scorned them as 'artificial
products' and he refused to use anything but warm water for shaving;
he claimed that this was the best way to avoid needless irritation
of his skin. He was revolted by artificial dentures, and when his
own teeth began to fall out he absolutely refused to do anything
about replacing them. But he was fond of joking about his toothless
mouth. To a druggist who was advertising a new mouthwash he
offered a certificate confirming his readiness to pay $1000 to
anyone who would find a single bad tooth in his mouth. He could
well offer it because there were hardly any teeth left.

Up to his twenty-fifth year he had worn glasses. Then he discarded
this 'artificial product' claiming that it merely caused headaches.
He preferred to train his own eyes to see anything he wished to see.

In art and literature too he hated anything 'unnatural'. He was
too much of a logician to be amused by a paradox, however 'brilliant'. When someone showed him a collection of particularly witty
aphorisms he scornfully declared that he could be just as 'witty'
by turning every one of them upside down, (and there he wasn't
far wrong).

He didn't like antiques either, and he refused to be impressed by
anything that was considered remarkable merely for the patina of
venerable age. 'Show me a new machine', he would say, 'a new
invention, a new idea, but leave the dead wood of the past to the
dead.'

He had a peculiar sense of order which was based on logic rather
than tidiness; this was quite in keeping with his own *Kampf* philosophy and its thesis about the 'economy of means' and the need to
concentrate one's time and energy on the things that matter. His
own desk may have seemed horribly untidy to anybody else, but
he could not be bothered to waste time in 'tidying' it. He was
satisfied that usually and at a moment's notice he could find anything he really wanted there. He never minded being forgetful
and negligent about trivialities, so long as he kept his mind concentrated on vital matters.

He could certainly be as absent-minded as any professor. During
the very hot summer of 1911 the 'buffalo-belt' was all the rage,
and every well-dressed gentleman would wear it in lieu of a waistcoat. Martha had bought a particularly nice one for Emanuel,
of pure black silk. The Laskers were about to make an important

call, and Emanuel was to look his best; but they were well on their way when Martha noticed to her dismay that he wasn't wearing the precious new belt; he wasn't wearing a waistcoat either. Martha reproached him, but her husband stubbornly insisted that he had put on that newfangled thing. He had done it merely to please her, he clearly remembered it, and he could always trust his memory. When they got home it appeared that Lasker was quite right. He *had* put the belt on, but he was wearing it under his shirt.

Lasker got immense pleasure out of 'proving his point' in such a way. There was indeed something roguishly boyish in his sense of humour. He liked to go to the circus merely to watch the clowns and to ponder about the common sense emphasized in their antics. He was fond of children too, and they liked him because he treated them quite naturally and never 'talked down' to them.

One day, seeing a boy beating up a smaller one in the next-door garden, he ran to pull them apart and he addressed the big one angrily: 'What are you trying to prove by beating up this small chap? If you want to show your strength and courage and can't think of anything better than that, you are a miserable ruffian.' Then he turned to the smaller boy: 'Why are you crying? Because you feel ashamed? It's the other boy who should be ashamed of himself. But even a small boy must learn to defend himself, even if he gets a beating. So don't cry!'

A significant little story because it contains two of the main planks of Lasker's philosophy: 'Balance of Position' and 'Struggle': the moral demand for maintaining one's position in life, and the equally strong moral demand to earn it by fighting for it.

CHAPTER TWENTY-ONE

Lasker's Bid for Poultry-farming

Towards the end of his first year of married life, Lasker once again went to America, and this time he took his wife along. They went in state on one of the big liners, and Lasker much enjoyed his long conversations with his neighbour at table, Thomas A. Edison. Poor Martha, being seasick most of the time, could take little part in this intellectual fare, still less in the culinary one, enhanced by the choice delicacies which Mr Ritz, another fellow-passenger, insisted on sending to her stateroom. He had a pedigree cow from one of his own dairy farms on board, so as to be sure of a daily supply of fresh milk.

Lasker had promised his mother-in-law to invent a new game for her, and he employed the leisure of the pleasant sea voyage in keeping his promise. The old lady was very fond of bowling, and Lasker designed a similarly unassuming but somewhat more tricky and stimulating game. In honour of his mother-in-law he called it 'Lina Solitaire', and for many years, particularly in Berlin, it was much in vogue as a popular pastime. Lasker himself liked to play it whenever he felt tired and in need of light relaxation.

In New York the Laskers put up at the Astor Hotel, and once again Emanuel embarked on a lengthy tour of lectures and exhibitions all over the East coast and the Middle West. Martha used to join him on the more extended tours, but sometimes she stayed behind in New York. It so happened that she did so one day in November when Lasker had to fulfil an engagement in Philadelphia. He had to spend the night there, but next morning —it being Martha's birthday—the liftboy knocked at her door with a big bunch of flowers and the message: 'Dr Lasker sends you these'. Martha was delighted that her husband, despite his preoccupation, had not forgotten the day, and she gave the boy a generous tip. But he would not budge from the door.

'What is it?' asked Frau Lasker, 'what do you want?'

'The flowers aren't paid for, madam. $2.25 please!'

Martha could not help laughing. It was so typical of Emanuel. Having paid for her own birthday present Martha promptly presented the bill on her husband's return. He paid up at once, and by way of compound interest he added a handsome gold brooch.

Wherever he was, he never forgot his wife's birthday. It was one of his superstitiously 'sacred' days. Many years later it so happened that, once again on the eve of her birthday, he had to give a simultaneous performance. This time it was at Amsterdam, and Martha was present. Lasker was a fairly slow simultaneous player and by midnight the performance, started at eight, was only just reaching its climax, with Lasker's intense concentration demanded on most of the forty boards mobilised against him. Even so, he had a sharp eye on the clock, and on the stroke of midnight he left the board he was just engaged on and walked across the hall to where his wife was seated; to the great delight of the cheering crowd he gave her a birthday kiss and, forthwith, hurried back to make his move and to pass on to the next board.

Normally, though, it was not advisable to disturb his concentration at the chess-board. Even the clatter of a teaspoon or the rustling of a newspaper could drive him to distraction and send him into a fit of anger. It was certainly no bliss to be his companion in the course of a tournament. Yet, he insisted on Martha acting as his 'guardian angel' during every important game, and even on less important occasions he was irritated and restive whenever he lacked her company. No one knew as well as she did how to gauge his every mood, to talk at the right time, to be silent at the right time, and to act at the right time. She knew that a tournament would absorb all his nervous energy, and she never minded his being 'hopelessly lost to the idiocy of chess', as he would put it after the end of the tournament. By then he was his old friendly self again, a charming companion and always eager to take her on his beloved long country walks.

It seems indeed remarkable that, with all his *penchant* for smoky cafés, Lasker was very much an out-door type, profoundly fond of nature. It was perhaps one of the expressions of his constant yearning to get away from the atmosphere of chess which never lost its fascination for him. Thus he was for ever torn between these two extremes, and after his return from that 1912 tour of the USA he gave some tangible form to his perennial longing to 'get away from it all'. Some twenty miles from Berlin, on a little hill surrounded by woods, the Laskers purchased a strip of land. They had a large if somewhat wildly romantic garden there and a small cottage. No telephone, no city-lights, no chess—no chess-café at any rate.

Lasker was quite taken with his new role as a farmer. He was going to plant his own cabbages, to dig his own potatoes. But the way he set about it certainly wasn't the sensible one of hiring a reliable gardener or farmer who could have taught him the rudiments of that new and mysterious game. No, he got himself a library of agricultural literature and volumes of the relevant trade papers, and forthwith plunged into the study of whatever the intelligent man should know about the history of gardening and the theory and practice of sowing and harvesting. He purchased some cattle and poultry and having thus made sure of a steady supply of manure he proceded to cultivate his garden, to tend his apple-trees, and to plant peaches, strawberries, and even asparagus.

It might have been an excellent scheme, and with a bit of luck even a profitable one. But alas, the man who was one of the profoundest mathematicians of his time was sadly deficient in the arithmetics of market-gardening. He was cheated all along the line, people pinched his pears and peaches, dealers swopped his cows and hens for inferior breeds; and Lasker sought some consolation in what he considered the only rational explanation of his misfortunes. 'Surely they must be very poor devils', he said, 'if they cannot make ends meet without robbing me.'

Martha took a less charitable view of the situation, and when the home-grown potatoes reaching her Berlin flat straight from her own farm seemed to average the size of a walnut she considered it poor solace to hear Emanuel quote the famous German proverb; 'It is the dumbest peasant who grows the biggest potatoes.' She said that it was precisely such a 'dumb peasant' that Emanuel could do with, as an advisor. Anyway, she harboured a healthy scepticism about the longevity of her husband's agricultural dream.

But before the 'experiment' was definitely shelved Emanuel had one last fling as a poultry-breeder. He had studied a good many books about the breeding of pigeons and already in his fertile imagination he saw the glorious Lasker-pigeons carry off all the gold and silver medals at next year's Berlin Poultry Show. It just meant seeing about as many moves ahead as he would in any minor chess-combination. To begin with, he made the first move of purchasing a very pretty couple of pigeons; his second was to closet the birds in a comfortably roomy cage; the third was obviously to feed them properly and to keep the cage neat and clean. So far, so good; but here the combination seemed to develop a flaw. For many weary and anxious months nothing happened at all, except the daily feeding and cleaning. But then, that was merely a repetition of move No. 3. The great Berlin Poultry Show which was to see the triumph of the Lasker-pigeons had come and gone. At long last, Emanuel decided to seek the best available expert advice and while the expert examined the two birds merrily pecking away in their spotless cage, Dr Lasker wrinkled his high brow and shook his fine head.

'I am amazed', he said, 'that these two birds haven't started breeding yet.'

'I would be even more amazed if they had', said the expert; 'they happen to be cock-pigeons, both of them, and their chances of progeny would seem to be extremely slight.'

Whereupon Emanuel Lasker 'resigned' this particular gambit by releasing the two birds and giving up all hopes of the world championship in poultry-breeding.

CHAPTER TWENTY-TWO

The Most Thrilling Tournament

Lasker was enjoying his 'holiday' from chess; it was one of the longest of many such interruptions of his career, and for once he could well afford to stay away from tournaments and matches for nearly five years.

He spent much time on one of his philosophical works *Das Begreifen der Welt*, yet such was the irony of his fate that even in the realm of abstract thought he could never quite get away from the game that obsessed him. He could and did stay away from tournament chess, but he must have felt an irresistible urge to justify the time he had spent at chess-boards all his life, and significantly he did it by elevating chess (or, more precisely, the concept of mental and intellectual struggle) into the realm of philosophy, and this is the gist of most of his philosophical essays.

Even so, he much enjoyed such work and the recognition given to it; he felt duly honoured by being elected a member of the Berlin Kant Society, lectured there and elsewhere on philosophical problems, and did a good deal of work in the sphere of pure mathematics.

Those last few years before the war were pleasant enough, and in spite of sinister portents such as the Balkan wars, few thought of the conflagration to come; least of all the European chess-fraternity which was enjoying an extremely busy time. Some of the stars of the young generation were coming to the fore, particularly Rubinstein who gained first honours in all the four great tournaments of 1912 and was rightly considered the most worthy contender to challenge Lasker for the title.

But there was yet another, an even younger man whose sudden rise to grandmastership had been most spectacular: Raoul José Capablanca, a Cuban barely out of his 'teens who, after a smashing match-victory over Marshall, had been admitted to the great San Sebastian Tournament of 1911 and had carried away the first prize, ahead of almost all the great masters of the day—all, except Lasker.

In the spring of 1914, the wealthy St. Petersburg Chess Club organised a tournament in which Lasker, at long last, agreed to compete and thereby to meet both Rubinstein and Capablanca. Among the other competitors there were such world-famous masters as Tarrasch, Marshall, Bernstein, Janowski, Nimzowitsch and a very young Russian student of whom great things were expected, Alexander Alekhine. But neither Schlechter nor Spielmann was there, neither Maroczy nor Duras nor any other citizens of the Austro-Hungarian Empire whose relations with Russia were very strained; for this was only a few months before Serajevo.

But the chess-fraternity wasn't much concerned with the animosities of world politics, it had its own to gossip about, and one of the less pleasant aspects of the great St Petersburg tournament was the fact that Lasker and Capablanca, the two chief contenders, were not on speaking terms. They had accused one another of unfairness in some rather protracted and acrimonious negotiations for a title match that had come to nought. But now, at any rate, they were to meet in the great tournament, and with them the other and perhaps the worthiest claimant for the title, Akiba Rubinstein.

Since in the absence of all the Austro-Hungarian masters there were only eleven competitors the tournament was so arranged that the first five were to go on playing a double round tournament among each other. The idea, of course, was to make the event a more convincing trial of strength than a relatively short one-round tournament in which a point or two dropped by some unexpected defeat or poor starting form may well prove an insuperable handicap. However, the arrangement proved to be most ill-advised, in as much as Rubinstein, for once not his usual reliable self, started so badly that he failed to qualify for the final test. It was the first failure in his career, and the tournament was thereby robbed of the keenly and confidently expected thrill of seeing the three undeniably greatest players of the time fighting it out in the final.

For a while it almost looked as if there was to be the even greater shock of seeing the world-champion also drop out of the final. Lasker, of course, was usually a slow starter, and in most of his great tournament triumphs he had required a few days to reach his best form. But never had his start been as shaky as in that vital tournament at St. Petersburg.

True enough, he scored a victory in the first round, but that was against Blackburne, the septuagenarian British master who had merely been invited on the strength of his past glory. That game was a 'push-over', but even in the second round the world champion was hard put to get away with a draw against Nimzowitsch, and in the third round he had quite a struggle to secure a draw against Frank Marshall, so easily and decisively beaten in their match. It was only in the fourth round that Lasker reached his best form by beating the great Rubinstein in a beautiful game and with consummate mastership, thereby taking his revenge for the defeat he had suffered from the same crafty opponent five years earlier in that same Petersburg Club room.

Poor Rubinstein, having had none too propitious a start either (with a couple of draws in his first few rounds), was so shaken by his fourth round defeat that he lost again in the next round and failed to qualify among the first five. But Lasker too had yet to face some stiff trials. In the next round he met Capablanca—their first meeting, eagerly watched by the entire chess-world—and after hovering on the brink of defeat for most of the game he just managed to scrape a draw. The next opponent was young Alekhine who, unbeaten yet, was leading the field along with Capablanca. For once Lasker had much the better of it, but unlike his usual self, he over-pressed the attack, overlooking an elegant little ma- noeuvre which gave the crafty young Russian a chance to get away with a 'perpetual check' and a draw.

So the world champion was still behind Capablanca and Alekhine, and coming up against Dr Bernstein in the next round Lasker was determined to score a much needed point: playing with great care, he built up a position which, after 35 moves, seemed to have all the makings of a win.

Oddly enough Lasker, a rationalist if ever there was one, was strangely superstitious where his wife was concerned; he firmly believed that, so long as she was in the room, he could never lose a game, (and indeed, he never had). On this vital day, Martha had promised to stay within sight, even though not next to the board: for being no chess player herself she would have been bored to dis- traction had she not been permitted to walk around the hall and talk (or rather whisper) to friends.

'He's got him licked', they told her; 'Bernstein is bound to resign in a few moves' said another expert. With that reassurance, and since it was very stuffy in the room Martha thought she might as well go out for a few minutes to get a breath of fresh air. She went for a stroll, and when she came back after about half an hour she turned to one of the expert friends.

'Well, hasn't he resigned yet?' she asked with a radiant smile.

'Indeed he has, isn't it terrible?'

'Terrible? Why, what's so terrible about it?'

'But don't you know yet?' said the friend. 'Lasker has lost.'

Martha Lasker stood dumbfounded. It wasn't the defeat so much that irked her as her own guilty feeling of having let Emanuel down in his hour of need. There and then she vowed that it must never happen again, but then that didn't restore to the score-board the vital point thrown away. Poor Martha had a black day, even though, in point of fact, Emanuel hadn't noticed her absence. What had happened was simply that, in a clearly won position, he had made one of his very rare blunders, an inexplicably careless move which threw away the attack and cost him a pawn and finally the game.

At that stage of the tournament it was a very serious loss indeed, for it threw him back to sixth place, and unless he pulled himself together in the remaining three rounds he might easily share Rubinstein's fate and fail to qualify for a place in the final. He did, of course, make the mighty effort required of him, and looking back at the event now we might well call his unexpected loss against Bernstein a blessing in disguise; for had he won that game his truly superhuman effort would not have been necessary, and we would have missed what will probably for ever remain the most dramatic and thrilling 'spurt' in the history of chess.

Yet, on the day after the Bernstein catastrophe there was no inkling of a turn for the better. Lasker was up against Tarrasch and soon got himself into a most unfavourable position. One more defeat, and he would have been hopelessly out of the running. But this time Lasker was helped by his lucky star rather than his ingenuity. Tarrasch simply overlooked a none too complex winning continuation and had to be content with a draw. But that modest half point, so luckily garnered, still merely sufficed to keep the world-champion in the sixth place of the score-board. With only two more rounds to go Lasker had to win both games, so as to make absolutely sure of his inclusion among the first five. This he did without undue strain, for one of the remaining opponents was Gunsberg who was at the bottom of the table and hadn't won a single game; the other one was Janowski, and Lasker knew how to deal with him in no uncertain manner. So the score after eleven rounds was: Capablanca 8, Lasker und Tarrasch 6½ each, Alekhine and Marshall 6 each. The young wizard from Cuba hadn't lost a single game, he was playing with inexorably meticulous precision; and since he led the field by 1½ points it was generally considered almost impossible even for a Lasker in his greatest form—and he certainly seemed very far from that—to catch up so substantial an advantage in a mere eight rounds.

On the first day of the final, Capablanca had the 'bye', while Lasker scored a very fine and well deserved victory against Alekhine. Then he had to meet Capablanca who, playing White, soon began to pile on the pressure in what seemed to him (and undoubtedly was) a very promising position. It was only when Lasker made a somewhat queer Rook move that the coolly calculating Cuban was disconcerted. It was a very deep and subtle move, but in point of fact—as Tarrasch later proved by a thorough analysis in his book of the tournament—it wasn't an altogether correct move, and by taking certain risks Capablanca might have won a piece and the game. But the Cuban had a deeply rooted aversion to 'Greek gifts', preferring to keep to his own safe and steady path.

It was a sticky wicket for the world champion, but Lasker was never perturbed by such positions, indeed he sought them and gloried in them, so long as he had a chance of mixing things up and complicating matters, and this he did by nonchalantly giving two pieces for a rook. This happened round about the thirtieth move, and for fully seventy further moves Capablanca tried to translate his slight material advantage into some clearly won ending; for hour after gruelling hour he tried until, after a hundred moves had been made he had to admit that the uncanny man on the other side of the board had, once again eluded him and got away with a draw. It had been truly a battle of giants, and what was more: a battle of diametrically opposed personalities and concepts of the game.

After the next round the distance between the two contenders was once again 1½ points, for Lasker had had his 'bye' and Capablance had beaten Tarrasch. Next day, what with Lasker beating Tarrasch and Capablanca prevaling over Marshall, they were still as far apart as ever, and it was only in the next round that, by beating Marshall the world champion could catch up half a point against his young rival, for Capablanca had to be content with a draw against Alekhine.

Here is what Tarrasch had to say about it in the book of the tournament:

'Defending a Queens Pawn game against Marshall, Lasker once again played on unorthodox lines and went all out to win. He dared an awful lot, and it may well have proved fatal for him. But then, just this is his style. If I were to assess it objectively I certainly could not call it the correct way of playing chess, and to be successful it invariably requires some unvoluntary co-operation on the opponent's part. But this, oddly enough, is never lacking for Lasker. It seems amazing and yet, one cannot withold one's admiration. So as to persuade Lasker to compete in this tournament the Committee have paid him an unprecedented sum of money, more than four thousand roubles. *I do not consider this excessive.* (Tarrasch's italics). He would well deserve an even bigger bonus for the splendid games he has played in this tournament.'

This seems all the more remarkable when considering the lifelong animosity between the two men and the acerbity so frequently to be found in Tarrasch's previous observations about Lasker.

Thus the 'half time' of the Final had been reached with a score of: Capablanca 11, Lasker 10, Alekhine 8½, Marshall 7, Tarrasch 6½. Only four more rounds were to be played, and for the Cuban to be still a full point ahead seemed to be an even more decisive advantage than his 1½ points lead when there were still eight games to be played. Capablanca still hadn't lost a single game and was playing with the clockwork precision of a perfectly adjusted machine. To catch up with him seemed a hopeless task, even for Lasker at his best; unless, of course, one was prepared to accept at its face value the proud claim stated in one of his philosophical essays: 'I deny that there is any problem of any importance that would prove to be insoluble.'

The second half of the Final was opened by yet another typical Lasker victory, this time against Alekhine; and once again, Tarrasch could not but admire:

'Another remarkable specimen of Lasker's style when going all out for a win. Defending a Ruy Lopez against Alekhine he seemed reduced for a long time to just about maintaining the balance in positions so precarious that many another would have faltered. But in the end it was his opponent who was lured into the abyss by a chimera . . . . .'

Capablanca had his 'bye' in that round, and so both he and the world-champion had 11 points, the vital difference being that Capablanca had still another four games to play, and Lasker merely three; and since they were to meet again in the next round it was quite obvious that this final meeting was to be decisive.

So once again the champion found himself in the unenviable position of having to stake everything on one card. He had to play for a win *a tout prix*, as a mere draw would have left his rival in a lead which, so near the end, would have been decisive. To *have* to win, and against Capablanca of all people, was a formidable task! For here was neither a bundle of nerves, like Janowski at Cambridge Springs 1904, nor the lackadaisical Teichmann of St. Petersburg 1909, nor the modestly diffident Schlechter of the 1910 match; but Capablanca, a young man of perfect self-assurance and iron nerve, passionately ambitious and yet coolly relying on the precision of his masterful technique. The entire chess world watched with bated breath, and this was a sporting event with so dramatic a climax as to thrill millions who knew little or nothing about chess.

This was the most important game in the world champion's career, and it is significant that it is even more remarkable for Lasker's subtle psychology than for his prowess at chess. Considering that a draw was no good to him at all—for with the rest of the field far behind he could be sure of the second prize even if he lost the game—and that he happened to have the White pieces, everyone expected him to risk one of those do-or-die attacks right from the start. Almost anybody else would have done it in such circumstances, but not Lasker. To everybody's surprise he chose the 'Exchange Variation' of the Ruy Lopez, generally considered to be rather tame and dull because it involves the exchange of Queens as early as on the sixth move. It is the sort of variation that one might well expect to be chosen by a player who wished to avoid any risk and to keep the draw safely in hand; it was, in fact, the sort of variation that, in the circumstances of that game, might have pleased Capablanca, had he had the White pieces.

Even so, however dull and tame that variation may seem, it certainly contains at least one drop of poison, though its effect, if any, is far from instantaneous. What happens is that, by means of the early exchange of the Queens, White secures a pawn position which, (provided he can keep it unchanged) will give him an end-game advantage. But then the sixth move may be a little early to think of the end-game, for much might happen before it is reached; and moreover, the price White has to pay for that long-term chance is to leave Black his pair of Bishops and some rather favourable and immediate attacking chances. In fact, Black is given not merely the chance to attack, he is almost obliged to do so; he must strive either to win in the middle-game, thereby making White's end-game advantage illusory; or to use his middle-game attack to rectify the pawn skeleton and thereby restore the equilibrium for the end-game. This is the more usual outcome, and while the variation offers no untractable problems either to White or to Black, it is certainly one to be favoured by Black if he happens to be aggressively minded. It is, indeed, the very kind of variation which, in the circumstances of that vital game, Lasker should have been expected to choose, had *he* had to play Black.

We can now gauge the subtlety of Lasker, the psychologist. Accustomed to playing the man rather than the board he would certainly do so on this vital occasion. He would not ask himself: 'What is the objectively most favourable variation, preferably one in which I can surprise my opponent by some clever novelty?' That is how almost any other chess master would have approached the task, but not Lasker. He simply asked himself: 'What is my opponent's present state of mind, and how can I worry him most?'

To so shrewd a psychologist the answer was simple enough.

Capablanca didn't want to take any chances, he didn't want to win at all, he was desperately eager for a draw. Hence, what Lasker did was to saddle his opponent with a variation in which the very logic of the position required him to go in for an attack he was most reluctant to wage. Moreover, having worried him by his choice of opening, Lasker confused him even more by treating the early middle-game on rather unorthodox lines. For the first time the young Cuban, usually so cool and unperturbable, showed signs of nervousness and when he eventually tried his counter-attack on the Queen's-wing his game was already going to pieces. It was Capablanca's first defeat for many a year, and when he laid down his King and silently rose from his chair he was deadly pale. Since the two masters were not on speaking terms they did not shake hands, and Capablanca silently left the board; but now the pent-up excitement in the overcrowded hall relieved itself in a burst of cheering and applause that went on for minutes on end: a truly unheard of spectacle at a chess-tournament where usually even a whisper is frowned on.

Of course the tournament wasn't over yet. By beating his rival the world-champion had merely caught up with him. They now had 12 points each, and since there were two more rounds to be played the result was still in doubt and the most probable outcome seemed a tie for first and second place. But such was the emotional shock Capablanca had suffered that next day the unexpected happened. He lost to Tarrasch who thereby scored his only win the in 'Final', and since Lasker won his game against Marshall he was now leading by a full point, with only one more round to go. Capablanca was still so shaken that he very nearly lost to Marshall, but he finally managed to save and even to win the game. As for Lasker he took no chances this time and drew his game with Tarrasch, the half point being just sufficient to ensure his first prize in the tournament, the final score being: Lasker 13½, Capablanca 13, Alekhine 10, Tarrasch 8½, Marshall 8.

It goes without saying that the tournament, so munificently arranged by the wealthy Petersburg Club, was concluded by a none the less munificent banquet. Martha Lasker was among those who reported it in the Press, and here is a relevant quotation.

'During the dinner I asked Emanuel to let bygones be bygones and to make it up with Capablanca. Without a word he rose and, carrying his glass of champagne, he walked over to where Capablanca was seated, drank his health and offered his hand. I was very happy to see the two men smile at one another in a friendly chat, and this public act of reconciliation was loudly cheered by all those present at that large banquet.'

Almost exactly twenty years had passed since Lasker won the title. For him they had been rich in adventure and endeavour; and he had staunchly defended his proud title in a good many matches, as well as proving his supremacy in some of the greatest tournaments. True enough, at London 1899 and Paris 1900 he had outclassed everybody else whereas now he had just managed to win by the smallest possible margin; but even so, that Petersburg tournament was not only one of the most sensational of all times, it was also one of the world champion's most convincing personal tests. After all, he was now 46, almost old enough to be the father of some of those brilliant young masters knocking at the gate.

To have held on to the world championship for twenty years was a great enough achievement, to be still worthy of the title was an even greater tribute to his personality no less than to his prowess as a chess-player.

ST. PETERSBURG 1914

Preliminary	1	2	3	4	5	6	7	8	9	10	11	
1 Capablanca . . .	×	½	½	1	½	1	½	1	1	1	1	8
2 Lasker	½	×	½	½	½	0	1	½	1	1	1	6½
3 Tarrasch	½	½	×	½	½	1	½	1	1	0	1	6½
4 Alekhine	0	½	½	×	1	½	1	½	½	½	1	6
5 Marshall	½	½	½	0	×	1	½	½	1	1	½	6
6 Bernstein	0	1	0	½	0	×	½	½	½	1	1	5
7 Rubinstein . . .	½	0	½	0	½	½	×	½	½	1	1	5
8 Nimzovitch . . .	0	½	0	½	½	½	½	×	0	½	1	4
9 Blackburne . . .	0	0	0	½	0	½	½	1	×	0	1	3½
10 Janowski	0	0	1	½	0	0	0	½	1	×	½	3½
11 Gunsberg	0	0	0	0	½	0	0	0	0	½	×	1

The first five players qualified for a final, and their scores were carried forward

Final	1	2	3	4	5	Final	Prelim.	TOTAL
1 Lasker	×	½1	11	1½	11	7	6½	13½
2 Capablanca . . .	½0	×	½1	10	11	5	8	13
3 Alekhine	00	½0	×	11	1½	4	6	10
4 Tarrasch	0½	01	00	×	0½	2	6½	8½
5 Marshall	00	00	0½	1½	×	2	6	8

GAME 44

RUY LOPEZ

LASKER–RUBINSTEIN

St. Petersburg 4th round,
26th April 1914

1) P—K4	P—K4
2) Kt—KB3	Kt—QB3
3) B—Kt5	P—QR3
4) B—R4	Kt—B3
5) 0—0	Kt×P
6) P—Q4	P—QKt4
7) B—Kt3	P—Q4
8) P×P	B—K3

9) P—B3   B—QB4
10) QKt—Q2   0—0
11) B—B2   Kt × Kt

This exchange is not so good for Black since it helps to develop the opponent. He ought to have played 11) ...P—KB4.

12) Q × Kt   P—B3

There are other moves here but none better than this one. After the opening of the B-diagonal, Black is threatened by mating attacks.

13) P × P   R × P

It would probably have been better to retake with the Q.

14) Kt—Q4   Kt × Kt

That way he is saddled with a permanently backward P on the open QB file, thereby establishing a clear and finally decisive advantage for White. He might have avoided it by 14) ...Kt—K4.

15) P × Kt   B—Kt3?
                       (B—Q3!)
16) P—QR4   R—Kt1
17) P × P   P × P
18) Q—B3   Q—Q3
19) B—K3   B—KB4

He should have played ...R—QB1 so as to try a push of the QBP whenever possible.

20) KR—B1   B × B
21) R × B   R—K1
22) QR—QB1   KR—K3
23) P—R3   R—K5
24) Q—Q2   QR—K3
25) R—B6

That's a move I can't possible approve of. To allow his Rooks to be swapped for the op-

ponent's queen could only deprive him of his best attacking chance. Nor would the win of the QKtP have made up for it.

25) .....   Q—Q2?

Oddly enough, Rubinstein passes up this excellent opportunity.

26) R × R   Q × R
27) Q—Q3   Q—K1
28) Q—B3   K—B2

The K stands rather exposed here, thereby facilitating the exchange of Queens so scrupulously avoided by Black.

29) Q—Q3   K—Kt1
30) Q—B3   Q—K3
31) R—R1   Q—K1
32) K—B1   P—R3
33) Q—Q3   K—B2
34) R—B1   K—Kt1
35) Q—Kt3   Q—B2
36) R—Q1   P—B3

This rather weakens the Q-wing. He should have played 36) ...Q—Q2.

37) P—B3   Q—B3
38) Q—Q3   R—K2
39) B—B2   Q—Q3

So as to stop the Bishop from coming to KKt3 an K5, but it would have been better to use his B for that purpose.

40) Q—B2   K—B2
41) R—B1   R—K3
42) Q—B5 ch   R—B3
43) Q—K5

Thereby he achieves the exchange of Queens, for if Black tries to avoid it, White will play R—K1 and B—R4 with a dominating position.

Position after White's 59th move

| 43) | ..... | R—K3 |
| 44) | Q × Q | R × Q |

Now Lasker has got the ending he wanted and he will soon be able to materialise the advantage of his better pawn position.

45)	K—K2	K—K2
46)	K—Q3	R—Kt3
47)	P—KKt3	R—B3
48)	P—B4	K—Q2
49)	R—K1	R—B1
50)	R—QR1	P—R4

This merely facilitates the emergence of a passed Pawn for White. It's usually a good rule for pawns to remain passive on their minority wing.

51)	B—K3	P—Kt3
52)	R—KB1	K—Q3
53)	P—KKt4	P × P

| 54) | P × P | P—B4 |

At long last Black manages to secure a counter chance. But now it's too late. Perhaps it was better to play 54) ...K—K3 so as to delay the emergence of a passed Pawn, but in the long run the game would seem to be untenable.

55)	P × P ch	B × P
56)	B × B ch	K × B
57)	P—B5	P × P
58)	P × P	R—B3
59)	R—B4	P—Kt5

Somewhat better would have been 59) ...P—Q5; 60) K—K4, R—Q3; 61) R—B3. That way Black might have had some slight chances of a draw, but only—as exhaustive analysis has proved—in the case of some slight slip or other on White's part.

| 60) | P—Kt3 |

Now a Zugzwang position has been reached.

60)	.....	R—B2
61)	P—B6	K—Q3
62)	K—Q4	K—K3
63)	R—B2	K—Q3
64)	R—QR2	R—B2
65)	R—R6 ch	K—Q2
66)	R—Kt6	Resigns

(Notes by Dr. TARRASCH in the Book of the Tournament)

GAME 45

RUY LOPEZ

BERNSTEIN–LASKER

St. Petersburg, 8th round,
2nd May 1914

1)	P—K4	P—K4
2)	Kt—KB3	Kt—QB3
3)	B—Kt5	Kt—B3
4)	0—0	P—Q3
5)	P—Q4	B—Q2
6)	Kt—B3	B—K2

7) R—K1   P×P
8) Kt×P   0—0
9) B×Kt

This position is so advantageous for White as to give him the choice of several good continuations. He may well retreat the B to B1 so as to avoid it being swapped, leaving Black in his cramped position. Equally good is P—QKt3 and B—Kt2, but even Kt×Kt as well as the text move B×Kt are quite good enough.

9) .....   P×B
10) B—Kt5   P—KR3
11) B—R4   R—K1
12) P—K5

Looks daring but seems to be quite sound. Black mustn't take the P since this would mess up his Pawn formation.

12) .....   Kt—R2
13) B—Kt3   P—QR4

A queer move, and yet one that turns out to be very good indeed. I should have probably played 13) ...B—R5.

14) Q—Q3   B—KB1
15) P×P   P×P
16) R×R   Q×R
17) Kt—B3   B—Kt5!

Very well parried. If he pushed the QP he would have to allow White's Kt—K5.

18) R—Q1   P—Q4

Having now a Pawn in the centre, Black is getting slightly the better of it.

19) P—KR3

Here I should have preferred 19) R—K1 followed by Kt—K5.

19) .....   B×Kt
20) Q×B   Kt—Kt4
21) Q—Q3   P—R5
22) K—B1   Q—B1
23) Kt—K2   Q—Kt2

Now Lasker's idea in pushing the QRP becomes evident. He wants to open the R-file.

24) P—Kt3   Kt—K5
25) B—B4   B—B4
26) B—K3   B×B
27) Q×B   P×P
28) RP×P   R—R7

The Black pieces are somewhat better posted and White will now have to loosen his K-position so as to drive the Kt from its dominant post.

29) P—KB3   Kt—Kt4
30) Q—Q3   Kt—K3
31) Kt—Kt3   R—R1
32) R—K1   Q—Kt5
33) Kt—K2   Q—B4
34) P—B3   Q—Q3

Position after White's 35th move

35) Kt—Q4   Q—R7?

A hallucination. Black overlooked that three moves later there would be no mate on his

KKt8 since the White K can escape to Kt3. By playing 35) ...Q—Kt6 Black could have further strengthened his position and almost certainly won the game. As it is, he will now lose his attack as well as a pawn and thereby the game.

36) Kt × Kt   R—R7
37) R—K2   R—R8 ch
38) K—B2   P × Kt
39) Q—Kt6!   Q—B2
40) Q × KP ch   K—R1
41) P—QKt4   R—R1
42) Q—K3   Q—Q1
43) Q—Q4

So as to stop the check on KR4. Instantly White threatens R—K6, attacking two Pawns.

43) .....   K—R2
44) P—R4

White deprives the opponent's Queen of every chance to attack.

44) .....   Q—Q2
45) Q—Q3 ch   K—R1
46) Q—K3   R—QB1
47) Q—K7   Q—B4
48) Q—Q6!   Q—B1
49) Q—Q7

Now White completely dominates the situation. Black can hardly budge.

49) .....   P—B4
50) P—Kt5   P—Q5
51) P × P   R—Q1
52) Q—K7   Q × Q
53) R × Q   R × P
54) P—Kt6   R—QKt5
55) P—Kt7   K—R2
56) P—R5!   Resigns

What with Black being only able to move the R, White can simply bring his K over to the Q-wing and win without any trouble.

(Notes by Dr. TARRASCH in the Book of the Tournament)

GAME 46

QUEEN'S GAMBIT DECLINED

JANOWSKI–LASKER

St. Petersburg, 10th round, 5th May 1914

1) P—Q4   P—Q4
2) Kt—KB3   P—QB4
3) P—B4   P—K3
4) P—K3   Kt—QB3
5) B—Q3   Kt—B3
6) 0—0   B—Q3
7) P—QKt3   0—0
8) B—Kt2   P—QKt3
9) QKt—Q2   B—Kt2
10) Kt—K5

However unpleasant the look of this knight, Black mustn't take it for it would be even worse to have an enemy P on his K4 driving away Black's KKt and thereby robbing his K of its only protection.

10) .....   Q—K2

Threatening ...P × QP followed by ...B—R6.

11) P—QR3   QR—Q1
12) Q—B2   QP × P
13) Kt(2) × P

That Kt gets well into play, but it would have been even better to retake with the P since the two centre Pawns would have constituted a permanent latent threat for Black. Moreover White would not have lost control of Q5 where Black pieces can now settle down most effectively.

13) . . . . .   P × P
14) P × P   R—B1
15) Q—K2   B—Kt1
16) P—B4   Kt—Q4
17) QR—K1

Having played P—KB4 he should be consistent and push on, for even though Black would have an adequate defence by . . . P × KBP; 18) B × P, QR—K1, White at least would have had some open files for attack and his QP would have been a passed pawn.

17) . . . . .   P—B4

Very well played. By blocking the White KB he puts paid to his opponent's every attacking chance. It's not too big a price for that to make his KP backward and to yield his K4 to the opponent.

18) Q—Q2

This move clearly proves that he can't very well get on with the attack.

18) . . . . .   Kt × Kt
19) Kt × Kt

It would have been better to retake with the QP for that way he would have got rid of his isolated Pawn which is now merely a source of weakness. Moreover, his own pawn would have exercised more pressure on K5 and his QB's diagonal would have been lengthened.

That way he needn't have lost the game.

19) . . . . .   P—QR3

Presumably so as to follow up with . . . P—QKt4 and B—R2 but it will never come to that.

20) B—Kt1

After this the P on QR3 can't easily be covered and Lasker is quick to grasp such a tactical chance.

20) . . . . .   B—Q3
21) Kt—B4

Not 21) P—QKt4 so as not to give Black the chance to give up two pieces for a Rook and two Pawns.

21) . . . . .   P—QKt4
22) Kt—R5   B—R1
23) P—QKt4   Kt—Kt3!

All this is beautiful positional play. He wants to get the B to Q4 where the weak Pawn at K3 will be covered; and as an equivalent for the strongly posted enemy Kt on his QB5 he will have his own similarly posted.

24) Kt—Kt3   B—Q4
25) Kt—B5   Kt—B5
26) Q—B3

Now White threatens to obtain a tangible advantage by 27) Kt × P followed by P—Q5. Moreover, QR6 is attacked.

26) . . . . .   R—KB3!

Parrying the one threat and ignoring the other, since Kt × RP could be countered by sacrificing the B on KKt7 and regaining the piece by . . . Q—Kt2 ch.

27) B—B1   P—QR4

28) R—B2	P × P
29) P × P	R—R1
30) B—R2	Q—KB2
31) B × Kt	B × B
32) B—Kt2	R—Kt3
33) R—R1	

This is definitely disadvantageous for White. He shouldn't have deprived himself of the possibility of B—QB1.

33)	R × R
34) B × R	Q—B2!

What with White's KB4 not easily to be covered, Lasker shrewdly espies another tactical chance.

35) Q—K3	R—Kt5

Of course not 36) Kt × KP on account of ...Q—K2.

36) P—Kt3	P—Kt4!

Very daring but quite correct and, indeed, decisive. The

Position after Black's 36th move

GAME 47

QUEEN'S GAMBIT DECLINED

LASKER–TARRASCH

St. Petersburg, 15th round,
14th May 1914

KKtP mustn't be taken on account of the threatened B-sacrifice on Kt6. White's onl.y chance is the following counter-attack, but however dangerous that might look, Lasker can cope with it.

37) P—Q5	B × QP
38) Q—Q4	P × P
39) Q—R8 ch	K—B2
40) Q × P ch	K—K1
41) Q—R8 ch	B—B1
42) B—K5	Q—B2
43) R × P	R × R
44) B × R	

White has regained his P and now threatens B—Q6. But Black has an absolutely murderous card up his sleeve.

44)	Q—KKt2!

Forcing an immediate decision upon the opponent. He has either to swap Queens (with an obviously lost ending) or to submit to a mating attack.

45) Q—R5 ch	K—Q1
46) B—Kt5 ch	K—B2
47) B—B4 ch	B—Q3
48) B × B ch	K × B
49) Q—R4	Q—R8 ch
50) K—B2	Q—Kt7 ch
51) K—K1	Q—B8 ch
52) K—K2	B—B5 ch
	Resigns

(Notes by Dr. S. TARRASCH in the Book of the Tournament)

1) P—Q4	P—Q4
2) Kt—KB3	P—QB4
3) P—QB4	P—K3
4) P × QP	KP × P
5) P—KKt3	Kt—QB3

6) B—Kt2   Kt—B3
7) 0—0   B—K2
8) P×P   B×P
9) QKt—Q2   P—Q5

Usually in this variation, what with the White Kt on QB3, this move wins a tempo which makes all the difference and gives Black the superior position. Here, however, the move loses an important tempo which should have better been used for development.

10) Kt—Kt3   B—Kt3
11) Q—Q3!

Lasker now refutes the ill-considered P-push very shrewdly. Since his P would get lost by R—Q1, Black must go in for an unfavourable exchange.

11) .....   B—K3
12) R—Q1   B×Kt
13) Q×B

Here, as will soon be evident, the White Q is excellently placed.

13) .....   Q—K2

So as to dodge the attack of the KP. Black's position now looks reasonably good, but he is a tempo behind in development and that makes all the difference.

14) B—Q2   0—0
15) P—QR4!

A very subtle move, the force of which Black fails to recognise. The P is to push on to R6 so as to loosen the position of the Black pieces, particularly the QKt. Naturally Black must not take the KP since

16) R—K1, Q—R3; 17) B—KB1 would cost him the Q.

Position after White's 15th move

15) .....   Kt—K5

It would have been best to stop the further advance of the P by either ...B—B4 or ...P—QR3 but White would have had the better game in any case; Black's position, though, may still have been tenable, whereas now it breaks down very quickly.

16) B—K1   QR—Q1?(B1!)
17) P—R5   B—B4
18) P—R6   P×P

After ...P—Kt3 White would still maintain his advantage by 19) Q—QR4 followed by 20) P—QKt4.

19) QR—B1   R—B1
20) Kt—R4

Forcing material gain, since White threatens to win the Kt or the B.

20) .....   B—Kt3
21) Kt—B5   Q—K4
22) B×Kt   Q×B
23) Kt—Q6   Q×P
24) Kt×R   R×Kt

For the loss of the exchange Black, at any rate, has a strong passed pawn which might enable him to save the game so long as he can avoid the exchange of rooks.

25) Q—Q5   Q—K3
26) Q—B3

At this juncture the exchange of queens would not be quite favourable enough for White.

26) .....   P—R3
27) B—Q2   Kt—K4
28) R × R ch   Q × R
29) Q—K4   Kt—Q2
30) R—QB1   Q—B1
31) B × P!   Kt—B4

If ...P × B White would regain the piece by 32) Q—Kt4 ch.

32) Q—Kt4   P—B4
33) Q—Kt6   Q—B2
34) Q × Q ch   K × Q
35) B—Kt5   Kt—Q6
36) R—Kt1

Not, of course, R—B2 since

Black would win a piece by ...Kt—K8 followed by ...Kt—B6 ch.

36) .....   K—K3
37) P—Kt3   K—Q4
38) P—B3   P—R4
39) P—R4   Kt—B4
40) P—R5   P—Q6

Black is hopelessly lost since there is no way to stop White from getting a passed Pawn on the K-wing.

41) K—B1   P—R5
42) P × P   Kt × P
43) B—B6!   K—K3
44) B × P   K—B2
45) B—K5   Kt—B4
46) R—Q1   Resigns

Obviously the QP will get lost. A beautifully-played game, but then almost all of Lasker's games in this Tournament are worthy of a World Champion.

(Notes by Dr. TARRASCH in the Book of the Tournament)

GAME 48

QP GAME

MARSHAL—LASKER

St. Petersburg, 16th round, 15th May 1914

1) P—Q4   Kt—KB3
2) P—QB4   P—Q3
3) Kt—QB3   QKt—Q2
4) Kt—B3   P—K4
5) P—K3   B—K2
6) B—Q3   0—0
7) Q—B2   R—K1
8) 0—0   B—B1

What with his somewhat unorthodox opening, Black is rather cramped. [*As a matter of fact Lasker was simply a few decades ahead of his time, his defence being quite fashionable these days. R.T.*]

9) Kt—KKt5

Marshall starts a violent attack which would seem to be perfectly justified. Yet in the midst of it, just as if Lasker had exercised a spell on him, he falters, and all of a sudden it is the World Champion who has the winning advantage.

9) .....   P—KKt3
10) P—B4   P × QP

11) P×P   B—Kt2
12) P—KB5

Marshall could still complete his development by B—Q2 and QR—K1 without the slightest risk, but now he throws caution to the wind. What with his K5 being mainly defended by the QP, Black will try to eliminate the defending Pawn by ...P—QB4; and if he can do that and get his own Kt to K4 before White's attack has prospered, he will be on top.

12) .....   Kt—Kt5
13) Kt—B3   P—B4
14) P×KtP   KBP×P
15) P—KR3?

Very feebly played and almost inexplicable except for Lasker's queer knack of 'willing' his opponents to make weak moves. Against any other opponent Marshall almost certainly would have played 15) B—Kt5, gaining the advantage in every variation. It looks almost like witchcraft.

15) .....   P×P

Of course!

16) B—Kt5

Too late!

16) .....   Kt—K6!
17) Q—B2   Q—Kt3
18) Kt—Q5   Kt×Kt
19) P×Kt   Kt—B4

Now Black is well developed and a P up, but he still has to face some danger on his K-Wing.

20) QR—Q1   B—Q2
21) Q—R4   B—R5

Position after Black's 21st move

21) ...Kt×B followed by ...B—Kt4 would be refuted by R—Kt3.

22) B×P

White's best chance in the circumstances.

22) .....   P×B
23) B—Q8

Winning the Q, but at much too high cost.

23) .....   Q×B
24) Kt—Kt5   Q×Kt
25) Q×Q   B×R
26) Q×P   B—B7

White was threatening to win by R—KB7, but Black can well afford to return one of his pieces.

27) Q×B   P—Q6
28) Q—Q1   P—R4
29) Q—Kt4   R—KB1
30) R—Q1   QR—K1
31) Q—Kt6   R—K7
32) R—KB1

Nor can he save the game by sacrificing the exchange since 32) ...R—K8 ch followed by ...B—K4 ch would lead to mate.

32)	P—Q7	35) Q—Q8 ch	K—R2
33) R × R ch	K × R	36) Q—R4 ch	B—R3
34) Q × P ch	K—Kt1	Resigns	

(Notes by Dr. S. TARRASCH in the Book of the Tournament)

GAME 49

RUY LOPEZ

ALEKHINE–LASKER

St. Petersburg (17th round),
17th May 1914

1)	P—K4	P—K4
2)	Kt—KB3	Kt—QB3
3)	B—Kt5	P—QR3
4)	B × Kt	QP × B
5)	Kt—B3	P—B3
6)	P—Q4	P × P
7)	Q × P	Q × Q
8)	Kt × Q	B—Q3

Now we have the standard position of the exchange variation except that White has added the good developing move Kt—QB3 and Black the ugly move . . . P—KB3

9)	B—K3	Kt—K2
10)	0—0—0	0—0
11)	Kt—Kt3	

So as to play B—B5 which cannot be forestalled by . . . P—Kt3. What now follows is a most interesting sequence of thrusts and counter-thrusts with the World Champion always seeming (but merely seeming!) to have the worst of it.

11)	. . . . .	Kt—Kt3
12)	B—B5	B—B5 ch
13)	K—Kt1	R—K1
14)	KR—K1	P—QKt3
15)	B—K3	B—K4
16)	B—Q4	Kt—R5

It is now evident that it would have been better for White to castle K-side.

17)	R—Kt1	B—K3
18)	P—B4	B—Q3
19)	B—B2	Kt—Kt3

Now White is getting embarrassed about covering the KBP. Obviously 20) P—KKt3 would make the Black QB far too strong, whereas the disadvantage of pushing the KBP is the resulting backwardness of the KP.

20)	P—B5	B × Kt
21)	RP × B	Kt—B1
22)	B × P	B × P
23)	R—R1	P × B
24)	R × B	P—QKt4

Black has not only wriggled out of his precarious position but he has actually now got the better of it, his opponent's KP being very weak indeed.

| 25) | R—K1 | Kt—Q2 |
| 26) | Kt—Q1 | P—QR4 |

Black might have been expected to play simply for the gain of the KP, but he does nothing of the kind; he prefers going in for a somewhat belated attack on the K; a dangerous undertaking, since it permits the opponent to get rid of his backward P and to start a counter-attack on the K-wing.

27)	R—R3	P—Kt5
28)	Kt—B2	Kt—B4
29)	R(3)—K3	P—R5
30)	P×P	Kt×P
31)	P—K5	P×P
32)	R×P	R(K1)—Kt1

It certainly required some courage to give up the open file as simply as all that. But then Black has got the attack he wanted and just now he threatens a mating attack starting with Kt—B6 ch.

33)	Kt—K4	P—Kt6
34)	R—K2(forced)	Kt—Kt3

The tempting Kt-sacrifice on Kt7 followed by R—R7 ch would not be as good as it looks, since White could stifle the attack by a counter sacrifice of his own Kt.

35)	P×P	Kt—Q4
36)	P—KKt4	P—R3
37)	P—Kt5	P×P
38)	Kt×P	Kt—B3
39)	R—K7	

With the threat of Kt—K6 and R—Kt2. But since Black can parry all this quite comfortably, it would have been better for White to attack the BP by 39) R—B2.

39)	.....	R×P
40)	R—Kt2	Kt—Q4
41)	R—Q7	

Now the threat is Kt—K6 with a mating attack, but Black soon puts a stop to that.

41)	.....	R—Q6!!

An extremely shrewd move! He threatens to win either the one R or the other by Kt-checks on K6 or QB6 alter-

Position after Black's 41st move

natively; and if White tries to dodge both checks by K—B1 he gets into a mating net by means of ...R—R8 ch and Kt—Kt5. This is altogether brilliant play on the part of the World-Champion.

42)	R×Kt(forced)	R×R
43)	Kt—K6	K—B2(best)
44)	R×P ch	K—B3
45)	R—QB7	R—Q3
46)	Kt—B5	K×P

We now get to the second phase of this extremely difficult game: an ending never before experienced in chess-literature. What with being the exchange up and only one P left, Black's problem, of course, is how to force the exchange of Rooks. If he were faced with a B rather than a Kt the game could never be won.

47)	R—B7 ch	K—K4
48)	K—B2	R—KR3
49)	Kt—Q3 ch	K—Q3
50)	R—B5	R—QKt1
51)	K—B3	K—B2
52)	R—B7 ch	K—Kt3

53) R—Q7

This, of course, would seem to be the most agreeable position for the R but Black can easily rob him of so much space to move in. He will aim to pin the Kt at, say, KR6 and then get his other R on to the Q-file at, say, Q4. That would be one of the winning positions, but it is by no means as simple as all that.

53) .....   R—R6
54) R—Q4   R(1)—KR1
55) R—Kt4 ch   K—B2
56) K—B2   R(1)—R5
57) R—Kt3

Now the mobility of the R has been considerably restricted.

57) .....   R—R7 ch
58) K—B3   R(5)—R6
59) R—Kt4   R—R4
60) R—Kt4   R(7)—R6
61) K—B2   R—Q4
62) Kt—B4   R—B4 ch
63) K—Kt1   R—R8 ch
64) K—R2   R—R4 ch
65) K—Kt3   R—Kt4 ch
66) K—B3   K—Kt3
67) Kt—Q3   R—R6
68) K—B2   R—Q4
69) R—Kt4 ch   K—B2
70) R—Kt3   R—R7 ch
71) K—B3   K—Q3
72) R—R3   R—Kt7
73) R—R1   R—Kt6
74) R—Q1   K—B2
75) R—Q2   K—Kt3
76) R—Q1   K—Kt4

Now the position is becoming precarious. Should White again play R—Q2 he will be beaten by ...R—B4 ch; 78) K—Kt3, R—B5 etc.

77) K—B2   K—B5
78) P—Kt3 ch

Thereby Black has forced a significant weakening of the White position.

78) .....   K—Kt4
79) R—Q2   R—R6
80) R—Q1   R—R7 ch
81) K—B3   R—Q1
82) R—KKt1   R—R6
83) R—Q1   R(Q1)—KR1

Now Black threatens to force the exchange of rooks by ...R—R8 etc.

84) R—KKt1   R(1)—R4
85) K—B2   R—Q4
86) R—Q1   R—KKt4
87) R—Q2?

A mistake which leads to a quick loss. The R should have left the Q-file. Then Black would have had to double rooks on the 7th and to bring his K to Q4. Even so it would have still been far from easy to force the win.

87) .....   R(6)—Kt6!
88) Kt—B1   R—Kt7
89) Kt—K2   K—Kt3

Resigns

Now, no more disturbed by the threat of the Kt-check, Black can force the exchange of Rooks, whereafter a win is, of course, quite easy.

(Notes by Dr. S. TARRASCH in the Book of the Tournament)

GAME 50

RUY LOPEZ

LASKER–CAPABLANCA

St. Petersburg, 18th round,
18th May 1914

1)	P—K4	P—K4
2)	Kt—KB3	Kt—QB3
3)	B—Kt5	P—QR3
4)	B × Kt	QP × B
5)	P—Q4	P × P
6)	Q × P	Q × Q
7)	Kt × Q	B—Q3
8)	Kt—QB3	Kt—K2
9)	0—0	0—0
10)	P—B4	R—K1

More forceful would have been
10) ...B—B4. Lasker's ex-
cellent next move stops it.

11)	Kt—Kt3	P—B3

An unnecessarily defensive
move since 12) P—K5 could
be merely agreeable for Black
by giving him important
squares for his pieces. Capablanca's over-cautious play in
this game was, of course, due
to the fact that he merely
required a draw. [*According to
Capablanca's own notes the
next move was very well considered since by Kt—KKt3 and
by fianchettoing his QB he
hoped to exercise pressure on
the opponent's P-centre. R.T.*]

12)	P—B5	

What with making the KP
backward and the square K5
weak, this seems a surprising
move. Yet on second thoughts,
its advantages outweigh its
disadvantages. There is more
space for the White B, and as

for the Black QB and Kt they
are being gravely hampered in
their mobility. Moreover, by
dominating the K6, White is
amply compensated for the
weakness of his K5.

12)	.....	P—QKt3

I should have preferred ...B—
Q2 and ...QR—Q1. I think
it was a wrong conception for
the Black QB to give up
command of the vital square
K3.

13)	B—B4	B—Kt2

Black should have made the
exchange himself. Sure enough,
he is now getting rid of his
double Pawn but his Q3 will
be permanently weak. [*Lasker
thought that the line suggested
by Reti would have been rather
favourable for him. R.T.*]

14)	B × B	P × B
15)	Kt—Q4	QR—Q1
16)	Kt—K6	R—Q2
17)	QR—Q1	Kt—B1
18)	R—B2	P—QKt4
19)	R(2)—Q2	R(2)—K2
20)	P—QKt4!	K—B2
21)	P—QR3	B—R1
22)	K—B2	R—R2
23)	P—Kt4	

The centre locked, White can
safely exploit his advantage of
space for a break-through on
the K-Wing. Black's counter-
measures on the Q-Wing will
soon prove quite inadequate.

23)	.....	P—R3
24)	R—Q3	P—QR4
25)	P—KR4	P × P
26)	P × P	R(2)—K2
27)	K—B3	R—Kt1

Position after Black's 32nd move

28) K—B4   P—Kt3
29) R—Kt3   P—Kt4 ch
Now White will open the KR file with decisive advantage. Hence it would have been rather better for Black to open the Kt file by 29) ...KtP×BP. After the next move he hasn't a hope against Lasker's perfect end-game technique.
30) K—B3   Kt—Kt3
31) P×P   RP×P

32) R—R3!
Much stronger than taking the QP which would have given Black counterchances by ...R—R1 and ...Kt—B5.
32) .....   R—Q2
33) K—Kt3!
He is planning P—K5 hence, the K must not be exposed to a discovered check by the B.
33) .....   K—K1
34) R(1)—KR1   B—Kt2
35) P—K5!   QP×P
36) Kt—K4   Kt—Q4
37) Kt(6)—B5   B—B1
Black must give up the exchange in preference to losing a whole piece by 38) Kt×B, R×Kt; 39) Kt—Q6 ch etc.
38) Kt×R   B×Kt
39) R—R7   R—B1
40) R—R1   K—Q1
41) R—R8 ch   B—B1
42) Kt—B5   Resigns

(Notes by RICHARD RETI in *Masters of the Chess-board*)

CHAPTER TWENTY-THREE

Stepping Down from the Throne

When the war broke out Lasker, always cosmopolitan and a globe-trotter, found himself in his own country, and forced to stay put for some time.

The war put a sudden stop to the uninterrupted sequence of international events in recent years; and for almost all professional masters, it meant the drying up of their main source of livelihood, as well as their main occupation. Lasker never regretted long spells of absence from competitive chess and, though deeply worried by the war, settled down to the sort of life and work he enjoyed more than any other.

In November 1914 he joined the panel of the *Lessing Hochschule*—one of Berlin's more eminent Institutes for Further Education—and started a series of popular lectures on philosophy, and at the same time he started work on the most ambitious of his philosophical essays, *Die Philosophie des Unvollendbar*. But what he enjoyed more than anything at that time (and for seven years to come) was his unremitting labour on a verse-drama, a rather deep and subtle piece, a profound attempt at symbolising man's vain efforts through all recorded history to master nature's never-yielded secrets. He wrote this piece in collaboration with his brother Berthold, and we have yet to see the somewhat ludicrously dramatic circumstances in which, many years later, Emanuel was to spoil an important game at the Moscow tournament when overjoyed by the telegram that, at long last, the play was to have a Berlin production.

Public chess events were few and far between, one of the more noteworthy ones being a match between Tarrasch and Mieses which the Doctor won very convincingly by seven wins, four draws and only two losses. Since he seemed to be in excellent form his friends eagerly arranged a match with the world-champion. It wasn't to be a title match, though, merely a sequence of six games, and the proceeds were to go to some war charity.

Lasker readily agreed, and the games were played in Berlin in 1916. The first game was a draw, but then Tarrasch lost one after another, and with $\frac{1}{2} : 5\frac{1}{2}$ the result was even more shattering for him than that of the second title-match for Steinitz. But most inexplicable of all for Tarrasch was the fact that in almost every one of the games he lost, he had achieved a perfectly satisfactory and sometimes even the better position. That great exponent of chess theory could never grasp that a game of chess—particularly with Lasker on the other side of the board—was no abstract analysis in a vacuum but a mental struggle between human beings. While Tarrasch never got beyond the concept of Euclid's geometry, Lasker's 'relativism' anticipated Einstein's theories, at least so far as the chess-board was concerned.

Meanwhile, in blockaded Central Europe living conditions went from bad to worse, and while many people suffered from malnutrition none did more so than a host of unemployed chess masters. At last, in the spring of 1918 the Berlin Chess Fraternity managed to organise a small double-round tournament in which four prominent masters competed. Vidmar won it, ahead of Schlechter, Mieses and Rubinstein. No one among the chess players, in those harsh times, had suffered more physical privation than Schlechter; but that frail and amiable Viennese was too proud to ask for help, and at Christmas 1918 he literally starved to death.

A few months earlier he had competed in the last of his many tournaments, arranged in Berlin in October, just a few weeks before the end of the war. It was once again a double-round event for four grandmasters, and one of them was the world champion. The other competitors were Rubinstein, Schlechter and Tarrasch who only managed to score three draws. He too was very depressed, since his deeply loved and gifted son had been killed in action. Tarrasch, at that time, did not suffer material want—after all, he always had his doctor's practice to fall back on—but he was a very ardent German patriot, and he was deeply worried by his country's military defeat. As a chess player he was merely the shadow of his great past.

BERLIN 1918

		1	2	3	4	
1	Lasker	×	$\frac{1}{2}\frac{1}{2}$	$\frac{1}{2}$1	11	4$\frac{1}{2}$
2	Rubinstein	$\frac{1}{2}\frac{1}{2}$	×	1$\frac{1}{2}$	$\frac{1}{2}$1	4
3	Schlechter	$\frac{1}{2}$0	0$\frac{1}{2}$	×	$\frac{1}{2}\frac{1}{2}$	2
4	Tarrasch	00	$\frac{1}{2}$0	$\frac{1}{2}\frac{1}{2}$	×	1$\frac{1}{2}$

The Berlin tournament, not surprisingly, turned out to be a duel between Lasker and Rubinstein. They met in the first round and fought a stiff battle ending in a draw. Next day Lasker beat Tarrasch and Rubinstein scored against Schlechter, but on the third day each of the two leaders had to be content with a draw. Then they came up against one another, and again a draw was the result. It was in the fifth round that Lasker forged ahead by beating Tarrasch whilst

Rubinstein could only draw against Schlechter. In the final round, what with both leaders beating their opponents, Lasker maintained his narrow lead, with the result: Lasker 4½, Rubinstein 4, Schlechter 2, Tarrasch 1½. A booklet of the tournament contains all the games with Lasker's annotations, but the quality of the games undoubtedly reflects the nervous tension of the time. Anyway, it was the world champion's seventh victory in a first-rate masters' tournament, no mean achievement for a man approaching his fiftieth birthday.

His most welcome birthday present, no doubt, was the publication of his ambitious essay *Die Philosophie des Unvollendbar* which, as the very title implies, marks a sceptical advance beyond his own concept of 'machology'. He was still convinced that mankind can be trained to approach perfection; but merely to approach it, never to achieve it beyond that final margin of the unattainable. Nietzsche said: 'If there were gods, how could I bear not to be a God? Hence, there are no gods'. Lasker admitted God, but denied man's right to strive for unattainable God-like perfection. Yet, his philosophy was far from being pessimistic. Indeed, he postulated man's duty always to strive for the attainable, thereby to ensure the steady progress of pushing the 'unattainable' margin further and further away.

Lasker was happy about the four years' carnage, at long last, having come to an end, but he was far from happy about the social insecurity and moral laxity so significantly ripe in the immediate aftermath of the war. In the chess world the new generation was coming to the force, and ageing Tarrasch could never understand how Alekhine, Nimzowitsch, Reti, Bogoljubov and other young men could scorn so many of his principles and yet go from one victory to another. They liked to be called Neo-Romanticists, and it may well be that their provocatively bizarre style was formed by the still fresh memories of the caveman tactics in trench warfare no less than by the insatiably romantic lust for adventure as reflected in the gambling dens, the dance clubs and the jazz-parties of the post-war period. Moreover, there were more chess professionals than ever, young men uprooted by the war years, unable to settle down to some proper job in the economic upheaval of Central Europe's postwar inflation, and more or less hopelessly trying to make a living out of chess, even though tournaments and matches were nowhere near as generously financed as they used to be when a hundred mark note was still the equivalent of five golden sovereigns. The cake was much smaller than it used to be, but there were more than ever trying to snatch a crumb of it.

Of the great pre-war stars of chess, only Lasker and Capablanca still seemed in full fettle; and the Cuban, of course, though a grand-master of ten years' standing, was only thirty at the war's end and a contemporary of the rising rather than the old generation. He was at the height of his physical and mental powers, he was very ambitious and moreover, unlike most chess masters, he was of independent means since the Cuban Government, rightly proud of the world-fame he had earned for his country, had given him a post in the diplomatic service.

Small wonder that soon after the war an almost world-wide clamour began for a title match between the world champion and Capablanca. There was also Rubinstein, of course, and there were many who said that, on the strength of his pre-war triumphs, his was the prior claim for challenging the champion. But Rubinstein too, although barely forty at that time, was merely a shadow of his glorious past. He had been, even in his hey-day, an extremely sensitive person, diffident to the point of timidity, and the war years had fully unsettled him emotionally. He suffered from grave mental depressions and disorders, and while he did, from time to time, show sparks of his erstwhile genius, even in the nineteen-twenties his great career was practically at an end, long before he reached his fiftieth year in the early thirties. But even ten years earlier he was in no condition to be seriously considered as a claimant for Lasker's title.

So there was only Capablanca as the obvious contender, and negotiations for the match were duly started and unduly protracted. There was no love lost between the two men, even though their erst-while differences had been patched up at the banquet concluding the St. Petersburg tournament just before the war. Finally, after long and fruitless efforts to come to mutually satisfatory terms, Lasker threw quite a bombshell by publishing a statement solemnly renouncing his title for good and all. Having held the world championship for more than twenty-five years—so he said—he felt the time ripe for a younger man to hold the title, and since at the present time Capablanca seemed the most worthy claimant he, Emanuel Lasker, was herewith formally and voluntarily relinquishing the world-championship and conceding it to Raoul José Capablanca.

Since at that time our present *Fédération International des Echecs* was not yet in existance and there was neither an official international organisation nor any universally recognised ruling for governing the 'chess-world'; since Lasker had won (and frequently staked) his title by private enterprise, it could well be argued that the world champion was perfectly entitled to deal with it as he pleased, and even to renounce it and to confer it on somebody else. It *could*

so be argued, and Lasker certainly did so, but the majority of the
chess fraternity all over the world did not like the idea of a title
'conferred', they wanted to see it won, they wanted 'to see blood';
and finally, Lasker yielded to the clamour.

All through his professional career Lasker had worked for chess
masters to be remunerated on a scale commensurate with the pleasure
they gave to millions all over the world; since gaining the title he had
insisted on making himself 'rare' enough to be able to hold out for
his own terms, and—unlike most of his colleagues who were forced
by economic necessity to accept practically any offer—he could well
afford to bide his time and to say 'No'. For that reason Lasker was
often accused of being mercenary, but there can be no doubt that
in the first two decades of his world championship Lasker has
benefitted his colleagues even more than himself. None of them,
of course, was in as good a bargaining position as a world champion
who also happened to be a man of independent means; yet they all
profited from the general rise of tournament prizes and performance
fees largely due to his efforts.

Having agreed to play a title-match against Capablanca, Lasker
once again held out for his own terms. After all, the match was to
take place in the wealthiest Casino of Cuba, and they could well
afford the sum of $20.000, with a minimum guarantee of $11.000
for Lasker. Compared with the fortunes available for other sporting
events of comparable world-wide interest, the sum of $20.000
seemed far from exorbitant, but it was certainly the greatest financial
reward ever offered in the realm of chess; and this time, for once,
Lasker could well do with the money, for in Germany the rapid
inflation of the mark was playing havoc with whatever financial
stability the savings and the property of the middle classes had provided. Frau Lasker was no longer a well-to-do woman, and a substantial sum of dollars would restore, for some time at any rate,
the financial security that was vanishing with the fast devaluation of
the German currency.

So Lasker went to Cuba to play the match, but he didn't feel very
happy about it. He was a stubborn man and, having once declared
that he no longer considered himself world champion and that he
conceded his title to the younger man, he stuck to his declaration
even though the chess world refused to accept it. He was prepared,
as ever, to do his best, but he was far from being imbued with that
indomitable fighting spirit that had successfully carried him through
all his previous tests and never failed him in a real emergency.

Moreover he soon began to see that he had been unwise not to
listen to those of his friends who had warned him that the late

spring in Cuba is hot and enervating for a man used to a more Northern climate; nor did he feel very happy in the luxurious atmosphere of the Casino where people would stroll in from the bar or the roulette tables to glance at the two famous chess matadors; then, as likely as not, they would have a bet on whatever they expected to be the next move, and if it bored them to wait they would stroll back to baccarat and roulette.

It wasn't what Lasker would have considered a 'congenial' atmosphere, but he coped as well as he could, and the first four games, each of them a stiff positional struggle, were all drawn. In the fifth game, as in that fatal game of the Schlechter-match Lasker, messed up a perfectly good position and finally had to yield the point to Capablanca's unerring technical precision.

With the score at 1 : 0 against the champion, they fought four more hard-contested games, each one ending in a draw, and then came the tenth game, the one in which, eleven years earlier, Lasker had had to stake everything to restore his fortunes. He tried it again, but this time it was not to be. True, he obtained a fairly good position, but he spoiled it, and Capablanca got and took his chance of a successful counter-attack.

So the score was 2 : 0 for the challenger, with eight draws. Still not an irretrievably hopeless score in so long a match, but Lasker was evidently suffering from fatigue. He managed to draw the next two games, but then he lost the thirteenth and the fourteenth. It was now getting on for May, and the 52-year-old champion was feeling the strain of the unaccustomed semi-tropical climate. He suggested continuing the match in New York or Philadelphia, but Capablanca insisted on completing the contract with the Cuban Casino. Whereupon Lasker resigned the match there and then, stubbornly refusing to play another game.

It was the one and only time he ever disappointed his public; for only fourteen games, less than half the stipulated number of thirty had been played. Even so, at that stage of the match the challenger's lead of four points was so convincing that to equal it would have been almost a physical impossibility for a Lasker at the top of his form; and he was far from that. In point of fact, Lasker returned to Europe, a sick man. He had to go to hospital for several months, and after that he had to take the cure at Karlsbad before fully restoring his health.

GAME 51

TWO KNIGHTS DEFENCE

TARRASCH–LASKER

3rd game of 2nd match, Berlin 1916

1) P—K4	P—K4
2) Kt—KB3	Kt—QB3
3) B—B4	Kt—B3
4) Kt—B3	Kt × P

One of the rare cases where this move, not recommendable as a rule, proves highly successful.

5) Kt × Kt

The counter sacrifice 5) B × P ch etc. is no good for White since it opens an important file for Black and helps to develop him.

5)	P—Q4
6) B—Q3	P × Kt
7) B × P	B—Q3
8) P—Q4	

With the Black centre P adequately secured, White must hurry up to liquidate the centre. Not so good would be 8) 0—0, giving Black a chance of ...B—KKt5 with the threat of ...P—KB4.

8)	P × P
9) Kt × P	

B × Kt ch would have been better.

9)	0—0!
10) B—K3	

A weak move. It was important to play B × Kt but, in any case, the White position has its weak spots.

10)	Q—R5!
11) B × Kt	P × B
12) P—KKt3?	

This opens up all the White squares for the opponent's B, but then P—KR3 would be almost as bad, inviting a subsequent B-sacrifice. Best, probably, was 12) Q—Q2, R—QKt1; 13) 0—0—0.

12)	Q—R6
13) Q—K2	P—QB4
14) Kt—Kt3	B—Kt5
15) Q—B1	Q—R4

Position after White's 16th move

16) Kt—Q2	R—K1!

'Action Stations' for the final assault.

17) KR—Kt1	QR—Kt1
18) Kt—B4	B—K4!
19) P—KR3	B × RP
20) Q—K2	B—Kt5
21) Q—Q3	QR—Q1
22) Kt × B	

Q—Kt3 would be countered by ...B—Q1.

22)	R × Q
23) Kt × R	R × B ch !

Resigns

After P × R, he is anihilated by ...Q—R7. A dashing game on the World-Champion's part.

(Notes by Dr. S. TARTAKOWER)

GAME 52

QUEEN'S GAMBIT DECLINED

LASKER–TARRASCH

Berlin, Oct. 1918 tournament

2nd round

1)	P—Q4	P—Q4
2)	Kt—KB3	P—QB4
3)	P—B4	P—K3
4)	P×QP	KP×P
5)	Kt—B3	Kt—QB3
6)	P—KKt3	Kt—B3
7)	B—Kt2	B—K2
8)	0—0	0—0
9)	P×P	B×P
10)	B—Kt5	P—Q5

Trying to get the initiative, but the disadvantage of the move is its opening up the long diagonal for the White KB.

11)	Kt—K4	B—K2
12)	B×Kt	B×B
13)	R—B1	R—K1

Position after White's 14th move

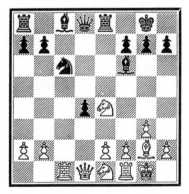

14) Kt—K1

This Kt aims at Q3 where it will exercise considerable pressure. Black is already in difficulties.

14)	.....	B—B4?

If this were possible all would be well but alas, it's *not* possible. The best move in the circumstances was 14) ...R—Kt1.

15)	Kt—B5	B—B1(best)
16)	Kt×P	B×Kt
17)	R×Kt	Q—R4
18)	P—QR3	QR—Kt1
19)	R—B2	B—R3
20)	Kt—Q3	B×Kt
21)	Q×B	KR—QB1
22)	R(1)—B1	R×R
23)	R×R	P—KR3
24)	B—K4	

The rest is mere routine. White must utilise his extra pawn, but in that sort of position it would be fatal to rush matters. Moreover, Black still puts some hope in the differing colour of the squares dominated by the Bishops.

24)	.....	R—K1
25)	P—QKt4	Q—K4
26)	B—B3	B—Q1
27)	R—B5	Q—K2
28)	R—QKt5	Q—B3

...B—Kt3 would be countered by 29) P—QR4.

29)	R—KB5	Q—QKt3
30)	R—QKt5	Q—KB3
31)	P—QR4	Q—Q3
32)	Q—B4	B—B3
33)	B—Q5	R—K2
34)	R—B5	R—Q2
35)	P—R5	

White is angling for the most favourable position to push his QKtP.

35)	.....	P—Kt3

Securing the Black K, but

opening up new avenues of attack for White, such as P—R4—R5 etc.

36)	P—R4	B—K4
37)	K—Kt2	K—Kt2
38)	B—K4	Q—K2
39)	B—B6	R—Q1
40)	B—Q5	Q—B3
41)	R—B6	Q—B4
42)	R—B5	Q—B3
43)	B—B3	P—Q6

A grand gesture, but tantamount to suicide. Black should wait for White to indicate his plan of attack and meanwhile the best he could do was 43) ...P—KR4 so as to stop the White KRP. As for the threatened advance of the White QKtP, there is nothing that Black can do about it except to try not to make things too easy for White.

44)	P×P	B—Q5
45)	R—B6	Q—K4
46)	R—B7	Q—B3
47)	P—Kt5	P—Kt4
48)	P×P	P×P
49)	Q—R2	R—KR1
50)	B—Q5	R—KB1
51)	P—Kt6	P×P
52)	P—R6	P—Kt5
53)	P—R7	Q—R3
54)	K—B1	Q—Q3
55)	R×P ch	R×R
56)	B×R	Resigns

(Notes by Dr. LASKER in the Book of the Tournament)

GAME 53

QUEEN'S GAMBIT DECLINED

LASKER–SCHLECHTER

Berlin tournament, last round October 1918

1)	P—Q4	Kt—KB3
2)	Kt—KB3	P—Q4
3)	P—B4	P—K3
4)	B—Kt5	P—B4
5)	BP×P	KP×P
6)	Kt—B3	B—K3
7)	P—K3	QKt—Q2

That Kt belongs at QB3 so as to exert pressure on his Q5. At Q2 it merely hampers Black's other pieces.

8)	B—Kt5!	P×P
9)	KKt×P	B—K2
10)	P—B4!	P—QR3
11)	P—B5	

If 11) B—R4 Black could play ...B—KKt5 followed by ...P—QKt4 thereby just managing to defend himself.

11)	.....	P×B
12)	P×B	Kt—K4
13)	B—B4(best)	Kt—Kt3
14)	P×P ch	K×P
15)	0—0	

By Kt×P White could have grabbed the Pawn immediately but he prefers to take it later in a more comfortable position.

15)	.....	P—Kt5
16)	Kt(3)—K2	R—K1
17)	R—B1	R—QB1
18)	Q—Kt3	Q—Q2
19)	R×R	R×R
20)	B—Kt5	K—Kt1
21)	B×Kt	B×B
22)	Q×KtP	Kt—K4
23)	P—QKt3	Kt—B3
24)	Q—Q2	

From here up to the adjournment on the 30th move White's
play is amazingly feeble. Obviously 24) Q—Kt5 was indicated so as to maintain the
pressure.

24)	Kt×Kt
25) P×Kt	R—K1
26) Kt—B3?(Kt3!)	Q—Kt5
27) R—B4	Q—K3
28) R—B1	Q—Kt5
29) R—Q1?	

Here White should continue
29) R—B4, Q—K3; 30) P—
KR4 with a still far superior
position.

29)	B—Kt4

Position after White's 30th move

30) Q—Q3	B—K6 ch?

White's threat of Q—Kt5
frightens Black off the strong
move ...R—K6. He could
have played it with impunity
since after 31) Q—Kt5, P—R4!;
32) R—QB1, K—R1! Black
would have a winning game.

31) K—R1	Q×P

But not B×QP on account of
32) P—KR3.

32) Q—Kt5	Q—K4
33) R×P	Q—K2
34) R—Q7	Q—B3
35) R—Q1	R—KB1
36) Kt—Q5	Q—B7
37) Kt×B	Q×Kt
38) P—KR3	P—QKt3
39) Q—Q3	Q—B7
40) P—QR4	P—R3
41) Q—Q4	Q—K7
42) K—R2	K—R1
43) R—Q3	R—B3
44) R—K3	Q—B8
45) R—K8 ch	K—R2
46) Q—K4 ch	P—Kt3

46) ...Q—B4; 47) Q×Q ch,
R×Q; 48) R—K6, P—QKt4:
49) R—K2 etc. would give
White a winning end-game
since his King threatens to go
to QKt4; hence the Black
King will be forced over to the
Q-wing whereupon White
simply gives up the QRP and
then plays havoc with his King
among the enemy Pawns.

47) R—K7 ch	R—B2
48) R—K6	R—B3
49) Q—Kt7 ch	R—B2
50) Q—Kt8	P—QKt4
51) P×P	Q—B5 ch
52) Q×Q	R×Q
53) R—K7 ch	K—Kt1
54) P—Kt6	Resigns

(Notes by Dr. LASKER in the Book
of the Tournament)

GAME 54

QUEEN'S GAMBIT DECLINED

CAPABLANCA—LASKER

5th match game Havana
4th April 1921

1)	P—Q4	P—Q4
2)	Kt—KB3	Kt—KB3
3)	P—B4	P—K3
4)	B—Kt5	QKt—Q2
5)	P—K3	B—K2
6)	Kt—B3	0—0
7)	R—B1	P—QKt3

A move of questionable merit. The safe move is 7) ...P—QB3.

8)	P×P	P×P
9)	Q—R4	P—B4

I had to go in for the P-sacrifice since after ...B—Kt2; 10) B—R6 Black would have had some rather weak squares at QR3 and QB3. Nor does 9) ...Kt—QKt1 seem very attractive.

10)	Q—B6	R—Kt1
11)	Kt×P	B—Kt2

Black has an attack of sorts, but Capablanca knows how to

Position after White's 13th move

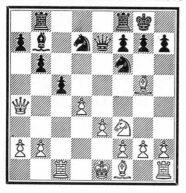

cope. It may have been best for me here to play for a draw by 11) ...Kt×Kt; 12) Q×Kt, B—Kt2; 13) B×B, Q×B; 14) Q—Kt5, Q×Q etc.; a variation which I think is credited to Teichmann.

12)	Kt×B ch	Q×Kt
13)	Q—R4	QR—B1

Black could easily equalise here by 13) ...B×Kt; 14) KtP×B, P×QP etc.

14)	Q—R3!	Q—K3
15)	B×Kt!	Q×B
16)	B—R6!	

Now I was in a quandary; 16) ...P×P being ruled out on account of 17) R×R, R×R; 18) 0—0.

16)	.....	B×Kt
17)	B×R	R×B
18)	P×B	Q×BP
19)	R—KKt1	R—K1
20)	Q—Q3	P—Kt3
21)	K—B1	R—K5
22)	Q—Q1	Q—R6 ch
23)	R—Kt2	Kt—B3
24)	K—Kt1	P×P
25)	R—B4!	

Excellent. Now ...R—Kt5 would be bad on account of 26) R—B8 ch.

25)	.....	P×P
26)	R×R	Kt×R
27)	Q—Q8 ch	K—Kt2
28)	Q—Q4 ch	Kt—B3
29)	P×P	Q—K3
30)	R—KB2	P—KKt4
31)	P—KR4	P×P?

Not so good. Better ...K—Kt3; 32) P×KtP, Kt—K5.

32)	Q×RP	Kt—Kt5
33)	Q—Kt5 ch	K—B1

34) R—B5

Here 34) R—Q2 might have been better since it would have forced me to play ...P—B3, weakening the K.

34)	.....	P—KR4(best)
35)	Q—Q8 ch	K—Kt2
36)	Q—Kt5 ch	K—B1
37)	Q—Q8 ch	K—Kt2
38)	Q—Kt5 ch	K—B1
39)	P—Kt3	Q—Q3
40)	Q—B4	Q—Q8 ch
41)	Q—B1	Q—Q2
42)	R × P	Kt × P
43)	Q—B3	Q—Q5
44)	Q—R8 ch	K—K2

45) Q—Kt7 ch   K—B1?

An incredible blunder. By ...K—K3 or ...K—B3 Black could have avoided the fatal exchange of Queens. It has been suggested that I made this crude mistake owing to time pressure. That was not so. I had well over 15 minutes to think about the move, but the trouble was that I was unable to think.

46) Q—Kt8 ch   Resigns

(Notes by Dr. LASKER in The Book of the Match)

GAME 55

QUEEN'S GAMBIT DECLINED

LASKER–CAPABLANCA

10th match game Havana, 11th April 1921

1)	P—Q4	P—Q4
2)	P—QB4	P—K3
3)	Kt—QB3	Kt—KB3
4)	B—Kt5	B—K2
5)	P—K3	0—0
6)	Kt—B3	QKt—Q2
7)	Q—B2	P—B4
8)	R—Q1	Q—R4
9)	B—Q3	P—KR3
10)	B—R4	BP × P
11)	KP × P	P × P
12)	B × P	Kt—Kt3
13)	B—QKt3	B—Q2
14)	0—0	QR—B1
15)	Kt—K5	B—Kt4
16)	KR—K1	QKt—Q4
17)	B(3) × Kt	

White got out of the opening with a superior position but he

Position after Black's 16th move

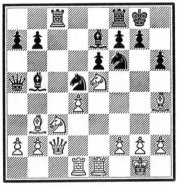

misses his chance. The young Hungarian Master Breyer (shortly before his untimely death) has indicated the correct continuation. White should have played QB × Kt, then if Black retakes with the Kt White could win by 18) Kt—Kt6; and if 17) ...B × B then 18) B × Kt, P × B; 19) Q—B5 etc. [Black could avoid any *disadvantage by countering 19) ...B—B3 etc. as indicated by Golombek in 'Capablanca's 100 Best Games'. R.T.]*

17) .....   Kt×B
18) B×B   Kt×B
19) Q—Kt3   B—B3
20) Kt×B   P×Kt
21) R—K5   Q—Kt3
22) Q—B2   KR—Q1
23) Kt—K2

Here I began to play poor chess. After all the R had gone to K5 with the idea of getting to QB5 hence 23) Kt—QR4 was the obvious move.

23) .....   R—Q4
24) R×R?

Even worse than the preceding move. Correct was 24) R—K3, then if ...Kt—B4 then 25) R—QKt3 and White will gain time for a counter-attack.

24) .....   BP×R

Now Black has re-united his Pawns and dominates the Q-wing.

25) Q—Q2   Kt—B4
26) P—QKt3

Mediocre chess. This advance could have waited. Much better was 26) P—KKt3.

26) .....   P—KR4
27) P—KR3?

Undoubtedly bad since it enables Black to retard the White pawns by ...P—R5. It was essential to play 27) P—KKt3.

27) .....   P—R5!
28) Q—Q3   R—B3
29) K—B1   P—Kt3
30) Q—Kt1   Q—Kt5

31) K—Kt1?

The K was quite well posted. White should have played 31) Q—Kt2.

31) .....   P—R4!

This decides the issue. Black now wins the game very prettily, and right up to the ending the crystal-clear logic of his manoeuvres is very attractive.

32) Q—Kt2   P—R5
33) Q—Q2   Q×Q
34) R×Q   P×P
35) P×P   R—Kt3
36) R—Q3   R—R3
37) P—KKt4   P×P e. p.
38) P×P   R—R7
39) Kt—B3   R—QB7
40) Kt—Q1   Kt—K2
41) Kt—K3   R—B8 ch
42) K—B2   Kt—B3
43) Kt—Q1   R—Kt8!

Avoiding the little trap I had put up in case of 43) ...Kt—Kt5; 44) R—Q2, R—Kt8; 45) Kt—Kt2, R×Kt?; 46) R×R, Kt—Q6 ch; 47) K—K2, Kt×R; 48) K—Q2 and the Kt has no escape.

44) K—K2?   R×P
45) K—K3   R—Kt5
46) Kt—B3   Kt—K2
47) Kt—K2   Kt—B4 ch
48) K—B2   P—Kt4
49) P—Kt4   Kt—Q3
50) Kt—Kt1   Kt—K5 ch
51) K—B1   R—Kt8 ch
52) K—Kt2   R—Kt7 ch
53) K—B1   R—B7 ch
54) K—K1   R—QR7
55) K—B1   K—Kt2
56) R—K3   K—Kt3

57) R—Q3	P—B3	65) R—Q3	P×P
58) R—K3	K—B2	66) R×P	K—B4
59) R—Q3	K—K2	67) R—Q1	P—Q5
60) R—K3	K—Q3	68) R—B1 ch	K—Q4
61) R—Q3	R—B7 ch	Resigns	
62) K—K1	R—KKt7		
63) K—B1	R—QR7		
64) R—K3	P—K4		

(Notes by Dr. LASKER in the Book of the Match)

CHAPTER TWENTY-FOUR
Triumphant Come-back

Steinitz was fifty-eight when he lost the title, six years older than his conqueror when he met the same fate. Yet, while Steinitz went on from tournament to tournament, desperately trying to gain new laurels and to wipe out the stigma of his defeat, Lasker was in no such hurry. He took the loss of his title as calmly as he had accepted his set-back at Cambridge Springs. But then he was only thirty-six and now he was getting on for fifty-three. How long could he afford to wait before staging a come-back? Lasker continued to bide his time. There were attractive tournaments in Budapest and in the Hague that year, and during the next a great tournament in Pistyan, an even greater one in London, more in Teplitz-Schönau and in Vienna, while 1923 started with a major tournament at Karlsbad. Lasker had invitations to almost every one of these attractive events, but he just couldn't be bothered. Steinitz wouldn't have missed any of these opportunities, Lasker missed them all. He could afford to wait.

He was kept busy enough by his mathematical and philosophical work, and in collaboration with his brother Berthold he spent a great deal of time and labour on their verse-drama. Moreover he took an ever growing interest in bridge and soon ranked as one of the best and shrewdest players in his country. But then he was a master of most card and board games and he was assiduously doing a bit of research on the theory of each of them. Only chess was completely neglected, and so far as that greatest of all games was concerned, the ex-champion certainly seemed to emulate Achilles sulking in his tent.

Meanwhile, the new generation of up and coming grandmasters were throwing their weight about, and such 'neo-romanticists' as Reti, Nimzowitsch, Bogoljubov, Alekhine, Tartakover were going from strength to strength and finding holes in the allegedly infallible theories of the 'Tarrasch School'. As for Tarrasch himself he could no longer cope with those rebellious youngsters; even Rubinstein was relegated to a back-seat, and it was on ever rarer occasions that he would show some flashes of his erstwhile genius.

Capablanca, having upheld the supremacy of his title with a magnificent victory in the great London tournament of 1922, had retired to his diplomatic post in Cuba and seemed to have every intention of keeping as aloof from the hurly-burly of the chess-arena as his predecessor.

Eventually the time came when Lasker could no longer resist the lure of the sixty-four squares, and it caused a sensation in the chess-world when the news got round that Lasker had accepted an invitation to play in a tournament. It happened in the summer of 1923 at Moravska Ostrava where, to celebrate the jubilee of the local Club, some Czech coal barons had provided a sufficient sum of money to stage quite a remarkable tournament. There were most of the leading lights of the 'Neo-Romanticists', such as Reti, Grünfeld, Tartakower and those strong Russian emigrés Bogoljubov and Selesniev; there was Spielmann who might well be dubbed an 'Old Romanticist', and there was Euwe, the up and coming young Dutchman. As for the pre-war generation there were Rubinstein, Tarrasch and Wolf; there were also a few gifted Czechoslovaks, and above all—there was Lasker.

As usual, he didn't start too well, having to concede a draw to Hromadka, one of the outsiders. But then, by beating Euwe, Bogoljubov and Tartakower, he pulled up his socks; and he jolly well had to, so as to keep the pace set by Reti who won game after game and seemed to be running away from the field. But Lasker doggedly held on, and when the two leaders met in the ninth round it was evident that this would be the 'decider' of the whole tournament.

Frau Martha Lasker, as usual, sat in a quiet corner not too near the board but within her husband's sight, busy with her knitting. From time to time she would send Emanuel a cup of coffee or a cigar, for ever since, at a certain great tournament, a stranger had offered him an opium-scented cigar Lasker would never touch one unless it was handed him by his wife. From time to time, while his opponent was thinking, he would walk over to his wife for a brief whispered chat. He did so as his momentous game against Reti was reaching the critical stage.

'How is it?', she asked. 'People say your position is not so good.'

'Do they?' said Lasker with a smile. 'Well, I'm not particularly worried about it; in fact, I rather like it.' And, of course, he did win the game.

It was certainly the decisive game of the tournament but it was remarkable in more than that respect; for here was a clash between the leading exponent of the 'New School' and a man who could not properly be pigeonholed into any one 'School', being the foremost exponent of his own theory that a game of chess, irrespective of theoretical notions, is above all an struggle between two personalities.

Now what about the 'New School', those 'Neo-Romanticists' and 'Hypermoderns' who gave old Tarrasch so much cause for worry? What was so 'new' about them? And how have the 'hyper-modern' notions of the nineteen-twenties stood the test of the subsequent decades? They have stood it very well, and have become part and parcel of more recent theoretical thought, the only difference being that no one any longer makes as much fuss about them as their progenitors (very pardonably) did in the early nineteen-twenties; and when shorn of some rather highfalutin' phraseology, which was all the rage when the 'hypermodern' ideas were really new, one of their main points can be boiled down to the simple statement—'simple' and obvious for a long time now—that in certain circumstances it may be more convenient and efficacious to dominate the centre of the chess-board with some of one's pieces rather than prematurely occupying it with one's Pawns.

Lasker proved that he could cope with the 'Hypermodern Neo-romanticists' as well as he had coped with Steinitz and Tarrasch; and for a man of his age to have gone through so strong a tourna-ment without a loss and to have won it with a comfortable margin and the convincing score of eight wins and five draws was certainly a most remarkable achievement. Small wonder that the chess frater-nity all over the world clamoured for another meeting of the present and the former world champion; and while there seemed to be no chance yet of another Lasker–Capablanca match, there soon came an opportunity for those two to meet in a tournament.

It was the great New York tournament of 1924, and apart from bringing about this sensational meeting, it was conspicuous for the attendance of Alekhine, Reti, Marshall, Maroczy and other great players. Moreover, since there were only eleven competitors, it was possible to make it a double-round event and thereby an even more convincing test of strength.

Lasker was looking forward to the American trip, for he hadn't crossed the Atlantic in twelve years. The last time his wife had been with him, but this time she stayed at home. The European masters met in Hamburg, passage having been booked for all of them on a Hapag liner; but Lasker, had he been less energetic a person, would have certainly missed the boat. He was touring Finland, prior to the American trip, and the ship on which he was leaving the country got icebound in the harbour. He had cut things rather fine, and would inevitably have missed his connection to Hamburg, unless he took some drastic action. This he did by leaving the boat at once and venturing a march of several miles across the ice, and on to the nearest railway station. Thus he just managed to make

MORAVSKY-OSTRAVA 1923

		1	2	3	4	5	6	7	8	9	10	11	12	13	14	
1	Lasker	—	1	½	½	1	1	1	1	½	½	1	½	1	1	10½
2	Reti	0	×	½	½	½	1	1	½	1	½	1	1	1	1	9½
3	Grünfeld	½	½	×	1	½	½	½	½	½	½	1	1	½	1	8½
4	Selesniew	½	½	0	×	1	½	0	1	½	½	½	1	1	½	7½
5	Euwe	0	½	½	0	×	½	½	½	0	1	½	1	1	1	7
6	Tartakower	0	0	½	½	½	×	½	½	1	1	½	1	½	½	7
7	Bogoljubow	0	0	½	1	½	½	×	0	1	1	0	0	1	1	6½
8	Tarrasch	0	½	½	0	½	½	1	×	1	0	1	0	½	1	6½
9	Spielmann	½	0	½	½	1	0	0	0	×	1	1	½	0	1	6
10	Rubinstein	½	½	½	½	0	0	0	1	0	×	½	1	½	½	5½
11	Pokorny	0	0	0	½	½	½	1	0	0	½	×	1	½	½	5
12	Hromadka	½	0	0	0	0	0	1	1	½	0	0	×	1	½	4½
13	Wolf	0	0	½	0	0	½	0	½	1	½	½	0	×	1	4½
14	Walter	0	0	0	½	0	½	0	0	0	½	½	½	0	×	2½

NEW YORK 1924

		1	2	3	4	5	6	7	8	9	10	11	
1	Em. Lasker	×	½1	1½	½1	11	11	11	½1	½1	½1	11	16
2	Capablance	½1	×	½½	½½	01	½1	11	11	1½	½1	½1	14½
3	Alekhine	0½	½½	×	½½	10	1½	½½	½½	11	½½	11	12
4	Marshall	½0	½½	½½	×	½1	0½	01	½0	½1	1½	11	11
5	Reti	00	10	01	½0	×	½½	01	11	10	10	11	10½
6	Maroczy	00	½0	0½	1½	½½	×	01	½½	11	½1	10	10
7	Bogoljubov	00	00	½½	10	10	10	×	01	11	½1	01	9½
8	Tartakower	½0	00	½½	½1	00	½½	10	×	10	0½	½1	8
9	Yates	½0	0½	00	½0	01	00	00	01	×	11	½1	7
10	Ed. Lasker	½0	½0	½½	0½	01	½0	½0	½1	00	×	0½	6½
11	Janowski	00	½0	00	00	00	01	10	½0	½0	1½	×	5

a train connection to Hamburg, in time to catch his boat. Had he missed it—since there were no trans-Atlantic flights yet at that time— he would have missed the tournament. Moreover, most of his luggage was already on board the Hapag Liner.

It was a good deal of luggage, for Frau Martha, provident as ever, had seen to it that her husband was well provided not merely with all the books he would wish to have but also with other necessities and luxuries. Being evidently under the misapprehension that passengers on Transatlantic Liners aren't properly fed, she had packed all manner of delicacies for him, nor had she forgotten a number of eggs from their own chicken-farm. It was certainly a sufficient number to provide for his breakfast on every day of the journey, and indeed each egg was duly marked with the date on which it was meant to be consumed as well as some message or advice in Martha's hand. Hence, every morning at the breakfast table his colleagues would ask Lasker: 'Well, what's the news from your wife to-day?' Whereupon Lasker would look at the egg of the day and read either some sentimental message, such as 'Forget me not', or some useful advice, such as 'Don't smoke too much!' or 'Give the steward your laundry!'

The sensation of the tournament was Capablanca's uncommonly bad start, so unlike his customary clockwork precision. His scoring a mere draw in each of the first four rounds was still considered his methodical way of 'warming up' for so long a tournament, but the real sensation came in the fifth round when the World-Champion lost to Reti. It was Capablanca's first defeat for many a year, and as for the tournament score it meant that with two points out of five he was well behind in the field. However, far from discouraged by so catastrophic a start, the champion now showed his mettle by scoring ten wins and five draws in the remaining fifteen games.

However, he had Lasker to contend with, and even that splendid recovery wasn't good enough to catch up with such an adversary; for this time Lasker was in splendid form from the beginning. His loss to Capablanca in their second game had little bearing on the result as it was his only loss in the tournament, and since he merely gave away six half-points and scored thirteen wins Lasker finished with the magnificent score of 16 points (80 %!), 1½ points ahead of Capablanca who, in turn, was 2½ points ahead of Alekhine and the rest.

Lasker got a triumphant reception when he returned home. To have so convincingly won two grandmaster-tournaments within less than a year was clear enough evidence that he was still the rightful claimant for the title he had held so long, and that a return match with Capablanca was overdue.

Lasker was perfectly willing to play such a match, but he was too proud to hunt around for 'backers'. He made it clear that if the chess world wanted the match it was up to them to organise it and to find the necessary funds. But alas, while there was a great deal of talk about it, it never came to pass. Not that it worried Lasker, for he was busy enough with the kind of work that mattered more to him than chess.

GAME 56

ALEKHINE DEFENCE

LASKER–TARRASCH,

2nd round at Moravska-Ostrava, July 1923

1) P—K4	Kt—KB3
2) P—K5	Kt—Q4
3) P—QB4	Kt—Kt3
4) P—Q4	P—Q3
5) P—B4	P×P
6) BP×P	Kt—B3
7) B—K3	B—B4
8) Kt—QB3	P—K3
9) Kt—B3	B—QKt5
10) B—Q3	

Better B—K2 at once. But then White's position is not so good altogether. [*According to modern theory White does have the better game after 10) B—K2 Black should have played 9) ...B—K2 followed by ...0—0. R.T.*]

10) ...	B—Kt5
11) B—K2	B×Kt
12) P×B	Q—R5 ch
13) B—B2	Q—B5
14) KR—Kt1	

The great tactician Lasker is of course fully aware of being in a fairly awkward position; hence, he seeks counter chances at the cost of a Pawn.

14)	0—0—0
15) R—Kt4	Q×RP
16) R—R4	Q—Kt7
17) B—B1	Q—Kt4
18) Q—B2	P—KR4
19) R—Q1	Q—R3
20) P—R3	B—K2
21) R—R3	B—Kt4
22) Q—K4	P—B3

So far Black has played very well indeed but now he should have played ...B—QB8.

23) P×P	Q×P
24) B—K2	Q—B4?

A grievous strategical error. Black is now saddled with a very poor end-game.

Position after Black's 24th move

25) Q×Q	P×Q
26) B—Q3	P—Kt3
27) Kt—K2	P—R5

28)	P—B4	B—B3
29)	P—Kt4	K—Kt1
30)	P—Q5	Kt—K2
31)	K—B1	Kt(3)—B1

The Black Pawns on the K-wing are practically worthless whereas White is very strongly placed on the Q-wing.

| 32) | P—Kt5 | P—B3? |

This is almost tantamount to suicide. After 32) ...Kt—Q3 followed by ...Kt—K5 he still had a playable game.

33)	KtP×P	P×P
34)	R—Kt1 ch	K—R1
35)	Kt—Q4	B×Kt

36)	B×B	R—R2
37)	B—K5	Kt—Q3

Black is hopelessly lost.

38)	P—B5	Kt—Kt2
39)	P—Q6	Kt—Q4
40)	R—B1	R—KB1
41)	B—R6	Kt—B3
42)	B(5)×Kt	R×B
43)	R—K3	R—B1
44)	R(1)—K1	R(2)—R1
45)	P—Q7	K—Kt1
46)	R—K8 ch	K—B2
47)	B×Kt	Resigns

Lasker has played the ending with consummate mastery.

(Notes by RICHARD TEICHMANN)

GAME 57

RUY LOPEZ

LASKER—BOGOLJUBOV

Moravska-Ostrava, 4th round, July 1923

1)	P—K4	P—K4
2)	Kt—KB3	Kt—QB3
3)	B—Kt5	P—QR3
4)	B—R4	Kt—B3
5)	0—0	B—K2
6)	R—K1	P—QKt4
7)	B—Kt3	P—Q3
8)	P—B3	0—0
9)	P—Q4	P×P

More solid and certainly more usual is 9) ...B—Kt5.

10)	P×P	B—Kt5
11)	Kt—B3	Kt—QR4
12)	B—B2	P—B4
13)	P×P	

Lasker, of course, is never afraid of simplification since somehow he manages to squeeze an advantage out of

a position reduced to practically nothing. The text move at any rate gives White certain pressure.

| 13) | ..... | P×P |
| 14) | P—K5! | |

Cramping Black's game; from now on he hardly gets a chance to breathe.

14)	.....	Q×Q
15)	R×Q	Kt—Q2
16)	P—KR3!	

Forcing Black to retreat since ...B×Kt; 17) R×Kt would cost a piece.

16)	.....	B—K3
17)	Kt—Q5!	B×Kt
18)	R×B	Kt—Kt3
19)	R—Q1	QR—Q1

It may have been better first to play 19) ...P—KR3.

20)	B—Kt5!	P—B3(forced)
21)	P×P	B×P
22)	B×B	P×B

First tangible result: The Black

K-wing P-formation is getting messed up.

23) QR—B1   Kt(3)—B5

Moreover Black will be worried a great deal about the dislocation of his Knights.

24) P—QKt3   Kt—Q3
25) R—O5   Kt(4)—Kt2
26) QR—Q1   P—Kt5

With a chronic weakness of his K-wing Black is forced to strive for a counter chance on the Q-Wing, thereby loosening and still further weakening his position.

27) B—Q3   R—R1
28) R—K1   P—QR4
29) R—K7   R—B2
30) R × R   Kt × R?

After this momentary lapse of his fairly energetic defence further calamities pile up for Black, and what with the White R penetrating first one and then another Pawn will get lost. He should not, however, under any circumstances,

Position after White's 32nd move

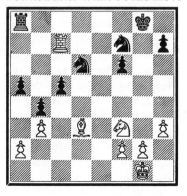

have given up the Kt-position at his Q3. Hence 30 ...K × R would have been better; and then, if 31) B × RP, Black might have had certain counter chances ...P—QR5

31) R—Q7   Kt(Kt2)—Q3
32) R—B7   R—Q1
33) B—R6!(R × P?) R—R1
34) B—K2   R—QB1
35) R—R7   Kt—K4
36) Kt × Kt   P × Kt
37) B—Kt4

Lasker is inexorable. Even before deigning to take the first Pawn (QRP) the next one on the QB file is being prepared for the slaughter.

37) .....   R—B3
38) B—Q7   R—Kt3
39) R × P   Kt—K5
40) B—B5   Kt—B6
41) R × P   R—Kt4

One last vague attempt to save himself, but Lasker is in no conciliatory mood. The rest is silence!

42) R—B8 ch   K—Kt2
43) R—B7 ch   K—B3
44) B × P   R—Q4
45) R—B4   Kt × P
46) P—B4   P × P
47) R × P ch   K—Kt2
48) B—B2   R—Q7
49) R—B2   R—Q5
50) B—B5   Kt—B6
51) B—K6   and soon resigned

(Notes by Dr. S. TARTAKOWER in *Die Hypermoderne Schachpartie*)

GAME 58

QUEEN'S GAMBIT DECLINED

RETI–LASKER

Moravska-Ostrava, 9th round, July 1923

Decisive game of the tournament

1) Kt—KB3   P—Q4
2) P—Q4

Reti refrains from playing his very own opening. Against such an opponent he prefers to steer the game into ordinary QP channels.

2) .....   Kt—KB3
3) P—B4   P—B3
4) Kt—B3   P×P

The late Alapin's posthumous triumph since this move, after having been discredited for many years, does seem to save the honour of the opening. By accepting the gambit Black becomes the attacker and the game speedily turns into a hell for leather fight.

5) P—K3   P—QKt4
6) P—QR4   P—Kt5
7) Kt—R2   P—K3
8) B×P   B—K2

According to Dr. Tarrasch ...QKt—Q2 is better so as to prepare for ...P—QB4, thereby stopping White's push in the centre. Anyway after the text move White's superiority is soon evident.

9) 0—0   0—0
10) Q—K2   QKt—Q2
11) P—QKt3   P—QR4
12) B—Kt2   P—B4
13) KR—Q1   Q—Kt3
14) Kt—B1   B—R3

Lasker has dealt with this difficult opening in his own unorthodox way and actually achieved some concrete advantage but now he runs head on against the forceful resistance of a brilliant opponent.

15) P×P?!
15) .....   Kt×P

At first sight it would seem to be odd enough to help the enemy Kt into such a dominating position against one's own pawn at Kt3 but the move is really quite subtle in as much as it increases the activity of the QB and also brings about a dominating Kt position on QB4.

16) Kt—K5   B×B
17) Kt×B   Q—R3

The idea being ...R—QB1 followed by ...Kt×P thereby winning a Pawn; hence White eliminates this dangerous Knight.

18) B—Q4   KR—B1

The great tactician begins to visualise a new target and proceeds to go after it with admirable tenacity. Instead of the merely static efficacy on QB4 the other Kt is to have some dynamic effect by worrying the opponent from QB6

19) B×Kt   B×B
20) Q—B3   B—K2!

Facilitating the manoeuvre ...Kt—Q4—B6 before the opponent can permanently stop it by Kt—Q3—K5, threatening KB7.

21) Kt—Q3

Here Reti scorned playing for a draw by 21) Kt—K2.

21)	....	Kt—Q4
22)	Kt(Q3)—K5	B—B3
23)	P—K4	Kt—B6

From here Lasker has a pretty strong hold on the game even though Reti in his own notes considers this as a 'mere spot of middle game complications' while emphasising the strength of his own inviolable Kt on QB4.

24)	R—Q6	Q—Kt2
25)	R—K1	B×Kt
26)	Kt×B	QB2!

Coping with the threat of R—Q7, protecting all his weak spots and attacking at the same time.

27)	Kt—B4	P—K4!

Otherwise White would fortify his position by 28) P—K5 hence it would be very dangerous to go Pawn snatching by 27) ...Kt×P; 28) P—K5!, R—Q1; 29) R(1)—Q1, Kt—QB3: 30) R—Q7!, and White would win. Now however Black aims at getting control of the Q-file by means of ...R—Q1 to say nothing of further tremendous complications. A typical Lasker move!

28)	Q—B5	

Threatening R—Q7 and at the same time attacking the KP. Here Reti thought that his great opponent had made a bloomer.

28)	.....	Kt—K7 ch
29)	K—B1?	

Lasker knew very well what he

Position after Black's 28th move

was doing and it is Reti now who makes the decisive mistake, being also in terrible time trouble. He ought to have played 29) R×Kt, Q×R; 30) Q×BP ch!, K—R1!: 31) Q—Q5!, with a good chance of securing the draw in spite of being the exchange down. Even better perhaps, (as Tarrasch later found in a thorough analysis) might have been 29) K—R1 leaving White finally a Pawn up even though Black should have the draw well in hand.

29)	.....	Kt—Q5
30)	Q×P	Kt×P
31)	Kt—Kt6	Kt—Q7 ch!
32)	K—Kt1	Kt—B5
33)	Kt×Kt	

33) Kt×R would be countered by ...Q×R; all of which Lasker must have seen on his 27th move.

33)	.....	Q×Kt
34)	Q—KB5	

Since what with his strong QKtP, the end-game would be

a clear win for Black it is obvious for White to avoid the threatened exchange of Queens and to seek his salvation in pushing the KP and attacking for all he is worth.

34)	.....	QR—Kt1
35)	P—K5	P—Kt6
36)	P—K6	P×P
37)	R(6)×P	R—B1
38)	Q—K5	Q—B7
39)	P—B4	P—Kt7
40)	R—K7	Q—Kt3

41)	P—B5	Q—KB3
42)	Q—Q5 ch	K—R1
43)	R—Kt7	Q—B6!

Resigns

A little early but with good reason for after 44) R—KB1, Q—K6 ch; 45) K—R1, Q—B8; 46) K—Kt1, P—R3!; 47) P—B6, R×R; 48) Q×R, R×P White would soon be at the end of his tether. A hard game!

(Notes by Dr. S. TARTAKOWER in *Die Hypermoderne Schachpartie*)

GAME 59

SICILIAN

WOLF–LASKER

12th round at Moravsky-Ostrava, July 1923

1)	P—K4	P—QB4
2)	Kt—QB3	Kt—QB3
3)	P—KKt3	P—KKt3
4)	B—Kt2	B—Kt2
5)	P—Q3	P—Q3
6)	Kt(1)—K2	Kt—B3
7)	0—0	0—0
8)	P—KR3	Kt—K1!

This is much stronger than ...B—Q2; 9) B—K3, P—KR3; 10) Q—Q2, K—R2; 11) P—KB4 etc. (Tarrasch–Spielmann, Mannheim 1914).

9)	B—K3	Kt—Q5!

An outpost very effective in this variation and stopping the push of the QP.

10)	K—R2	

White's position could have been strengthened by 10) P—KKt4 followed by Kt—Kt3 and P—KB4.

10)	.....	B—Q2
11)	Q—Q2	R—B1!

Superficially Black's best chance would seem to be ...P—KB4 and ...P—K4 but Lasker has other plans and systematically strengthens his Q—Wing position.

12)	Kt—Q1	B—QB3
13)	Kt—Kt1	P—Q4!

Opening up the game and definitely taking the initiative.

14)	P—QB3	Kt—K3
15)	P×P	B×QP
16)	P—B3	

Bottling up his own pieces.

16)	.....	Kt—Q3
17)	Kt—B2	Kt—B4
18)	Kt—Kt4	Q—Q3
19)	Kt—K2	P—KR4!
20)	Kt—R6 ch	Kt×Kt
21)	B×Kt	

(See diagram on following page)

21)	.....	P—R5!

Opening the R-file with decisive effect.

22)	B×B	Kt×B
23)	Q—B4	P×P ch

Position after White's 21st move

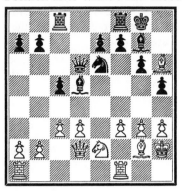

24) Q×P   P—K4!
25) K—R1   KR—K1

26)	QR—Q1	Q—KB3
27)	Q—B2	Kt—K3
28)	R—Q2	K—Kt2
29)	K—R2	QR—Q1
30)	P—R3	R—KR1
31)	R—K1	Kt—Kt4
32)	Kt—Kt1	Q—B5 ch
33)	K—R1	B×P!

The *coup de grâce*. A beautifully consistent game on Lasker's part.

34)	B×B	Kt×P
35)	Q—K3	Kt—Kt4 ch
	Resigns	

(Notes by Dr. TARTAKOWER in *Die Hypermoderne Schachpartie*)

GAME 60

CARO–KANN

LASKER–TARTAKOWER,

Last round at Moravska-Ostrava, July 1923

1)	P—K4	P—QB3
2)	P—Q4	P—Q4
3)	P×P	P×P
3)	B—Q3	Kt—QB3
5)	P—QB3	Kt—B3
6)	B—KB4	P—KKt3
7)	P—KR3	B—Kt2
8)	Kt—B3	Kt—K5

A leap into the unknown, but Lasker refutes it in no uncertain manner.

9)	QKt—Q2	P—B4
10)	0—0	0—0
11)	Kt—K5!	

Most masters, (to quote Maroczy's notes in the Book of the Tournament) would have concentrated on dominating the K-file so as to keep the pressure on Black's backward pawn but Lasker has his own ideas.

11)	.....	Kt(3)×Kt
12)	QB×Kt	B×B
13)	P×B	Kt×Kt
14)	Q×Kt	P—B5?

Burning all his boats behind him since obviously the text move weakens his Pawn formation. More solid would have been 14) ...P—K3; 15) QR—Q1, Q—B2 followed by ...B—Q2 although even then the immobility of his B would have reduced Black to a long stretch of passive resistance.

15) QR—Q1

Anticipating ...B—KB4 and threatening 16) P—QB4 Black now has the choice of several moves, and he picks the weakest one.

| 15) | ..... | Q—B2? |

Equally bad was ...P—B6,

refuted by 16) B—K4! Black ought to have played ...B—K3, a dare-devil attack being his only chance in the circumstances.

16)	KR—K1	P—K3
17)	QR—B1!	Q—Q1
18)	B—K2	Q—R4?
19)	P—QKt4	Q—B2

Position after Black's 19th move

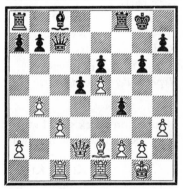

20) P—B4!

As elegant as it is forceful. By 20) Q—Q4 he would have given Black a chance to consolidate his position by ...Q—QKt 3.

20)	.....	Q×KP
21)	P×P	Q—Q3
22)	B—B3	R—Q1
23)	Q—Q4!	

The *coup de grâce*. Black is hopelessly tied up since ...P×P is ruled out on account of 24) B×P ch etc.

23)	.....	B—Q2

24) Q—B5!

The simplest way. Black can no longer avoid the loss of the Pawn.

24)	.....	Q×Q
25)	P×Q	QR—B1
26)	P—B6	P×P
27)	P×P	B—K1
28)	P—B7	R—Q2(forced)
29)	R×P	

The point of the advance. White begins to reap the fruits of his labour.

29)	.....	B—B2
30)	R(6)—QB6	B—Q4

That costs a second pawn, but what with the threat of B—Kt4 Black had no alternative. Obviously 30) ...P—KR4 would have been countered by R—QB4 and B—Kt2.

31)	B×B ch	R×B
32)	R—R6	K—B2
33)	R×RP	K—K2
34)	R—R4	P—Kt4
35)	R(R4)—B4	K—Q2
36)	R—B5	

Cruel but efficient! The rest is silence!

36)	.....	R×R
37)	R×R	R×P
38)	R×R ch	K×R
39)	K—B1	K—Q3
40)	K—K2	K—K4
41)	P—QR4	K—Q5
42)	K—B3	Resigns

(Notes by Dr. S. TARTAKOWER in *Die Hypermoderne Schachpartie*)

GAME 61

QUEEN'S GAMBIT DECLINED

ALEKHINE–LASKER

New York, 3rd round, March 1924

1) P—Q4   P—Q4
2) P—QB4   P—K3
3) Kt—KB3 Kt—KB3
4) Kt—B3   QKt—Q2
5) P×P

That exchange may well wait until White can make it in particularly favourable circumstances. Meanwhile the best move here would be B—Kt5.

5) .....   P×P
6) B—B4

Here too the pinning move B—Kt5 would be rather more recommendable. As it is Black can comfortably equalise in various ways.

6) .....   P—B3
7) P—K3

Should White play 7) P—KR3 so as to keep his B, a good line would be ...B—K2; 8) P—K3, Kt—K5! followed by ...P—KB4 as first introduced by H. Wolf at Teplitz-Schönau, 1922. Now Black forces an exchange not too unfavourable for him even though it is at the expense of his development.

7) .....   Kt—R4
8) B—Q3?

Of three possibilities this was undoubtedly the least favourable. He should have played either B—Kt3 or B—K5. White plays this game somewhat irresolutely and inconsistently.

8) .....   Kt×B

9) P×Kt   B—Q3
10) P—KKt3?

Now, all of a sudden he desists from his original intention of Kt—K5 because he didn't like the idea of having to counter ...Q—R5 11) P—KKt3, Q—R6 by 12) Q—B2. The strong position of his Kt might have recompensed White for the weakness of his White squares.

10) .....   0—0
11) 0—0   R—K1
12) Q—B2   Kt—B1
13) Kt—Q1

Nor would 13) Kt—Kt5 be much better even though it has been suggested by various commentators. The sequel might have been ...P—KKt3; 14) R—K1, P—B3; 15) Kt—B3, B—Kt5; 16) R×R, Q×R; 17) R—K1, Q—Q2; Simplest and best for White under the circumstances would have been 13) KR—K1.

13) .....   P—B3!
14) Kt—K3   B—K3
15) Kt—R4?

Loss of time. It is due to his insistence on getting the initiative in spite of his inferior opening play that White's game will now disintegrate with surprising rapidity. With some more passive play on White's part (such as 15) KR—Q1 with the idea of countering ...B—KB2 by 16) B—B5) it wouldn't have been quite so easy for Black to get an attack going.

15) .....   B—QB2

More precise perhaps was ...P—QR4.

16) P—QKt4   B—Kt3
17) Kt—B3   B—KB2!

Position after Black's 17th move

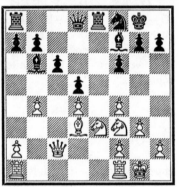

18) P—Kt5?

The decisive mistake. True enough Black has much the better of it but by 18) KR—Q1, B—KR4; 19) B—K2, the game was still tenable. After the text move Black forces some further loosening of the White K-wing and then wins quite easily.

18) .....   B—KR4!
19) P—Kt4   B—KB2
20) P×P   R—B1
21) Q—Kt2   P×P
22) P—B5

Otherwise the Kt wll decisively enter via K3.

22) .....   Q—Q3

The threat being ...Q—KB5.

23) Kt—Kt2   B—B2
24) KR—K1   P—KR4!
25) P—KR3

By means of a double Pawn

sacrifice such as 25) P—KKt5, P×P; 26) Kt—K5, Kt—Q2; 27) P—KB4 etc. the threatening mating attack might be parried for the time being, but in the long run that wouldn't help much.

25) .....   Kt—R2
26) R×R ch   R×R
27) R—K1   R—Kt1
28) Q—B1   Kt—Kt4
29) Kt—K5

Or 29) Kt×Kt, Q—R7 ch; 30) K—B1, P×Kt; 31) Kt—K3, Q×RP etc.

29) .....   P×Kt
30) Q×Kt   P—K5
31) P—B6   P—Kt3

Even after ...Q×BP White would have had to resign pretty soon. It was only ...Q—R7 ch that Black had to beware of since 32) K—B1, Q—R8 ch; 33) K—K2, P×Bch; 34) K×P, Q×RP ch; 35) Kt—K3, K—B1; 36) Q×KtP ch, K—K1; 37) K—B2! would have turned the tables.

32) P—B4   RP×P!

Lasker finds the shortest way to victory. Moves such as ...P×P e.p. or ...P×B would not have been quite as immediately decisive.

33) B—K2   P×P
34) B—R5   R—Kt7!
35) Kt—R4   Q×P(B5)
36) Q×Q   B×Q

Resigns

(Notes by ALEKHINE in the Book of the Tournament)

GAME 62

SICILIAN

JANOWSKI–LASKER

4th round, New York, March 1924

1) P—K4	P—QB4
2) Kt—KB3	Kt—QB3
3) P—Q4	P×P
4) Kt×P	Kt—B3
5) Kt—QB3	P—Q3
6) B—K2	P—K3
7) 0—0	B—K2
8) B—K3	0—0
9) Q—Q2	

(*According to modern theory 9) P—KB4 followed by Q—K1—Kt3 is considered stronger. R.T.*)

9)	P—QR3
10) QR—Q1	

By allowing the opponent to complete his development undisturbed, White almost imperceptably slips into an inferior position. Here he certainly ought to have played 10) P—KB3 so as to be able to counter ...Q—B2 by 11) Kt—R4.

10)	Q—B2
11) Kt—Kt3	P—QKt4
12) P—B3	R—Q1
13) Q—K1	

The White pieces have nothing to bite at and they are hampered in their mobility. The text move's demonstration against QKt6 means no real harm to Black.

13)	Kt—K4
14) Q—B2	R—Kt1
15) B—Q3	Kt—B5
16) B—B1	B—Kt2
17) Q—Kt3	QR—B1
18) KR—K1	

All that so as to be able at long last, to play P—KB4 with the possibility of more or less bogus threats. Compared with this the co-operation of the Black pieces strikes one as very harmonious indeed.

18)	Kt—Q2
19) P—B4	B—KB3

Threatening 20) ...Kt×KtP and thereby forcing White to give the opponent the advantage of two Bishops.

20) B×Kt	P×B
21) Kt—Q2	Q—R4
22) Kt(2)—Kt1	Kt—B1
23) B—K3	Q—Kt5
24) B—B1	Kt—Kt3
25) Q—B2	B—R5!
26) P—KKt3	B—KB3
27) P—QR3	Q—R4
28) B—K3	Q—R4!
29) B—Kt6	R—Q2
30) R—Q2	B—B3!
31) R(1)—Q1	B—K2
32) P—QR4	

Janowski has exploited his inferior position for all it was worth and for the time being he has certainly managed to cramp the Black pieces a bit; yet, he can never get over the inherent disadvantage of his game, viz his weakness on the White squares due to the disappearance of his KB; and this in the end will be the cause of his downfall.

32)	R—Kt2
33) P—R5	P—B4!
34) Q—K3	P—K4!

Yielding his Q4 but on the other hand denuding the White K, the more so since the White pieces are engaged on the Q wing. Lasker's play, considering his opponent's energetic resistance is most impressive.

35) R—KB1   KP×P
36) KtP×P   B—B1
All of a sudden the co-operation of both Rooks is secured.

37) Kt—Q5   R—KB2
38) Kt(1)—B3   R—K1!
39) Q—Q4
The irrelevant QBP is a poor exchange for the centre Pawn. Yet the obvious 39) Kt—B7 would have been refuted by an unanswerable sacrifice of the exchange, ...R×P; 40) Kt×R, P×Kt etc.

39) .....   P×P
40) Q×BP   B—Q2
41) B—K3   Kt—R5
42) R(2)—B2   B—R6
43) Kt×P
Obviously he can't help losing the exchange, but before helping himself to it Lasker forces

Position after White's 48th move

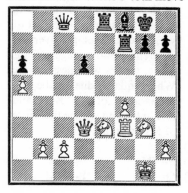

an advantageous simplification.

43) .....   Q—Kt5 ch!
44) Kt—Kt3   Kt—B4
45) R—B3   B×R
46) Q×B   Kt×B
47) Kt×Kt   Q—B1!
48) Q—Q3   Q—B4?
A mistake which may well have robbed Black of the fruits of his deep strategy. The correct move was ...P—Q4.

49) Q—Q2?
White counters blunder with blunder overlooking the obvious 49) Kt—K4 which would have given him a defensible game. In view of the threat of 50) Kt—Kt5 Black would have only had the choice of either returning the exchange or giving the Queen for two Rooks. In both cases, in view of White's insecure K position, Black would still have had an advantage. But the win, if at all possible, would have been far from easy.

49) .....   P—Q4
Now however it is quite simple since the advancing Pawn gives Black another strong weapon. It will only take a few moves to make White's position quite hopeless.

50) K—Kt2   P—Q5
51) Kt—Kt4   B—Q3
52) Kt—B2   Q—Q4
53) P—B4
Desperation.

53) .....   Q×BP
54) Kt(3)—K4   Q—Q4
55) Kt×B   Q×Kt

56)	Kt—Q3	Q—Q4	64)	Q—Q1	R—KB3
57)	K—Kt3	R—B3	65)	Kt—Q3	P—Kt4!
58)	K—B2	R—R3	66)	Kt—B5	Q—Q4
59)	P—R3	R—KB3	67)	Kt—Q3	P×P
60)	K—Kt3	R—Kt3 ch	68)	Kt×P	Q—K5
61)	K—B2	R—K6!		Resigns	
62)	Kt—K5	Q—K5			
63)	P—Kt4	P—R4			

(Notes by ALEKHINE in The Book of the Tournament)

GAME 63

RUY LOPEZ

EM. LASKER–ED. LASKER

New York, 6th round, March 1924

1)	P—K4	P—K4
2)	Kt—KB3	Kt—QB3
3)	B—Kt5	P—QR3
4)	B—R4	Kt—B3
5)	0—0	B—K2
6)	R—K1	P—QKt4
7)	B—Kt3	0—0
8)	P—B3	P—Q3
9)	P—KR3	Kt—QR4
10)	B—B2	P—B4
11)	P—Q4	Q—B2
12)	QKt—Q2	BP×P
13)	P×P	B—Q2
14)	Kt—B1	KR—B1
15)	R—K2	Kt—R4

The P-sacrifice intended with this move is very brilliant and interesting even though, in the long run, it turns out to be incorrect;

[*a claim yet to be proved; see note for Black's 30th move. R.T.*]

16)	P×P	P×P
17)	Kt×P	

Lasker, never frightened by complications, calmly helps himself to the Pawn presented to him; and he *will* soon get the better of the ensuing complications.

17)	.....	B×P
18)	Kt×P!	

There is the horrible threat 19) Q—Q5.

18)	.....	B—K3
19)	Kt—Kt5	B—B5
20)	B—Q3	R—Q1
21)	R—B2!	

More favourable for White than an immediate exchange of QB4.

21)	.....	Kt—B5
22)	B×Kt	Q×B
23)	Kt—R3	Q—K4
24)	B×B ch	Kt×B
25)	Q—K2	

White is a healthy Pawn up and it should not take him long now to expel the Black Kt from its dominating position. Black would not seem to have quite sufficient recompense for the Pawn by his temporary domination of the Black squares.

25)	.....	R—Q5
26)	P—B3	QR—Q1
27)	QR—B1	B—B4
28)	K—R1	B—Kt5

Black's efforts would seem to

have made the threat of P—QKt3 even more menacing. The text move intends to provide entry for the Black Knight at Q7 but even that should not alter the fate of the game.

29) P—QKt3   Kt—Q7

After ...Kt—Kt3 30) R—QB6, White would have been able to force the exchange of one Rook, thus relieving the pressure on the Q-file. The text move gets the Kt into a *cul de sac*.

30) Kt—K3!

The threat now is R—Q1, chasing the Bishop off his diagonal and winning a piece. Black puts his trust in what he considers a very subtle defensive resource but these hopes soon go awry.

30) .....   B—R6

'*I had no more time left to figure through 30) ...Kt×KP 31) P×Kt, R×P; 32) R—B8, R—K1!! which would have won a solid pawn and the game*', says Edward Lasker in his book '*Chess Secrets*'. *Should that be the refutation of the combination started on the 17th move? (R.T.)*.

31) R—Q1   B—Kt5
32) P—R3!

This manoeuvre had to be worked out very carefully.

32) .....   B—R4
33) P—QKt4   B—B2

The mate now threatened cannot very well be parried by 34) Kt—Kt4 on account of

...Kt×P!, but White has a much more effective rejoinder.

34) P—B4!   Kt×P!(forced)
35) K—R2!(best)   R×R
36) Kt×R!(P×Q?)   Q—K2

Position after Black's 36th move

37) R×B?

Thereby he robs himself of the fruits of his excellent play. By simply playing 37) Kt(1)—B2, R—Q5; 38) Q—K3 he could win a piece and the game. After the text move the win would seem to be very difficult, to say the least.

37) .....   Q×R
38) Q×Kt   Q—B5
39) Q—K7

Neither here nor later could White win by an exchange of Queens since Black would win the QRP and the remaining material would not be sufficient. In desperately avoiding the exchange White gradually drifts into a position which cannot properly be won at all. He *wants* to win though, hence the *tour de force* on his 51st move.

39)	Q—B1
40) Kt(1)—B2	P—R3
41) Q—R7?(Kt—K4!)	Q—K3
42) Q—Kt7	Q—Q4!
43) Q—Kt6	

Obviously the exchange of Queens was tantamount to accepting the draw.

43)	R—Q3
44) Q—K3	R—K3
45) Q—QB3	Q—B5

Within the last eight moves the Black position has quite considerably improved.

46) Q—B3	Q—B3
47) Q—Q3	R—Q3
48) Q—Kt3 ch	Q—Q4
49) Q—Kt1	R—K3

Now the R is ready for a counter attack (particularly on the QRP) and unless White is willing to agree to a draw by repetition he will have to conjure up something or other.

50) Kt—Kt4   R—K7!

Black has rightly assessed the harmlessness of the sacrifice intended by his famous opponent and he calmly goes in for it; the more readily since otherwise, what with the strong position of his Kt at K5, White may still have had a small winning chance.

51) Kt×P ch?

The hopes based on this combination must needs be thwarted by the fact that the Kt, in view of the insecure K position, cannot properly join in the attack. As a matter of fact in persistently avoiding any chance of a draw White will come very near losing the game.

51)	P×Kt
52) Q—Kt6 ch	K—B1
53) Q×P ch	K—K1
54) Q—Kt6 ch	K—Q1
55) Q—Kt3	R—K1
56) Q—B2	R—Kt1
57) Q—Kt2	

Here too 57) Q—Kt6 ch, etc. would have forced the draw.

57) .....   Q—Q3!

Avoiding further checks and once again forestalling the co-operation of the Knight.

58) Q—B3	K—Q2
59) Q—B3	K—B2
60) Q—K4	R—Kt2
61) Q—B5?	

White has consistently materialised his plan and by means of the subtle manoeuvring of his Queen he has secured the Kt's co-operation after all. Even so this now appears to be not all that important, and certainly not worth the loss of the QRP.

61) .....   R—K2!

62) Kt—Kt5

There was still time to secure the Q-wing with 62) Q—B2 ch, K—Q1; 63) Q—B3. The Kt manoeuvre was tempting enough but it may well have cost him the game.

62)	R—K6
63) Kt—K4	Q—K2!
64) Kt—B6	K—Kt1!

That seals the fate of the QRP; ever since the 38th move Black has defended himself quite excellently and now he has reached what ought to be a winning position.

65) P—Kt3   R×RP
66) K—R3   R—R8

By 66) ...Q×P he would have allowed White to secure a draw by perpetual check but Black, of course, is now trying to win the game.

67) Kt—Q5   R—R8 ch
68) K—Kt2   Q—KR2
69) Q×Q(forced)   R×Q
70) K—B3   K—Kt2
71) P—Kt4   K—B3
72) K—K4   R—R1?

This plausible move gives White a hidden and subtle chance of a draw. He ought to have played 72) ...R—Q2 thereby forcing either the retreat of the Kt or the removal of the R from its seventh rank.

73) Kt—K3!   R—K1 ch
74) K—Q4   R—Q1 ch
75) K—K4

White will not have his K separated from the passed pawns under any circumstances and, in the end, this tactic proves to be right. A forced win for Black seems no longer evident and the text move after a keen but short struggle will lead to a clearly drawn position. [A perfectly correct observation but 'after the event'. During the game neither Alekhine nor Capablanca or any other of the grandmasters assembled were that sure of the draw. As a matter of fact big bets were

layed on the younger Lasker to win the game but then, to a certain extent, the wish may have been father to the thought! —Translator's note]

75) .....   P—R4!
76) P×P   P—Kt5
77) P—R6(best)   K—B4
78) P—R7!   P—Kt6
79) Kt—Q1   R—QR1
80) P—Kt5   R×P
81) P—Kt6   R—Q2
82) Kt—Kt2   R—Q7
83) K—B3!

The point of Emanuel Lasker's brilliant defence. Naturally on account of 84) P—Kt7 the Knight is taboo and if Black wishes to continue playing for a win he has to allow the opponent's K to approach his passed pawns.

83) .....   R—Q1
84) K—K4   R—Q7
85) K—B3   R—Q1
86) K—K4   K—Q3

Both Pawns are lost but the final position, oddly enough, cannot be won in spite of the substantial material superiority

87) K—Q4   R—QB1
88) P—Kt7   K—K3
89) P—Kt8(Q) ch   R×Q
90) K—B4   R—Kt6!
91) Kt—R4   K—B4
92) K—Kt4   K×P
93) Kt—Kt2   K—K5
94) Kt—R4   K—Q5
95) Kt—Kt2   R—KB6

A last attempt to get the King across to Q7 but meanwhile White will have time to get his K to Kt2 and after that

Black will no longer be able to make any headway. An extraordinarily interesting ending.

96)	Kt—R4	R—K6
97)	Kt—Kt2	K—K5
98)	Kt—R4	K—B6
99)	K—R3	K—K5
100)	K—Kt4	K—Q5
101)	Kt—Kt2	R—R6
102)	Kt—R4	K—Q6
103)	K × P	K—Q5 ch
	Drawn	

(Notes by ALEKHINE in the Book of th Teournament.)

GAME 64

SLAV DEFENCE

MARSHALL–LASKER

9th round, New York, March 1924

1)	P—Q4	P—Q4
2)	P—QB4	P—QB3
3)	P × P	P × P
4)	Kt—QB3	Kt—KB3
5)	Q—Kt3	P—K3
6)	B—B4	Kt—B3
7)	Kt—B3	B—K2
8)	P—K3	Kt—KR4

Probably the best defence since Black retains the two Bishops with good chances of a Kingside attack. The fact that White will soon obtain a decisive advantage is merely due to a tactical slip on Black's part.

9)	B—Kt3	O—O
10)	B—Q3	P—B4

The threat being ...Kt—B3—K5. White is quite right to get rid of this tiresome Kt at once.

11)	B—K5	Kt—B3
12)	B × Kt!	R × B
13)	R—QB1	B—Q3
14)	Kt—QR4	

A cunning move! Black was just about to complete his development rather favourably by playing his QB via Q2 and K1 over to KR4 so as to utilise it for an imminent K-wing attack. Now by the very threat of posting his Kt on QB5 White distracts the opponent's Q to his QR4 whereafter ...B—Q2 is ruled out by Q × KtP. Of course Black could then restore the old position by ...Q—Q1 but White was right to hope that his opponent would not accept an immediate draw, the less so since White seemed to have lost a tempo.

14)	.....	Q—R4 ch
15)	Kt—B3	

After 15) K—K2 Black could have forced an exchange of the White KB by ...Kt—Kt5, since obviously 16) B—Kt1 was ruled out on account of ...P—QKt3; 17) P—QR3, B—R3 ch, etc.

15)	.....	R—Kt1?

Black is overrating his position and thereby soon drifts into disadvantage, (certainly not by the manoeuvre ...Kt—KR4 and ...P—KB4 which has been criticised by various commentators). What Black should have played in these circumstances was either 15) ...Q—Q1; (putting White into the same old quandary if he insisted on playing for a win) or 15) ...Q—Kt5 which would have relieved the pressure on QKt2 as well.

16) 0—0

Now we can see the disadvantage of Black's last move, robbing his Bishop of the retreat at Kt1. White is now threatening Kt—Kt5 either so as to exchange or to occupy the square K5.

16) .....   P—QR3
17) Kt—QR4   B—Q2
18) Kt—B5   Q—B2

A sad necessity since ...B—K1 would be refuted by 19) Kt×P, Q—B2; 20) Kt×B! R×Q; 21) Kt×B, followed by Kt× R ch etc.

19) Kt—K5

With the occupation of this key point White obtains a far superior position. Obviously if Black were to go in for winning a P on his K4 he would lose the exchange.

19) .....   B—K1
20) P—B4

By 20) Kt×KP, R×Kt; 21) Q×P, Q—K2; 22) B×P, Kt—Q1 23) B×R ch he could gain some material but since Black, with his two Bishops, would have retained good defensive chances, White wisely prefers his simple text move.

20) .....   Q—K2
21) P—QR3

Black cannot afford a merely passive resistance since White would simply clear his QKt-file for a push of the Pawn and the final break-through on the Q-wing.

21) .....   R—R3

Starting a wing attack which in view of White's powerful centre would seem to be condemned to failure; however there is nothing else that Black could do.

22) R—KB2   P—KKt4
23) P—Kt3   K—R1?

Even after 23) ...P×BP 24) P×P, K—R1; 25) R—Kt2 White would have much the better of it.

24) Q—Q1!

Preparing for P—QKt4 and thereby forcing the opponent to take drastic counter measures.

24) .....   P×P
25) Kt×Kt!   P×Kt

More obvious was ...B×Kt; 26) P×P, B—K1 etc. But there is much to be said for the idea of having the R co-operate on the Kt-file at once. He should not have given up his R-Pawn, though, on his next move.

26) KP×P   Q—KKt2?

The decisive mistake since now Black loses a Pawn without any equivalent at all. By ...P—QR4 he could still have put up more determined resistance whereas now White ought to win quite easily.

27) B×RP   B—R4
28) Q—Q2   R—Kt1

29) B—K2!   B—K1

The implied threat of ...R × RP can be parried without any difficulty and certainly was not worth a Pawn.

30) Q—K3   R—B3

The KP wasn't really threatened by the Kt yet, but by his following move White forces Black to provide further coverage.

31) B—B1   Q—K2

32) P—QR4

Against the further advance of this Pawn Black would seem to be completely defenceless.

32) .....   P—KR4

33) R—Kt2

Having achieved a clearly winning position White starts to get flustered. Or course here as well as on the next move the advance of the passed Pawn was indicated the more so since Black doesn't really threaten anything on the other wing.

33) .....   P—R5

34) Kt—Q3?

Fiddling and quite unnecessary too but even such unprecise play still ought to suffice to materialise White's superiority.

34) .....   Q—QR2!

35) P—Kt3   R—Kt2

36) Kt—K5   P × P

37) P × P   Q—Kt3

38) P—R5!

Since now the pawn as such cannot be easily exploited White rightly uses it for opening new files.

38) .....   Q × RP

39) Kt × P   Q—Kt3

40) Kt—K5   R—QB2

40) ...Q—Kt2 would simply be countered by 41) R—QKt1 and the push of the passed pawn.

41) R × R   Q × R

42) P—KKt4!   P × P

43) Kt × P!

This move, condemned by various critics, is in fact the quickest road to victory. After 43) R × P Black could have held out a little longer by ...R—R3 44) Q—Kt3, B—KB2! etc.

43) .....   R × P

44) Q × P?

A mistake which jeopardises the win. By 44) B—Q3! with the threat of 45) Q—R3 ch etc. he could have won at once.

44) .....   R × B ch!

45) K × R   B—Kt4 ch!

Evidently it was this check that Marshall had overlooked having only considered 45) ...Q—B8 ch 46) Q—K1, B—Kt4 ch; 47) K—B2, Q—B5 ch 48) K—Kt1, Q × P ch: 49) K—R1, which indeed would have given him an easy win.

46) R—K2

The only chance since 46) K—B2, Q—B7 ch 47) K—B3, Q—Q8 ch would have been even more unpleasant.

46) .....   B × R ch

47) Q × B   Q—B2 ch

48) Q—B2   K—Kt2

...Q × Q ch 49) K × Q would be quite wrong because the

Black QP could then no longer be saved.

49) Kt—K3   B—B5?

A slip which once again saddles him with what ought to be a lost position. In point of fact he could have forced the draw here by the very subtle 49) ...B—R6! as indicated by Edward Lasker. [50) Q×Q ch, K×Q 51) Kt×P, B—Kt7 etc.]

50) K—K2!

After this there would seem to be no adequate defence against Q—Kt2 ch.

50) .....   Q—B2
51) Q—Kt2 ch   K—B1

Position after Black's 51st move

52) Kt×P?

Incredibly artificial play. After 52) Q×P, B×Kt; 53) K×B Black would have had to resign pretty soon as the few 'spite-checks' left to him would soon be exhausted. Now, how-ever, Lasker grasps his chance immediately and forces the draw in a very subtle way.

52) .....   Q—B7 ch
53) K—B3   B—Q7!

The one and only move but quite sufficient.

54) Q—B1

Even 54) Q—B2, Q—Q6 ch 55) K—Kt2 ch, K—K1; wouldn't have been good enough.

54) .....   Q×P ch
55) K—K2 ch

Or 55) K—K4 ch, K—K1; 56) Q—KB6, Q—Kt8 ch; 57) K—K5, Q—Kt1 ch; 58) K—B5, Q—B1 ch; 59) K—K4, Q—Q1!; with a perfectly ade-quate defence.

55) .....   K—K1
56) Q—B5

True enough White will now win a piece but even this is not sufficient to force the win.

56) .....   Q—B5 ch
57) K×B   Q×P ch
58) K—K2   Q—B5 ch
59) K—B2   Q—B4 ch
60) K—Kt2   Q—Q3
61) K—B3   K—Q1!

Preparing for the subsequent neat little stalemate trap.

62) K—K4   Q—K3 ch!
Drawn

(Notes by ALEKHINE in the Book of the Tournament)

GAME 65

FRENCH DEFENCE

LASKER–RETI

10th round, New York, March 1924

1)	P—K4	P—K3
2)	P—Q4	P—Q4
3)	Kt—QB3	Kt—KB3
4)	B—Kt5	B—Kt5
5)	Kt—K2	P×P
6)	P—QR3	B—K2
7)	B×Kt	P×B

*More usual these days is
...B×B; 8) Kt×P, Kt—B3!*
(R.T.)

8) Kt×P   P—KB4

And here the appropriate move
is ...P—QKt3 (R.T.)

9) Kt(4)—B3   B—Q2

That way, White unnecessarily
hampers the development of
his Q-wing. For whatever piece,
B or Kt, now comes to QB3,
it will always give the White
QP a chance to push on with
the gain of a tempo. The
proper move was 9) ...P—
QKt3.

10) Q—Q2   B—Q3

11) 0—0—0   Q—K2?

Losing another tempo. It
would have been much better
to secure the centre by ...P—
QB3. He should avoid castling
altogether; such as 11) ...P—
QB3; 12) Kt—Kt3, Q—R5;
13) Q—K1, K—Q1, followed
by ...P—QR4, as well as
...Kt—QR3. That way he
may well have managed in due
time to conjure up a sort of
attack on the Q-wing.

12) Kt—Kt3

The threat being Kt×KBP,
P×Kt; 14) R—K1, B—K3;
15) P—Q5 with advantage for
White.

12)	.....	Q—R5
13)	Q—K1!	Kt—B3?

Giving the opponent the
chance of opening more lines;
something that, what with the
insecure position of his King,
Black should have avoided at
all costs. He should have
played 13) ...Q—B5 ch followed by ...Kt—QB3.

14)	Kt×P	Q—B5 ch
15)	Kt—K3	Kt×P
16)	P—KKt3	Q—K4
17)	B—Kt2	Kt—B3
18)	P—B4	Q—Kt2
19)	Kt—Kt5!	0—0

By 19) ...0—0—0, Black
might have put up some stiffer
resistance.

20)	Kt×B	P×Kt
21)	R×P	KR—Q1
22)	Q—Q2	B—K1
23)	R—Q1	KR—B1

Position after Black's 23rd move

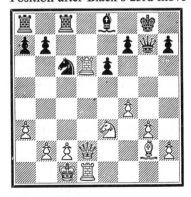

24) P—B5!

Starting the final attack which

will lead to success within a few moves.

24)	P—K4
25) P—B6	Q—B1
26) Kt—B5	K—R1
27) Q—Kt5	R—B2

Losing a Rook, but the position was hopeless anyway.

28) B×Kt	R×B
29) R—Q8	R(3)—B1
30) Q—Kt7 ch	Q×Q
31) P×Q ch	K—Kt1
32) Kt—K7 ch	Resigns

(Notes by ALEKHINE in the Book of the Tournament)

GAME 66

RUY LOPEZ

LASKER–JANOWSKI

12th round, New York, April 1924

1) P—K4	P—K4
2) Kt—KB3	Kt—QB3
3) B—Kt5	P—QR3
4) B—R4	Kt—B3
5) 0—0	P—Q3
6) R—K1	B—Kt5
7) P—B3	B—K2
8) P—KR3?	

A mistake. That move certainly shouldn't be played until Black has castled.

8)	B—R4
9) P—Q3	Q—Q2

A subtle move, making Black's advantage quite evident. His idea is an immediate attack on the K-wing by ...P—KKt4, possibly after preparation by ...P—KR3. Another object of Black's move is to stop White's P—KKt4 as well as to prepare for 0—0—0. Lasker immediately recognises his danger and tries to meet the threat by exchanges.

10) B×Kt	Q×B
11) B—Kt5	B—Kt3
12) QKt—Q2	P—KR3

13) B×Kt	B×B
14) Kt—B1	0—0
15) Kt—K3	

White has no unassailable space for his Knights and hence no proper co-operation for his pieces. The Black Bishops, on the other hand, are very strongly posted.

15)	QR—K1
16) Q—Kt3	B—Q1
17) Q—Q5?	

After this second slip, White has a strategically lost game. Since Black wasn't yet threatening anything, White, rather than go in for that unfavourable exchange of Queens, should have tried for some counter-play on the Q-wing, starting with a push of the QRP.

17)	Q×Q
18) Kt×Q	P—KB4
19) Kt—Q2	B—B2!

Forestalling the manoeuvre P×P, coupled with Kt—K4 etc.

20) Kt—K3	P—B5!

What with his cramped position, White will not, in the long run, be able to cope with both threats of a break-through

by ...P—Q4 and ...P—
KKt4. Janowski's play, up to
his 38th move, (when he
actually reaches winning position) is most impressive.

21) Kt(3)—B4   B—B3
22) P—QR4

This move's only object is to
worry the opponent a little
about coverage for his QKt2.
It just goes to show how
hopeless White's position
really is.

22) .....   R—Q1
23) Kt—R5   R—Kt1
24) Kt—B3   P—KKt4
25) Kt—R2   P—R4
26) Kt—B4   B—K3
27) P—B3

Now the Kt on R2 will be
excluded for a very long time
from any co-operation in the
centre. But then, the Kt is
badly needed to stop ...P—
Kt5.

27) .....   KR—Q1
28) R—K2   K—B2
29) P—R5   R—Kt1
30) R—R4   QR—Q1

So as to hand the job of
covering QKt2 to the Bishop.

31) R—Kt4   B—B1
32) P—QKt3   R—R1

He threatens doubling Rooks
on the KR-file, followed by
...P—Kt5.

33) Kt—Kt2

The idea being Kt—Q1—B2.

33) .....   P—Q4!

Perfectly timed.

34) P×P

Otherwise, after ...QP×P;
35) QP×P, Black would win

by his domination of the Q-file,
whereas 35) BP×P would be
countered by ...P—Kt5.

34) .....   R×P
35) R—B4   P—B3
36) P—QKt4

To bottle up the R that way
would seem to be somewhat
dangerous for White.

36) .....   B—B4
37) R—Q2   R(1)—Q1

Here White should have lost
a P without any equivalent
whatever.

38) K—B2   R—Kt4?

Having played extremely well
so far, Black now begins to
'fiddle' by a series of oddly
artificial moves. And even
though for a long time yet, he
still has the win safely in hand,
it will become more and more
difficult until finally the tables
will be turned on him entirely.
The proper move, of course,
was, 38) ...B×P; 39) Kt×B,
R×Kt; 40) R×R, R×R; 41)
K—K2, P—K5, and Black
would remain a P up in a much
superior position.

39) K—K2   R(4)—Q4

Black now sees that 39)
...B—K3 would really threaten
nothing, since after 40) ...B×
R; 41) P×B, his own R would
get lost as well.

40) K—Q1

It is certainly Lasker's best
chance in that way to tempt
Fate, or rather the opponent,
as to whether he will take the
P at Q3 with what should have
been a winning position.

40) .....   K—K3?

Naturally he should have played ...B×P. The sequel might have been 41) Kt×B, R×Kt; 42) R×R, R×R ch; 43) K—B2, P—K5!, and White musn't play 44) Kt—B1 on account of ...P×BP etc.

41) K—B2   B—K2

The Black position is so strong that even this move, coupled with the next one, should be good enough to force the win.

42) Kt—B1   P—B4!

The threat being 43) ...P×P; 44) P×P, R—Kt4; 45) K—Kt3, R—Q5! etc.

43) P×P   B×P
44) R—R4   R(1)—Q2
45) R—Q1   B—QR2

This is rather better than B—K2, which would have given White a chance to put up some defence by 46) P—QB4, followed by Kt—R2.

46) R—R3   P—Kt5
47) RP×P   P×P
48) P—B4   R(4)—Q3
49) Kt—Q2

For the first time in this game, one of the Knights gets a look-in.

49) .....   B—K6?

It would have been much better either to play 49) ...R—R2, or better still ...B—Q5; 50) Kt—K4, B×Kt; 51) K×B, B×Kt; 52) P×B, R—R2, with a very favourable ending.

50) R—KR1   P×P
51) P×P   R—Kt2
52) R—R2   B—Kt8

Here, and in his next moves,

Black is chasing a chimera. But by now, it was very difficult to win the game at all. If ...R—Kt6, White would have countered 53) R—QKt3, and then if 53) ...R—Q2, White, by means of 54) Kt—R4, would have had various counter-chances.

53) R—K2   R—Kt6

Losing a tempo quite unnecessarily. Much better chances were offered by ...R—Q1, followed by ...R—Kt1.

54) Kt—Q1!   R—Q2
55) R—Kt3   R(2)—Kt2
56) Kt—B3!

Now White is definitely saved.

56) .....   B—K6
57) Kt—Q5   R—Kt7

Position after Black's 57th move

58) R×B!

This combination, long prepared and patiently worked for, should win a P for White. Even so, this should hardly be enough to force the game. But Black by now is so utterly demoralised as to lose a piece quite unnecessarily.

58)	P×R	71) Kt—K4	R—Q6
59) R—Kt6 ch	K—Q2!	72) R×P	R—QKt7
	(K—B2?)	73) Kt—B5	R×P
60) Kt×P	K—B2?	74) R—K8 ch	K—B2

An utterly incomprehensible move which would seem to make any further resistance hopeless. After ...R—K7!; 61) R×KtP, K—B3; 62) R×R, R×Kt; 63) Kt—K4, R×BP, the game would probably have come to be drawn.

75) R—K6	R—QB7
76) Kt×P ch	K—Kt2
77) Kt(6)—B5 ch	K—R2
78) R—K7 ch	K—R1
79) Kt—R4	R—KR7

61) Kt×B	R—R2
62) Kt—Q6	R(2)—R7
63) Kt—K4	R—R8
64) K—B3	R—B8 ch
65) K—Kt4	R—Q8
66) Kt—Kt3	R×QP
67) R×P ch	K—B1
68) R—B7	R—QKt7
69) Kt—B5	R—Q3
70) R—B5	R—K7

Black has shrewdly put up a little stalemate trap: 80) Kt—Kt6, K—Kt1; 81) P—R6??, R×Kt ch; 82) K×R, R—Kt7 ch etc. But Lasker isn't likely to fall for a thing like that.

80) Kt(3)—B5	K—Kt1
81) R—Kt7 ch	K—B1
82) P—R6	Resigns

(Notes by ALEKHINE in the Book of the Tournament)

GAME 67

SICILIAN

LASKER–BOGOLJUBOV

13th round, New York, April 1924

1) P—K4	P—QB4
2) Kt—KB3	P—K3
3) P—Q4	P×P
4) Kt×P	Kt—KB3
5) B—Q3	Kt—B3
6) Kt×Kt	KtP×Kt
7) 0—0	B—K2?

The correct move was 7) ...P—Q4. Black should have moved his KB only after White's 8) Q—K2. After the text move the Black QP will be permanently backward and, moreover, he will be inevitably weakened on the Black squares.

8) P—K5!	Kt—Q4
9) Q—Kt4	P—Kt3
10) Kt—Q2	P—KB4

Even though every immediate danger on the K-wing is thereby eliminated, the future of the QP looks bleaker still. However, in making this move Black was following up a certain tactical idea.

11) Q—B3	Kt—Kt5

The idea being either to secure the two Bishops or to win a P to make up for his unfavourable Pawn formation.

12) Kt—B4	B—R3

The threat now being 13) ...B×Kt as well as 13)

...Kt×BP. Obviously White could easily parry both threats by means of 13) Q—K2 but he prefers a rather more energetic continuation.

13) B—Q2!

An interesting sacrifice of a Pawn, the idea being to exploit the opponent's weakness in the centre by means of speedily mobilising all his available pieces as well as deplacing the Black Kt.

13) .....   Kt×BP

Black accepts the sacrifice in the hope that by being able in due time to return the P he might have some chance of improving his position. It is most interesting to see how Lasker scotches this notion.

14) QR—Q1!   0—0
15) Kt—Q6!

Now the deeper idea of the sacrifice becomes quite clear. It is the precarious position of the Kt which White will exploit for the achievement of some decisive advantage; as for the backward QP, Black can now secure it by blocking the file.

15) .....   Kt—Q5
16) Q—K3   B×B
17) Q×B   B×Kt

Practically every one of Black's moves is forced. Obviously he mustn't play 17) ...P—QB4 since 18) B—KR6, B×Kt; 19) P×B, R—KB2; 20) P—QKt4 would regain the P with a splendid position.

18) P×B   P—K4

19) KR—K1   Q—B3
20) B—B3

Now we can see the result of the attack so flawlessly carried through with such inconspicuous means. Black has no adequate defence against such threats as P—KB4 or Q—B4ch, nor can he improve his inferior position by returning his material gains.

Position after White's 20th move

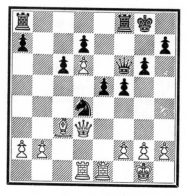

20) .....   QR—K1
21) P—B4!   Q—R5

Or ...Q—KB2; 22) R×P, R×R?; 23) Q×Kt and wins.

22) Q—B4 ch   Kt—K3
23) B×P   K—B2

This doesn't seem to make much sense. It was certainly preferable to play 23) ...Q—Q1.

24) R—K3!

The threat being 25) R—KR3.

24) .....   Q—Q1
25) R—QKt3   Q—R4?

The invasion of the Rook at QKt2 had to be stopped at all costs. ...Q—R1 certainly would have put up some more tenacious resistance.

26) R—Kt7   Q—B4 ch
27) R—Q4!

This subtlety was evidently overlooked by Black when he made his 25th move. He only allowed for the immediate exchange of Queens which, indeed, might have given him some reasonable drawing chances.

27) .....   R—Q1
28) P—QKt4   Q × Q
29) R × Q   P—Kt4
30) R × RP   Kt × P

He should certainly have saved his QBP by ...K—Kt3. What with the opponent's two united passed Pawns, his position is now quite hopeless.

31) B × Kt   P × B
32) R × QBP   R—KKt1

This R manoeuvre doesn't lead to anything. But whatever Black plays, it doesn't really much matter anyway by now.

33) K—B2   R—Kt3
34) P—Kt5   K—K3
35) R—B2   R(3)—Kt1
36) K—B3

This prolongs the struggle quite needlessly. Much simpler would have been 36) P—QR4, R—QR1; 37) R × R, R × R; 38) R—QB4, followed by K—B3 and a very simple win.

36) .....   R—QR1!
37) R—K2 ch   K × P
38) R—Q2 ch   K—B4

39) R(2) × P   K × P
40) R × R   R × R
41) R × P   R—R6 ch!

A little *finesse*. After ...R × P; 42) R—Kt7, R—R5; 43) R—Kt5 Black would have had to resign at once. Now he can still hang on to his last P for a while.

42) K × P   R × P
43) R—Kt7   R—B7 ch
44) K—K5   P—B5!
45) K—K4!   K—B4

45) ...P—B6 would be countered by 46) P × P, R × P; 47) R—QB7 and wins at once.

46) P—R4   K—Q3
47) P—R5   R—B8
48) R—Kt4   R—KR8?

But here, if he wanted to play on at all, he had to go in for ...P—B6; 49) P × P, K—K3. As it is, and what with the White K stepping up, he hasn't the ghost of a chance.

49) R—Kt5   R—R5
50) K—B5   K—K2
51) K—Kt6   K—B1
52) R—R5   R—R7
53) R—R2   P—B6
54) R—R8 ch   K—K2
55) P × P   R—Kt7 ch
56) K—B5   R—KR7
57) R—R7 ch   K—K1
58) K—Kt6   R—Kt7 ch
59) K—B6   R—KB7
60) R—R8 ch   K—Q2
61) R—R3   Resigns

(Notes by ALEKHINE in The Book of the Tournament)

GAME 68
RETI
RETI-LASKER

New York, 16th round, April 1924

1) Kt—KB3   P—Q4
2) P—B4   P—QB3
3) P—QKt3   B—B4
4) P—Kt3   Kt—B3
5) B—KKt2   QKt—Q2
6) B—Kt2   P—K3
7) 0—0   B—Q3
8) P—Q3   0—0
9) QKt—Q2

9) *Kt—QB3 is preferable with the idea of then countering ...P—K4 by 10) P×P, P×P; 11) P—K4! hence Black's best answer would be 9) ...Q—K2* (R.T.)

9) .....   P—K4!
10) P×P   P×P
11) R—B1   Q—K2
12) R—B2

Playing according to his very own system Reti is soon forced into a line which at best seems to promise him the chance of the draw.

12) .....   P—QR4!

Yielding his QKt4 but at the same time weakening the opponent's corresponding square as well as his QKtP. On the whole this would seem to be good business for Black.

13) P—QR4   P—R3

Preparing for the following retreat of the Bishop thereby strengthening the threat of ...P—K5 since the White Kt would no longer attack the Bishop from Q4.

14) Q—R1   KR—K1
15) R(1)—B1   B—R2
16) Kt—B1

Providing against the now fairly strong threat of ...P—K5—K6.

16) .....   Kt—B4

By means of 16) ...P—K5; 17) P×P, P×P; 18) Kt—Q4, P—K6; 19) Kt×P, B×R; 20) R×B, Black could have won the exchange but as then the White Bishops might have been fairly powerful Lasker prefers, quite rightly, to do without this material gain and to increase the pressure instead.

17) R×Kt

With excellent positional judgement White seeks his salvation in a sacrifice facilitating the elimination of one of the centre pawns.

17) .....   B×R
18) Kt×P   QR—B1
19) Kt—K3   Q—K3
20) P—R3

White hasn't anything really to show for the exchange and has to wait and see for the time being. Even so, the seemingly harmless text move is not without an idea which, oddly enough, Dr. Lasker fails to recognise.

20) .....   B—Q3?

An error which might have had grievous consequences. What Black ought to have done was ...P—QKt3 so as to secure the Q-wing as well as the position of the Bishop. After 21) P—Q4 he could still

have got sufficient counter play
by occupying his K5.

21) R × R   R × R
22) Kt—B3?

White fails to grasp his opportunity with the fairly obvious
Kt(5)—Kt4,   Kt × Kt;   23)
P × Kt he could get a second
pawn for the exchange thereby
eliminating any risk of loss to
say the very least. His poor
text-move is almost incomprehensible but now Lasker
gets his teeth into the game
and won't let go.

22) .....   B—K2
23) Kt—Q4   Q—Q2
24) K—R2?

Beginning a somewhat artificial manoeuvre the inadequacy of which is proved by
Lasker with admirable precision. White might have had
more chances of a draw by
24) Kt—Kt5.

24) .....   P—R4

This advance and the following
exchange will deprive the
White King of one of his
protecting Pawns which will
prove to be decisive. It is now
clear that the King stood
much safer on Kt1 and should
have remained there.

25) Q—R1

A move that 'looks good' but
effects nothing. Black could
have simply covered the P by
...R—Q1 but what he actu-
ally plays is much more consistent and energetic.

25) .....   P—R5
26) Kt × P   P × P ch

27) P × P   Kt × Kt
28) B × Kt   B—B3!

This horrible pin will mark the
downfall of White in spite of
his now very brilliant defence.

29) B × P   R—B4
30) B—R6!

The threat being 31) Q—R8 ch
etc.

30) .....   B—Kt3
31) Q—Kt7   Q—Q1
32) P—QKt4

But not 32) P—K3 on account
of ...B × Kt; 33) B × B, R—
B7 ch; 34) K—R1, Q—Q3;
etc.

32) .....   R—B2

Position after White's 33rd move

33) Q—Kt6   R—Q2!

The point of Lasker's winning
manoeuvre. After the exchange
of Queens White must not play
35) Kt—B6 since ...R—Q3
36) B × B, R × Kt would cost
him the other Bishop. Hence
he must concede to the opponent his immensely strong
passed pawn which will bring
about the decision in a few
moves.

34) Q×Q ch   R×Q
35) P—K3   P×P
36) K—Kt2   B×Kt
37) P×B

The more obvious 37) B×B wouldn't have saved the game either. True enough the combination starting with 37) ...R×B could not then have forced the issue, but by the simple B—KB4 followed by ...B—Q2 Black would have still won quite comfortably by means of his passed Pawn.

37) .....   B—B4
38) B—Kt7   B—K3

So as to counter 39) P—R5 by ...B—Q4 ch, etc.

39) K—B3   B—Kt6
40) B—B6   R—Q3
41) B—Kt5   R—B3 ch
42) K—K3   R—K3 ch
43) K—B4

He has no adequate move left since 43) K—B3 is countered by ...B—Q8 ch etc. and 43) K—Q2 by ...R—Kt3 44) P—Kt4, R—KR3; winning a pawn.

43) .....   R—K7
44) B—B1   R—B7
45) B—K3   B—Q4
Resigns

(Notes by ALEKHINE in the Book of the Tournament)

GAME 69

ENGLISH

TARTAKOWER–LASKER

21st round, New York, April 1924

1) P—QB4   P—K4
2) P—QR3   Kt—KB3
3) P—K3   B—K2
4) Q—B2   0—0
5) Kt—QB3   P—Q3
6) Kt—KB3   R—K1
7) B—K2   B—B1
8) 0—0   Kt—B3
9) P—Q4   B—Kt5
10) P—Q5

If White had tried to maintain the tension by 10) R—Q1, Black might well have replied ...P—K5, but there is much to be said for the text move which seems to promise White a comfortable initiative on the Q-wing.

10) .....   Kt—K2
11) P—R3   B—Q2
12) Kt—KR2   Q—B1
13) P—K4   Kt—Kt3
14) P—B4?

He misjudges the position. It would have been wiser to let sleeping dogs lie on the K-wing and to start activities on the Q-wing by 14) P—QKt4. True enough, it wouldn't have been easy to break through on the QB-file, but at any rate it would have been a plan consonant with the positional possibilities. As for the text move, White was probably tempted by the temporary gain of space, but he allows the opponent some more vital and permanent advantages: the domination of the Black squares and the weakness of

White's QB4. It is quite remarkable how Lasker proceeds to exploit these minute advantages.

14) .....   P×P
15) B×P   Kt×B
16) R×Kt   B—K2!

The beginning of a deeply considered and typically Laskerian regrouping manoeuvre by means of which every trace of danger is eliminated on the K-wing.

17) R(1)—KB1   R—B1
18) Q—Q3   B—K1
19) Q—Kt3   Q—Q1
20) Kt—Q1   Kt—Q2
21) Kt—K3

White under-estimates the force of the counter move. By 21) Kt—B3 or also by 21) P—KR4 he might at least have avoided material disadvantage, even though nis positional inferiority was no longer to be denied.

21) .....   B—Kt4
22) R—Kt4

22) R—KB5 would have been countered by ...B—KR5 followed by ...Kt—K4. By his text move, White hopes for a chance of sacrificing the exchange with some advantage. In point of fact, Lasker will take it in his very own way and without leaving the opponent any chance at all.

22) .....   P—KB3

The threat being 23) ...P—KR4.

23) Q—B2   P—KR4
24) R—Kt3   P—R5!

Certainly not: ...B—R5 which, after 25) R×P ch, would have given White some chances.

25) R—Kt4   B—R4

Thereby the fate of the game is sealed.

26) Kt—B5   B×R
27) Kt×B   Q—K1
28) B—B3   Kt—K4
29) Kt×Kt   Q×Kt
30) Kt×RP   B×Kt
31) Q×B

In the course of the liquidation, Black has given up one of his Pawns, but the position is now so much simplified that the exploitation of his material advantage won't give him any trouble at all.

31) .....   P—KB4!

This would seem to be the shortest way to victory.

32) P×P   R×P
33) R—K1   Q×KtP
34) B—Kt4   Q—Q5 ch
35) K—R2   R(1)—KB1
36) Q—K7   Q—B5 ch
37) K—R1   R—K4
38) R×R

Putting his last hope in the QP. After 38) B—K6 ch, K—R2; 39) R—KKt1, Black wins quite easily by ...Q—B7 etc.

38) .....   P×R
39) Q×BP   P—K5!
40) Q—K7

(See diagram on following page)

40) .....   Q—B3!

The *coup de grâce*. The ending is easily won for Black after 41) Q×KP, Q—B8 ch; 42)

K—R2, Q—B5 ch; 43) Q×Q,
R×Q etc.

41)	Q×KtP	Q—R8 ch
42)	K—R2	Q—K4 ch
43)	K—Kt1	R—Kt1
44)	Q—Q7	R—Kt8 ch
45)	K—B2	P—K6 ch
46)	K—K2	R—Kt7 ch
47)	K—K1	Q—B6 ch
48)	K—B1	Q—B8 ch
	Resigns	

(Notes by ALEKHINE in The Book
of the Tournament)

Position after White's 40th move

GAME 70

RUY LOPEZ

LASKER–MARSHALL

Last round, New York, 1924

1)	P—K4	P—K4
2)	Kt—KB3	Kt—QB3
3)	B—Kt5	P—QR3
4)	B×Kt	QP×B
5)	P—Q4	B—Kt5

This somewhat queer gambit
is not recommendable since all
that Black gets for his pains is
the labour of trying to regain
the gambit Pawn, with more
or less success. It would have
been much better and simpler
to play ...P×P leading to the
exchange of Queens and the
standard line of this variation.

6)	P×P	Q×Q ch
7)	K×Q	0—0—0 ch
8)	K—K1	

Much better than K—K2 which
would give Black the chance by
means of ...P—KB3, either
to regain his Pawn at once, or
to open the centre files.

8)	.....	B—QB4
9)	P—KR3	B—R4
10)	B—B4	P—B4

An interesting move and as
likely as not Black's most
promising continuation. 11)
P×P would now be countered
by ...B×Kt; 12) P×B,
KKt—K2 meaning that he
would still maintain some
pressure on the KB-file.

| 11) | QKt—Q2 | Kt—K2 |
| 12) | B—Kt5! | |

The threat being 13) Kt—QKt3
as well as P×P, thereby
forcing the exchange of the
tiresome QB.

12)	.....	B×Kt
13)	P×B	KR—K1
14)	R—Q1	

But not 14) P×BP on account
of ...R—Q4.

| 14) | ..... | P×P |
| 15) | P×P | |

If 15) Kt×P instead the answer
is ...B—Q5 whereas now
White can counter this by
playing his Kt to QB4.

15)	P—R3
16) B—R4	B—Q5
17) Kt—B4	P—KKt4

Position after Black's 17th move

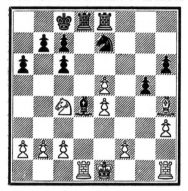

18) P—QB3!

This, at long last, clears the situation, for the subsequent exchange will strengthen White's centre position quite considerably. Nor will it make much difference that Black, in the further course of the game, does succeed in regaining his gambit Pawn after all.

18)	Kt—Kt3
19) P × B	

Simplest.

19)	Kt × B
20) K—K2	R—Q2
21) P—B3!	Kt—Kt3

If ...R(1)—Q1 White could continue by 22) P—Q5, P × QP; 23) P—K6, etc.

22) Kt—K3

By means of 22) P—QKt4 White could have easily avoided the following liquidation in the centre but there was really no need for it since he maintains his advantage in any case.

22)	P—B4
23) P × P	Kt—B5 ch
24) K—B2	R × R
25) R × R	R × P

He could have offered somewhat better resistance by ...Kt × P ch; 26) K—Kt3, Kt—B5; 27) Kt—Q5, Kt—Kt3;

26) Kt—Q5!   Kt × P ch

Now the Kt remains locked out and White will achieve two united passed Pawns; but even if the Kt had retreated White could have easily won by 27) P—Kt4.

27) K—Kt3   P—Kt5

That is the resource that Black had relied on [28) P × P, Kt—Kt4] etc., but Lasker's next move puts paid to these hopes.

28) Kt—B6!	P—KR4
29) P—B4	R × BP
30) R—K1!	

But certainly not at once P—K5 on account of 30) ...P—R5 ch; 31) K × RP, Kt × P etc.

30)	R—QKt4
31) P—K5	K—Q1
32) Kt × RP	K—K2
33) P—B5	Kt—Kt4

Otherwise the further advance of the passed Pawn would be immediately decisive.

34) K × P	Kt—R2
35) Kt—B4	R × KtP
36) Kt—Q5 ch	K—Q2
37) P—K6 ch	K—Q3
38) P—K7!	K × Kt
39) R—K6!	

Now Black has to give up his

Rook for the passed Pawn which obviously makes any further resistance hopeless.

39) .....   R—Kt7 ch
40) K—B4   R—Kt1
41) P—K8(Q)   R × Q
42) R × R   P—B4
43) R—Q8 ch   K—B3
44) R—KR8!   Resigns

For he is going to win the Knight into the bargain!

(Notes by ALEKHINE in the Book of the Tournament)

CHAPTER TWENTY-FIVE

Another Great Success

The year after his great triumph in the New York tournament must have been one of the happiest in Lasker's life. Having revealed his undiminished stature as a chess master for all the world to see by winning two great international tournaments in quick succession, he was happy to devote himself to the things that mattered more to him, his research on mathematical and philosophical problems, and above all the verse-drama on which he and his brother Berthold had lavished so much time and care these last six or seven years.

It was a five-act drama entitled *Vom Menschen die Geschichte* and it dealt with man's quest, through the ages, for unattainable perfection—a futile, and yet very exhilarating and glorious quest. It was a poetic dramatisation of Lasker's own philosophy of the '*Unvollendbar*', and at last, after much revision and polishing, the two brothers (and Berthold's wife, that ethereally subtle poetess Else Lasker–Schüler) were satisfied with the result of their seven years' labour, and Martha Lasker started negotiations for getting the play produced.

At that time, in the early autumn 1925, Lasker received an invitation to attend a great international tournament at Moscow, and eager for first hand impressions of the new Soviet State (then still in its infancy) he gladly accepted. But Martha stayed behind, so as not to interrupt the delicate negotiations for the production of the play.

More than thirty years have passed since that first great tournament staged in the USSR, and while for many years now we have come to recognise the consistent and lavish efforts made by the Soviet authorities for sponsoring and organising chess in their own country, we mustn't forget that it took decades to establish their present supremacy in the realm of chess. In 1925 it was still a long way from a chess organisation comprising millions of graded players, thousands of master-candidates, hundreds of masters, and a score of officially and internationally recognised grandmasters. The 1925 tournament was one of the first big steps towards this achievement but even then there were quite a few young Russian players still unknown outside their own country, who were soon to show their mettle. Meanwhile, there were only two Russian-born players who were world-famous, Alekhine and Boglojubov, and both of them were 'White Russians' in exile. But, Bogoljubov, though soon later to be naturalised in Germany, was still the top player of his native country for that one great tournament, and indeed that Moscow tournament turned out to be far and away the greatest success of his career.

Apart from him, ten other 'Western' masters had been invited, foremost among them the world champion Capablanca and his predecessor Emanuel Lasker; the others included such famous grandmasters as Marshall, Rubinstein, Reti, Tartakower. Certainly a fine enough galaxy of talent for the rising Russian generation to learn a thing or two, (which, indeed, was the reason why the Soviet authorities had not grudged the foreign currency required to invite all those stars). Yet, it soon appeared that some of those young Russians hadn't much to learn, and it certainly caused a world-wide sensation when the great Capablanca who had only lost one tournament game in ten years was soundly and brilliantly trounced by two players no one had ever heard of, one Verlinsky and one Iljin-Genevsky.

More than once in chess history one of the less consistently successful grandmasters has outgrown his own stature, as it were, and scored the one glittering and unsurpassable success of a life-time. It happened to Pillsbury at Hastings, 1895, to Marshall at Cambridge Springs, 1904, and to Bogoljubov at Moscow, 1925. Usually a somewhat erratic player found as often among the 'also-runs' as among the first three or four, Bogoljubov just couldn't do wrong this time, winning game after game, with few draws in between, and apparently running away from the field.

As for Capablanca, handicapped by his two unexpected defeats early in the tournament, he was trailing two or three points behind, and it was some time before, by a determined victory over the leader, he managed to creep up a bit. Meanwhile only Lasker, a mere point or two behind, could keep up the murderous pace set by the leader, and he actually caught up with him when Bogoljubov suffered a defeat by Reti.

From now on, with only eight more rounds to go, everybody expected Lasker to get into the lead and to hold on to it and increase it in one of those 'finishing spurts' he had so often achieved in the final stage of a big tournament; and Lasker seemed to have every intention as well as the will-power of doing so when next day, playing young Torre, he had much the better of a difficult game, deliberately complicated in true Lasker fashion. As was his wont he was 'egging on' his opponent to an unsound attack which, ultimately, would seal the attacker's doom, when just as the game was reaching

MOSCOW 1925

		1	2	3	4	5	6	7	8	9	10	11	12	13	14	15	16	17	18	19	20	21	
1	Bogoljubov	×	½	0	½	1	1	0	½	1	1	½	½	1	1	1	1	1	1	1	1	1	15½
2	Lasker	½	×	½	1	½	0	½	1	½	1	1	1	1	1	0	½	1	½	½	1	1	14
3	Capablanca	1	½	×	1	1	½	½	½	½	0	1	½	½	0	½	½	1	1	1	1	1	13½
4	Marshall	½	0	0	×	½	0	1	1	½	0	1	1	1	1	1	1	½	½	0	1	1	12½
5	Tartakower	0	½	0	½	×	½	1	½	½	½	½	1	1	1	½	1	1	½	½	½	½	12
6	Torre	0	1	½	1	½	×	½	0	½	½	0	½	½	1	1	½	0	1	1	1	1	12
7	Reti	1	½	½	0	0	½	×	1	0	1	1	½	0	½	½	1	1	1	½	½	½	11½
8	Romanowsky	½	0	½	0	½	1	0	×	1	0	½	0	0	1	1	1	1	1	1	½	1	11½
9	Grünfeld	0	½	½	½	½	½	1	0	×	1	½	0	½	½	½	1	1	½	½	½	½	10½
10	Iljin Genevsky	0	0	1	1	½	½	0	1	0	×	½	½	1	0	0	½	1	½	½	1	1	10½
11	Bogatyrtchuk	½	0	0	0	½	1	0	½	½	½	×	1	½	½	½	1	½	½	½	½	1	10
12	Rubinstein	½	0	½	0	0	½	½	1	1	½	0	×	0	0	1	0	0	1	1	1	1	9½
13	Spielmann	0	0	½	0	0	½	1	1	½	0	½	1	×	0	1	½	½	½	1	0	1	9½
14	Verlinsky	0	0	1	0	0	0	½	0	½	1	½	1	1	×	1	½	0	½	1	1	0	9½
15	Löwenfisch	0	1	½	0	½	0	½	0	½	1	½	0	0	0	×	1	1	½	½	1	½	9
16	Rabinowitsch	0	½	½	0	0	½	0	0	0	½	0	1	½	½	0	×	1	1	½	1	1	8½
17	Yates	0	0	0	½	0	1	0	0	0	0	½	1	½	1	0	0	×	½	1	0	1	7
18	Gotthilf	0	½	0	½	½	0	0	0	½	½	½	0	½	½	½	0	½	×	1	0	½	6½
19	Sämisch	0	½	0	1	½	0	½	½	½	½	½	0	0	0	½	½	0	0	×	1	0	6½
20	Dus-Chotimirsky	0	0	0	0	½	0	½	0	½	0	½	0	1	0	0	0	1	1	0	×	1	6
21	Subarev	0	0	0	0	½	0	½	0	½	0	0	0	0	1	½	0	0	½	1	0	×	4½

its crisis a messenger entered the room and put a telegram on Lasker's table.

While his opponent was brooding over the dangerously compromised position Lasker idly and somewhat absent-mindedly opened the telegram. It was from his wife and it told him that her negotiations had been successfully concluded, the verse-drama was to be produced, rehearsals were to start soon.

Lasker had never been seen to show his feelings in public as he then did, but he was serenely happy; these were probably the happiest minutes of his life, for that play meant a great deal to him, and its forthcoming production meant the fulfilment of a dream he had hardly expected to come true. Pacing the lobby excitedly and telling all his friends the great news he had received, Lasker was informed that his opponent had made his move and that it was time to return to the game. This, of course, was one of the very rare, if not the only exception to Lasker's iron rule never to allow his concentration to be disturbed during a tournament game. Moreover, his present game, at that precise juncture, required his utmost concentration.

He tried as hard as he knew how, but unable to banish the happy news from his thoughts he made one careless move, and that was enough for young Torre to win the game, while at the next board Bogoljubov was scoring yet another of his many victories. From now on there was nothing to stop him and no one to catch up with him. He won the tournament with the magnificent score of $15\frac{1}{2}$ points (out of 20), Lasker being second with 14, and Capablanca close on his heels with $13\frac{1}{2}$.

A man of fifty-eight need not be ashamed of such a result in such company, and the chess world remarked the significant fact that this was the third consecutive time that Lasker had come out of a tournament ahead of the man who had deprived him of his title. There was a clamour for a return match, but Lasker didn't much worry about it, nor was he very disappointed about his failure to win the first prize at Moscow. He was far too happy about the forthcoming production of his verse-drama.

It duly took place, and it received respectful notices in the more sophisticated organs of the Press. But then it was hardly to be expected that a play of that type—more aptly to be called a sequence of dialogue in verse—would draw the queues that line up for the long run of some popular musical comedy.

GAME 71

RUY LOPEZ

LASKER–ROMANOVSKY

3rd round, Moscow 1925

1)	P—K4	P—K4
2)	Kt—KB3	Kt—QB3
3)	B—Kt5	Kt—B3
4)	0—0	B—K2
5)	R—K1	P—Q3
6)	P—B3	0—0
7)	P—Q4	Kt—Q2

This system of defending the Ruy was Tchigorin's favourite, even through most other Grandmasters never fancied it much. Black must certainly play with great precision so as to equalise.

8)	QKt—Q2	B—B3
9)	Kt—B1	Kt—K2
10)	Kt—Kt3	P—B3
11)	B—R4	P—KKt3

More cautious would be 11) ...Kt—KKt3.

12)	B—R6	R—K1?

Black ought to choose the lesser of the two evils by playing ...B—Kt2. Now his

Position after Black's 19th move

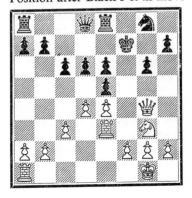

KB2 will be very weak indeed.

13)	B—Kt3	Kt—B1
14)	B—Kt5	B×B
15)	Kt×B	Kt—K3
16)	B×Kt	B×B
17)	Kt×B	P×Kt
18)	Q—Kt4	K—B2
19)	R—K3	Kt—Kt1
20)	P×P	P×P
21)	Kt—R5!	Kt—B3

To take the Kt would be tantamount to suicide, the sequel being 22) Q×P ch, K—Kt2; 23) R—Kt3 ch, K—R1; 24) Q—KB7, R—K2; 25) R×Kt ch and wins easily.

22)	Kt×Kt	K×Kt
23)	R—Q1	Q—B2
24)	R(3)—Q3	

By finally occupying and dominating the open Q-file, White's strategic advantage is quite sufficient for him to continue the attack at leisure.

24)	.....	R—K2
25)	P—KR4	K—Kt2
26)	P—R5	R—KB1
27)	P×P	P×P
28)	Q—Kt5	R—KR1

This is forced on account of the threatened 29) R—KR3.

29)	R—Kt3	R—R3
30)	R—B3	R—K1
31)	R(1)—Q3	Q—K2
32)	Q×KP ch	K—Kt1
33)	R—R3	R×R
34)	R×R	Q—Kt2
35)	Q—Kt5	P—K4
36)	R—Q3	K—R2
37)	Q—Kt4	Q—B3
38)	R—Q7 ch	R—K2
39)	R—Q8	K—Kt2
40)	Q—R3	K—B2

41)	Q—R6	Q—Kt2
42)	Q—K3	Q—B3
43)	Q×P	Q—B5
44)	Q—K3	Q×Q
45)	P×Q	K—B3
46)	R—Q6 ch	K—Kt4
47)	P—R4	K—R4
48)	K—B2	R—B2 ch
49)	K—Kt3	R—K2
50)	P—R5	K—Kt4
51)	P—Kt4	K—R3
52)	P—R6	P×P
53)	R×P	R—QR2

54)	R—B5	R—K2
55)	K—Kt4	R—K3
56)	P—B4	R—K1
57)	P—Kt5	P×P
58)	P×P	R—K3
59)	R—Q5	R—K2
60)	P—Kt6	R—QKt2
61)	R—Kt5	K—Kt2
62)	K—Kt5	K—B2
63)	R—Kt1	K—Kt2
64)	R—Kt2	Resigns

(Notes by BOGOLJUBOV in The Book of the Tournament)

GAME 72

SLAV

RUBINSTEIN–LASKER

6th round, Moscow 1925

1)	P—Q4	P—Q4
2)	P—QB4	P—QB3
3)	P—K3	Kt—B3
4)	Kt—QB3	P—K3
5)	Kt—B3	QKt—Q2
6)	B—Q3	P×P
7)	B×BP	P—QKt4
8)	B—K2	

White has played the opening somewhat passively. The usual continuation here is 8) B—Q3, P—QR3; 9) P—K4, P—QB4; 10) P—K5 etc.

8)	.....	P—QR3
9)	0—0	B—Kt2
10)	P—QKt3	

(*More promising is 10) P—K4, P—QB4; 11) P—K5, Kt—Q4; 12) P—QR4!, P—Kt5; 13) Kt—K4. R.T.*)

10)	.....	B—K2
11)	B—Kt2	0—0
12)	Kt—K5	P—B4

13)	B—B3	Q—B2
14)	Kt×Kt	Kt×Kt
15)	Kt—K4	

White fondly imagines to have the better game and refrains from further exchanges.

15)	.....	QR—Q1
16)	R—B1	Q—Kt1
17)	Q—K2	P×P
18)	P×P?	

Quite unnecessarily White saddles himself with a weak pawn. He should have played 18) B×QP and after ...P—K4 he could have equalised at once by 19) B—QB5!

18)	.....	R—B1
19)	P—Kt3	

In guarding against the threat of ...Kt—B5 White has weakened the long diagonal.

19)	.....	Q—R1
20)	K—Kt2	KR—Q1
21)	R×R	R×R
22)	R—B1	R×R
23)	B×R	P—R3
24)	B—Kt2	Kt—Kt3

25) P—KR3
Why not simply Kt—B5?
25) .....   Q—B1
26) Q—Q3   Kt—Q4!
The idea being to provoke
P—R3.
27) P—R3   Kt—Kt3
28) K—R2   B—Q4
29) K—Kt2   Q—B3
30) Kt—Q2   P—QR4
31) Q—B3
White's position has come to
be very uncomfortable and the
text move is very well exploited
by Lasker.

Position after White's 31st move

31) .....   B×B ch!
The exchange of Queens would
be much weaker since White
could then retake with the
King but if now 31) Q×B
then ...Kt—Q4 33) Q—K4,
P—KB4! and Black will win.
32) Kt×B   Q×Q
33) B×Q   P—R5!
If now P—Kt4 Black will win
the RP by means of ...Kt—B5
and that of course is only
possible because the White Kt
has been shrewdly deviated
to KB3.

34) P×P   P×P
35) K—B1
White hastens to get his King
to help in the defence; 35)
B—Kt4 would have been
countered by ...B×B, 36)
P×B, P—R6 etc.
35) .....   B×P
36) K—K2   K—B1
37) K—Q3   Kt—Q4
38) B—K1   B—Q3
39) K—B4   K—K2
40) Kt—K5   B×Kt
41) P×B   K—Q2
42) B—Q2   P—R4
43) B—B1   K—B3
44) B—R3   Kt—Kt3 ch
45) K—Q4   K—Kt4
46) B—B8   Kt—B5
47) K—B3   P—Kt3
48) P—B4   Kt—K6
49) K—Q3   Kt—Q4
Threatening P—KR5 and if
White were trying to stop this
by 50) P—R4 then ...Kt—Kt3
followed by ...Kt—QB5, the
Black Kt finally aiming at his
KB4.
50) B—R3   P—R5
51) P×P   Kt×P ch
52) K—K4   Kt—R4
Of course not ...Kt×RP on
account of 53) K—B3 followed
by K—Kt3, K—B2; and fur-
ther persecutions of the Kt.
53) K—B3   K—B5
54) B—Kt2   K—Kt6
55) B—R1   P—R6
56) K—Kt4   K—B7
57) K—Kt5   K—Q6!
Resigns

(Notes by BOGOLJUBOV in the Book
of the Tournament)

GAME 73

SICILIAN

ILJIN–GENEVSKY–LASKER

8th round, Moscow 1925

1) P—K4   P—QB4
2) Kt—QB3   P—K3
3) Kt—B3   P—Q3
4) P—KKt3
   With 4) P—Q4, P × P; 5) Kt × P etc. he could enter well-trodden paths.
4) .....   Kt—KB3
5) B—Kt2   B—K2
6) 0—0   0—0
7) P—Kt3
   White is trying to avoid the weakness of QB4, so often a source of embarrassment of this opening.
7) .....   Kt—B3
8) B—Kt2   B—Q2
9) P—Q4   P × P
10) Kt × P   Q—R4
11) Q—Q2   QR—B1
12) QR—Q1   K—R1
   So as to guard against the threat 13) Kt × Kt, followed by Kt—Q5.

Position after White's 13th move

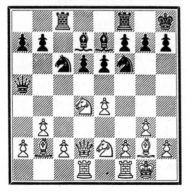

13) Kt(3)—K2!   Q × P
   A rather odd combination of Lasker's which happens to turn out very well indeed; yet, it was fairly risky to give up the Q for and R and a B even though Black does secure a fairly sound position. Lasker probably wished to avoid the exchange of Queens because he considered it to give White a superior position.
14) R—R1   Q × B
15) KR—Kt1   Q × R ch
16) R × Q   KR—Q1
17) P—QB4   Kt—K1
18) P—B4
   White is trying to force matters thereby weakening his K position; a very much safer move was 18) Kt × Kt.
18) .....   P—QR3
19) K—R1   Kt—B2
20) Q—K3   R—QKt1
21) R—Q1   Kt—Kt5
   Whereas Black is strengthening his position with every move White seems to shove around his pieces rather aimlessly.
22) Q—QB3   P—QR4
23) R—R1
   That Rook had no business here!
23) .....   P—QKt3
24) Q—K3?
   A regrettable mistake thereby cutting short a game that had promised to become very interesting and instructive.
24) .....   P—K4!
   Black now wins the exchange and thereafter the ending presents no trouble at all.

25)	Kt—B5	B×Kt	35) Q×Kt	R×Kt
26)	P×B	Kt—B7	36) B—B3	P—R5
27)	Q—QB3	Kt×R	37) P—R5	P—R6
28)	Q×Kt	B—B3	38) Q—K2	R(1)—Q1
29)	Q—KKt1	P—Q4	Resigns	
30)	P×QP	Kt×P		
31)	P×P	B×P		
32)	P—KKt4	P—B3		
33)	P—R4	P—QKt4		
34)	Kt—Q4	Kt—K6!		

A game showing Lasker, the great tactician, at his very shrewdest.

(Notes by Bogoljubov in the Book of the Tournament)

GAME 74

RUY LOPEZ

Lasker–Bogatirtchuk

9th round, Moscow 1925

1) P—K4 P—K4
2) Kt—KB3 Kt—QB3
3) B—Kt5 P—QR3
4) B—R4 Kt—B3
5) 0—0 B—K2
6) R—K1 P—Q3
7) P—B3 Kt—Q2

The so-called Tchigorin defence but 7) ...B—Q2 was simpler.

8) P—Q4 B—B3
9) QKt—Q2 P—QKt4
10) B—Kt3 Kt—R4

If ...P×P White counters 11) P×P and the QP then is of course taboo.

11) B—B2 P—B4

Not so good in this position, as convincingly demonstrated by Lasker. The proper move was 11) ...0—0.

12) Kt—B1 0—0
13) P—QR4 B—Kt2
14) Kt—K3 Kt—Kt3
15) RP×P RP×P
16) Kt—Kt4 Kt—B3?

Black was already in consider-

Position after Black's 16th move

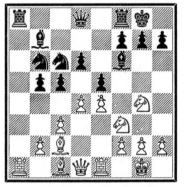

able difficulties, and his only chance was to continue 16) ...P×QP; the text move gives White an opportunity for a winning combination.

17) R×R Kt×R
18) Kt×B ch Q×Kt

Forced because 18) ...KtP×Kt 19) B—R6, R—K1 would lead to a win for White.

19) P—Q5 Kt—R2
20) B—Kt5 Q—Kt3
21) B—K7 P—B3

21) ...R—K1 would be countered by 22) Kt—KR4, Q—R3; 23) Kt—B5, Q—Kt3; 24) B×QP, etc.

22) B×QP!	R—Q1

...R—QB1 would be countered by 23) Q—QR1.

23) B×BP	Kt—B1
24) Q—K2	Q—K1
25) Kt—Q2	Kt—Q3
26) B—Q3	Kt—QB2
27) R—R1	Q—Q2

28) Kt—Kt3	K—R1
29) B—Kt6	R—R1
30) R×R ch	B×R
31) Kt—B5	Q—B1
32) P—QKt4	Resigns

(Notes by BOGOLJUBOV in the Book
of the Tournament)

GAME 75

SLAV

VERLINSKY–LASKER

10th round, Moscow 1925

1) P—Q4	P—Q4
2) Kt—KB3	Kt—KB3
3) P—B4	P—B3
4) Kt—B3	P×P
5) P—QR4	B—B4
6) P—K3	Kt—R3

The idea being to get the Kt
to Kt5. A very remarkable
novelty of Lasker's.

[*As a matter of fact the move
was first played by the Canadian
Maréchal.   R.T.*]

7) B×P	Kt—QKt5
8) 0—0	P—K3
9) Q—K2	B—K2
10) Kt—K5	0—0
11) P—K4	B—Kt3
12) Kt×B	RP×Kt
13) B—K3	Q—R4
14) KR—Q1	QR—Q1
15) P—B3?	P—B4
16) P—Q5	P×P
17) P×P	

Now White has an isolated
Pawn and his K position is less
secure than the opponent's;
moreover his pieces on the
open K-file are placed rather
awkwardly. It might have been
safer for him first to exchange
two pieces on Q5.

17)	P—R3
18) Q—KB2	Q—B2
19) QR—B1	KR—K1
20) P—KKt3	B—Q3

Position after Black's 20th move

21) B—B1?

Evidently so as to parry the
threat ...B×KtP followed by
...R×B but this could have
been more efficiently done by
21) K—Kt2; moreover it is no
proper threat at all. As a
matter of fact, White could
safely play 21) Kt—R2, (so as
to get rid of the awkward
Black Kt) and then ...B×
KtP would be a bad blunder

on account of 22) P×B, R×B; whereafter 23) P—Q6! would make nonsense of Black's entire combination. After the text move, though, White's game is hardly tenable.

21) .....   P—Kt3
22) P—R5
Desperation!
22) .....   P—QKt4
23) B—Kt2   B—B1
24) B—B4   Q×P
25) P—Q6   Q—Kt3
26) Kt—K4   Kt×Kt
27) P×Kt   B×P
28) B×B   R×B

29) R×R   Q×R
30) Q×P   Q×Q ch
31) R×Q   R—Q1
32) R—B3   R–Q8 ch
33) B—B1   R—K8!
34) R—B8 ch   K—R2
35) R—K8   R—Kt8
36) R—KB8   R×P
37) R×P   Kt—B3
38) R—B8   P—R4
39) P—R4   P—R5
40) B—R3   Kt—Q5
41) R—B8   Kt—K7 ch
Resigns

(Notes by BOGOLJUBOV in the Book of the Tournament)

GAME 76

QP GAME

TORRE–LASKER

12th round, Moscow 1925

1) P—Q4   Kt—KB3
2) Kt—KB3   P—K3
3) B—Kt5   P—B4
4) P—K3   P×P
Best here would be ...Q—Kt3 forcing White to play 5) Q—B1.
5) P×P   B—K2
6) QKt—Q2   P—Q3
Lasker treats the opening in a most unorthodox way. The text move aims at getting control of K4.
7) P—B3   QKt—Q2
8) B—Q3   P—QKt3
9) Kt—B4
Waste of time. The normal line of development is 9) Q—K2, B—Kt2; 10) 0—0 etc.
9) .....   B—Kt2
10) Q—K2   Q—B2

11) 0—0   0—0
12) KR—K1   KR—K1
13) QR—Q1   Kt—B1
14) B—B1   Kt—Q4!
15) Kt—Kt5?
White doesn't quite know how to continue now the unfavourable position of the Knight at QB4 is evident. Anyway 15) Kt—R3 was preferable.
15) .....   P—QKt4!
16) Kt—QR3   P—Kt5
This aims at the isolation of the White QP.
17) P×P   Kt×P
18) Q—R5?
Too exuberant. He would have better played B—QKt1.
18) .....   B×Kt
19) B×B   Kt×B
20) R×Kt   Q—R4!
Now the threat is 21) ...Q×R as well as ...P—KR3.
21) P—QKt4!
White copes with one of the

threats only, for obviously the Black Queen mustn't take the pawn on account of 22) R—Kt1, Q—R4; 23) Kt—B4, Q—R6! 24) R×B, Q×R; 25) Kt×P with a level game.

Position after White's 21st move

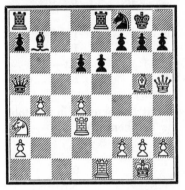

21)	.....	Q—KB4
22)	R—Kt3	P—KR3
23)	Kt—B4!	Q—Q4?

A decisive mistake. Black had to be content with equalising by 23) ...P×B.

| 24) | Kt—K3 | Q—Kt4 |

Now comes a shattering combination. But even by 24) ...Q×QP Black could no

longer save the game. White, (as indicated by the Russian master Sosin in *Shakmaty*) could win by 25) R—Q1!, Q—K5 (or Kt7) 26) B×RP, Kt—Kt3; 27) B—KKt5 with the threat R—KR3 etc.

25)	B—B6!	Q×Q
26)	R×P ch	K—R1
27)	R×P ch	K—Kt1
28)	R—Kt7 ch	K—R1
29)	R×B ch	K—Kt1
30)	R—Kt7 ch	K—R1
31)	R—Kt5 ch	K—R2
32)	R×Q	K—Kt3
33)	R—R3	K×B
34)	R×P ch	K—Kt4
35)	R—R3	KR—Kt1
36)	R—Kt3 ch	K—B3
37)	R—B3 ch	K—Kt3
38)	P—QR3	P—R4
39)	P×P	R×P
40)	Kt—B4	R—Q4
41)	R—B4	Kt—Q2
42)	R×P ch	K—Kt4
43)	P—Kt3	Resigns

A sensational game

(Notes by BOGOLUBOV in The Book of the Tournament)

GAME 77

RUY LOPEZ

LASKER–DUS-CHOTIMIRSKY

13th round, Moscow 1925

1)	P—K4	P—K4
2)	Kt—KB3	Kt—QB3
3)	B—Kt5	P—QR3
4)	B—R4	Kt—B3
5)	0—0	B—K2
6)	R—K1	P—QKt4
7)	B—Kt3	P—Q3
8)	P—B3	Kt—QR4
9)	B—B2	P—B4
10)	P—Q3	0—0
11)	QKt—Q2	R—K1
12)	Kt—B1	Q—B2
13)	B—Kt5	R—Kt1
14)	P—QR3	

A good alternative was 14) Kt—K3.

| 14) | ..... | B—K3 |

15) P—R3   P—R3
16) B—Q2

Lasker has played somewhat aimlessly so far evidently hoping that the opponent would hand him something to bite on; but he is now gradually getting the inferior game.

16) .....   Kt—B3
17) Q—K2   B—KB1
18) P—QR4? P—Kt5!
19) P—B4   Kt—Q2
20) B—K3   P—Kt3
21) Kt(3)—Q2 P—B4
22) P×P   P×P
23) Q—R5   Kt—B3
24) Q—Kt6 ch Q—Kt2
25) Q×Q ch B×Q
26) P—KB4?

This, as Lasker himself has pointed out, was a mistake. As a matter of fact by entirely passive play (such as, say P—KB3) the White game would hardly be tenable in the long run.

26) .....   Kt—Q2
27) QR—Q1 B—B2
28) Kt(2)—Kt3

If 28) P—QKt3, Black will win by ...P×KBP 29) B×BP, Kt—Q5 etc.

28) .....   P×P
29) B×P   Kt—Q5
30) Kt×Kt   B×Kt ch
31) K—R2   P—Kt6!

Now Black's advantage is very evident indeed and what with the White Bishop practically bottled up at Kt1, one would think that Black ought to have an easy win.

32) R×R ch B×R

33) B—Kt1 Kt—K4
34) Kt—Kt3 B—Kt3

But it wasn't quite so easy as all that. Black had to play very precisely and by ...B—Q2!; 36) P—R5, R—K1; 37) Kt—K2, B—KB3 he could have achieved a clearly winning position.

35) R—Q2   R—Kt5?

An entirely wrong plan which will finally turn the tables on Black. By 35) ...Kt—B2! he could have maintained his advantage.

36) Kt—K2 R×RP

A useful alternative was ...B—B7 37) Kt—B1, B—R5 etc.

37) Kt×B   P×Kt
38) P—B5

A powerful counter stroke!

38) .....   R—R8
39) P×P   Kt—Q2
40) R—Q1   B—B2

White's threat being 41) B—B2, R×R; 42) B×P ch followed by B×R.

Position after White's 41st move

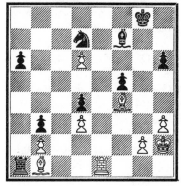

41) R—K1   P—QR4?

Having thrown away the win he now makes a decisive mistake jeopardising the draw too. By ...R—R4 42) R—K7, Kt—B1 Black could still have equalised.

42) R—K7   Kt—B4
43) B—K5!   R—R5
44) R—B7!   Kt—K3
45) P—Q7   R—Kt5
46) R—B8 ch   K—R2
47) R—R8 ch   K—Kt3
48) R—K8   R—Kt3
49) B—B4   Kt × B

50) P—Q8(Q)   R—QB3
51) R—K7   Resigns

(This is one of the most famous examples of Lasker's strength in an uphill struggle and of his uncanny gift of first saving a seemingly hopeless position and then actually proceeding to win it; the important point of course being that he very frequently let himself in for that sort of trouble quite deliberately so as to avoid a draw. Translator's Note).

GAME 78

QUEE'NS GAMBIT DECLINED

MARSHALL–LASKER

14th round, Moscow, 1925

1) P—Q4   P—Q4
2) P—QB4   P—K3
3) Kt—QB3   Kt—KB3
4) B—Kt5   QKt—Q2
5) P—K3   P—B3
6) P × P

This exchange is somewhat premature and merely helps the opponent's development. [but it is quite a popular move these days. R.T.]

6) .....   KP × P
7) B—Q3   B—Q3
8) Kt—B3   0—0
9) Q—B2   P—KR3
10) B—R4   R—K1
11) 0—0

A slightly preferable alternative may have been 11) 0—0—0.

11) .....   Kt—B1
12) P—K4?

Strategically unjustifiable; a

move that gives White no attack but just saddles him with a permanent weakness on Q4.

12) .....   P × P
13) Kt × P   B—K2
14) B × Kt

B—Kt3 was rather preferable.

14) .....   B × B
15) KR—K1   B—Kt5!
16) Kt × B ch   Q × Kt
17) Kt—K5   B—K3

Now, apart from various other advantages, Black has obtained control of his Q4.

18) R—K3   KR—Q1!
19) Q—B3   B—Q4
20) B—K4   Kt—K3
21) R—B3?

That costs him the QP. He certainly should have played Kt—KB3.

21) .....   Q—R5!
22) B × B   R × B

Now White can neither play Kt × BP (on account of ...Kt × QP nor R × BP (on

Position after Black's 36th move

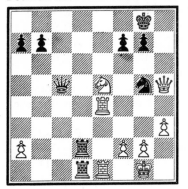

account of ...R × Kt); moreover that tiresome weakling
on Q4 is no longer defensible.

23) R—K1   Kt × P
24) R(3)—K3   R(1)—Q1
25) R—K4   Q—B3
26) Kt—Kt4
White hopes to get his R to
K7, a plan scotched by the
opponent's next move.
26) .....   Q—Kt3
27) P—KR3   P—KR4
28) Kt—K5   Q—Q3
29) Kt—B4   Q—Kt1!
Now R—Kt7 would be simply
countered by ...Kt—B4.
30) Kt—K5   Q—Q3
31) Q—B1   Q—B2
32) P—QKt4   Kt—K3!
33) Q—R3   R—Q8
Stopping 34) Q × RP on account of ...P—QB5; 35)
Q—K3, P—B5!; 36) R—B4,
Q × R; 37) Kt × Q, P—B7 and
wins.
34) P × P   Q × P?
Here Lasker starts a faulty
combination which should
have given White a chance to

equalise. By 34) ...Kt × BP
Black could have maintained
his advantage.
35) Q—KB3!   Kt—Kt4
36) Q × P   R(1)—Q7
That evidently was exactly
what Lasker bargained for!
37) Kt—Q3?
It seems incredible that as
brilliant a combinative player
as Marshall should fail to see
the subtle defence here at his
disposal; Q × Kt, Q × P ch; 38)
K—R2, R × R; 39) R × R,
P—B3!; but not Q × R which
would lose a piece on account
of 40) Kt—B3. This indeed
being the reason for the
unsoundness of the combination if only Marshall had seen
its weak spot.
37) .....   Kt × R
38) Kt × Q   R × R ch
39) K—R2   Kt × P
After ...R × BP White would
have had excellent drawing
chances by 40) Kt × Kt, R × Kt;
and 41) Q—Q5!
40) Q—B5   R—K1
41) Kt × P   Kt—Q8!
But not ...R × RP which
would give White a chance to
draw by 42) Kt—Q6, R—B1;
43) Kt—B8!
42) Q—B5   R—K3
43) Q—B1   Kt—K6!
Now White is completely
defenceless.
44) Q—B8 ch   K—R2
45) Q—B3   R—KKt3!
46) Q × Kt   R(7) × P ch
47) K—R1   R(7) Kt6
Resigns

(Notes by BOGOLJUBOV in the Book of the Tournament)

GAME 79

QUEEN'S GAMBIT DECLINED

LASKER–SPIELMANN

17th round, Moscow 1925

1)	P—QB4	P—K3
2)	P—Q4	P—Q4
3)	Kt—KB3	Kt—KB3
4)	B—Kt5	P—KR3
5)	B×Kt	Q×B
6)	Kt—B3	P—B3
7)	P—K3	Kt—Q2
8)	B—Q3	B—Kt5
9)	0—0	B×Kt
10)	P×B	P×P
11)	B×P	P—K4

He should have castled first before making this move. Now White will have the better end-game.

12)	P×P	Kt×P
13)	Kt×Kt	Q×Kt
14)	Q—Q4	Q×Q
15)	KP×Q	B—K3

The lesser evil since 15) ...0—0, could be answered by 16) KR—K1 followed by R—K7.

16)	KR—K1	K—Q2

Position after Black's 24th move

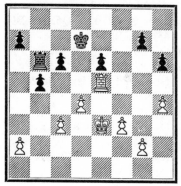

17)	B×B ch	P×B
18)	R—K5	KR—KB1
19)	R(1)—K1	QR—K1
20)	P—B3	R—B4
21)	K—B2	R×R
22)	R×R	

This R-ending is far from easy for Black but it is by no means lost yet.

22)	.....	P—QKt4
23)	K—K3	R—QKt1
24)	P—KR4	R—Kt3
25)	P—R4!	

Evidently Black's counter manoeuvre has not availed him much but now he should play ...P—QKt5 so as at least to keep his R mobile after 26) P×P, R×P; 27) R—QR5, R—Kt7; etc.

25)	.....	P—QR4?
26)	K—Q3	R—Kt1
27)	K—B2	R—Kt2
28)	P—QB4!	P×RP
29)	R×RP	R—Kt5
30)	K—Q3	K—B2
31)	P—B5!	K—Kt2
32)	K—K4	P—R4
33)	P—Kt4	P×P
34)	P×P	P—Kt3
35)	K—K5	R—B5
36)	P—R5?	

One of the very rare cases of Lasker playing an ending with lack of precision and thereby enabling the opponent to force the draw by a subtle manoeuvre. White could have won quite easily by 36) P—Kt5.

36)	.....	P×P
37)	P×P	R—B8?

Black misses his opportunity. It was only in the *post mortem*

that Spielmann found out how
he could have drawn the game
here by 37) ...R—Kt5! 38)
P—R6, R—Kt6! 39) R×P,
R—KR6; 40) K—Q6, R×P;
etc.

38) R×P	R—KR8

39) K—Q6	R×P
40) R—Kt4 ch	K—B1
41) K×BP	R—Q4
42) R—R4	K—Kt1
43) K—Kt6	Resigns

(Notes by BOGOLJUBOV in the Book
of the Tournament)

GAME 80

QUEEN'S GAMBIT DECLINED

BOGOLJUBOV–LASKER

20th round, Moscow, 1925

1) P—Q4	P—Q4
2) Kt—KB3	P—K3
3) P—B4	Kt—Q2
4) B—Kt5	

Simpler would be 4) Kt—QB3;
the usual continuation ...QP×
P; 5) P—K4, Kt—Kt3; 6)
B×P, Kt×B; 7) Q—R4 ch is
quite favourable for White.

4)	B—K2
5) B×B	Kt×B
6) Kt—B3	0—0
7) P—K3	P×P
8) B×P	P—QB4
9) 0—0	P×P
10) Q×P	Kt—QKt3
11) B—Kt3	Q×Q
12) Kt×Q	B—Q2
13) KR—Q1	KR—Q1
14) R—Q2!	B—B3
15) R(1)—Q1	QR—B1

If ...B or Kt to Q4 White
can get the better of it by 16)
Kt×KP!, P×Kt; 17) P—K4
etc.

| 16) P—K4 | B—K1 |
| 17) P—B3 | |

At this juncture Kt×P is no
longer quite so strong on

account of 17) ...R×R 18)
R×R, R×Kt; whereafter the
White Q-wing might be some-
what weak.

| 17) ..... | Kt—B3 |
| 18) Kt×P | |

By exchange at QB6 White
could produce a hopelessly
dull draw; so he grasps the last
opportunity for the sacrifice
on K6.

| 18) ..... | P×Kt! |

Now, of course, Lasker wishes
to avoid the exchange of one
of his Rooks a decision that
proves to be very wise. That
is why White would have done
better to sacrifice on K6 two
moves earlier.

19) B×P ch	K—B1
20) B×R	R×B
21) Kt—Kt5	Kt—B5
22) Kt—Q6	Kt×Kt
23) R×Kt	Kt—K4
24) R—Q8	R—B7
25) R(8)—Q2	R—B2
26) K—B2	K—K2
27) P—KR3	R—B3
28) P—B4	Kt—B2!
29) R—Q5?	

White seems to have the better
of it but that is a delusion. It
would have been safer to play
29) P—K5.

29)	.....	R—QR3
30)	P—R3	B—B3
31)	R(5)—Q4	R—Kt3

Position after White's 32nd move

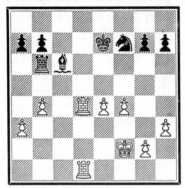

| 32) | P—QKt4 | P—QR4! |

Starting a very dangerous counter attack.

33)	P × P	R—R3
34)	R(1)—Q3	R × P
35)	K—B3	R—QB4
36)	P—KR4!	

White seeks his salvation by swopping as much as possible.

36)	.....	P—R4
37)	P—Kt4	P × P ch
38)	K × P	Kt—R3 ch
39)	K—Kt3	R—B8
40)	P—R4!	

White is even prepared to give up a Pawn so as to facilitate further exchanges.

| 40) | ..... | R—Kt8 ch |
| 41) | K—B3 | R—QR8 |

An alternative continuation would have been ...R—Kt5; 42) R—QKt4!, R × RP; 43) K—Kt3 which should give White a comfortable draw. As for 41) ...Kt—B4, Lasker himself suggested that 42)

R—QKt4, Kt × R 43) K × R would be good enough for White since Black would hardly retain sufficient material for a win.

| 42) | R—Q1 | |

Giving the opponent's R no chance to escape an exchange.

42)	.....	R—R6 ch
43)	R(1)—Q3	R × R ch
44)	R × R	Kt—B4

A last attempt; in view of the position of White's strong centre pawns 44) ...B × P would not have achieved more than a draw.

| 45) | P—KR5 | K—K3! |

Black was threatening to win by ...Kt—Q3; 47) R—Q4, Kt × KP!; 48) R × Kt ch, K—B4! as Lasker himself has pointed out 46) R—Q1, Kt—Q3; 47) R—KKt1 would be inadequate on account of ...K—B2; 48) R—K1, K—B3!

| 46) | R—B3! | Kt—Q3 |
| 47) | R × B! | |

Eliminating the villain of the piece and thereby forcing a draw.

47)	.....	P × R
48)	P—R5	P—B4
49)	P—QR6	Kt—Kt4
50)	K—K3	P—B5
51)	K—Q2	K—Q3
52)	K—K3	K—K3

Drawn

Now any attempt for Black to win would involve a grave danger of losing the game.

(Notes by BOGOLJUBOV in the Book of the Tournament)

CHAPTER TWENTY-SIX

Interlude of Bridge and Literature

There was quite a clamour for a Lasker–Capablanca return match and a great deal of talk and correspondence about it, but the required funds failed to come forth. No doubt, had Lasker been a Russian, the match would have been organised; and had he been a Dutchman, Holland's enthusiastic chess-fraternity would have found the funds, just as they did ten years later when Max Euwe's, their very own chess-hero's, bid for the world championship had to be financed.

But Lasker was a German citizen, and his country was in the throes of political strife and economic unrest; nor was it a time in most other countries when people might have felt inclined to back a thoroughly intellectual and not exactly lucrative show. It was the time when France was worried by the fall of the franc and Sweden by the Kreuger scandal; in the USA it was the time prior to the big 'slump' when bogus prosperity and prohibition caused gangsterism to flourish; in Central Europe it was a time for tycoons such as Castiglioni and Bosel to come to the fore, and in Italy it was a time when such men as Matteotti were murdered by those who prospered under Mussolini. It was a bad time and the portents of worse to come were much in evidence. It was certainly not a time in which much financial interest for a chess match could be roused.

Even though he never said much about it, there can be no doubt that Lasker was deeply disappointed by the failure to finance his return match against Capablanca; and while there had been many periods in his life when he kept more or less completely aloof from chess, they had never lasted quite as long as this, nor had he ever been so completely 'browned off' about chess and the 'chess-world' as he seemed to be for nearly a decade after his great successes in 1924 and 1925.

Some of his anger may have been due to a great deal of unpleasantness caused by the personal animosity of the committee organising the New York tournament of 1927. It was meant to be one of the greatest tournaments in chess history, and it seemed all set to be just that, since, among some other great masters, the list of competitors included Capablanca, the world champion and Alekhine (who was to wrest the title from him soon after that very tournament). Yet, the fact that neither Reti nor Bogoljubov were invited caused quite a stir in the chess-world, and the omission to invite Lasker caused a veritable outcry. The reason for the omission was entirely personal and had something to do with a quarrel during the 1924 New York tournament, of which the less said now the better. Anyway, in view of considerable public clamour the Committee tried to make up for their omission by sending Lasker a last minute invitation which he promptly declined.

There seems to be no doubt that, but for those personal animosities, Lasker would have liked to play in that tournament. As it was, he considered his career as a chess player at an end; and he certainly considered his *Chess-Manual* as his parting gift to the chess world. He had spent a long time writing it, and the first German edition had appeared at the end of 1925, at the beginning of that long retirement from active chess which he soon felt to be permanent.

The *Manual*—a bulky book of nearly 350 pages—is undoubtedly Lasker's most important work on chess, and indeed one of the most important books ever written on that subject; just like the same author's *Common Sense in Chess* [1] and unlike most other books on chess, the *Manual* is likely never to be 'dated', because it is a work dealing with general principles rather than with 'variations' which are often out of date within a few years of their being considered brand-new innovations.

The first English edition of the book appeared in 1932, and as they are significant a few passages from the author's preface may well be quoted here.

'. . . . . That after having written it in my mother tongue I should myself have re-written it in English does require explanation, even apology. Such at least is my sentiment, for I am by no means blind to the shortcomings of my diction, and I admire all languages in their purity and their noble life, and I love to see them used with the utmost art and sincerity and veneration.

But in the present case a difficulty arose. A translation by somebody foreign to the matter would have probably been, if conscentious, too literal. No translation, particularly no literal translation, can be accurate; it is in danger of reproducing the body, but not the essential thing, the soul of the book . . . . . I had the option of sacrificing the elegance or the meaning of what I desired to say. And I made, I trust, the right choice in preserving what seemed to me of greater value. On the other hand, after having lived a good part of my life in English-speaking countries,

(1) See p. 49.

I did not doubt that I should be capable of expressing myself definitely in the King's English.'

Even though completely aloof from competitive chess all through the second half of the twenties and the first three years of the thirties, Lasker was far from idle; nor did he devote all his time to his favourite mathematical and philosophical problems. It was in those years that he took a greater interests than ever in bridge: an almost professional interest, for not only did he write a fairly profound book on that game but he also raised his own prowess to a standard sufficient to make him eligible as the leader of the German team at the 'Bridge Olympics'. He also took an almost passionate interest in 'Go', for thousands of years the 'national pastime' of Japanese intellectuals and so difficult that those who were considered the masters of the game used to be granted royal honours. Among the few non-Japanese players who achieved some noteworthy prowess in that difficult game, Lasker certainly ranked very near the top. He also put a very lucid chapter on the rules of the game into his *Brettspiele der Völker*, a comprehensive work on the basic principles of the more important board-games, indeed a book rather similar in style and construction to his English book *Card Strategy*.

Lasker's almost devout attitude to '*Go*' and to the few real masters of that game was neatly revealed when, upon his return from Russia, one of his friends asked him whether he had used the opportunity of teaching the Russians some '*Go*'.

'Russia belongs to Asia', he answered, 'and Asia is the mother of all games. When one meets Asiatics one doesn't teach them any game, one learns it from them.'

From time to time Lasker accepted one or the other of numerous invitations to lecture or to give a performance of playing twenty to thirty players simultaneously. He did it if only the better to indulge his insatiable *wanderlust*, but as often as not he and Frau Martha would journey abroad for the sheer fun of it and unencumbered by any professional assignment. On one such occasion, in Madrid, he decided to pay a courtesy visit to the local chess club, but an overawed hall porter, without even listening to his name, refused to admit him, for it so happened that King Alfonso was a guest of the club that evening, and only members or specially invited guests were to be admitted. Lasker was just about to leave when he was recognised by one of the members passing through the hall. Now he was triumphantly admitted, and the club, that night, had two guests of honour, a King of Spain and a King of Chess. As a matter of fact, before the Laskers left Madrid, the club arranged a special banquet in their honour.

No less royal honours were accorded Lasker in Copenhagen, where the biggest hall in town was overcrowded when he gave a lecture. But what appealed to him much more than such professional engagements, however pleasing, was to roam around foreign cities at will; to go to Venice just to listen to the gondoliers' singing; to go up the *Jungfrau-Bahn* in Switzerland merely for the glorious view; to go to Vienna and Prague for the pleasure of seeing old friends, and to go to Rome for the thrill of exploring its historic relics. On one such visit, while visiting the catacombs, Martha Lasker felt rather annoyed by the ceaseless chatter of an uncommonly talkative guide. Since he happened to be a Trappist monk Emanuel drily remarked.

'No doubt, he is trying to make up for the long spells of silence imposed on him by his religious duties.'

In between such stimulating trips abroad Lasker would spend most of his time in his quiet study at Thyrow where the Laskers had their small farm and cottage and where, particularly in the summer, they would spend a good deal more time than at their flat in Berlin. In his study at Thyrow Lasker felt really at home and did most of his mathematical research and his philosophical writing, such as a number of essays on causality, published in 1928 and widely noted and debated. Here is a quotation which is significant of Lasker's way of thinking and of the fact that the thought (and the symbolism) of chess was never far from his mind.

'It is quite wrong to compare life with a game of chess in which Satan is playing for the opposite side. It is part of life's tragedy as well as its greatness that each of the forces opposing one another all through human history hoped to serve a good purpose. There seems to be an ethical motive in the con as well as the pro of most conflicts.'

Towards the end of that year 1928 Lasker was to celebrate his sixtieth birthday, but a few months earlier the death of his brother Berthold made him suffer the greatest bereavement of his life; for Berthold was more than a good brother, he had been his mentor in youth and his friend and collaborator all his life. Emanuel was abroad when the news reached him, and it cast a deep shadow over the birthday celebrations prepared at Amsterdam by an old and loyal friend of the Laskers, Strick van Linschooten, that most generous and able leader of Holland's chess-fraternity.

Lasker always felt particularly happy in Amsterdam, and was made most welcome there by his many admirers. It seemed, indeed, a pleasing idea to celebrate his sixtieth birthday at the very place where, almost exactly forty years earlier, he had embarked on his international career. But yet another shadow was to be cast upon that pleasant event, for on the way home the Laskers got the bad news that part of their home at Thyrow had been destroyed by fire and that Emanuel's aunt, the only surviving and dearly loved sister of his mother, had perished in the conflagration.

During the next three or four years the life of the Laskers was more quiet than ever. They spent most of their time at Thyrow and did not go abroad as often as they used to, while Emanuel's name was publicly mentioned much less often than before. He liked it that way, he enjoyed his quiet retirement in the country, but his fertile brain was no less active than before.

It was a time when he developed a growing interest in tinkering with all manner of inventions; and, never a man to do anything half-heartedly, he devoted himself to his new interests as passionately and methodically as he knew how.

Next to his study at Thyrow he fitted out a small laboratory, and, oddly enough, one of the first ideas to which he devoted many months of patient research and construction was a machine meant to trace the exact location of a gun by means of the sound of its fire. It was a sort of radar anticipated, but he never took out a patent. He also constructed an electro-magnetic burglar alarm, the amusing point being that, in lieu of a bell or a siren, he fitted the recorded sound of some very fierce dogs barking.

Being as fond of coffee as most chess players he never tired of experiments to find the perfect way of making it. He carefully tested the water of different districts as well as all manner of recipes for making coffee; and having studied all available literature on the subject he finally constructed a very special sort of coffee-grinder which he claimed to be more efficient than any other.

Rather more elaborate (and expensive) were his efforts to modernise the famous 'Chess-Automaton' of the early nineteenth century —a machine hiding a chess master who 'miraculously' beat all comers—by radio-electric means. By means of a complicated system of mirrors Lasker finally constructed the model of a machine devised to facilitate a sort of radio-simultaneous performance of up to twenty games. He meant to present the machine at the New York World Exhibition of 1939, but he couldn't be bothered to look for the financial backing.

'Why is it', asked his wife,' 'that with all those inventions of yours you have never managed to become a rich man?'

'But I am rich', he answered; 'I am rich in ideas and plans, and that gives me all the happiness I want.'

CHAPTER TWENTY-SEVEN

Driven into Exile

It may well be that, but for the stormy events of 1933, Lasker would have lived out his life contentedly in the quiet retirement of his country home. But it was not to be, and for the Laskers, no less than for so many German Jews and other anti-Nazis, the advent of the Hitler régime meant the loss of their property and citizenship, it meant being uprooted from their home and forced into exile.

Emanuel Lasker was sixty-five years old when, all of a sudden, he found himself deprived of the solid 'bourgeois' background that had been providing security for his old age. As an old man he suddenly found himself as poor as he had been as a boy; worse than that, he found himself without a home, with the ruins of his material life behind him and nothing to look forward to. Steinitz had been a younger man when he lost an imaginary kingdom in the realm of chess, but in an otherwise fairly stable world; and yet, for Steinitz the shock was so great that it broke his heart and sent him out of his mind. Not so Lasker when he had to face an infinitely more precarious situation. It was now that he showed his mettle: ready to tackle the problem, to accept the challenge and never, so long as he lived to resign the game of chess that was the pattern of his life. He decided to make a fresh start, and often those days —so he liked to tell his friends with a smile—he was reminded of that children's ditty which had so impressed him when he first learned English that he never forgot it.

> *I played with my blocks, I was but a child.*
> *What towers I raised, what castles I piled!*
> *But they tottered and fell-all my building in vain,*
> *And my father said kindly, we'll try it again.*

So he returned to the saving grace of his youth, to his first and perennial love: the chess-board. For nearly nine years he had kept completely aloof from the chess world, and meanwhile a great deal had changed.

Capablanca was no longer the world-champion; in 1927, having held the title for only six years, he had relinquished it to that fiery and adventurous genius, Alexander Alekhine. Tarrasch was dead, Reti was dead, Nimzovitsch was at death's door. Tarrasch had lived to the age of 72, just long enough to see the first year or two of the

Nazi régime. He had been an almost jingo-patriotic German all his life, proud of his only son's heroic death for the fatherland in the first war; and yet he lived to see himself deprived of his own chess journal, to be kicked out of his very own chess club, to be ostracised in his private life as well as in his medical profession. It was a sad end for a man who, with all his human failings, was a very great chess master and a great personality.

The new world champion's rivals were, almost all of them, members of the young generation which had, meanwhile, come to the fore. One of the 'oldest' of them was Max Euwe, the erudite Dutchman, already in his thirties; but Flohr of Czechoslovakia, Kashdan of the USA, Stolz and Stahlberg of Sweden, and that rising star of the USSR, Mikhail Botvinnik were even younger. Younger still were those budding grandmasters of the USA, Reuben Fine and Samuel Reshevsky, and youngest of all was Paul Keres, a chess genius from Esthonia, barely out of his' teens. And here now, ready to match his strength with all those youthfully ambitious giants of the chess world came old Emanuel Lasker, a world champion of the previous century, sixty-five years of age.

When Lasker accepted the invitation to play in the great tournament arranged at Zurich in the summer 1934 to celebrate the anniversary of the local Club, there wasn't a chess player anywhere in the world who wasn't surprised and thrilled; but even the old man's most sanguine well-wishers hardly expected him to show much of his erstwhile prowess. After all, it was nine years since Lasker had played any serious chess, and apart from being nine years older he was unlikely to have recovered from the recent shock of being deprived of his home, his property, his country. All this must surely be too much of a handicap when facing some of the world's greatest players, such as Alekhine, the world champion, Euwe and Flohr, both of them worthy contenders for the title, young Stahlberg as well as some senior grandmasters such as Bernstein, Bogoljubov, Nimzovitch and quite a few other masters. Sixteen competitors! Fifteen hard games to be played! It seemed a formidable undertaking for an old and tired man.

Even so, on the eve of the tournament Lasker was as calm as ever, and while he had no illusions about his chances he had sufficient confidence to predict that he considered himself capable of winning fifth prize.

In the first round Lasker had the Black pieces against Euwe, the Dutchman who, a year later, was to wrest the title from Alekhine; a man who at that time was not merely the most erudite theoretician but one of the strongest players in the world. He was at his very prime, 33 years old, almost exactly half his opponent's age. Small wonder that, 'on book form', the young contender for the world-championship was hot favourite against the old ex-champion. But the unexpected happened, for the old man played one of the finest games of his life. In an extremely complex position—the kind of position he loved—Lasker offered a positional Queen-sacrifice of uncommon depth and beauty. It wasn't the sort of short-term combination reaping immediate results in the shape of material gain or a mating attack, it was a rather long-term scheme, leading to slow but inexorable attrition of an opponent who finally could no longer resist the decisive break-through. When Euwe resigned the game, the audience almost went into hysterics of excitement and enthusiasm.

Next day Lasker had to face another star of the young generation, Salo Flohr, forty years his junior and one of the most consistently successful grandmasters of the time, who had to work hard to escape with a draw against the uncanny old man. Another win, and a most exciting one too, against Bernstein, and Lasker was actually leading the field, and millions of his admirers all over the world began to keep their fingers crossed and to believe in the miracle that he would keep it up and would run away with the tournament as he had so often done in the past.

Lasker himself, of course, knew better than anybody that he just hadn't the stamina to sustain the prodigious effort of the first week, and that a reaction was bound to come. It did come, slowly he fell back and was caught up by the three young grandmasters Alekhine, Euwe and Flohr as well as by Bogoljubov. Even so he kept well in the running and ended up fifth, precisely as he had predicted; the final score being Alekhine 13, Euwe and Flohr 12 each, Bogoljubov 11½, Lasker 10, Bernstein and Nimzovitch 9 each, Stahlberg 8 and so on.

At the concluding banquet Lasker made a speech in praise of the world champion's well deserved victory; whereupon Alekhine rose to speak. 'Emanuel Lasker', he said, 'has been my teacher all my life. But for him I would not be what I am. His book on the Petersburg tournament of 1909 has been a sort of catechism for me all my life. I have studied, again and again, every one of the ideas Lasker has expressed in that book, and for years I have had the book with me day and night. The very idea of chess as an art form would be unthinkable without Emanuel Lasker.'

GAME 81
QUEEN'S GAMBIT DECLINED

EUWE–LASKER

1st round, Zurich, July 14th, 1934

1)	P—Q4	P—Q4
2)	P—QB4	P—K3
3)	Kt—QB3	Kt—KB3
4)	B—Kt5	QKt—Q2
5)	P—K3	P—B3
6)	Kt—B3	B—K2

[In the Orthodox Defence P—QB3 is usually played only after Black has castled and when White has chosen the main variation 7) R—B1, since the continuation in the text affords White a great choice of lines. After 5) ...P—B3 it is best to go in for the Cambridge Springs Defence, 6) ...Q—R4. G.S.]

7)	Q—B2	0—0
8)	P—QR3	R—K1
9)	R—B1	

[A good continuation is also 9) R—Q1!. G.S.]

9)	.....	P×P
10)	B×P	Kt—Q4
11)	B×B	Q×B
12)	Kt—K4!	

[A very strong move, since Black, once White has played P—QR3, no longer has the opportunity that normally occurs in the Kt—K4 variation, first used by Alekhine, of exchanging Queens by Q—Kt5 ch. G.S.]

12)	.....	Kt(4)—B3
13)	Kt—Kt3	P—B4

Black might try to relieve his position by 13) ...P—QKt3 followed by ...B—Kt2. Any-

way, White has got out of the opening in a distinctly superior position.

[The other attempt at breaking open the position by 13) ...P—K4 fails because of 14) Kt—B5. G.S.]

14)	0—0	P×P
15)	Kt×P	Kt—Kt3
16)	B—R2	R—Kt1

[After 16) ...B—Q2; 17) Q—B7! would have been awkward for Black. G.S.]

17)	P—K4	

[White strives after a King-side attack. More logical would have been an attack on Black's undeveloped Queen-side by Q—Q2, followed by Q—R5. G.S.]

17)	.....	R—Q1!

[Lasker immediately takes defensive measures. With the text move he ensures a safe retreat for his Knight. G.S.]

18)	KR—Q1	B—Q2
19)	P—K5	

Letting go of the square Q5 without a proper quid pro quo. He should have played the Queen to K5 via QB7.

19)	.....	Kt—K1
20)	B—Kt1	P—Kt3
21)	Q—K4	B—R5

[Lasker procures himself counter-chances by weakening White's Pawn formation on the Q-wing. G.S.]

22)	P—Kt3	B—Q2
23)	P—QR4	Kt—Q4
24)	B—Q3	QR—B1
25)	B—B4	B—B3
26)	Kt×B	P×Kt
27)	R—Q3	Kt—Kt5

Position after White's 35th move

28) R—KB3

Certainly more consistent than an exchange of Rooks. Even so, it can't avail him much.

28) .....   R—B2

29) P—R4

[White plays logically for the attack, but finds it difficult to attain anything against Black's solid position. G.S.]

29) .....   R(2)—Q2

30) P—KR5   Q—Kt4

31) R—K1   R—Q5

32) P×P   RP×P

[Lasker rightly avoids 32) ...R×Q; 33) P×BP ch, K—B1; 34) P×Kt=Q db ch, K×Q; 35) Kt×R. G.S.]

33) Q—K2   R—Q7

34) Q—B1?

This almost incomprehensible retreat is refuted by Lasker's very beautiful combination.

[With 34) Q—K3, White could have escaped into a tenable end-game. Now Lasker obtains a decisive advantage by means of a fine and deeply calculated combination. G.S.]

34) .....   Kt—B7!

35) Kt—K4   Q×P!!

Willynilly, White must accept this sacrifice. The almost clock-work precision in the co-operation of Black's pieces is most attractive.

36) Kt—B6 ch   Q×Kt

37) R×Q   Kt(1)×R!

[Still stronger than 37) ...Kt× R(K8), followed by R—Q8. G.S.]

38) R—B1

[This loses quickly, but even the end-game continuation, 38) R—K2!, R—Q8; 39) R×Kt, R×Q ch leads to a won position for Black. G.S.]

38) .....   Kt—K5

39) B—K2   Kt—Q5

[The Black pieces co-operate in an aesthetic and instructive manner. G.S.]

40) B—B3   Kt×BP

41) Q—B4   Kt—Q6

42) R—B1   Kt—K4

43) Q—Kt4   Kt(4)×B ch

44) P×Kt   Kt—K7 ch

45) K—R2   Kt—B5 ch

46) K—R1   R(7)—Q5!

[Lasker is weaving a mating net. G.S.]

47) Q—K7   K—Kt2

48) Q—B7   R(1)—Q4

49) R—K1   R—KKt4

50) Q×BP   R—Q1!

Resigns

The finish is easily comprehensible. Lasker has played this game with iron consistency.

(Notes by ALEKHINE in the Book of the Tournament, and bracketed notes by G. Stahlberg in 'Chess and Chessmasters' [Bell & Sons,-London])

GAME 82

RUY LOPEZ

GROB-LASKER

3rd round, Zurich, 16th July 1934

1)	P—K4	P—K4
2)	Kt—KB3	Kt—QB3
3)	B—Kt5	P—QR3
4)	B—R4	Kt—B3
5)	0—0	B—K2
6)	R—K1	P—QKt4
7)	B—Kt3	P—Q3
8)	P—B3	Kt—QR4
9)	B—B2	P—B4
10)	P—Q3	

This is a thoroughly sound system, provided one can steer the game into some well planned channels.

10)	.....	Kt—B3
11)	QKt—Q2	0—0
12)	P—KR3	

Why that? Surely there was no need to be afraid of ...B—KKt5 which could have been answered 13) Kt—K3 if only he had made the proper move 12) Kt—B1 at once.

12)	.....	Q—B2
13)	P—QR4	

White loses more precious time. The QR-file means nothing to him just now. He still should have played Kt—B1.

13)	.....	B—K3
14)	Kt—B1	Kt—Q2

So as to clear up the situation on the Queen's wing before proceeding in the centre by say ...P—Q4.

15)	Q—K2	Kt—Kt3
16)	P×P	P×P

17)	B—K3?	

17) B—Q2 would have been better. (See White's next but one move).

17)	.....	P—Q4
18)	P×P	B×QP
19)	B—Q2	R×R
20)	R×R	P—B4

Now Black's domination of the centre is quite evident.

21)	P—QKt3	

Bottling up that hapless KB even more, but then he is hard put to it for some sensible move anyway.

21)	.....	B—Q3

Even so Black maintains sufficient positional advantage. Yet it may have been more precise to play ...K—R1 so as to keep the QB by ...B—Kt1 whenever White played Kt—K3.

22)	Kt—K3	P—Kt5
23)	Kt—B4	K—R1
24)	R—K1	

That attack against the KP doesn't lead to anything. After 24) B—Q1 he may have retained future chances of utilising that Bishop somehow.

24)	.....	Kt—Q2
25)	Kt×B	Q×Kt
26)	R—R1	Kt—B3

(See diagram on following page)

27)	R—R6	

Black would seem to have a winning position anyhow but there was no need yet for White to give up the exchange. On the other hand it may well be that the text move was a mere oversight. The rest requires no explanation.

Position after Black's 26th move

| 27) | ..... | P×P |
| 28) | B×P | Kt—Q5 |

29)	B×Kt	Q×R
30)	B×BP	R—K1
31)	P—QKt4	Kt—Q2
32)	Q—Q1	Kt×B
33)	P×Kt	Q—R6
34)	Kt—Kt5	P—R3
35)	P—Q4	P—K5
36)	P—R4	P—K6!
37)	Kt—R3	P×P ch
38)	Kt×P	Q—KKt6
39)	B—K4	B×B
40)	Kt×B	R×Kt
	Resigns	

(Notes by ALEKHINE in the Book of the Tournament)

GAME 83

QUEENS INDIAN

LASKER–GYGLI

4th Round, Zurich, July 17th 1934

1)	P—QB4	Kt—KB3
2)	Kt—KB3	P—K3
3)	P—KKt3	P—QKt3
4)	B—Kt2	B—Kt2
5)	0—0	B—K2
6)	Kt—B3	0—0

This game is most characteristic of Lasker's shrewd tactics as a fighter and psychologist. By the very act of keeping his opponent unmolested in the centre, he gradually puts him to sleep, as it were, and finally strangles him. Even here, and still on the next move, Black could and should have played ...P—Q4 with the idea of countering Kt—K5 by ...P—QB3 as well as ...Q—QB1.

7)	Q—B2	P—Q3?
8)	P—Kt3	QKt—Q2
9)	B—Kt2	R—K1
10)	QR—Q1	B—KB1
11)	KR—K1	

A concentration of forces, rather significant for Lasker.

11)	.....	P—Kt3
12)	P—Q4	B—Kt2
13)	P—K4	

All of a sudden, White is in full control of the centre, which means that strategically the battle is as good as over.

13)	.....	R—KB1
14)	B—QR3	Q—Kt1
15)	P—K5	Kt—K1
16)	Kt—K4	P—QR3

(See diagram on following page)

| 17) | P—B5 | |

As the sequel shows, this turns out to be quite good enough to win the game in the end. Yet the mere fact that in 16 moves Black has got nowhere

Position after Black's 16th move

and never ventured beyond his third line should have met with some more drastic punishment. White might well have played 17) P—KR4, whereupon ...P—KR3 would be ruled out on account of 18) P—R5, P—KKt4; 19) Kt× KtP etc. Black's game would soon have gone to pieces.

17)	KtP × P
18) KP × P	P × P(Q3)
19) P × P	B × Kt
20) R × B	Kt × P
21) B × Kt	P × B
22) R—QB4	

The P majority on the Q-wing and the so much more effective position of his pieces, secures White's decisive advantage in the middle game as well as for the ending.

22)	R—R2
23) R × P	Kt—Q3
24) Kt—Q4	

Forcing a further exchange which will leave White a strong Bishop as against a short-legged Knight.

24)	B × Kt
25) R × B	Kt—Kt4
26) R—Q1	R—B2
27) R × R	Q × R
28) Q × Q	Kt × Q
29) R—Q6	R—Kt1
30) R—B6	R—Kt2
31) R × KP	Kt × R

Slightly better drawing chances might be offered by 31) R × KtP. From now on, White has nothing more to worry about.

32) B × R	P—QR4
33) K—B1	K—B1
34) K—K2	K—K2
35) B—Q5	Kt—B2
36) B—B4	P—B3
37) K—K3	K—Q3
38) K—Q4	K—B3
39) B—Q3	Kt—K3 ch
40) K—B4	P—B4
41) B—B1	Kt—B2
42) B—Kt2 ch	K—Q3
43) P—B4	P—R3
44) P—KR4	Kt—K3
45) K—Kt5	Kt—Q4 ch
46) K × P	Kt—K7
47) K—Kt6	Kt × P
48) P—R4	Kt—R4
49) P—R5	Kt × P
50) P—R6	Kt—K3
51) P—R7	Kt—B2
52) P—R8(Q)	Resigns

(Notes by Alekhine, in the Book of the Tournament)

GAME 84

NIMZO-INDIAN

LASKER–HENNEBERGER

6th round, Zurich, 19th July, 1934

1) P—Q4   Kt—KB3
2) P—QB4   P—K3
3) Kt—QB3   B—Kt5
4) Kt—B3

(*More popular these days is
4) P—K3.   R.T.*)

4) .....   B×Kt ch
5) P×B   P—Q3
6) P—Kt3   0—0
7) B—Kt2   Q—K2
8) B—QR3   QKt—Q2

In spite of the opponent's
counter measures Black is
intent on ...P—K4. It would
have been better to forego this
move for the time being and
to develop by 8) ...P—B4
followed by ...Kt—QB3.

9) Kt—Q2!   P—K4
10) 0—0   R—K1

...P—K5 would be countered
by 11) P—K3.

11) P—K3   P—B4

So he is playing it after all but
now the awkwardly posted
QKt is hampering the co-
operation of the other pieces.

12) R—Kt1   Kt—Kt3?

That will cost him a pawn but
then Black's position is quite
inferior by now anyway. The
best he could have done was
...Q—Q1—B2 and possibly
...R—Kt1 and ...P—QKt3.

13) P×BP   P×P
14) R—Kt5!   B—Q2
15) B×P   Q—K3
16) R—Kt4   B—B3

17) B×Kt   B×B
18) K×B   P×B
19) Q—B2

It is still by no means easy to
make something out of White's
slight material advantage. Lasker does so with considerable
tactical skill.

19) .....   KR—Q1
20) P—B3!

Coupled with the following
move this is quite sufficient to
secure the White K position.

20) .....   R—Q3
21) KR—B2   R(1)—Q1
22) Kt—K4   Kt×Kt
23) Q×Kt   Q—Q2

A fairly meaningless demonstration! Anyway if White
continued by Q×P? it would
merely come to an exchange
of his KP for the opponent's.

24) R(4)—Kt2   P—B3
25) P—B5

White's winning chances are
getting more and more tangible. Already a passed Pawn is
in the offering.

25) .....   P×P
26) R×P   Q—K3
27) P—Kt4!

So as to counter ...R—Q7 by
28) R—R7.

27) .....   R—Q6
28) P—QB4   P—Kt3
29) R—Kt8!

Yet another step forward.

29) .....   K—Kt2
30) R×R   R×R
31) R—QKt2   K—R3
32) K—Kt3   R—Q8
33) P—KR4   R—Kt8 ch
34) K—R2   R—Q8

35) K—Kt3   R—Kt8 ch
36) R—Kt2!
This had to be worked out very precisely.
36) .....   P—B4
Position after Black's 36th move

37) Q—Q5!
If now ...Q×Q 38) P×Q, R—Q8; White certainly must-

not play P—K4?, P×P; 40) P×P, R—Q5; which would give Black a reasonable chance for a draw. The proper continuation would be 39) P—R4! R×P; 40) R—QR2, whereafter the passed Pawn would soon decide the issue. After the exchange of Rooks though it is even simpler.

37) .....   R×R ch
38) K×R   Q—QR3
39) Q—Kt8!
The coup de grâce!
39) .....   Q×RP ch
40) K—R3   Q—R2
41) Q—KB8 ch   resigns
Obviously ...Q—Kt2 is countered by 42) P—Kt5 ch. One of Lasker's best games at Zurich.

(Notes by ALEKHINE in the Book of the Tournament)

GAME 85

FRENCH DEFENCE

BERNSTEIN–LASKER

7th round, Zurich, 20th July 1934

1) P—K4   P—K3
2) P—Q4   P—Q4
3) Kt—QB3   Kt—KB3
4) B—Kt5   B—K2
5) P—K5   KKt—Q2
6) B×B   Q×B
7) Q—Kt4
A more usual move is 7) Q—Q2 or P—B4. R.T.)
7) .....   0—0
8) Kt—B3   P—QB4
9) B—Q3   P—B4
10) P×P e. p.   R×P

Black might have played just as favourably ...Kt×P. It just goes to prove that White's 7th move was not much good.
11) Q—R4   Kt—B1
12) P×P   Q×P
13) 0—0
After 13) 0—0—0, Kt—B3; 14) KR—K1, B—Q2, etc. White could not quite as easily exchange on K5.
13) .....   Kt—B3
14) QR—K1   B—Q2
15) Kt—K5   Kt×Kt
16) R×Kt   Q—Kt3
The threat being Kt—K4.
17) R—K3
Having nothing much to show

against the opponent's flexible P centre White must try to hold the position by some rather artificial means. The text move, of course, provides indirect cover for the QKtP viz: ...Q×P? 18) R—Kt1, Q—R6; 19) Kt×QP with the threat of B×RP ch etc.

17) .....   B—K1
18) R—Kt3   B—Kt3
19) Q—Kt4   R—Q1
20) P—QKt3

Here or on the next move one would expect him to play Kt—Q1 with a chance of subsequently centralising the Kt rather than displacing it on the R-file.

20) .....   R—Q2
21) Kt—R4   Q—Q3
22) R—B3   B×B

More advantageous for Black would seem to be ...R×R 23) Q×R, P—K4 etc.

23) P×B   R—R3

The Rook has no business here. It would have been best for Black to seize the open file by ...R×R; 24) Q×R, R—QB2 etc.

24) Q—Kt3   P—K4
25) R—K3   P—QKt4?

A very risky move which ought to have given him rather more trouble than it did. By far the smaller evil was 25) ...Kt—Kt3.

26) Kt—B3   Kt—Kt3
27) P—Q4!

Clearly refuting the opponent's last moves.

27) .....   P×P

28) Kt×KtP   Q—B4

After the exchange of Queens he would love the QP just as well.

Position after Black's 28th move

29) Q—Kt8 ch

A regretable miscalculation. White overlooks the next but one move of his opponent and thereby, instead of winning a Pawn, he loses a piece. After 29) R—K8 ch, Kt—B1 30) Q—Q3! White's win would have been a matter of mere routine, but now having grasped his fortuitous chance Lasker wont let it go any more.

29) .....   Kt—B1
30) R—B3   R—Kt3
31) Q—K8   R—KB3!

Poor horsey, he is done for!

32) R×R   P×R
33) Q—K2   P—QR3
34) Kt×P   Q×Kt
35) Q×P   Q—K4
36) Q—Q3   Kt—K3
37) P—Kt3   P—Q5
38) R—B1   Q—Q4
39) P—KR4   K—Kt2

40) R—K1	Kt—B4
41) Q—Q1	P—Q6
42) P—QKt4	Kt—K5!

43) Q—B3	Kt—B6
44) Q—Kt4 ch	K—B2
Resigns	

(Notes by ALEKHINE in the Book of the Tournament)

GAME 86

CARO–KANN

LASKER–MÜLLER

13th round, Zurich, July 26th, 1934

1) P—K4	P—QB3
2) Kt—QB3	P—Q4
3) Kt—B3	P×P
4) Kt×P	B—B4
5) Kt—Kt3	B—Kt3
6) P—KR4	P—KR3
7) Kt—K5	B—R2
8) Q—R5	P—KKt3

Black already has a pretty poor position.

9) Q—B3

I rather prefer this move to 9) B—B4 as suggested by so many commentators. Black could simply counter ...P—K3 and then what?

[*Modern theory suggests 10) Q—K2! with the threat of Kt×KBP* (R.T.)]

9)	Kt—KB3

10) Q—Kt3

Surely he could do better than go on this snatching expedition. After 10) B—B4, P—K3; 11) P—Q4 White would have a splendid position without the slightest risk.

10)	Q—Q4
11) Q×P	Q×Kt ch
12) B—K2	Q—Q3
13) Q×R	Q—B2
14) P—R4	

The only move to stop the Black Kt coming across to QKt3.

14)	B—Kt2
15) R—QR3	0—0

Black misses his chance. He should have first played 15) ...KKt—Q2, castling only after 16) P—R5; in that case the White Queen would be far from happy.

16) R—Kt3

Even now the White position is by no means easy but Lasker copes with admirable tactical skill.

16)	P—Kt4
17) P×P	P×P
18) Q—Kt7	Q—B5
19) R—Kt4	Q—Q3
20) P—Q3	QKt—Q2
21) P—QB3	Kt—B4
22) Q×RP	Kt—Q4

Position after Black's 22nd move

23) R×B!

Certainly the simplest way; in the end White will be some Pawns up with a perfectly safe position.

23) .....   K×R
24) Kt—B5   Q—K4
25) Q×Kt   Q×Kt
26) R—Kt4   Q—K3

27) R×P   P—B4
28) Q—B4   R—B3
29) Q—R4 ch   R—R3
30) R×B ch   K×R
31) Q×R ch   Q×Q
32) B×Q ch   Resigns

(Notes by ALEKHINE in The Book of the Tournament)

CHAPTER TWENTY-EIGHT

Holding his Own in Moscow

The old man had lost his home and his property. Both his Berlin flat as well as the farm at Thyrow was confiscated by the Nazis, and so was his bank account. The wheel had turned full circle, and once again Emanuel found himself in the position he had to face nearly fifty years earlier; and as the boy Lasker, willy-nilly, had to depend on chess for a living, so did the old man.

Once again a great international tournament was being organised in Moscow and Emanuel Lasker, of course, was among the foreign guests. They were received with great acclaim, accommodated in the best hotel and given four days of rest and sightseeing before the tournament began.

This was the first occasion for foreign observers to note the enormously growing popularity and indeed the mass appeal of chess in the USSR. 'Lasker is being lionised in Moscow', wrote a British newspaper correspondent, 'no less than a Hollywood star in America'. The crowd called him 'Starishok', which means something like 'dear little old man', and on one occasion when the car hadn't arrived, the master's admirers were determined to carry him home shoulder-high. Fortunately, the timely arrival of the car saved him from this flattering but precarious situation.

Among Lasker's competitors were such celebrated grandmasters as Capablanca, Flohr and Spielmann, to say nothing of Russia's own budding star Mikhail Botvinnik. But there were also some other famous international masters, such as Lilienthal, Pirc, Stahlberg and quite a galaxy of young Russians whose names were soon to have as much international renown as they already enjoyed in their own country. With twenty competitors, there were nineteen games to be played, an average daily stint of eight hours. Quite a feat for an old man, and this is what Paul Hugo Little had to say about it in the American *Chess-Review*:

'..... Lasker was 67, and yet he all but won the tournament. Botvinnik and Flohr shared 1st and 2nd prize with 13 points and only ½ point behind came Lasker with six wins, thirteen draws and not a single loss. And one of his victories was against Capablanca who came ½ point behind the man from whom he had taken the world-championship fourteen years earlier'.

This was the fourth time these two met in a tournament after

their title match, and for the fourth time Lasker came out ahead of
the man who was twenty years his junior. Just as in his youth and
early middle age Tarrasch had been his 'arch-rival', now in the
autumn and winter of his life it was Capablanca. He not only beat
him in that exciting race but also in their individual encounter,
capturing his Queen and winning as magnificently as he had done
twenty-one years earlier at St. Petersburg, in 1914.

The final score was Botvinnik and Flohr, 13 each; Lasker 12½,
Capablanca 12, Spielmann 11, Kan and Löwenfisch 10½ each,
Lilienthal, Ragosin and Romanovsky 10 each etc. This time, as at
Zurich, Lasker had shown his mettle right from the start, and even
in the first round he defeated the very strong young Russian Kan
by means of a positional Queen-sacrifice, reminiscent of his great
first round game against Euwe at Zurich. But this time he stayed
the course, and for the whole of three or four gruelling weeks
kept up with the fast pace of the leaders. Indeed, he was in the lead
most of the time, and had he won his game against Botvinnik as he
should have, he would have shared first and second with Flohr,
and Botvinnik would have been third. It was a very small slip that
enabled his redoubtable opponent to escape with a draw in a lost
position.

When after this game one of his friends remarked to Lasker:
'This fellow Botvinnik really was exceedingly lucky', Lasker answered: 'Yes, he is lucky to be such an exceedingly strong player'.
This remark is significant of Lasker's fine sense of sportsmanship,
but how can one explain the fact that a near-septuagenarian could
hold his own with some of the world's strongest masters, forty
years his juniors?

Certainly this old man understood the trend of a time which was
no longer his, better than some of the young generation who belonged
to it. Small wonder that Lasker's personality and his very existence
had the effect of a tonic on so many of the younger generation
and that he was more revered now than ever before. He had come to
be both the most popular and the most sincerely and universally
loved man in the entire chess world; he had come to be a symbol and
almost a legend. And yet, what he made for his material needs
was a tiny fraction of the sums spent on any professional tennis
circus or any second-rate hit-tune.

Rather significant of the material difficulties that he had to
contend with, is a passage from Culbertson's book *Strange Lives
of One Man*. The famous bridge-champion met Lasker in London,
and this is what he has to say about it.

'There was one thing that made me feel sad. Doctor Emanuel

Lasker, who for so many years was chess champion of the world, came to see me. I was delighted to meet a man I had greatly admired since my youth. Mentally he was still a giant in chess as well as in the philosophy of cards and card-games. Lately things had been going pretty badly for him and if it hadn't been for bridge they would have been much worse.

"Mr. Culbertson", he said, "I would like to teach bridge. I understand that you issue certificates to teachers after proper examination. I would like to take the examination with you privately".

"Why, Doctor! Who am I to give you an examination? It's for you to give me an examination, and I would be honoured, I assure you."

"I am very serious, Mr Culbertson. Your certificate would help me to get pupils. You have a big name."

I thought of his years of brilliant and faithful service to hundreds of thousands of chess-players and to the noble game itself that had fascinated the best minds for centuries and in which there were but few equals to Doctor Lasker. I thought of the rewards in chess and in bridge and somehow felt ashamed.

As I was silent, I heard his voice repeating timidly, "Will you give me an examination, Mr Culbertson, please?"

I gave him an honorary certificate.'

To imagine Lasker's indomitable pride bowed by such circumstances is not a pleasant thought, and it is scant solace to remember that Rembrandt and Mozart, Spinoza and Diogenes and a host of other great men lived in penury too. All his life, Lasker had worked to raise the economic standard of chess masters, all his life the sad spectacle of Steinitz's beggarly old age had been a warning example to him. He had been determined to safeguard his declining years from want, and yet here he was, nearly seventy, having to start all over again to work hard for a living. But work he did; he would not accept alms from anybody and he certainly earned his daily bread.

The prize money of the great Moscow tournament was a welcome asset to the Laskers' budget. Moreover, the organisers of the tournament, delighted with his magnificent performance, invited him and his wife to be the Government's guests for a combined sight-seeing tour and rest cure. They went to see the sulphur springs at Kislovodsk and Piatigorsk in the Caucasus, and Emanuel gave a simultaneous performance in a huge hall, so crowded that little boys climbed the chandeliers so as not to miss the great event.

After this pleasant trip Lasker received a most flattering offer from the Moscow Academy of Science. He was to become a member of the Academy, there to continue some of his mathematical research. Lasker accepted the offer, and while it was arranged for him to establish permanent residency in Moscow he was to have sufficient leave of absence to comply with his lecture commitments and to see his friends in the Western World.

He made several such trips, and never failed to visit Vienna where on one such occasion he met Paul Keres, then barely out of his 'teens and already recognised as an international master and a budding grandmaster. Between the old man and the boy it was a case of mutual sympathy at first sight, soon developing into sincere friendship; and, considering the difference between their ages of nearly fifty years, it bridges a span of chess history from the days of Zuckertort and Steinitz right up to the mid-20th century.

It was on that same trip to Vienna that Lasker, in one of his nightly spells of feverish work on mathematical problems, solved a particularly difficult assignment he had undertaken for the Moscow Academy. He was very happy about this success, and delighted that he could once more afford to play chess for fun rather than a living, and only when he felt like it. He did, indeed, attend yet another strong Moscow tournament in the spring of 1936. But this time, as at Zurich, he could stand the pace only for the first week or two, being too exhausted toward the end of the tournament to keep up with the leaders. That tournament was a great success for Capablanca who won it with 13 points, ahead of Botvinnik (12), Flohr (9½), Lilienthal (9), Ragosin (8½), Lasker (8), Eliskases, Kan, Löwenfisch, Rjumin (7½ each) etc. It was the first time that Emanuel Lasker failed to be among the prize-winners of a chess tournament.

GAME 87

QUEEN'S GAMBIT DECLINED

KAN–LASKER

1st round, Moscow, 15th Febr. 1935

1) P—Q4	P—Q4
2) P—QB4	P—QB3
3) P×P	P×P
4) Kt—QB3	Kt—QB3
5) Kt—B3	Kt—B3
6) B—B4	B—B4

As always, Lasker is satisfied with simple openings. (R.Fine)

7) Q—Kt3
A faulty idea.   (R.F.)

7)	Kt—QR4
8) Q—R4 ch	B—Q2
9) Q—B2	R—B1
10) P—K3	P—QKt4!
11) P—QR3	P—K3
12) B—Q3	B—K2

Black has captured the iniative. (R.F.)

13) Kt—K5	Kt—B5
14) Q—K2	0—0
15) 0—0	B—K1
16) QR—B1	Kt—Q2
17) Kt×Kt(B4)	

So far the game resembles Spielmann-Pirc, 1931 but now

Position after White's 34th move

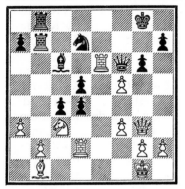

White ought to continue 17) B—QKt1.

17)	KtP × Kt
18) B—Kt1	P—B4!
19) P—B3	Kt—Kt3
20) B–B2	B—Q3
21) B × B	Q × B
22) QR—Q1	B—Q2
23) Q—Q2	

He certainly ought to play 23) P—K4.

23)	B—B3
24) KR—K1	QR—Q1
25) R—K2	R—Q2
26) R(1)—K1	P—Kt3
27) R—Q1	R—Kt1
28) Q—K1	R(2)—QKt2
29) R(1)—Q2	Kt—Q2
30) B—Kt1	P—K4!
31) Q—Kt3	Q—K3?

A mistake; correct was 31) ...Q—B3! (R.F.)

32) P—K4	

White has delayed this move far too long. Now it has got to be done to avoid suffocation.

32)	KP × P!?

Complications were always Lasker's forte. (R.F.)

33) P × BP?	Q—B3

Kan blunders also. The right way was 33) P × QP! Q—B3; 34) P × B, P × Kt; 35) R × Kt, R × P; 36) R × R, R × R; 37) Q—K1!, with an easy win. From now on Lasker regains his composure and finishes in wonderful style. (R.F.)

34) R—K6	P × Kt!!
35) R × Q	P × R
36) R × P ch	

The only chance. If 36) B—B2, Kt × R. (R.F.)

36)	P × R
37) Q × P ch	K—B1
38) Q—Q6 ch	K—K1
39) B—B2	

Threatening P—B6 as well as Q × B. (R.F.)

39)	R—Kt3!
40) P—B6	K—Q1
41) P—B7	K—B1
42) P—B8(Q) ch	Kt × Q
43) Q × Kt ch	K—Kt2
44) Q—B6	K—R3!

This King has come a long way. 45) Q—Q4 could now be countered by ...R × P 46) Q × QP, B—R5; this indeed being threatened anyway.

45) Q—Q6	R—K1

Preferable to 45) ...B—R5; 46) Q × P. (R.F.)

46) P—KR4	R—K8 ch
47) K—R2	R—QB8
48) B—B5	

The last gasp. (R.F.)

48)	P—Q8(Q)
49) B—B8 ch	K—R4
Resigns	

(Notes by REUBEN FINE in 'The World's Great Chess Games' (André Deutsch 1952) and from *Wiener Schachzeitung* 1935)

GAME 88

QUEEN'S GAMBIT ACCEPTED

CHEKOVER—LASKER

4th round, Moscow
February 18th, 1935

1) P—QB4	Kt—KB3
2) Kt—QB3	P—K3
3) Kt—B3	P—Q4
4) P—Q4	P×P
5) P—K4	B—Kt5
6) B—Kt5	P—B4!
7) B×Kt	

7) B×BP!, P×P 8) Kt×P, Q—R4; 9) B×Kt! is considered to be favourable for White. (R.T.)

7)	Q×B
8) B×P	P×P
9) Q×P	Kt—B3
10) Q×Q	P×Q

The good old 'Vienna variation'.

11) QR—B1	B—Q2
12) 0—0	QR—B1
13) P—QR3	B—Q3

Position after White's 21st move

14) Kt—K2	Kt—K4
15) Kt×Kt	B×Kt
16) B—Kt5	R×R
17) B×B ch	K×B
18) R×R	R—QB1!
19) R×R	K×R
20) P—QKt3	K—B2
21) K—B1	P—Kt4!

Securing a definite end-game advantage.

22) K—K1	B—Kt7
23) P—QR4	P×P
24) P×P	K—B3
25) K—Q2	K—B4
26) Kt—B3	

Probably 26) K—B2, B—R8; 27) K—Kt3, would have been better.

26)	K—Kt5
27) Kt—Kt5	P—QR4
28) Kt—Q6	K×P
29) K—B2	

Forced since otherwise 29) ...K—Kt6.

29)	B—K4
30) Kt×P	B×P
31) Kt—Q8	P—K4
32) Kt—B6	B—Kt8
33) P—B3	B—B4
34) Kt—Kt8	K—Kt4
35) P—KKt4	B—K2
36) P—Kt5	P×P
37) Kt—Q7	B—Q3
38) Kt—B6	K—B5!

Resigns

For obviously 39) Kt×P is countered by ...B—K2.

(Notes by *Wiener Schachzeitung* 1935)

GAME 89

SCOTTISH

SPIELMANN–LASKER

8th round, Moscow
February 24th, 1935

1) P—K4   P—K4
2) Kt—KB3   Kt—QB3
3) P—Q4   P×P
4) Kt×P   Kt—B3
5) Kt—QB3   B—Kt5
6) Kt×Kt   KtP×Kt
7) B—Q3   P—Q4

[A trenchant reply. But the more reserved 7) ...P—Q3 has some hidden resources. 500 M.G.]

8) P×P   Q—K2 ch

What with the immediate exchange of Queens, this leads to a variation usually considered the dullest of this opening. It is all the more surprising how, after a very few moves, the fighting spirit of those two Masters conjures up positions of an almost uncanny tension.

9) Q—K2   Q×Q ch

Best here is 9) ...P×P. (R.T.)

10) K×Q   P×P

If Black is out for a draw he should exchange on his QB6. *Actually, exchange on Black's QB6 followed by 11) ...P×QP; 12) B—QR3! is rather advantageous for White. (R.T.)*

11) Kt—Kt5

[Suddenly the fight flares up. If 11) ...B—R4; 12) B—KB4, and Black is prevented from castling. 500 M.G.]

11) .....   K—Q1

12) R—Q1   P—B3
13) P—QB3   R—K1 ch
14) K—B1   B—B1
15) Kt—Q4   K—B2
16) B—B4 ch   K—Kt3

[An heroic decision. More prosaic is, clearly, 16) ...B—Q3; 17) B×B ch, K×B; 18) Kt—B5 ch, B×Kt; 19) B×B, and the consequence might easily be a dull draw. 500 M.G.]

17) P—QR4   P—QR4
18) P—QKt4!

[In the sequel White succeeds in creating dangerous mating nets, in spite of the absence of Queens. 500 M.G.]

18) .....   P×P

[For instance, if 18) ...B—Q2; 19) P×P ch, R×P (not 19) ...K×P; 20) B—B7 mate, nor 19) ...K—B4; 20) Kt—Kt3 mate); 20) KR—Kt1 ch, K—R2; 21) B—B7, and wins. 500 M.G.]

19) P—R5 ch!

[This Pawn is taboo, for if 19) ...R×P; 20) R×R, K×R; 21) B—B7 ch, K—R5; 22) R—R1 mate. 500 M.G.]

19) .....   K—Kt2
20) P×P   Kt—K5

Giving Spielmann the chance of a pretty sacrificial attack. By 20) ...B—Q2 Black certainly would have protected his QBP, but he would have had to face White's attack on the QKt-file without any counter-play whatever.

21) Kt×P!

For Black to survive so

shattering an attack borders on the miraculous. Obviously he musn't accept the sacrifice since ...K×Kt; 22) QR—B1 ch, K—Q2; 23) B—Kt5 ch, K—K2; 24) R—B7 ch would win easily.

21) .....   P—Kt4!

Perched over the very edge of the abyss, Lasker now pulls out every trick of his uncanny powers of defence. First of all the Bishop is to be pushed off his diagonal.

22) B×Kt   R×B
23) Kt—Q8 ch   K—R3

Position after Black's 23rd move

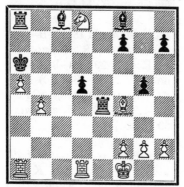

24) B×P

I cannot imagine any Grandmaster who wouldn't have played just this move, for after all White will come out 2 Pawns up with an end-game that would seem to be an almost certain win. However, as the further course of the game shows, this is not so. The P at QKt4 will prove untenable, QR5 will be very weak and there will always be the latent

threat of the opponent's QP. [This temporarily wins a second Pawn, but it allows the opponent some breathing space, for the consolidation of his position. The win was obtainable, in a blaze of glory, by 24) R×P, R×B; 25) P—Kt5ch K—R2; 26) R—B1, with fatal threats, or 24) ...B×P; 25) B×P, and the struggle is hopeless for Black. 500 M.G.]

24) .....   B—K3
25) Kt—B6   B—Kt2!

[Turning the Bishop to account on the long diagonal is much better than 25) ...B×P; 26) QR—Kt1, etc. 500 M.G.]

26) QR—B1   R—QB5
27) B—K3

[He still seeks complications. It would have been wiser to have played for the end-game, by 27) R×R, P×R; 28) Kt—Q4, B×Kt; 29) R×B, K—Kt4; 30) B—Q2, etc., as now White's victory is by no means assured, in spite of his two extra Pawns, by reason of the Bishops of opposite colours. 500 M.G.]

27) .....   K—Kt4
28) Kt—R7 ch   K×P
29) B—Kt6   R—B6!
30) R—Kt1 ch   R—Kt6
31) Kt—B6 ch   K—R5
32) B—Q4

[White sees that, in spite of the Black King's exposed position, there is no possibility of applying the final sanctions, and so he decides on liquidation. 500 M.G.]

32) .....   R×R
33) R×R   B×B
34) Kt×B   R—R3

[Neither 34) ...R×P; 35) R—R1 ch, K—Kt5; 36) Kt—B6ch, etc., nor, evidently, 34) ...K×P; 35) R—R1 ch, followed by R×R, is admissible here. 500 M.G.]

35) R—R1 ch   K—Kt5
36) K—K2

White may have had some better chances by steering into a R ending with 36) Kt×B! and 37) P—Kt4.

36) .....   B—Q2
37) Kt—B2 ch?

[Too hesitating. He should have fortified his position by 37) K—Q3, R×P; 38) Kt—B2 ch, K—Kt4; 39) R×R ch, K×R; 40) K—Q4, with every chance of a win, or 37) ...B—R5; 38) R—QB1, R×P; 39) Kt—B6 ch, B×Kt; 40) R×B, R—R7; 41) R—B6,

with good practical chances. 500 M.G.]

37) .....   K—B6
38) Kt—K3   B—Kt4 ch
39) K—K1   P—Q5
40) R—B1 ch

[The plausible 40) Kt—Q5 ch would even lose; 40) ...K—Kt7; 41) R—Q1; R—K3 ch; 42) K—Q2, R—K7 mate. 500 M.G.]

40) .....   K—Q6
41) R—Q1 ch   Drawn

[But 41) ...K—K5 would be useless, because of 42) Kt—B2, P—Q6; 43) P—B3 ch (an important check); 43) ...K—K4 (or 43) ...K—B5; 44) Kt—Q4); 44) Kt—Kt4, R—Q3; 45) P—R6, etc. Draw. A grand fight. 500 M.G.]

(Notes from *Wiener Schachzeitung*. Bracketed notes by S. TARTAKOWER and J. DU MONT in '500 Master Games of Chess' (Bell & Sons, London).)

GAME 90

FRENCH DEFENCE

LASKER–CAPABLANCA

9th round, Moscow
February 27th, 1935

1) P—K4   P—K3
2) P—Q4   P—Q4
3) Kt—QB3   B—Kt5
4) Kt—K2   P×P
5) P—QR3   B—K2
6) Kt×P   Kt—KB3
7) Kt(2)—B3   QKt—Q2

A move that looks natural and good enough and yet may not be best. There is much to be said for Alatorzev's system 7) ...0—0 followed by ...Kt—QB3.

8) B—KB4   Kt×Kt
9) Kt×Kt   Kt—B3
10) B—Q3   0—0
11) Kt×Kt ch   B×Kt
12) P—QB3   Q—Q4

Black is banking on 13) 0—0, P—QB4; which would be good enough for him, but Lasker doesn't oblige.

13) Q—K2!   P—B3
14) 0—0   R—K1

15) QR—Q1   B—Q2

Thereby admitting that the Black QB must remain bottled up; hence the opening cannot have been treated properly.

16) KR—K1

According to Rabinovitch 16) B—K5, what with the threat of P—QB4 and Q—K4 would have been stronger.

16) .....   Q—QR4

17) Q—B2   P—KKt3

Black had the choice of two evils to weaken his K-wing. Had he played ...P—KR3 instead, 18) Q—K2 followed by Q—K4 would have been most disagreeable.

18) B—K5   B—Kt2

19) P—KR4!

A bugle call for attack!

19) .....   Q—Q1

20) P—R5   Q—Kt4

21) B×B   K×B

22) R—K5   Q—K2

23) R(1)—K1   R—KKt1

24) Q—B1!   QR—Q1

25) R(1)—K3   B—B1

26) R—R3   K—B1

Position after Black's 28th move

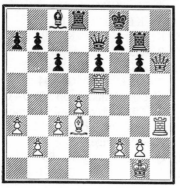

27) Q—R6 ch   R—Kt2

28) P×P   RP×P

29) B×P!

A very pretty and decisive sacrifice, or rather the offer of one, for Black could not possibly accept it on account of 30) Q—R8 ch

29) .....   Q—B3

30) R—KKt5!   K—K2

The only thing Black could have tried against the threat of R—B3 was 30) ...R—Q4; A little trap, for R—B3 would fail against ...Q×R 32)P×Q, R×R; 33) Q×R, R×B and Black would win. But White of course after ...R—Q4 would simply play 31) R×R, BP×R 32) Q—R8 ch etc.

31) R—B3   Q×R(B6)

32) P×Q   R(1)—Kt1

Black's best chance in the circumstances.

33) K—B1   R×B

34) R×R   R×R

35) Q—R2

He could have simplified matters by 35) Q—KB4.

35) .....   K—Q2

36) Q—B4   P—B3

37) P—B4   P—R3

38) Q—R4   R—Kt4

39) Q—R7 ch   K—Q1

40) Q—R8 ch   K—B2

41) Q×P   R—KB4

So far it is a brilliantly played game, particularly on Lasker's part, but from now on, for well over 20 moves, he does nothing to materialise his advantage; however there is a very good reason for this.

Since it was particularly important for Lasker to win this game he wished to avoid the slightest risk of a slip due to fatigue; hence he very shrewdly 'plays out time' waiting for the adjournment.

42)	Q—Kt7 ch	B—Q2
43)	K—K2	K—B1
44)	Q—R8 ch	K—B2
45)	Q—R2 ch	K—B1
46)	Q—Q6	R—KR4
47)	K—K3	R—KB4
48)	K—K4	R—KR4
49)	Q—B8 ch	K—B2
50)	Q—B4 ch	K—B1
51)	Q—Q6	R—KB4
52)	K—K3	R—KR4
53)	K—Q3	R—KB4
54)	K—K2	R—KR4
55)	K—Q2	R—KB4
56)	K—K3	R—KR4
57)	Q—B8 ch	K—B2
58)	Q—B4 ch	K—B1
59)	Q—Q6	R—KB4
60)	Q—Kt3	R—KR4
61)	Q—Kt4	R—KB4
62)	Q—Kt8 ch	K—B2
63)	Q—Kt3 ch	K—B1
64)	Q—Kt6	Resigns

Here the game was adjourned but Capablanca resigned it before the resumption. Of course it was not difficult for White to force the win by, say 64) ...K—B2. 65) Q—Kt3 ch, K—B1; 66) K—Q3, R—R4; 67) K—B3, R—KB4; 68) K—Kt4, R—KR4; 69) P—QB5!, R—Q4; 70) K—R5, followed by K—Kt6 etc.

(Notes from *Wiener Schachzeitung* 1935)

GAME 91

QUEEN'S GAMBIT DECLINED

VERA MENCHIK—LASKER

10th round Moscow,
February 28th, 1935

1)	P—Q4	Kt—KB3
2)	Kt—KB3	P—Q4
3)	P—B4	P—K3
4)	B—Kt5	QKt—Q2
5)	P—K3	P—B3
6)	Kt—B3	Q—R4
7)	B×Kt	Kt×B
8)	B—Q3	P×P
9)	B×BP	P—QR3

More usual is ...B—QKt5. The text move is evidently meant to prepare for ...P—QKt4 or ...P—QB4 but it doesn't come to that.

10)	0—0	B—K2
11)	P—QR3	0—0
12)	P—QKt4	Q—B2
13)	P—K4	P—QR4!
14)	Q—Kt3	R—Q1
15)	KR—B1	

Better QR—B1 or even P—Kt3.

15)	.....	Q—B5!

This throws the lady off her balance.

16)	P—K5	

Preferable was B—Q3 followed by Kt—K2.

16)	.....	Kt—Q4
17)	B×Kt?	KP×B
18)	P—Kt5	B—Q2
19)	Kt—QR4	QR—Kt1!

20) Kt—Kt6?

Now White is drifting into the inferior position. She should have played 20) P—Kt6, followed by Q—K3.

Position after White's 20st move

20) . . . . .   B—KKt5!
21) P×P

The QP is not easily defensible. e.g.: 21) R—Q1, B×Kt 22) KtP×B, P—KB3! etc.

21) . . . . .   P×P
22) R×P   B×Kt

23) Q×B   Q×QP
24) R—Q1   Q×P

What with the Pawn being taboo on account of the mate on the base line, Black's advantage is now materialised.

25) P—Kt3   P—Q5
26) Q—Q3   B—B3
27) R(1)—QB1   Q—K1!
28) Q—KB3?

Kt—QR4 was better. Under no circumstances should she have allowed the P to advance.

28) . . . . .   P—Q6
29) R×B

Looks very good, but it isn't quite good enough.

29) . . . . .   P—Q7!
30) R—Q1   P×R
31) Kt—Q5   R×Kt!
Resigns

For obviously Q×R is followed by 32) ...Q—K8 ch.

(Notes from the *Wiener Schachzeitung*)

GAME 92

Q. GAMBIT ACCEgPED

BOTVINNIK–LASKER

14th round, Moscow
March 6th, 1935

1) P—Q4   P—Q4
2) P—QB4   P×P
3) Kt—KB3   Kt—KB3
4) Q—R4 ch   QKt—Q2
5) Q×BP   P—K3
6) P—KKt3   P—B4
7) P×P   B×P
8) B—Kt2   0—0
9) 0—0   Q—K2

10) Kt—B3   P—KR3
11) P—K4   P—K4
12) Kt—QR4!

Getting rid of one of the Bishops since obviously 12) ...B—Q3 would be countered by 13) Kt—KR4!

12) . . . . .   R—K1
13) Kt—R4   Kt—Kt3!
14) Q×B   Kt×Kt
15) Q×Q   R×Q
16) P—Kt3   Kt—B6
17) B—QR3   R—K1
18) B—Kt2   Kt(6)×KP
19) KR—K1   P—KKt4

20) Kt—B3	B—B4		36) K—B1	K—Kt3
21) Kt×KP	QR—Q1		37) B—Kt2	R—B2
22) P—KKt4!	B—R2		38) P—KR4!	P—KR4!

23) P—B3   Kt—B4
24) B—KB1   Kt—Q4
25) B—B4   Kt—K3
26) QR—Q1   Kt(3)—B5
27) Kt—Q7!   R×R ch
28) R×R   B—Q6
29) Kt—B6 ch

There isn't anything to be gained by this. White should be content with the small advantage to be had by 29) B×Kt, Kt×B; Kt—QB5!

29) .....   Kt×Kt
30) B×Kt   R—QB1
31) B—Q4   B×B
32) P×B   P—Kt3!

Lasker is now evidently not content to secure a draw by ...R×QBP; 33) R—K8 ch, K—R2; 34) R—R8 ch, K—Kt3; 35) R—Kt8 ch, etc.

33) R—K4   Kt—K3
34) B—B6   R—B4
35) P—QR3   K—R2

Position after Black's 37th move

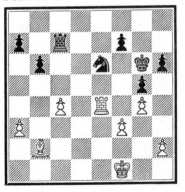

38) P—KR4!   P—KR4!

But certainly not ...P×RP; 39) P—KB4, Kt—Kt2; 40) P—B5 ch, etc.

39) RP×P   P×P
40) R×P   K—B4!

White has been getting the worst of it and his QBP is definitely weak.

41) R—R4   Kt—B5(best)
42) R—R7   K—K3?

Lasker would almost certainly have won the game (and thereby the tournament) by ...K×KtP.

43) B—B1   Kt—Kt3

Now ...R×P 44) B×Kt, R×B; 45) K—B2, R—R5; would merely lead to a draw.

44) P—B4

That saves him and very nicely too, ...R×P being countered by 45) P—B5 ch etc.

44) .....   P—Kt4
45) K—K2   P×P
46) K—Q1   K—B4
47) K—B2   Kt—B1

Or ...Kt×P; 48) B×Kt, K×B; 49) P—Kt6!

48) R—R6   Kt—K3
49) R—B6 ch   K—K5
50) P—Kt6!   Kt—Q5 ch
51) K—B3   P×P
52) R×P   Kt—K7 ch
53) K—B2   Drawn

For ...Kt×P is countered by 54) R—Kt4, R—B7; 55) K—B3

(Notes from the *Wiener Schachzeitung*)

GAME 93
SICILIAN

LASKER–PIRC

Last round Moscow 1935

1) P—K4	P—QB4
2) Kt—KB3	Kt—QB3
3) P—Q4	P×P
4) Kt×P	Kt—B3
5) Kt—QB3	P—Q3
6) B—K2	P—K3
7) 0—0	P—QR3
8) B—K3	Q—B2
9) P—B4	Kt—QR4

The usual thing in the Scheveningen variation is first to play 9) ...B—K2 whereupon White continues 10) Q—K1!, Kt—R4; 11) R—Q1, Kt—QB5; 12) B—QB1. It was just this that Pirc wished to avoid by his new move. Most of the critics have taken a dim view of it, but they may well be influenced by the negative result in this particular game.

10) P—B5

Lasker attacks with all the youthful exuberance of his 67 years.

10) ..... Kt—B5

More chances are given by 10) ...P—K4; 11) Kt—Kt3, Kt—B5; 12) B×Kt, Q×B, when White has to choose between 13) Q—B3, P—R3! and the pawn sacrifice, 13 Kt—Q2, Q—Kt5; 14) P—QR3, Q×KtP; 15) Kt—R4, Q—Kt4; 16) P—B4, Q—B3; 17) Kt—Kt6, R—QKt1, and the question as to who has the better of it is far from clear. (G.

Stahlberg in 'Chess and Chess-masters')

11) B×Kt	Q×B
12) P×P	P×P?

A weak move beautifully refuted by Lasker. Black should have played ...B×P, however unattractive it may seem.

Position after Black's 12th move

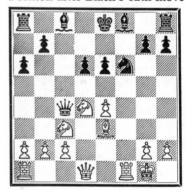

13) R×Kt!!

Here Lasker might have quoted Steinitz: 'I may be an old man but I am still able to bite if anyone puts his finger in my mouth!'

13)	P×R
14) Q—R5 ch	K—Q1

Other K moves are no better: 14) ...K—Q2; 15) Q—B7 ch, B—K2; 16) Kt—B5, R—K1; 17) Kt×P, or 14) ...K—K2; 15) Kt—B5 ch!, P×Kt; 16) Kt—Q5 ch, and White wins. (G. Stahlberg in 'Chess and Chess-masters').

15) Q—B7	B—Q2

After 15) ...B—K2 there follows 16) Kt—B5, Q—B2; 17) Kt—QR4, R—B1; 18) Q×RP, and Black is defence-

less. (G. Stahlberg in 'Chess and Chess-masters').

16) Q×P ch   K—B2
17) Q×R   B—R3
18) Kt×P ch!

(Notes by *Wiener Schachzeitung* and G. STAHLBERG).

Putting paid to Black's very last chance.

18) .....   Q×Kt
19) Q×R   B×B ch
20) K—R1   Resigns

GAME 94

FRENCH DEFENCE

LASKER–ELISKASES

3rd round, Moscow, May 16th 1935

1) P—K4   P—K3
2) P—Q4   P—Q4
3) Kt—QB3   Kt—KB3
4) B—Kt5   B—K2
5) P—K5   KKt—Q2
6) B×B   Q×B
7) Q—Q2   0—0
8) Kt—Q1

An old fashioned move hardly ever used these days, the usual thing being 8) P—KB4.

8) .....   P—KB3!
9) P×P   Kt×P
10) B—Q3   Kt—B3
11) Kt—KB3   P—K4
12) P×P   Kt×P

Position after Whites' 14th move

13) Kt×Kt   Q×Kt ch
14) Q—K3   Kt—Kt5?

Black has got slightly the better of it but the exchange of Queens is hardly likely to maintain the advantage. His best chance was 14) ...Q—KR4 15) 0—0, P—QKt3 to be followed up by ...B—Kt2, ...QR—K1, and ...P—QB4.

15) Q×Q   Kt×Q
16) 0—0   Kt×B
17) P×Kt   P—Q5

A double-edged move but then Black *was* fishing for trouble. It would have been much safer to play ...R—K1.

18) P—B3!   R—K1
19) Kt—B2   R—K6

All according to plan. The Rook is not to be cut off by Kt—K4.

20) QR—B1   P—B3
21) R—B4!   B—K3
22) R×P   B×P
23) R—Q7

By means of 23) Kt—K4, R—K7; 24) R—Kt4, P—QKt4; 25) Kt—QB3, etc. White could win a Pawn but only at the cost of the opponent's Q-wing Pawns getting very strong.

23) .....   P—QKt4
24) Kt—K4   B—Q4!

25) R—Q1   R—K7
26) Kt—B3!   R×P
27) Kt×B   P×Kt
28) R—QB1
Very well played for now
Lasker succeeds in getting
both his Rooks onto the 7th.

28) .....   K—R1?
The losing move. In such a
position timidity does not pay.
Black's one and only chance
was to play his own card
pushing the passed QRP. That
way the weaving of White's
mating net would be stopped
in the very nick of time and
White would have to be content with a draw by perpetual
check.

29) R(1)—B7   R—KKt1
30) R×RP   P—R3
31) P—R4!
Certainly not 31) R×QP on
account of ...R—K1! 32)
P—KR4, R(1)—K7 and Black
would have turned the tables
on White.

31) .....   P—Kt5
32) R(R7)—Kt7   P—Kt6
33) K—R2!
The Pawn wont run away and

Lasker wisely prefers to secure
his K position first.

33) .....   R—Q7
The beginning of the end, nor
would 33) ...R—QKt8 be
any better since after 34)
R×P, P—Kt7; 35) R—Q7
Black would get into *zugzwang*.

34) R×QKtP   R—K1
35) R(3)—Kt7   R×P
36) R×P   R—Q1
Obviously the RP cant be
saved by ...R—K3 either.

37) R—R7 ch   K—Kt1
38) R×P   R—K6
39) R(6)—R7   P—Q5
40) R(R7)—Q7
Simplest.

40) .....   R(6)—K1
41) P—R5   P—Q6
42) P—R6   R×R
He has no option since after
...P—Q7 he would be mated
in 4 moves.

43) R×R   R—K3
44) R×P   R×P ch
And since the game was to be
adjourned at this stage Black
resigned before White had
made his move. A typical
Lasker game.

CHAPTER TWENTY-NINE

A Great Farewell Performance

It was indeed the first time, and it was to remain the only time that Lasker, in a tournament career encompassing nearly half a century, failed to be among the prize-winners. For even a few months later, in August 1936, he once again amazed the chess world by a performance no one could possibly expect of him.

It happened at Nottingham where a tournament was held reminiscent of the (then) unsurpassed quality of the first great Hastings tournament of 1895. True, there have been, more recently, 'Candidates' Tournaments' consisting exclusively of those grandmasters eligible to challenge the world champion; but when it comes to awarding the plum for the 'greatest chess-tournament ever', in 1936, the Nottingham Tournament was certainly just that; and even now it is unique for a circumstance unlikely to be repeatable for generations to come, for it is certainly the only tournament in chess history that could boast the attendance of as many as five world champions, past, present, and future. There were Lasker, Capablanca and Alekhine, each of them an ex-holder of the coveted title, there was Euwe, the reigning world champion who had taken the title from Alekhine the year before, only to lose it back to him the year after, and there was Botvinnik who was to earn the title a few years later. Moreover, there were Reshevsky, Fine and Flohr, each of them a worthy contender for the title, to say nothing of older grandmasters, such as Vidmar, Bogoljubov, Tartakover.

While everyone was delighted to see Lasker among the competitors there was hardly anybody who expected him to score more than 50 per cent, let alone end up among the prize-winners after fourteen gruelling rounds in so stiff a competition.

The first round seemed to justify the pessimism of the old man's many well-wishers, for he got a cruel beating by the American grandmaster Reuben Fine, forty-six years his junior. But Lasker accepted this defeat with his usual philosophical calm, and when facing Bogoljubov in the next round, he trounced him in no uncertain manner, thereby revenging the defeat he had suffered at the same opponent's hands two years earlier at Zurich. Then came two quick and sound draws against Tartakover and Alekhine, and then yet another defeat inflicted by the young Czechoslovak grandmaster Salo Flohr. The next opponent was Capablanca who seemed quite

glad to escape with a quick and painless draw. It wasn't before
the next round, the seventh, that Lasker proved himself still capable
of his old wizardry by beating Tylor in a beautiful and typical game
at the end of which his opponent was completely 'tied up' and forced
to move to his own doom.

So, at the end of the first half of the tournament Lasker had
scored 3½ out of 7, just 50 per cent and certainly no outstanding
achievement by Lasker's own standards. In the eighth round he had
his 'bye', and by then Euwe was leading with the splendid score of
6 points out of seven games, (having already had his own 'bye').
Botvinnik had 6 points out of 8, closely followed by Fine's 5½ (8)
and Reshevsky's 5 (8). Hence, Lasker was well among the 'also-
runs', and for his many well-wishers this was even more depressing-
since it seemed only natural to expect that in the final stage of the
tournament the physical strain might begin to tell on a man of
sixty-eight.

Moreover, the old man's next game was against as dangerous an
opponent as Botvinnik who, being well in the running for first prize,
was determined to play for a win as sharply as he knew how. But
Lasker met this challenge so incisively that the Russian grandmaster all but lost and had to be glad to escape with a draw. It was
a magnificent fight and it raised the old man's spirits to such an
extent that, next day, he beat the British master Sir George Thomas
quite comfortably, and very neatly too. So, for the first time in this
badly started tournament, he had got beyond the 50 per cent border,
having now reached a score of 5 out of 9, and being not quite so far
behind the two leaders Botvinnik and Euwe who had 6½ points each.

But in the very next round came the inevitable reaction to the
exertion of the last days, and, suffering evidently from fatigue,
Lasker lost to Reshevsky in little over twenty moves; he had never
been so badly beaten in his life. Yet, refusing to be disconcerted by
such a shock, the indomitable old man was at his best again next day
when, playing Euwe, the world champion, he built up a perfectly
sound and very 'drawish' position. As a matter of fact, Lasker
offered a draw but his opponent, desperately eager to reduce the
narrow lead of his rivals and fighting for every half point, refused
the offer. He cannot have held much hope of winning the game,
but it so happened that on the very next move he made one of his
rare mistakes. A mere oversight gave his wily opponent the chance
of winning a piece, and Lasker grabbed that chance with alacrity.
Euwe resigned at once and that half point 'thrown away' was to cost
him his chance of a share in the first prize.

Lasker serenely went on to win his last two rounds against Winter and Alexander, and had actually achieved what seemed a miracle at the beginning of the tournament: he had caught up with the leaders every one of whom ranked among the world's top-players and was by decades his junior. The final score was Botvinnik and Capablanca, 10 each, Euwe, Fine, Reshevsky 9½ each, Alekhine 9, Flohr and Lasker 8½ each. Merely 1½ points' difference among the first eight, but then came a significantly wide gap of 2½ points separating, Vidmar (6), Bogoljubov and Tartakover (5½) and the rest of them from the leaders. It was a significant gap because it proved so clearly the extent to which that leading group of world-beaters had out-classed all the others; to have maintained his place among those leaders at the age of sixty-eight was, perhaps, one of the greatest achievements in Lasker's long career as a tournament player. It was his last too, for it was the last tournament he ever played in, and certainly a most worthy conclusion to one of the greatest tournament records ever achieved by any one player.

In those days Lasker was still bristling with energy and the sheer joy of life; and while his remaining span of life, alas, was limited to far too few years he was still full of plans and did a great deal of work. He travelled as much as ever, he lectured a good deal, he published a number of essays, he began work on a new book, and he even planned to compete in yet another chess tournament which was to be held in Moscow in the spring of 1937. But it was postponed by a year, and by then world affairs were in a pretty grim state, and there were plainly visible portents of struggles uglier and bloodier than those on the sixty-four squares.

The Laskers had gone back to Moscow and Emanuel, busy with his mathematical work at the Academy had no inkling of yet another unexpected change. Here is what Frau Lasker recorded about that fateful decision.

'It was August 1937, and a very hot day in Moscow. Late that afternoon Emanuel and I went for our daily walk in the great park near our house. We sat down on a bench, both lost in thought and not very talkative.'

"Well, my dear", Emanuel said suddenly. "We are getting to be quite elderly people. You'll be seventy in November. What do you want for your birthday? It's a unique occasion and you should have a unique gift."

"Well", I answered on the spur of the moment, "if money is no object I'd like a trip to America."

"Done", said Emanuel, and we were both very happy at the thought of seeing my daughter's family once again, and so many of our old friends. My daughter was in Amsterdam at the time, and we arranged to meet her there and to make the sea-voyage together.

We left Russia at the end of October, and as we meant to be back in February we took little luggage along. We had our return tickets too, and as for our Moscow household we left it in the care of Julie, our cook. We merely went for a trip, but fate had decided differently.

On the way to Holland we had to go in a round-about manner, crossing a good many borders; for we did not want to set foot in Nazi-Germany. When we finally got to Chicago we had a wonderful time with the grandchildren, and Emanuel finished his book *Das Weltbild des Spielers*. In Chicago too, I celebrated my seventieth birthday.

Soon after, Emanuel had to go to New York for a simultaneous performance in a chess club as well as a lecture at Columbia University. I joined him in New York a week or two later, and there I was gripped by quite a nasty influenza. I had some heart trouble too and had to go to hospital. We had to postpone our departure until I was fit enough to travel, but I never did get fit enough, and the doctors finally decreed that any long voyage had to be ruled out. So we had to resign ourselves to realising that we had reached the end of our peregrinations. We decided to stay in New York, and we sent for our furniture. That's how America came to be the last port of call in Lasker's life."

Hence, once again, the circumstances of the septuagenarian were completely changed, and from the quiet backwater and material security of his Moscow study he found himself transplanted to another continent and to the need once again to resume the struggle of life. True, he had his relations in America and many friends, he had his brain and his pen and his chess all of which combined to secure a moderately comfortable living. Yet, it is a sobering thought that, at the end of so successful a life a man so rich in fame and honours should have had to work for his daily bread.

But Lasker liked it that way; he would never accept charity, and he enjoyed his work. To have to travel from one lecture platform to another and to keep on with his chess-assignments rejuvenated him, even though a simultaneous performance was a strain for his old legs rather than his ever young brain, for to go from board to board and round and round for hours on end may tot up to a walk of a mile or two.

Yet he took it all in his stride, with his customary nonchalance as well as absent-mindedness. One day when he had to go to Boston for a simultaneous performance he had just left their New York

NOTTINGHAM 1936

		1	2	3	4	5	6	7	8	9	10	11	12	13	14	15	
{1	Botvinnik	×	½	½	½	½	½	½	½	1	1	1	1	1	1	½	10
{2	Capablanca	½	×	½	½	1	1	0	½	1	½	½	1	1	1	1	10
3	Euwe	½	½	×	½	1	0	½	0	1	½	1	1	1	1	1	9½
4	Fine	½	½	½	×	½	½	½	1	½	1	½	1	1	½	1	9½
5	Reshevsky	½	0	0	½	×	1	½	1	1	1	½	1	1	1	½	9½
6	Alekhine	½	0	1	½	0	×	1	½	½	1	1	½	1	½	1	9
7	Flohr	½	1	½	½	½	0	×	1	1	1	½	0	0	1	1	8½
8	Lasker	½	½	1	0	0	½	0	×	½	1	½	1	1	1	1	8½
9	Vidmar	0	0	0	½	0	½	0	½	×	1	½	½	1	½	1	6
10	Bogoljubow	0	½	½	0	0	0	0	0	0	×	½	1	1	1	1	5½
11	Tartakower	0	½	0	½	½	0	½	½	½	½	×	0	0	1	1	5½
12	Tylor	0	0	0	0	0	½	1	0	½	0	1	×	½	½	½	4½
13	Alexander	0	0	0	0	0	0	1	0	0	0	1	½	×	½	½	3½
14	Thomas	0	0	0	½	0	½	0	0	½	0	0	½	½	×	½	3
15	Winter	½	0	0	0	½	0	0	0	0	0	0	½	½	½	×	2½

apartment to catch his train. It was a hot day, and Martha discovered that Emanuel had gone without his coat which contained his passport as well as his money. In great excitement she hurried after him and just caught up with him on the subway station.

'What on earth would you have done?' she exclaimed.

Emanuel calmly replied that he had enough money in his trouser-pockets to pay for the fare to Boston; and there he would get his fee.

'But you couldn't appear for a public performance in your shirt-sleeves', cried Martha.

'Why not?' countered Emanuel; 'It's a hot day. Besides, I could always borrow someone else's coat. It would make no difference to the quality of the games.'

Lasker was also a frequent and ever welcome guest at the Manhattan Chess Club and the Marshall Chess Club in New York, and towards the end of 1940 a short match was arranged with his old friend and adversary Frank Marshall who was nearly ten years his junior. Alas, the match was never finished, as, very soon after it started, Lasker was stricken by his mortal illness. Thus only one game of the match was played, and it was won by Marshall with all the cleverness of his tricky style. Thus this great and lovable master won the first and the last game he ever played against Lasker, the first at Paris 1900, the last at New York 1940. But out of the twenty-two match and tournament games these two old warriors played in the intervening forty years, Marshall could not win a single one. He drew ten, and he lost twelve.

GAME 95

QUEEN'S GAMBIT DECLINED

LASKER–BOGOLJUBOV

2nd round, Nottingham
August 11th, 1936

1)	Kt—KB3	P—Q4
2)	P—B4	P—K3
3)	P—Q4	Kt—KB3
4)	Kt—B3	P—B3
5)	B—Kt5	QKt—Q2
6)	P—K3	Q—R4
7)	Kt—Q2	P×P

Now White can no longer keep his Bishops, but he gets a fairly strong centre.

8)	B×Kt	Kt×B
9)	Kt×P	Q—B2
10)	R—B1	Kt—Q4

A very strong move, thwarting White's plans on the Q-wing.

11)	B—Q3	Kt×Kt
12)	P×Kt	

Here the strength of Black's 10th move becomes fully apparent. Being unable to retake with the R, White is forced to block his QB line, thereby depriving himself of any activity on the Q-wing.

12)	.....	B—K2
13)	0—0	0—0

14) P—B4
Lasker seeks compensation on the K-wing.

14) ..... P—KKt3
So as to stop White from pushing his KBP and opening the file.

15) Kt—K5 B—R6
This move doesn't seem to make much sense. Much better was 15) ...P—QB4 followed by P—QKt3. The KB might well have been played to Kt2 via B3 so as to strengthen the defence.

16) R—QB2 P—B3
17) Kt—B4 B—K2
18) P—K4 P—QB4
19) P—B5
What with White attacking on the K-wing, and the Black counter-demonstration in the centre, the fight is hotting up.

19) ..... P—QKt4
20) Kt—K3 P×QP
21) P×QP Q—Kt3
22) B—K2 R—Q1
23) R—Q2 K—Kt2
24) B—B3 R—QKt1
25) K—R1 P—QR4
It looks a bit rash thus to neglect the defence of the K-wing; and by means of a few powerful moves Lasker will soon prove that the Black K-position could, indeed, do with some support.

26) P—Kt4 P—R5
27) P—K5!
This secures some decisive advantage for White.

27) ..... P×KP
28) QP×P R×R

29) Q×R?
Under considerable time pressure, Lasker makes a slip. He should have first played P—KB6 ch so as to scotch the subsequent counter-chance.

29) ..... B—Kt4!
Forcing White to give some additional support to his K3 which practically amounts to the White attack fizzling out.

30) R—K1 B—Kt2
31) B×B Q×B ch
32) K—Kt1 Q—B6
32) ...R—Q1 would, of course, be countered by P—B6 ch.

33) Q—Q4?
To guard against the threat of ...B×Kt, followed by ...Q—Kt5 ch. But White would have done better first to play P—B6 ch, so as to give Black no opportunity of easing his game by an exchange on his KB4.

33) ..... K—R3?
By ...R—Q1; 34) P—B6 ch, K—R3; 35) Q×R, B×Kt ch,

Position after Black's 33rd move

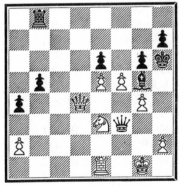

Black could have secured a comfortable draw.

34) P—B6!   R—KB1?

Now Black slips up under grievous time pressure. By 34) ...R—Q1 Black could still secure a draw, since 35) Q—R7 could be countered by R—Q2; 36) Q—B5, B—R5; 37) R—KB1, R—Q8! leading to perpetual check.

35) Kt—Kt2!

Scotching any chance of a counter-attack. There is nothing that Black can now do against the invasion of the White Q.

35) .....   R—B1

The idea being to swap rooks by 36) ...R—B8, but it won't come to that any more.

36) Q—Q7   R—KKt1
37) Q—KB7   Q—R1
38) P—R4   B—Q7
39) R—Q1!

Even more forceful than P—Kt5 ch.

39) .....   Q—QB1
40) R×B   Resigns

Since obviously 40) ...Q—B8 ch is countered by 41) K—R2, Q×R; 42) Q×R.

(Notes by Dr. EUWE in *De Schaakwereld* 1936)

GAME 96

FOUR GAME KNIGHTS

TYLOR–LASKER

7th round, Nottingham
August 17th, 1936

1) P—K4	P—K4
2) Kt—KB3	Kt—QB3
3) Kt—B3	Kt—B3
4) B—Kt5	B—Kt5
5) 0—0	0—0
6) P—Q3	P—Q3
7) B—Kt5	Kt—K2
8) Kt—KR4	P—B3
9) B—QB4	K—R1
10) P—B4	P×P
11) B×Kt	P×B
12) R×P	Kt—Kt3
13) Kt×Kt ch	BP×Kt
14) B—Kt3	Q—K2
15) Kt—K2	B—R4
16) P—B3	B—Q2
17) Kt—Kt3	B—B2
18) R—B2	K—Kt2

19) Q—K2	QR—K1
20) R(1)—KB1	B—K3
21) Q—B2	B—Kt3!
22) P—Q4	B—QB2
23) K—R1	P—KR4!
24) R—K1	Q—B2
25) R(2)—K2	B×B
26) P×B	Q—Q2
27) Kt—B1	R—K2
28) Q—Q3	R(1)—K1
29) Kt—Q2	P—Q4!

After all these careful preparations he now proceeds at long last to open up the game and thereby to give the B some considerable scope.

30) P×P	R×R
31) R×R	R×R
32) Q×R	Q×P
33) Q—K7 ch	Q—B2
34) Q—K4	

White avoids the exchange of queens as the ending would be not too favourable for him.

34) .....   Q—Q2
35) Kt—B3   K—B2!
36) P—B4

Kt—KR4 would have been refuted by 36) ...Q—Kt5!

36) .....   Q—K3
37) Q—Q3

He chooses to retreat, the alternative being 37) Q×Q ch, K×Q; 38) K—Kt1, K—B4; 39) K—B2, K—K5; 40) K—K2, P—Kt4!

37) .....   B—B5!

Stopping the approach of the opponent's K: 38) K—Kt1, Q—K6 ch; 39) Q×Q, B×Qch, followed by ...B—B8, anp wins.

38) P—Kt3   Q—K6!
39) Q—B3   B—R3
40) P—B5   Q—B7!
41) Q—B4 ch   K—Kt2
42) Q—Q3   B—K6

43) Q—Q1   P—QR4!

Zugzwang on a fairly crowded board.

Position after Black's 43rd move

44) P—QKt4   P×P
45) P—Kt3   K—R3

Resigns

Very neatly calculated.

(Notes by Eliskases in the *Wiener Schachzeitung*, 1936)

GAME 97

GRÜNFELD DEFENCE

Lasker–Botvinnik

9th round, Nottingham
August 20th, 1936

1) P—Q4   Kt—KB3
2) P—QB4   P—KKt3
3) Kt—QB3   P—Q4
4) Kt—B3   B—Kt2
5) B—Kt5

So as to avoid the beaten path.

5) .....   Kt—K5
6) P×P   Kt×B
7) Kt×Kt   P—K3
8) Kt—B3   P×P
9) P—K3

A very quiet position but by no means a dull one. Black has the two Bishops but White has a half-open file on the Q-wing which may well offer a chance for a minority attack on the Queen's wing.

9) .....   0—0
10) B—K2   P—QB3
11) 0—0   Q—K2
12) P—QR3   B—K3
13) R—B1   Kt—Q2
14) Kt—K1   Kt—Kt3!
15) Kt—Q3   QR—Q1
16) Kt—B5   B—B1
17) P—QKt4   Kt—B5

Black was of course well prepared for P—Kt4 and the tension now remains.

18)	Kt—Kt1	P—Kt3
19)	Kt—Kt3	B—R3
20)	R—K1	KR—K1
21)	Kt(1)—Q2	

That way White recovers control of his QB5 for obviously Black has to push the Pawn to support his Kt.

21)	.....	P—QKt4
22)	R—R1	B—QB1
23)	B—B1	Q—Q3
24)	Kt—B5	R—K2
25)	Kt(2)—Kt3	R(1)—K1
26)	Q—B1	P—B4
27)	Kt—Q3	P—Kt4

Black could not passively contemplate White's preparations for a Q-wing demonstration starting with P—QR4

28)	Q—B3	P—B5
29)	P×P	P×P
30)	R×R	R×R
31)	P—QR4	P—QR3
32)	P×P	RP×P
33)	R—R8	R—K1
34)	Q—B1	R—B1
35)	Q—Q1	

Not Kt×BP on account of 35) ...Kt—Kt3.

35)	.....	B—B4
36)	R×R ch	B×R
37)	Q—R5	Q—Kt3
38)	Q×Q ch	P×Q

39)	Kt×P	B×P
40)	B—Q3	Kt—Q7
41)	Kt×Kt	B×Kt
42)	B×B	P×B

Position after Black's 42nd move

43) Kt—K6!

The only move and very strong indeed. Black can just manage to escape with a draw.

| 43) | ..... | B—B6 |
| 44) | K—B1 | Draw agreed |

The sequel might be ...P—Kt5; 45) K—K2, P—Kt6; 46) K—Q3, P—Kt7; 47) K—B2, K—R2; and neither side will be able to make any headway. A very sound and solid game.

(Notes by HANS KMOCH in the Tournament Book of the *Wiener Schachzeitung*)

GAME 98

Q. GAMBIT DECLINED

LASKER–EUWE

13th round, Nottingham
August 25th, 1936

| 1) | P—Q4 | P—Q4 |
| 2) | P—QB4 | P—QB3 |

3)	Kt—KB3	Kt—B3
4)	P—K3	B—B4
5)	B—Q3	P—K3
6)	P×P	

The way White has treated the opening, he can't get much more out of it than equalisation.

6)	.....	B × B
7)	Q × B	KP × P
8)	Kt—B3	B—Q3
9)	0—0	0—0
10)	R—K1	QKt—Q2
11)	P—K4	

Necessary, even though he will be saddled with an isolated QP.

11)	.....	P × P
12)	Kt × P	Kt × Kt
13)	Q × Kt	

Obviously 13) R × Kt would be a bad blunder, giving Black a chance of winning immediately by ... Kt—B4.

13)	.....	R—K1
14)	Q × R ch	Q × Q
15)	R × Q ch	R × R
16)	K—B1	Kt—Kt3
17)	B—Q2	P—B3

Better was ...Kt—Q4; 18) R—K1, R—Q1.

18)	R—K1	R × R ch

With this last exchange, Black's minute advantage is practically reduced to naught. 18) ...R—Q1 would have been countered by 19) B—R5.

19)	Kt × R	K—B2
20)	K—K2	K—K3
21)	P—KR3	Kt—B5
22)	B—B1	B—B2
23)	K—Q3	B—R4??

A horrible mistake, particularly when considering the utter simplicity of the position. Translator's note: This almost incredible blunder has mean-

Position after Black's 23rd move

while come to be one of the classical instances of 'chess-blindness' from which sometimes even Grandmasters are not immune. In Euwe's case this was a particularly tragic lapse, since the $\frac{1}{2}$ point thus 'thrown away' robbed him of his chance of sharing first prize with Botvinnik and Capablanca.

24) P—QKt4!

Obviously winning a piece.

24)	.....	B × P
25)	Kt—B2	B—Q7
26)	B × B	Kt—Kt7 ch
27)	K—K2	K—Q4
28)	B—B1	Kt—B5
29)	K—Q3	Kt—Kt3
30)	Kt—K3 ch	K—K3
31)	Kt—B4	Kt—B1
32)	Kt—R5	Kt—Q3
33)	B—B4	Resigns

(Notes by HANS KMOCH in the *Wiener Schachzeitung*)

GAME 99

COLLE-SYSTEM

WINTER–LASKER

14th round, Nottingham
August 27th, 1936

1)	P—Q4	Kt—KB3
2)	Kt—KB3	P—Q4
3)	P—K3	P—K3
4)	QKt—Q2	P—B4
5)	P—B3	Kt—B3
6)	B—Q3	B—Q3
7)	0—0	0—0
8)	P×P	B×P
9)	P—K4	Q—B2
10)	Q—K2	R—K1

A novelty. The usual move (suggested by Alekhine) is ...B—Q3 followed by Kt—Kt5.

11)	P—K5	Kt—Q2
12)	R—K1?	

He should have first played Kt—QKt3 so as to give his QB some scope. Thereafter he could have secured his K5 by means of KR—K1 and B—KB4 with a reasonably good position.

Position after Black's 12th move

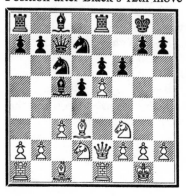

12)	.....	P—B3!
13)	Kt—Kt5?	

Much too optimistic. He should certainly have played 13) P×P. Evidently White is only considering ...P×Kt which after 14) Q—R5 and the subsequent B-sacrifice, would have given him a draw by perpetual check.

13)	.....	Q×P!

Forcing a winning endgame.

14)	B×P ch	K—B1
15)	Q×Q	Kt(2)×Q
16)	P—QKt4	B—Q3!

Lasker avoids the little trap his opponent had put up for him. It seemed that Black could win a piece by 16) ...P×Kt 17) P×B, P—KKt3. In point of fact though, White would not play 17) P×B; he would push the QKtP and regain his piece with considerable advantage. Of course Lasker doesn't fall for this, and by his next move he wins a P in very favourable circumstances.

17)	Kt(5)—B3	P—KKt3
18)	Kt—R4	K—Kt2
19)	P—KB4	K×B
20)	P×Kt	Kt×KP
21)	Kt(4)—B3	B—Q2
22)	Kt×Kt	B×Kt
23)	B—Kt2	

Completely hopeless position for White. He might as well have resigned here.

23)	.....	QR—B1
24)	R—K3	B—B5
25)	R—Q3	B—QKt4
26)	R—R3 ch	K—Kt2

27) P—R4	B—B5	39) R—K3	K—K2
28) Kt×B	R×Kt	40) K—K2	R—K5
29) R—Q1	B—K4	41) K—Q3	R×R ch
30) P—R5	R(1)—QB1	42) K×R	K—Q3
31) R—K1	R(1)—B3	43) K—Q3	K—B3
32) K—B1	P—KKt4	44) B—B1	K—Kt4
33) K—Kt1	P—Kt5	45) B—K3	P—R3
34) R—R4	R—B1	46) B—R6	P—B4
35) P—Kt3	R—KR1	47) B—Kt5	B—Kt2
36) R×R	K×R		Resigns
37) K—Kt2	K—Kt2		
38) K—B2	K—B2		

(Notes by HANS KMOCH in the *Wiener Schachzeitung*)

GAME 100

ENGLISH

LASKER–ALEXANDER

Last round, Nottingham
August 28th, 1936

1) P—QB4	P—K4
2) Kt—QB3	Kt—QB3
3) P—KKt3	P—KKt3
4) B—Kt2	B—Kt2
5) P—Q3	KKt—K2
6) B—Q2	0—0
7) Kt—B3	Kt—Q5
8) 0—0	P—QB3
9) R—B1	P—Q3

A more logical continuation was ...Kt×Kt ch followed by ...P—Q4.

10) P—QKt4	Kt×Kt
11) B×Kt	B—R6
12) R—K1	Q—Q2
13) P—Kt5	P—QB4

Oddly enough Black now finally renounces ...P—Q4 which he ought to have played several moves before.

14) Kt—K4	Q—B2
15) R—Kt1	B—Q2
16) Q—B1	P—Kt3?

Position after Black's 16th move

A very poor move which inevitably will cost him the exchange, the surprising point being merely this, that it's not the QR but the KR which will have to bite the dust.

17) B—Kt5!

Forcing the win, the threat being B×Kt as well as Kt—B6 ch followed by B×Kt and Q—R6.

17)	Kt—B4
18) Kt—B6 ch	B×Kt
19) B×B	QR—Kt1
20) B—Kt4	Kt—Kt2(forced)

21)	Q—R6	Kt—K1
22)	B—K7	Kt—Kt2
23)	B—B6	

This is merely to gain time and to see if may be the position will yield even more than a mere win of the exchange.

23)	.....	Kt—K1
24)	B—K7	Kt—Kt2
25)	B×R	

So it's 'only' the exchange after all.

| 25) | ..... | R×B |
| 26) | B—B3 | Kt—B4 |

27)	Q—Q2	Kt—Q5
28)	B—Kt2	B—B1
29)	P—K3	Kt—K3
30)	P—B4	B—Kt2
31)	P—QR4	P—B4
32)	B×B	Q×B
33)	Q—KKt2	Q—K2
34)	Q—Q5	Resigns

(Notes by Hans Kmoch in the *Wiener Schachzeitung*)

Translator's note:
This was the last of Lasker's tournament games.

GAME 100a

Q. GAMBIT DECLINED

MARSHALL–LASKER

New York, 1940

1)	P—QB4	P—K3
2)	Kt—KB3	Kt—KB3
3)	Kt—B3	P—Q4
4)	P—Q4	QKt—Q2
5)	B—Kt5	B—K2
6)	P—K3	0—0
7)	Q—B2	P—B4
8)	BP×P	Kt×P
9)	B×B	Q×B
10)	Kt×Kt	P×Kt

In spite of various transitions those two old warriors have finally steered into one of those old-fashioned variations they used to play so often some decades earlier.

11)	B—Q3	P—KKt3
12)	P×P	Kt×P
13)	0—0	P—Kt3
14)	QR—B1	P—QR4
15)	KR—Q1	B—Kt2
16)	Kt—Q4	KR—B1

17)	Q—K2	Q—B3
18)	P—KR3	R—B2
19)	R—B3	R(1)—QB1
20)	R(1)—QB1	Q—K4
21)	P—R3	P—R5
22)	B—Kt5	R—R1

Position after Black's 22nd move

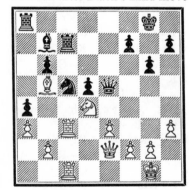

23) B×P!
A neat little combination securing a tangible advantage for White.

23)	.....	R×B
24)	P—QKt4	Q—K1
25)	Q—B2	R—K2

26) P×Kt   P×P
27) R×P   R×KP

Not quite good enough to turn the tables. This game (unpublished yet) is the very last match game Lasker played; an interesting point being that just as he lost the very first game he played against Marshall (Paris 1900) so he lost the very last game against him forty years later; but of the dozens of games they played in between Marshall could not win a single one. The little 'match' incidentally in which this game was played was never completed owing to Lasker's ill health. He died a few months after this game. He was 72 when the game was played, Marshall was 62.

28) P×R   Q×P ch
29) Q—B2   Q×Kt
30) Q×Q   R×Q
31) R—R5   R—QB5
32) R×R   P×R
33) R—QB5   B—R3
34) P—QR4   Resigns

The game was adjourned here, but Lasker obviously resigned it before resumption.

(Notes by the translator)

CHAPTER THIRTY

Working to the End

One of the last perfectly happy days in Lasker's life was his seventieth birthday which he celebrated at Christmas 1938, just about a year after his arrival in America. It was quite a party in the house of Harold M. Phillips, one of the oldest American friends of the Laskers, and well over three hundred guests had assembled to do sincere homage to the septuagenarian.

About a year later, Lasker's busy life was interrupted by the first signs of his illness. During one of his lectures he suddenly felt giddy, his voice became inaudible, and he could not go on. Irving Chernev, chess master and friend, took over, and the old man was packed off to bed. But he wouldn't give in yet, and after a day's rest he insisted on resuming his assignments; and after another restful week at the University of Hamilton—where the Laskers were the guests of Harold King, the President—Emanuel went back to his usual routine of classes, lectures and simultaneous exhibitions.

One of Lasker's last lectures was held at Chicago, and since the manuscript was preserved it might be interesting to quote a few significant passages in his own words:

I am very happy to have an opportunity of addressing citizens of the United States. Here I spent much of my time as a young man and here I learned to appreciate the spiritual freedom enjoyed by the citizens of this country. I came here to study mathematics, I won the world championship in chess and I returned to Germany to take a doctor's degree in philosophy. But America has always been one of my great loves, even though I have been a cosmopolitan all my life. That's how I was lucky enough to meet interesting people and to gain good friends all over the world.

As a young undergraduate I met Carl Ludwig Schleich. There isn't a doctor anywhere on earth who would not revere his name, for whoever is operated on by means of local anaesthetic and feeling no pain has to thank Schleich's great discovery for it. Yet, when he first presented the idea at a Berlin congress of doctors they wouldn't even discuss it, let alone give it a fair trial. He wrote a book about it, and when he couldn't find a publisher for it, he finally published it at his own risk and expense. It happened to be the standard work of a new branch of science, but do you think the author now received some official recognition and support? He didn't. Officialdom treated him no better than any genius ahead of their own narrow minds. Schleich was a poet too, and a fine writer, he was a great teacher and a lovable man. Had he lived in the United States he would have received sufficient support to be able to devote all his time to scientific research. In the Europe of those days he had to spend much of his time struggling for a living, and it was only in his ripe old age that officialdom granted him some reluctant recognition.

His fate is significant for the epoch in which he lived. It was the time after Bismarck's dismissal. It was a time in which mediocrity was at a premium and petty-bourgeois bogus-romanticism ran wild and was glorified right up to the throne. My brother Berthold was a medical genius, but he did not fare much better than Schleich. Rathenau was a great administrator and a benefactor of his country, yet for his pains he was murdered by those who were to reap high honour in the Third Reich.

I knew Walter Rathenau well. I met him in Moszkowski's house, along with Einstein. We had long discussions on philosophical problems, and while we argued fiercely and disagreed widely this tended to enhance rather than diminish mutual respect. It was the beginning of a long friendship with Moszkowski and several meetings with Einstein.

Einstein knew that I had raised certain objections against his theory, claiming that 'lim c equals infinity,' whereas he claims c to be finite. To my mind, Einstein's entire theory hinges on that question. I had talks with Michelson about it too, and I elaborated my thesis at a meeting of the Berlin Mathematical Society. A good many of Einstein's supporters were present on that occasion, and as many as fourteen of them attacked my thesis in the debate. However it was printed by the Society. I should have welcomed an opportunity of discussing it more thoroughly with Einstein himself. Maybe we would have got a small step or two nearer to truth.

Of famous men who were interested in chess I well remember the Viennese Rothschild, great-grandson of Amschel, one of the original Rothschild brothers. He was a leading member of the famous Vienna Chess Club, and almost daily he used to go there and spend four or five hours. He was usually surrounded by quite a flock of servants who would attend to their master's every wish and whim. He did a good deal for chess financially and supported a number of impecunious masters more or less generously. If only he had known that the Nazis were to rob him of his fortune anyway, he might have allocated a substantial part of it to a fund for the promotion of chess, such as Arthur Trebitsch had done, another wealthy Viennese who had a soft heart and an open purse for chess.

One of the most generous supporters of chess, of course, was the American Professor Rice who gave unstinted financial assistance to an entire generation of chess-masters. He was the inventor of the 'Rice Gambit' and he spent many thousands of dollars for that opening's thorough analysis. Speaking of generous American supporters of the game I must not fail to mention Mr. Rosenwald of Chicago who gave Sammy Reshevsky, the child prodigy, the chance of a sound education and thereby helped him to grow to the stature of the great master he now is; nor must I forget my own old friend Harold Phillips of New York who has done so much to sponsor the love of chess at American colleges. Finally let me pay my sincere tribute to a man who is in our midst to-night, our highly respected friend Addleman who, in his quiet and inconspicuous way, has done so much to materialise some of the greatest matches and tournaments of recent chess history.

As for the politicians and statesmen I had the good fortune of meeting, I should like to single out President Theodore Roosevelt. I was introduced to him while playing my match against Marshall at Washington. When in England in 1936 I had the most pleasing acquaintance of the Member of Parliament, Brigadier-General Spears. He invited my wife and myself to his house, and he wanted to know what we thought of the Hitler régime. May be he did not know that we were 'racially' persecuted. But my wife told him. 'General', she said, 'I am a Jewess. Yet, what ever blows and knocks I had to suffer I have never been unhappy and I am determined not to allow the dictators to spoil my joy of life. Nor shall we allow anybody to rob us of our faith in humanity and human decency.'

This is a sufficiently significant passage to conclude an account of Lasker's last public talk. As for his many American friends —and to name only a few of those not yet mentioned—there was Bigelow, his successor in conducting the chess-column of the 'New York Post'; there was Dr Platz who gave his blood when a last, vain attempt was made to save Lasker's life by a blood-transfusion; and there were Harry Grottowitz, Louis Wolff and Eva Robin who gave their loyal friendship as his life was drawing to a close.

Fortunately, he did not realise it until the very end. Even in 1940 the year before his death, he had a book published, *The Community of the Future*, a fairly ambitious work of nearly 300 pages and an attempt to analyse some of the economic and sociological problems of the time and to cure the recurrant cycles of slump and unemployment by cooperative means.

Nor was this indefatigable man without further literary plans, even in his seventy-second year. He meant to write a comprehensive treatise of mathematics in so popular a form as to make that difficult science and its awe-inspiring formulas palatable for the lay-mind. It would have been a most attractive book, to judge by the few chapters he still had the strength to write. Alas, the book remained unfinished, for he was disturbed more and more frequently by fits of giddiness which incapacitated him for days on end, though in between he would be his own bright self again.

Martha took him to see a specialist and then spoke to him alone. She knew now that it was hopeless, but Emanuel did not know it yet. On the way home he was as cheerful as ever, joking that he felt fifty-two because he had simply stopped counting twenty years ago.

A few days later was his birthday. Many friends came to see him, and most of them brought cigars. 'Now you have enough to last you to the next birthday', one of them said. But Lasker's mathematical mind would not stand for inaccuracy. 'If I smoke three each day', he said, 'they will last for five months and eighteen days.'

Darker days came, and then the end. He refused his food and he found it ever more difficult to speak. 'There's no more sense in it, my dear' he whispered to Martha; and now she knew that he knew it.

Next day Reuben Fine and his young wife came to see him for the last time. He could merely give them a feeble wave of his hand. When Fine had gone, Martha heard Emanuel whisper: 'A King of Chess.'

These were the last words he was heard to speak. He died next day, on 13 January 1941.

Postscript

When this book on Lasker first appeared in German it seemed obvious that so comprehensive an account of so interesting a life and so fascinating a personality must be given to the wider audience of the English-speaking world; it seemed all the more obvious since that world, for more than half his adult life, had provided the background of that truly cosmopolitan globetrotter.

Being myself a chess-addict (and a collector of chess books) I must have shared the impatience for an Anglo-American edition of Dr Hannak's book with thousands of persons similarly addicted;

but I had a personal reason for taking time off to do the job myself. I considered it a privilege since it gave me a welcome opportunity of discharging a personal debt of gratitude, apart from giving vent to the only bit of hero-worship I have ever indulged in.

The hero-worship requires no explanation for a chess player of my generation; as for the personal debt of gratitude it can be summed up in five words: Lasker warned me off bridge.

'Stop it before it begins to fascinate you', he told me in my early twenties; 'chess is quite bad enough for you. Chess *and* bridge is too much. Once you get the hang of bridge you'd be lost for any useful occupation.'

There and then I accepted such truly fatherly advice, and I have obeyed it ever since. But then I knew that Lasker was speaking from experience. He was an expert bridge player, and since no expert knowledge can be gained without a considerable outlay of time and since that was for ever Lasker's most precious commodity he had frequent cause to regret the time denied to his more important interests.

Yet so deeply ingrained was his aversion to any kind of dilletantism that he was congenitally unable to take up any pursuit —no matter if it was a science, an art-form, a language, or a mere game—without aspiring to perfect mastery of the subject.

Of this characteristic trait he once gave me a significant object lesson. We were sitting in a café, talking about a mutual acquaintance, a university professor much respected by Lasker for a recent philosophical treatise. Someone at the table—no chess player himself—mentioned that the professor was supposed to be very keen on chess, and since that was news to Lasker he turned to me for the only 'expert' confirmation available at that table.

'The professor never told me that he could play chess', he said; 'What sort of a chess player is he?'

I shrugged derisively.

'He is nowhere near to what you or even I would call a chess-player.'

'Well?', asked Lasker, peering at me earnestly and demanding the precise elucidation he required on any matter that interested him; 'Well then, what sort of a chess-player is he?'

My glance fell on some dominoes players engaged on a boisterous and evidently none too serious game at the next table.

'Well', I explained, 'He knows the rules of chess, but that's about all. He shoves the pieces about just like those dominoes players. He can't play proper chess at all, he plays a sort of dominoes with chess-men.'

I felt quite pleased with that impromptu definition of a chess-'duffer', but Lasker was far from pleased; he was quite angry.

'What do you know about dominoes?' he exclaimed. 'How dare you insult a very ingenious game of whose intricacies and subtleties you evidently haven't an inkling!' And forthwith, he treated us to a most thorough and lucid lecture on dominoes when played at the high level at which he mastered this and every other game he ever bothered about.

He had some deep theoretical knowledge and practical experience of a good many games including the most difficult of all, the Japanese 'Go'. Yet, while he would never rest content before having achieved complete mastery of any such game—mastery according to his own very exacting standards, truly 'grandmasterly' standards to use a convenient term of modern chess-phraseology—he could not but grudge the time inevitably spent on such minor pursuits; precious time taken from his major interests in philosophy and mathematics and from what he considered his real job in life.

With all his world-wide fame as the supreme champion and arbiter of the chess world, with all the irresistible fascination of the game and the time grudgingly devoted to tournaments and matches and to potboiler assignments of simultaneous performances and lectures on chess, he considered himself a philosopher and a mathematician rather than a chess-professional.

As for his philosophical and sociological essays, the less said about them the better; there is little original about them, and they are remarkable only for the dogged determination and the painstaking labour spent on them by a most lovable man, for ever an indomitable worker and a stubborn fighter who must needs attempt to elevate his theories of 'struggle' to a philosophical level; and who must needs assert and reassure himself with the conviction that his remarkable intellectual achievements were finding due recognition beyond that one sphere within whose relatively narrow and trivial compass his world-wide fame was so brilliantly and so permanently established.

It was somehow pathetic to see that intensely earnest man so deeply engrossed in a theoretical analysis of mere games and for ever attempting to 'repress', and at the same time to justify the very triviality of such pursuits and to claim recognition in the wider field of original philosophical thought. Yet, even the seven years of devoted labour lavished on his philosophical verse-drama would hardly have achieved a public performance and a modicum of *succès d'estime* if the author hadn't been Emanuel Lasker, famed the world over as the supreme champion at the game of chess.

While Lasker's excursions in the realm of creative philosophical thought have been somewhat overrated in his own mind as well as in the fulsome praise of his adulators, it seems an ironical point that his very real and highly remarkable eminence as a creative mathematician has never quite got the praise it deserves, not, at any rate, outside that small circle of experts who can live and breathe in the rarified atmosphere of higher mathematics.

True enough, everybody knows that Lasker was a mathematician of high professional calibre; but I for one—and I dare say this applies to many other lifelong admirers and to most readers of this book—I for one, (being no mathematician), was surprised to learn from a supremely expert source that some of Lasker's mathematical work was truly epoch-making; and that, even if he had never touched a chess-board in his life, his name would always rank among the immortals in the history of mathematics.

I owe this information to *Dr K. E. Hirsch*, Professor of Mathematics at London University and Hon. Secretary of the London Mathematical Society; and so as to emphasize (and elucidate) his point he has very kindly contributed the following brief outline of Lasker's lasting achievement in modern mathematical thought.

'Lasker's reputation as a mathematician is founded on a single paper. This is a monumental work of nearly one hundred pages Zur Theorie der Moduln und Ideale *and appeared in the* Mathematische Annalen, *vol. 60 (1905), pp. 20–116, one of the oldest and most distinguished mathematical research journals. The paper contains a full account of the results he had obtained in his doctoral dissertation of 1902, which is mentioned in the text (English edition, p. 87).*

It is quite a testimony to the high opinion which the editors of this periodical held of Lasker's work that they gave up so much space to it. Nowadays when a young mathematician wants to publish the contents of his Ph.D. thesis, he may find that he has to curtail his writing rather drastically. Lasker has also published a few other papers, but none of them reaches the same importance. There can be little doubt that if he had chosen to continue with his mathematical researches, he could have entered the academic career successfully. He himself was quite aware of the significance of his early discoveries. In his account of the match with Capablanca for the World Championship (Mein Wettkampf mit Capablanca, Berlin und Leipzig, 1922, p. 6) *he writes*: 'Ich hoffe, dass meine Philosophie des Unvollendbar, ja, auch meine Theorie der Moduln und Ideale, meinen Schachruhm lange überleben wird.' *While the world at large has not given recognition to his philosophical speculations, his mathematical achievements are still inherent in much of the algebraic research that is going on to the present day.*

It is impossible to give in non-mathematical terms the substance of the contribution Lasker has made to our mathematical knowledge, nor even to describe, however vaguely, the nature of his topic 'modules and ideals'. The reader may recall from his school days that Descartes in his creation of 'co-ordinate geometry' or 'analytical geometry' had achieved a fusion of Algebra and Geometry, where geometric objects are described and studied in algebraic language (for example, where 'curves' are given by 'equations'). In further pursuit of this central idea the impressive building of 'Algebraic Geometry' has been erected in the course of the centuries.

Now, when more and more equations in more and more unknown are given, it becomes a very difficult problem to identify the geometric object corresponding to them and to investigate its properties. Lasker is concerned with the algebraic side of this problem, with the task of resolving such systems of equations into simpler constituents. The situation bears a certain resemblance to the resolution of whole numbers into a product of numbers that cannot be further factorized, the so-called prime numbers (for example $360 = 2 \times 2 \times 2 \times 3 \times 3 \times 5$).

But while in the latter case this factorization can be effected in one way only, as Euclid had already proved, such a uniqueness does not hold in the objects of algebraic geometry, nor in certain more complicated number systems. To restore this desirable uniqueness the mathematicians of the nineteenth century had learned to consider, apart from the real factors, also certain 'ideal' factors or 'ideals'. When such an ideal is not amenable to factorization, it is called a prime ideal. Lasker introduced a weaker, but equally useful concept, that of a 'primary ideal'. It is this concept of a primary ideal that will always be linked with his name. True, many a younger mathematician who uses primary ideals as a matter of course, may not even know that the concept and the name are due to Lasker. But it is indeed, one of the most important tools of Modern Algebra which in turn is one of the pillars on which the whole building of mathematics rests.

It may be of interest to note that the ultimate combination of the arithmatical approach to ideal theory in higher number systems on the one hand, and of Lasker's approach by way of 'polynomial ideals' on the other hand, was the work of Emmy Noether (1882– 1935), the greatest woman mathematician the world has seen, and a daughter of Max Noether under whom Lasker took his degree of Ph.D.'

I welcome the opportunity of recording this one facet of Lasker's eminence unknown to many of his admirers. But then it was typical of him to be reticent about that particular sphere of his work. There was no false modesty about it, just common sense.

Like most great men he was fully aware of his worth and he liked to quote Goethe's famous dictum *Nur Lumpe sind bescheiden*. No doubt, he would discourse freely about his mathematical achievements when meeting a fellow-mathematician; but it would have been a waste of time with those of us lacking the expert knowledge to understand that part of his work.

Moreover, he was always brimming over with ideas and plans, and so varied were his interests, so universal his mind and his knowledge that he never lacked some absorbing topic of conversation with whoever happened to share his table at one of his favourite cafés in a good many cities of Europe and America.

He once did me the honour of suggesting collaboration on a book. Not on chess, of course, for chess in those days was very far from his mind, (nor was he likely to require anybody's collaboration for a book on chess). It was to be a book on Dostoievsky, and we spent one or two happy evenings at our café table discussing and planning the project.

Like so many plans of those days it came to nought, for it wasn't a very propitious time for planning anything except a speedy trip abroad. It was shortly before the advent of Hitler, and we knew that we would not have many more meetings; certainly not, at a Berlin café table.

A few years later I met Lasker for the last time when he passed through London on his way to the Nottingham tournament of 1936. It was to be the last of his many tournaments, the last (and by no means inglorious) page of a very glorious record.

All that remains to be done is to send the author of this book my compliments as well as my apologies for having dealt with his text in a somewhat free and easy manner. But then all I have to do in mitigation is to quote what our mutual hero wrote in the preface to his own English version of his 'Manual'.

'No literal translation can be accurate. It is in danger of reproducing the body, but not the essential thing, the soul of the book'.

As for 'the soul' of this book, I am not worried about it if it succeeds in making the memory of Emanuel Lasker come alive: a most interesting and very lovable man who, quite apart from his imperishable fame as a chess player, was one of the truly remarkable personalities of his time.

H. F.

A CATALOG OF SELECTED DOVER
BOOKS IN ALL FIELDS OF INTEREST

DRAWINGS OF REMBRANDT, edited by Seymour Slive. Updated Lippmann, Hofstede de Groot edition, with definitive scholarly apparatus. All portraits, biblical sketches, landscapes, nudes. Oriental figures, classical studies, together with selection of work by followers. 550 illustrations. Total of 630pp. 9⅛ × 12¼.
21485-0, 21486-9 Pa., Two-vol. set $29.90

GHOST AND HORROR STORIES OF AMBROSE BIERCE, Ambrose Bierce. 24 tales vividly imagined, strangely prophetic, and decades ahead of their time in technical skill: "The Damned Thing," "An Inhabitant of Carcosa," "The Eyes of the Panther," "Moxon's Master," and 20 more. 199pp. 5⅜ × 8½. 20767-6 Pa. $3.95

ETHICAL WRITINGS OF MAIMONIDES, Maimonides. Most significant ethical works of great medieval sage, newly translated for utmost precision, readability. Laws Concerning Character Traits, Eight Chapters, more. 192pp. 5⅜ × 8½.
24522-5 Pa. $4.50

THE EXPLORATION OF THE COLORADO RIVER AND ITS CANYONS, J. W. Powell. Full text of Powell's 1,000-mile expedition down the fabled Colorado in 1869. Superb account of terrain, geology, vegetation, Indians, famine, mutiny, treacherous rapids, mighty canyons, during exploration of last unknown part of continental U.S. 400pp. 5⅜ × 8½. 20094-9 Pa. $7.95

HISTORY OF PHILOSOPHY, Julián Marías. Clearest one-volume history on the market. Every major philosopher and dozens of others, to Existentialism and later. 505pp. 5⅜ × 8½. 21739-6 Pa. $9.95

ALL ABOUT LIGHTNING, Martin A. Uman. Highly readable non-technical survey of nature and causes of lightning, thunderstorms, ball lightning, St. Elmo's Fire, much more. Illustrated. 192pp. 5⅜ × 8½. 25237-X Pa. $5.95

SAILING ALONE AROUND THE WORLD, Captain Joshua Slocum. First man to sail around the world, alone, in small boat. One of great feats of seamanship told in delightful manner. 67 illustrations. 294pp. 5⅜ × 8½. 20326-3 Pa. $4.95

LETTERS AND NOTES ON THE MANNERS, CUSTOMS AND CONDITIONS OF THE NORTH AMERICAN INDIANS, George Catlin. Classic account of life among Plains Indians: ceremonies, hunt, warfare, etc. 312 plates. 572pp. of text. 6⅛ × 9¼. 22118-0, 22119-9, Pa. Two-vol. set $17.90

ALASKA: The Harriman Expedition, 1899, John Burroughs, John Muir, et al. Informative, engrossing accounts of two-month, 9,000-mile expedition. Native peoples, wildlife, forests, geography, salmon industry, glaciers, more. Profusely illustrated. 240 black-and-white line drawings. 124 black-and-white photographs. 3 maps. Index. 576pp. 5⅜ × 8½. 25109-8 Pa. $11.95

THE BOOK OF BEASTS: Being a Translation from a Latin Bestiary of the Twelfth Century, T. H. White. Wonderful catalog real and fanciful beasts: manticore, griffin, phoenix, amphivius, jaculus, many more. White's witty erudite commentary on scientific, historical aspects. Fascinating glimpse of medieval mind. Illustrated. 296pp. 5⅜ × 8¼. (Available in U.S. only)   24609-4 Pa. $6.95

FRANK LLOYD WRIGHT: ARCHITECTURE AND NATURE With 160 Illustrations, Donald Hoffmann. Profusely illustrated study of influence of nature—especially prairie—on Wright's designs for Fallingwater, Robie House, Guggenheim Museum, other masterpieces. 96pp. 9¼ × 10¾.   25098-9 Pa. $7.95

FRANK LLOYD WRIGHT'S FALLINGWATER, Donald Hoffmann. Wright's famous waterfall house: planning and construction of organic idea. History of site, owners, Wright's personal involvement. Photographs of various stages of building. Preface by Edgar Kaufmann, Jr. 100 illustrations. 112pp. 9¼ × 10.

23671-4 Pa. $8.95

YEARS WITH FRANK LLOYD WRIGHT: Apprentice to Genius, Edgar Tafel. Insightful memoir by a former apprentice presents a revealing portrait of Wright the man, the inspired teacher, the greatest American architect. 372 black-and-white illustrations. Preface. Index. vi + 228pp. 8¼ × 11.   24801-1 Pa. $10.95

THE STORY OF KING ARTHUR AND HIS KNIGHTS, Howard Pyle. Enchanting version of King Arthur fable has delighted generations with imaginative narratives of exciting adventures and unforgettable illustrations by the author. 41 illustrations. xviii + 313pp. 6⅛ × 9¼.   21445-1 Pa. $6.95

THE GODS OF THE EGYPTIANS, E. A. Wallis Budge. Thorough coverage of numerous gods of ancient Egypt by foremost Egyptologist. Information on evolution of cults, rites and gods; the cult of Osiris; the Book of the Dead and its rites; the sacred animals and birds; Heaven and Hell; and more. 956pp. 6⅛ × 9¼.

22055-9, 22056-7 Pa., Two-vol. set $21.90

A THEOLOGICO-POLITICAL TREATISE, Benedict Spinoza. Also contains unfinished *Political Treatise*. Great classic on religious liberty, theory of government on common consent. R. Elwes translation. Total of 421pp. 5⅜ × 8½.

20249-6 Pa. $6.95

INCIDENTS OF TRAVEL IN CENTRAL AMERICA, CHIAPAS, AND YUCATAN, John L. Stephens. Almost single-handed discovery of Maya culture; exploration of ruined cities, monuments, temples; customs of Indians. 115 drawings. 892pp. 5⅜ × 8½.   22404-X, 22405-8 Pa., Two-vol. set $15.90

LOS CAPRICHOS, Francisco Goya. 80 plates of wild, grotesque monsters and caricatures. Prado manuscript included. 183pp. 6⅜ × 9⅜.   22384-1 Pa. $5.95

AUTOBIOGRAPHY: The Story of My Experiments with Truth, Mohandas K. Gandhi. Not hagiography, but Gandhi in his own words. Boyhood, legal studies, purification, the growth of the Satyagraha (nonviolent protest) movement. Critical, inspiring work of the man who freed India. 480pp. 5⅜ × 8½. (Available in U.S. only)

24593-4 Pa. $6.95

ILLUSTRATED DICTIONARY OF HISTORIC ARCHITECTURE, edited by Cyril M. Harris. Extraordinary compendium of clear, concise definitions for over 5,000 important architectural terms complemented by over 2,000 line drawings. Covers full spectrum of architecture from ancient ruins to 20th-century Modernism. Preface. 592pp. 7½ × 9⅝. 24444-X Pa. $15.95

THE NIGHT BEFORE CHRISTMAS, Clement Moore. Full text, and woodcuts from original 1848 book. Also critical, historical material. 19 illustrations. 40pp. 4⅝ × 6. 22797-9 Pa. $2.50

THE LESSON OF JAPANESE ARCHITECTURE: 165 Photographs, Jiro Harada. Memorable gallery of 165 photographs taken in the 1930's of exquisite Japanese homes of the well-to-do and historic buildings. 13 line diagrams. 192pp. 8⅜ × 11¼. 24778-3 Pa. $10.95

THE AUTOBIOGRAPHY OF CHARLES DARWIN AND SELECTED LET-TERS, edited by Francis Darwin. The fascinating life of eccentric genius composed of an intimate memoir by Darwin (intended for his children); commentary by his son, Francis; hundreds of fragments from notebooks, journals, papers; and letters to and from Lyell, Hooker, Huxley, Wallace and Henslow. xi + 365pp. 5⅜ × 8. 20479-0 Pa. $6.95

WONDERS OF THE SKY: Observing Rainbows, Comets, Eclipses, the Stars and Other Phenomena, Fred Schaaf. Charming, easy-to-read poetic guide to all manner of celestial events visible to the naked eye. Mock suns, glories, Belt of Venus, more. Illustrated. 299pp. 5¼ × 8¼. 24402-4 Pa. $7.95

BURNHAM'S CELESTIAL HANDBOOK, Robert Burnham, Jr. Thorough guide to the stars beyond our solar system. Exhaustive treatment. Alphabetical by constellation: Andromeda to Cetus in Vol. 1; Chamaeleon to Orion in Vol. 2; and Pavo to Vulpecula in Vol. 3. Hundreds of illustrations. Index in Vol. 3. 2,000pp. 6⅛ × 9¼. 23567-X, 23568-8, 23673-0 Pa., Three-vol. set $41.85

STAR NAMES: Their Lore and Meaning, Richard Hinckley Allen. Fascinating history of names various cultures have given to constellations and literary and folkloristic uses that have been made of stars. Indexes to subjects. Arabic and Greek names. Biblical references. Bibliography. 563pp. 5⅜ × 8½. 21079-0 Pa. $8.95

THIRTY YEARS THAT SHOOK PHYSICS: The Story of Quantum Theory, George Gamow. Lucid, accessible introduction to influential theory of energy and matter. Careful explanations of Dirac's anti-particles, Bohr's model of the atom, much more. 12 plates. Numerous drawings. 240pp. 5⅜ × 8½. 24895-X Pa. $5.95

CHINESE DOMESTIC FURNITURE IN PHOTOGRAPHS AND MEASURED DRAWINGS, Gustav Ecke. A rare volume, now affordably priced for antique collectors, furniture buffs and art historians. Detailed review of styles ranging from early Shang to late Ming. Unabridged republication. 161 black-and-white draw-ings, photos. Total of 224pp. 8⅜ × 11¼. (Available in U.S. only) 25171-3 Pa. $13.95

VINCENT VAN GOGH: A Biography, Julius Meier-Graefe. Dynamic, penetrat-ing study of artist's life, relationship with brother, Theo, painting techniques, travels, more. Readable, engrossing. 160pp. 5⅜ × 8½. (Available in U.S. only) 25253-1 Pa. $4.95

HOW TO WRITE, Gertrude Stein. Gertrude Stein claimed anyone could understand her unconventional writing—here are clues to help. Fascinating improvisations, language experiments, explanations illuminate Stein's craft and the art of writing. Total of 414pp. 4⅝ × 6⅜. 23144-5 Pa. $6.95

ADVENTURES AT SEA IN THE GREAT AGE OF SAIL: Five Firsthand Narratives, edited by Elliot Snow. Rare true accounts of exploration, whaling, shipwreck, fierce natives, trade, shipboard life, more. 33 illustrations. Introduction. 353pp. 5⅜ × 8½. 25177-2 Pa. $8.95

THE HERBAL OR GENERAL HISTORY OF PLANTS, John Gerard. Classic descriptions of about 2,850 plants—with over 2,700 illustrations—includes Latin and English names, physical descriptions, varieties, time and place of growth, more. 2,706 illustrations. xlv + 1,678pp. 8½ × 12¼. 23147-X Cloth. $75.00

DOROTHY AND THE WIZARD IN OZ, L. Frank Baum. Dorothy and the Wizard visit the center of the Earth, where people are vegetables, glass houses grow and Oz characters reappear. Classic sequel to *Wizard of Oz*. 256pp. 5⅜ × 8. 24714-7 Pa. $5.95

SONGS OF EXPERIENCE: Facsimile Reproduction with 26 Plates in Full Color, William Blake. This facsimile of Blake's original "Illuminated Book" reproduces 26 full-color plates from a rare 1826 edition. Includes "The Tyger," "London," "Holy Thursday," and other immortal poems. 26 color plates. Printed text of poems. 48pp. 5¼ × 7. 24636-1 Pa. $3.50

SONGS OF INNOCENCE, William Blake. The first and most popular of Blake's famous "Illuminated Books," in a facsimile edition reproducing all 31 brightly colored plates. Additional printed text of each poem. 64pp. 5¼ × 7. 22764-2 Pa. $3.50

PRECIOUS STONES, Max Bauer. Classic, thorough study of diamonds, rubies, emeralds, garnets, etc.: physical character, occurrence, properties, use, similar topics. 20 plates, 8 in color. 94 figures. 659pp. 6⅛ × 9¼. 21910-0, 21911-9 Pa., Two-vol. set $15.90

ENCYCLOPEDIA OF VICTORIAN NEEDLEWORK, S. F. A. Caulfeild and Blanche Saward. Full, precise descriptions of stitches, techniques for dozens of needlecrafts—most exhaustive reference of its kind. Over 800 figures. Total of 679pp. 8⅛ × 11. Two volumes. Vol. 1 22800-2 Pa. $11.95
Vol. 2 22801-0 Pa. $11.95

THE MARVELOUS LAND OF OZ, L. Frank Baum. Second Oz book, the Scarecrow and Tin Woodman are back with hero named Tip, Oz magic. 136 illustrations. 287pp. 5⅜ × 8½. 20692-0 Pa. $5.95

WILD FOWL DECOYS, Joel Barber. Basic book on the subject, by foremost authority and collector. Reveals history of decoy making and rigging, place in American culture, different kinds of decoys, how to make them, and how to use them. 140 plates. 156pp. 7⅞ × 10¾. 20011-6 Pa. $8.95

HISTORY OF LACE, Mrs. Bury Palliser. Definitive, profusely illustrated chronicle of lace from earliest times to late 19th century. Laces of Italy, Greece, England, France, Belgium, etc. Landmark of needlework scholarship. 266 illustrations. 672pp. 6⅛ × 9¼. 24742-2 Pa. $14.95

ILLUSTRATED GUIDE TO SHAKER FURNITURE, Robert Meader. All furniture and appurtenances, with much on unknown local styles. 235 photos. 146pp. 9 × 12. 22819-3 Pa. $8.95

WHALE SHIPS AND WHALING: A Pictorial Survey, George Francis Dow. Over 200 vintage engravings, drawings, photographs of barks, brigs, cutters, other vessels. Also harpoons, lances, whaling guns, many other artifacts. Comprehensive text by foremost authority. 207 black-and-white illustrations. 288pp. 6 × 9. 24808-9 Pa. $8.95

THE BERTRAMS, Anthony Trollope. Powerful portrayal of blind self-will and thwarted ambition includes one of Trollope's most heartrending love stories. 497pp. 5⅜ × 8½. 25119-5 Pa. $9.95

ADVENTURES WITH A HAND LENS, Richard Headstrom. Clearly written guide to observing and studying flowers and grasses, fish scales, moth and insect wings, egg cases, buds, feathers, seeds, leaf scars, moss, molds, ferns, common crystals, etc.—all with an ordinary, inexpensive magnifying glass. 209 exact line drawings aid in your discoveries. 220pp. 5⅜ × 8½. 23330-8 Pa. $4.95

RODIN ON ART AND ARTISTS, Auguste Rodin. Great sculptor's candid, wide-ranging comments on meaning of art; great artists; relation of sculpture to poetry, painting, music; philosophy of life, more. 76 superb black-and-white illustrations of Rodin's sculpture, drawings and prints. 119pp. 8⅜ × 11¼. 24487-3 Pa. $7.95

FIFTY CLASSIC FRENCH FILMS, 1912–1982: A Pictorial Record, Anthony Slide. Memorable stills from Grand Illusion, Beauty and the Beast, Hiroshima, Mon Amour, many more. Credits, plot synopses, reviews, etc. 160pp. 8¼ × 11. 25256-6 Pa. $11.95

THE PRINCIPLES OF PSYCHOLOGY, William James. Famous long course complete, unabridged. Stream of thought, time perception, memory, experimental methods; great work decades ahead of its time. 94 figures. 1,391pp. 5⅜ × 8½. 20381-6, 20382-4 Pa., Two-vol. set $23.90

BODIES IN A BOOKSHOP, R. T. Campbell. Challenging mystery of blackmail and murder with ingenious plot and superbly drawn characters. In the best tradition of British suspense fiction. 192pp. 5⅜ × 8½. 24720-1 Pa. $3.95

CALLAS: PORTRAIT OF A PRIMA DONNA, George Jellinek. Renowned commentator on the musical scene chronicles incredible career and life of the most controversial, fascinating, influential operatic personality of our time. 64 black-and-white photographs. 416pp. 5⅜ × 8¼. 25047-4 Pa. $8.95

GEOMETRY, RELATIVITY AND THE FOURTH DIMENSION, Rudolph Rucker. Exposition of fourth dimension, concepts of relativity as Flatland characters continue adventures. Popular, easily followed yet accurate, profound. 141 illustrations. 133pp. 5⅜ × 8½. 23400-2 Pa. $4.95

HOUSEHOLD STORIES BY THE BROTHERS GRIMM, with pictures by Walter Crane. 53 classic stories—Rumpelstiltskin, Rapunzel, Hansel and Gretel, the Fisherman and his Wife, Snow White, Tom Thumb, Sleeping Beauty, Cinderella, and so much more—lavishly illustrated with original 19th century drawings. 114 illustrations. x + 269pp. 5⅜ × 8½. 21080-4 Pa. $4.95

SUNDIALS, Albert Waugh. Far and away the best, most thorough coverage of ideas, mathematics concerned, types, construction, adjusting anywhere. Over 100 illustrations. 230pp. 5⅜ × 8½. 22947-5 Pa. $4.95

PICTURE HISTORY OF THE NORMANDIE: With 190 Illustrations, Frank O. Braynard. Full story of legendary French ocean liner: Art Deco interiors, design innovations, furnishings, celebrities, maiden voyage, tragic fire, much more. Extensive text. 144pp. 8⅞ × 11¾. 25257-4 Pa. $10.95

THE FIRST AMERICAN COOKBOOK: A Facsimile of "American Cookery," 1796, Amelia Simmons. Facsimile of the first American-written cookbook published in the United States contains authentic recipes for colonial favorites—pumpkin pudding, winter squash pudding, spruce beer, Indian slapjacks, and more. Introductory Essay and Glossary of colonial cooking terms. 80pp. 5⅜ × 8½. 24710-4 Pa. $3.50

101 PUZZLES IN THOUGHT AND LOGIC, C. R. Wylie, Jr. Solve murders and robberies, find out which fishermen are liars, how a blind man could possibly identify a color—purely by your own reasoning! 107pp. 5⅜ × 8½. 20367-0 Pa. $2.50

THE BOOK OF WORLD-FAMOUS MUSIC—CLASSICAL, POPULAR AND FOLK, James J. Fuld. Revised and enlarged republication of landmark work in musico-bibliography. Full information about nearly 1,000 songs and compositions including first lines of music and lyrics. New supplement. Index. 800pp. 5⅜ × 8¼. 24857-7 Pa. $15.95

ANTHROPOLOGY AND MODERN LIFE, Franz Boas. Great anthropologist's classic treatise on race and culture. Introduction by Ruth Bunzel. Only inexpensive paperback edition. 255pp. 5⅜ × 8½. 25245-0 Pa. $6.95

THE TALE OF PETER RABBIT, Beatrix Potter. The inimitable Peter's terrifying adventure in Mr. McGregor's garden, with all 27 wonderful, full-color Potter illustrations. 55pp. 4¼ × 5½. (Available in U.S. only) 22827-4 Pa. $1.75

THREE PROPHETIC SCIENCE FICTION NOVELS, H. G. Wells. *When the Sleeper Wakes, A Story of the Days to Come* and *The Time Machine* (full version). 335pp. 5⅜ × 8½. (Available in U.S. only) 20605-X Pa. $6.95

APICIUS COOKERY AND DINING IN IMPERIAL ROME, edited and translated by Joseph Dommers Vehling. Oldest known cookbook in existence offers readers a clear picture of what foods Romans ate, how they prepared them, etc. 49 illustrations. 301pp. 6⅛ × 9¼. 23563-7 Pa. $7.95

SHAKESPEARE LEXICON AND QUOTATION DICTIONARY, Alexander Schmidt. Full definitions, locations, shades of meaning of every word in plays and poems. More than 50,000 exact quotations. 1,485pp. 6½ × 9¼. 22726-X, 22727-8 Pa., Two-vol. set $29.90

THE WORLD'S GREAT SPEECHES, edited by Lewis Copeland and Lawrence W. Lamm. Vast collection of 278 speeches from Greeks to 1970. Powerful and effective models; unique look at history. 842pp. 5⅜ × 8½. 20468-5 Pa. $11.95

THE BLUE FAIRY BOOK, Andrew Lang. The first, most famous collection, with many familiar tales: Little Red Riding Hood, Aladdin and the Wonderful Lamp, Puss in Boots, Sleeping Beauty, Hansel and Gretel, Rumpelstiltskin; 37 in all. 138 illustrations. 390pp. 5⅜ × 8½. 21437-0 Pa. $6.95

THE STORY OF THE CHAMPIONS OF THE ROUND TABLE, Howard Pyle. Sir Launcelot, Sir Tristram and Sir Percival in spirited adventures of love and triumph retold in Pyle's inimitable style. 50 drawings, 31 full-page. xviii + 329pp. 6½ × 9¼. 21883-X Pa. $7.95

AUDUBON AND HIS JOURNALS, Maria Audubon. Unmatched two-volume portrait of the great artist, naturalist and author contains his journals, an excellent biography by his granddaughter, expert annotations by the noted ornithologist, Dr. Elliott Coues, and 37 superb illustrations. Total of 1,200pp. 5⅜ × 8.
Vol. I 25143-8 Pa. $8.95
Vol. II 25144-6 Pa. $8.95

GREAT DINOSAUR HUNTERS AND THEIR DISCOVERIES, Edwin H. Colbert. Fascinating, lavishly illustrated chronicle of dinosaur research, 1820's to 1960. Achievements of Cope, Marsh, Brown, Buckland, Mantell, Huxley, many others. 384pp. 5¼ × 8¼. 24701-5 Pa. $7.95

THE TASTEMAKERS, Russell Lynes. Informal, illustrated social history of American taste 1850's–1950's. First popularized categories Highbrow, Lowbrow, Middlebrow. 129 illustrations. New (1979) afterword. 384pp. 6 × 9.
23993-4 Pa. $8.95

DOUBLE CROSS PURPOSES, Ronald A. Knox. A treasure hunt in the Scottish Highlands, an old map, unidentified corpse, surprise discoveries keep reader guessing in this cleverly intricate tale of financial skullduggery. 2 black-and-white maps. 320pp. 5⅜ × 8½. (Available in U.S. only) 25032-6 Pa. $6.95

AUTHENTIC VICTORIAN DECORATION AND ORNAMENTATION IN FULL COLOR: 46 Plates from "Studies in Design," Christopher Dresser. Superb full-color lithographs reproduced from rare original portfolio of a major Victorian designer. 48pp. 9¼ × 12¼. 25083-0 Pa. $7.95

PRIMITIVE ART, Franz Boas. Remains the best text ever prepared on subject, thoroughly discussing Indian, African, Asian, Australian, and, especially, Northern American primitive art. Over 950 illustrations show ceramics, masks, totem poles, weapons, textiles, paintings, much more. 376pp. 5⅜ × 8. 20025-6 Pa. $7.95

SIDELIGHTS ON RELATIVITY, Albert Einstein. Unabridged republication of two lectures delivered by the great physicist in 1920–21. *Ether and Relativity* and *Geometry and Experience*. Elegant ideas in non-mathematical form, accessible to intelligent layman. vi + 56pp. 5⅜ × 8½. 24511-X Pa. $2.95

THE WIT AND HUMOR OF OSCAR WILDE, edited by Alvin Redman. More than 1,000 ripostes, paradoxes, wisecracks: Work is the curse of the drinking classes, I can resist everything except temptation, etc. 258pp. 5⅜ × 8½. 20602-5 Pa. $4.95

ADVENTURES WITH A MICROSCOPE, Richard Headstrom. 59 adventures with clothing fibers, protozoa, ferns and lichens, roots and leaves, much more. 142 illustrations. 232pp. 5⅜ × 8½. 23471-1 Pa. $3.95

PLANTS OF THE BIBLE, Harold N. Moldenke and Alma L. Moldenke. Standard reference to all 230 plants mentioned in Scriptures. Latin name, biblical reference, uses, modern identity, much more. Unsurpassed encyclopedic resource for scholars, botanists, nature lovers, students of Bible. Bibliography. Indexes. 123 black-and-white illustrations. 384pp. 6 × 9. 25069-5 Pa. $8.95

FAMOUS AMERICAN WOMEN: A Biographical Dictionary from Colonial Times to the Present, Robert McHenry, ed. From Pocahontas to Rosa Parks, 1,035 distinguished American women documented in separate biographical entries. Accurate, up-to-date data, numerous categories, spans 400 years. Indices. 493pp. 6½ × 9¼. 24523-3 Pa. $10.95

THE FABULOUS INTERIORS OF THE GREAT OCEAN LINERS IN HISTORIC PHOTOGRAPHS, William H. Miller, Jr. Some 200 superb photographs capture exquisite interiors of world's great "floating palaces"—1890's to 1980's: *Titanic, Ile de France, Queen Elizabeth, United States, Europa,* more. Approx. 200 black-and-white photographs. Captions. Text. Introduction. 160pp. 8⅞ × 11¾. 24756-2 Pa. $9.95

THE GREAT LUXURY LINERS, 1927–1954: A Photographic Record, William H. Miller, Jr. Nostalgic tribute to heyday of ocean liners. 186 photos of Ile de France, Normandie, Leviathan, Queen Elizabeth, United States, many others. Interior and exterior views. Introduction. Captions. 160pp. 9 × 12. 24056-8 Pa. $10.95

A NATURAL HISTORY OF THE DUCKS, John Charles Phillips. Great landmark of ornithology offers complete detailed coverage of nearly 200 species and subspecies of ducks: gadwall, sheldrake, merganser, pintail, many more. 74 full-color plates, 102 black-and-white. Bibliography. Total of 1,920pp. 8⅝ × 11¼. 25141-1, 25142-X Cloth. Two-vol. set $100.00

THE SEAWEED HANDBOOK: An Illustrated Guide to Seaweeds from North Carolina to Canada, Thomas F. Lee. Concise reference covers 78 species. Scientific and common names, habitat, distribution, more. Finding keys for easy identification. 224pp. 5⅜ × 8½. 25215-9 Pa. $6.95

THE TEN BOOKS OF ARCHITECTURE: The 1755 Leoni Edition, Leon Battista Alberti. Rare classic helped introduce the glories of ancient architecture to the Renaissance. 68 black-and-white plates. 336pp. 8⅜ × 11¼. 25239-6 Pa. $14.95

MISS MACKENZIE, Anthony Trollope. Minor masterpieces by Victorian master unmasks many truths about life in 19th-century England. First inexpensive edition in years. 392pp. 5⅜ × 8½. 25201-9 Pa. $8.95

THE RIME OF THE ANCIENT MARINER, Gustave Doré, Samuel Taylor Coleridge. Dramatic engravings considered by many to be his greatest work. The terrifying space of the open sea, the storms and whirlpools of an unknown ocean, the ice of Antarctica, more—all rendered in a powerful, chilling manner. Full text. 38 plates. 77pp. 9¼ × 12. 22305-1 Pa. $4.95

THE EXPEDITIONS OF ZEBULON MONTGOMERY PIKE, Zebulon Montgomery Pike. Fascinating first-hand accounts (1805–6) of exploration of Mississippi River, Indian wars, capture by Spanish dragoons, much more. 1,088pp. 5⅜ × 8½. 25254-X, 25255-8 Pa. Two-vol. set $25.90

A CONCISE HISTORY OF PHOTOGRAPHY: Third Revised Edition, Helmut Gernsheim. Best one-volume history—camera obscura, photochemistry, daguerreotypes, evolution of cameras, film, more. Also artistic aspects—landscape, portraits, fine art, etc. 281 black-and-white photographs. 26 in color. 176pp. 8⅜ × 11¼. 25128-4 Pa. $13.95

THE DORÉ BIBLE ILLUSTRATIONS, Gustave Doré. 241 detailed plates from the Bible: the Creation scenes, Adam and Eve, Flood, Babylon, battle sequences, life of Jesus, etc. Each plate is accompanied by the verses from the King James version of the Bible. 241pp. 9 × 12. 23004-X Pa. $9.95

HUGGER-MUGGER IN THE LOUVRE, Elliot Paul. Second Homer Evans mystery-comedy. Theft at the Louvre involves sleuth in hilarious, madcap caper. "A knockout."—Books. 336pp. 5⅜ × 8½. 25185-3 Pa. $5.95

FLATLAND, E. A. Abbott. Intriguing and enormously popular science-fiction classic explores the complexities of trying to survive as a two-dimensional being in a three-dimensional world. Amusingly illustrated by the author. 16 illustrations. 103pp. 5⅜ × 8½. 20001-9 Pa. $2.50

THE HISTORY OF THE LEWIS AND CLARK EXPEDITION, Meriwether Lewis and William Clark, edited by Elliott Coues. Classic edition of Lewis and Clark's day-by-day journals that later became the basis for U.S. claims to Oregon and the West. Accurate and invaluable geographical, botanical, biological, meteorological and anthropological material. Total of 1,508pp. 5⅜ × 8½.
21268-8, 21269-6, 21270-X Pa. Three-vol. set $26.85

LANGUAGE, TRUTH AND LOGIC, Alfred J. Ayer. Famous, clear introduction to Vienna, Cambridge schools of Logical Positivism. Role of philosophy, elimination of metaphysics, nature of analysis, etc. 160pp. 5⅜ × 8½. (Available in U.S. and Canada only) 20010-8 Pa. $3.95

MATHEMATICS FOR THE NONMATHEMATICIAN, Morris Kline. Detailed, college-level treatment of mathematics in cultural and historical context, with numerous exercises. For liberal arts students. Preface. Recommended Reading Lists. Tables. Index. Numerous black-and-white figures. xvi + 641pp. 5⅜ × 8½.
24823-2 Pa. $11.95

HANDBOOK OF PICTORIAL SYMBOLS, Rudolph Modley. 3,250 signs and symbols, many systems in full; official or heavy commercial use. Arranged by subject. Most in Pictorial Archive series. 143pp. 8⅛ × 11. 23357-X Pa. $6.95

INCIDENTS OF TRAVEL IN YUCATAN, John L. Stephens. Classic (1843) exploration of jungles of Yucatan, looking for evidences of Maya civilization. Travel adventures, Mexican and Indian culture, etc. Total of 669pp. 5⅜ × 8½.
20926-1, 20927-X Pa., Two-vol. set $11.90

DEGAS: An Intimate Portrait, Ambroise Vollard. Charming, anecdotal memoir by famous art dealer of one of the greatest 19th-century French painters. 14 black-and-white illustrations. Introduction by Harold L. Van Doren. 96pp. 5⅜ × 8½.
25131-4 Pa. $4.95

PERSONAL NARRATIVE OF A PILGRIMAGE TO ALMANDINAH AND MECCAH, Richard Burton. Great travel classic by remarkably colorful personality. Burton, disguised as a Moroccan, visited sacred shrines of Islam, narrowly escaping death. 47 illustrations. 959pp. 5⅜ × 8½. 21217-3, 21218-1 Pa., Two-vol. set $19.90

PHRASE AND WORD ORIGINS, A. H. Holt. Entertaining, reliable, modern study of more than 1,200 colorful words, phrases, origins and histories. Much unexpected information. 254pp. 5⅜ × 8½.
20758-7 Pa. $5.95

THE RED THUMB MARK, R. Austin Freeman. In this first Dr. Thorndyke case, the great scientific detective draws fascinating conclusions from the nature of a single fingerprint. Exciting story, authentic science. 320pp. 5⅜ × 8½. (Available in U.S. only)
25210-8 Pa. $6.95

AN EGYPTIAN HIEROGLYPHIC DICTIONARY, E. A. Wallis Budge. Monumental work containing about 25,000 words or terms that occur in texts ranging from 3000 B.C. to 600 A.D. Each entry consists of a transliteration of the word, the word in hieroglyphs, and the meaning in English. 1,314pp. 6⅜ × 10.
23615-3, 23616-1 Pa., Two-vol. set $31.90

THE COMPLEAT STRATEGYST: Being a Primer on the Theory of Games of Strategy, J. D. Williams. Highly entertaining classic describes, with many illustrated examples, how to select best strategies in conflict situations. Prefaces. Appendices. xvi + 268pp. 5⅜ × 8½.
25101-2 Pa. $5.95

THE ROAD TO OZ, L. Frank Baum. Dorothy meets the Shaggy Man, little Button-Bright and the Rainbow's beautiful daughter in this delightful trip to the magical Land of Oz. 272pp. 5⅜ × 8.
25208-6 Pa. $5.95

POINT AND LINE TO PLANE, Wassily Kandinsky. Seminal exposition of role of point, line, other elements in non-objective painting. Essential to understanding 20th-century art. 127 illustrations. 192pp. 6½ × 9¼.
23808-3 Pa. $5.95

LADY ANNA, Anthony Trollope. Moving chronicle of Countess Lovel's bitter struggle to win for herself and daughter Anna their rightful rank and fortune—perhaps at cost of sanity itself. 384pp. 5⅜ × 8½.
24669-8 Pa. $8.95

EGYPTIAN MAGIC, E. A. Wallis Budge. Sums up all that is known about magic in Ancient Egypt: the role of magic in controlling the gods, powerful amulets that warded off evil spirits, scarabs of immortality, use of wax images, formulas and spells, the secret name, much more. 253pp. 5⅜ × 8½.
22681-6 Pa. $4.50

THE DANCE OF SIVA, Ananda Coomaraswamy. Preeminent authority unfolds the vast metaphysic of India: the revelation of her art, conception of the universe, social organization, etc. 27 reproductions of art masterpieces. 192pp. 5⅜ × 8½.
24817-8 Pa. $5.95

CHRISTMAS CUSTOMS AND TRADITIONS, Clement A. Miles. Origin, evolution, significance of religious, secular practices. Caroling, gifts, yule logs, much more. Full, scholarly yet fascinating; non-sectarian. 400pp. 5⅜ × 8½.

23354-5 Pa. $6.95

THE HUMAN FIGURE IN MOTION, Eadweard Muybridge. More than 4,500 stopped-action photos, in action series, showing undraped men, women, children jumping, lying down, throwing, sitting, wrestling, carrying, etc. 390pp. 7⅞ × 10⅝.

20204-6 Cloth. $21.95

THE MAN WHO WAS THURSDAY, Gilbert Keith Chesterton. Witty, fast-paced novel about a club of anarchists in turn-of-the-century London. Brilliant social, religious, philosophical speculations. 128pp. 5⅜ × 8½.

25121-7 Pa. $3.95

A CEZANNE SKETCHBOOK: Figures, Portraits, Landscapes and Still Lifes, Paul Cezanne. Great artist experiments with tonal effects, light, mass, other qualities in over 100 drawings. A revealing view of developing master painter, precursor of Cubism. 102 black-and-white illustrations. 144pp. 8¼ × 6⅜.

24790-2 Pa. $5.95

AN ENCYCLOPEDIA OF BATTLES: Accounts of Over 1,560 Battles from 1479 B.C. to the Present, David Eggenberger. Presents essential details of every major battle in recorded history, from the first battle of Megiddo in 1479 B.C. to Grenada in 1984. List of Battle Maps. New Appendix covering the years 1967–1984. Index. 99 illustrations. 544pp. 6½ × 9¼.

24913-1 Pa. $14.95

AN ETYMOLOGICAL DICTIONARY OF MODERN ENGLISH, Ernest Weekley. Richest, fullest work, by foremost British lexicographer. Detailed word histories. Inexhaustible. Total of 856pp. 6½ × 9¼.

21873-2, 21874-0 Pa., Two-vol. set $17.00

WEBSTER'S AMERICAN MILITARY BIOGRAPHIES, edited by Robert McHenry. Over 1,000 figures who shaped 3 centuries of American military history. Detailed biographies of Nathan Hale, Douglas MacArthur, Mary Hallaren, others. Chronologies of engagements, more. Introduction. Addenda. 1,033 entries in alphabetical order. xi + 548pp. 6½ × 9¼. (Available in U.S. only)

24758-9 Pa. $13.95

LIFE IN ANCIENT EGYPT, Adolf Erman. Detailed older account, with much not in more recent books: domestic life, religion, magic, medicine, commerce, and whatever else needed for complete picture. Many illustrations. 597pp. 5⅜ × 8½.

22632-8 Pa. $8.95

HISTORIC COSTUME IN PICTURES, Braun & Schneider. Over 1,450 costumed figures shown, covering a wide variety of peoples: kings, emperors, nobles, priests, servants, soldiers, scholars, townsfolk, peasants, merchants, courtiers, cavaliers, and more. 256pp. 8⅜ × 11¼.

23150-X Pa. $9.95

THE NOTEBOOKS OF LEONARDO DA VINCI, edited by J. P. Richter. Extracts from manuscripts reveal great genius; on painting, sculpture, anatomy, sciences, geography, etc. Both Italian and English. 186 ms. pages reproduced, plus 500 additional drawings, including studies for *Last Supper, Sforza* monument, etc. 860pp. 7⅞ × 10¾. (Available in U.S. only) 22572-0, 22573-9 Pa., Two-vol. set $31.90

THE ART NOUVEAU STYLE BOOK OF ALPHONSE MUCHA: All 72 Plates from "Documents Decoratifs" in Original Color, Alphonse Mucha. Rare copyright-free design portfolio by high priest of Art Nouveau. Jewelry, wallpaper, stained glass, furniture, figure studies, plant and animal motifs, etc. Only complete one-volume edition. 80pp. 9⅜ × 12¼. 24044-4 Pa. $9.95

ANIMALS: 1,419 COPYRIGHT-FREE ILLUSTRATIONS OF MAMMALS, BIRDS, FISH, INSECTS, ETC., edited by Jim Harter. Clear wood engravings present, in extremely lifelike poses, over 1,000 species of animals. One of the most extensive pictorial sourcebooks of its kind. Captions. Index. 284pp. 9 × 12. 23766-4 Pa. $9.95

OBELISTS FLY HIGH, C. Daly King. Masterpiece of American detective fiction, long out of print, involves murder on a 1935 transcontinental flight—"a very thrilling story"—NY Times. Unabridged and unaltered republication of the edition published by William Collins Sons & Co. Ltd., London, 1935. 288pp. 5⅜ × 8½. (Available in U.S. only) 25036-9 Pa. $5.95

VICTORIAN AND EDWARDIAN FASHION: A Photographic Survey, Alison Gernsheim. First fashion history completely illustrated by contemporary photographs. Full text plus 235 photos, 1840–1914, in which many celebrities appear. 240pp. 6½ × 9¼. 24205-6 Pa. $6.95

THE ART OF THE FRENCH ILLUSTRATED BOOK, 1700–1914, Gordon N. Ray. Over 630 superb book illustrations by Fragonard, Delacroix, Daumier, Doré, Grandville, Manet, Mucha, Steinlen, Toulouse-Lautrec and many others. Preface. Introduction. 633 halftones. Indices of artists, authors & titles, binders and provenances. Appendices. Bibliography. 608pp. 8⅜ × 11¼. 25086-5 Pa. $24.95

THE WONDERFUL WIZARD OF OZ, L. Frank Baum. Facsimile in full color of America's finest children's classic. 143 illustrations by W. W. Denslow. 267pp. 5⅜ × 8½. 20691-2 Pa. $7.95

FRONTIERS OF MODERN PHYSICS: New Perspectives on Cosmology, Relativity, Black Holes and Extraterrestrial Intelligence, Tony Rothman, et al. For the intelligent layman. Subjects include: cosmological models of the universe; black holes; the neutrino; the search for extraterrestrial intelligence. Introduction. 46 black-and-white illustrations. 192pp. 5⅜ × 8½. 24587-X Pa. $7.95

THE FRIENDLY STARS, Martha Evans Martin & Donald Howard Menzel. Classic text marshalls the stars together in an engaging, non-technical survey, presenting them as sources of beauty in night sky. 23 illustrations. Foreword. 2 star charts. Index. 147pp. 5⅜ × 8½. 21099-5 Pa. $3.95

FADS AND FALLACIES IN THE NAME OF SCIENCE, Martin Gardner. Fair, witty appraisal of cranks, quacks, and quackeries of science and pseudoscience: hollow earth, Velikovsky, orgone energy, Dianetics, flying saucers, Bridey Murphy, food and medical fads, etc. Revised, expanded In the Name of Science. "A very able and even-tempered presentation."—The New Yorker. 363pp. 5⅜ × 8. 20394-8 Pa. $6.95

ANCIENT EGYPT: ITS CULTURE AND HISTORY, J. E Manchip White. From pre-dynastics through Ptolemies: society, history, political structure, religion, daily life, literature, cultural heritage. 48 plates. 217pp. 5⅜ × 8½. 22548-8 Pa. $5.95

SIR HARRY HOTSPUR OF HUMBLETHWAITE, Anthony Trollope. Incisive, unconventional psychological study of a conflict between a wealthy baronet, his idealistic daughter, and their scapegrace cousin. The 1870 novel in its first inexpensive edition in years. 250pp. 5⅜ × 8½. 24953-0 Pa. $5.95

LASERS AND HOLOGRAPHY, Winston E. Kock. Sound introduction to burgeoning field, expanded (1981) for second edition. Wave patterns, coherence, lasers, diffraction, zone plates, properties of holograms, recent advances. 84 illustrations. 160pp. 5⅜ × 8¼. (Except in United Kingdom) 24041-X Pa. $3.95

INTRODUCTION TO ARTIFICIAL INTELLIGENCE: SECOND, EN-LARGED EDITION, Philip C. Jackson, Jr. Comprehensive survey of artificial intelligence—the study of how machines (computers) can be made to act intelligently. Includes introductory and advanced material. Extensive notes updating the main text. 132 black-and-white illustrations. 512pp. 5⅜ × 8½. 24864-X Pa. $8.95

HISTORY OF INDIAN AND INDONESIAN ART, Ananda K. Coomaraswamy. Over 400 illustrations illuminate classic study of Indian art from earliest Harappa finds to early 20th century. Provides philosophical, religious and social insights. 304pp. 6⅛ × 9⅜. 25005-9 Pa. $9.95

THE GOLEM, Gustav Meyrink. Most famous supernatural novel in modern European literature, set in Ghetto of Old Prague around 1890. Compelling story of mystical experiences, strange transformations, profound terror. 13 black-and-white illustrations. 224pp. 5⅜ × 8½. (Available in U.S. only) 25025-3 Pa. $6.95

PICTORIAL ENCYCLOPEDIA OF HISTORIC ARCHITECTURAL PLANS, DETAILS AND ELEMENTS: With 1,880 Line Drawings of Arches, Domes, Doorways, Facades, Gables, Windows, etc., John Theodore Haneman. Sourcebook of inspiration for architects, designers, others. Bibliography. Captions. 141pp. 9 × 12. 24605-1 Pa. $7.95

BENCHLEY LOST AND FOUND, Robert Benchley. Finest humor from early 30's, about pet peeves, child psychologists, post office and others. Mostly unavailable elsewhere. 73 illustrations by Peter Arno and others. 183pp. 5⅜ × 8½. 22410-4 Pa. $4.95

ERTÉ GRAPHICS, Erté. Collection of striking color graphics: Seasons, Alphabet, Numerals, Aces and Precious Stones. 50 plates, including 4 on covers. 48pp. 9⅜ × 12¼. 23580-7 Pa. $7.95

THE JOURNAL OF HENRY D. THOREAU, edited by Bradford Torrey, F. H. Allen. Complete reprinting of 14 volumes, 1837-61, over two million words; the sourcebooks for Walden, etc. Definitive. All original sketches, plus 75 photographs. 1,804pp. 8½ × 12¼. 20312-3, 20313-1 Cloth., Two-vol. set $120.00

CASTLES: THEIR CONSTRUCTION AND HISTORY, Sidney Toy. Traces castle development from ancient roots. Nearly 200 photographs and drawings illustrate moats, keeps, baileys, many other features. Caernarvon, Dover Castles, Hadrian's Wall, Tower of London, dozens more. 256pp. 5⅜ × 8¼. 24898-4 Pa. $6.95

CATALOG OF DOVER BOOKS

AMERICAN CLIPPER SHIPS: 1833–1858, Octavius T. Howe & Frederick C. Matthews. Fully-illustrated, encyclopedic review of 352 clipper ships from the period of America's greatest maritime supremacy. Introduction. 109 halftones. 5 black-and-white line illustrations. Index. Total of 928pp. 5⅜ × 8½.
25115-2, 25116-0 Pa., Two-vol. set $17.90

TOWARDS A NEW ARCHITECTURE, Le Corbusier. Pioneering manifesto by great architect, near legendary founder of "International School." Technical and aesthetic theories, views on industry, economics, relation of form to function, "mass-production spirit," much more. Profusely illustrated. Unabridged translation of 13th French edition. Introduction by Frederick Etchells. 320pp. 6⅛ × 9¼. (Available in U.S. only)
25023-7 Pa. $8.95

THE BOOK OF KELLS, edited by Blanche Cirker. Inexpensive collection of 32 full-color, full-page plates from the greatest illuminated manuscript of the Middle Ages, painstakingly reproduced from rare facsimile edition. Publisher's Note. Captions. 32pp. 9⅜ × 12¼.
24345-1 Pa. $4.95

BEST SCIENCE FICTION STORIES OF H. G. WELLS, H. G. Wells. Full novel The Invisible Man, plus 17 short stories: "The Crystal Egg," "Aepyornis Island," "The Strange Orchid," etc. 303pp. 5⅜ × 8½. (Available in U.S. only)
21531-8 Pa. $6.95

AMERICAN SAILING SHIPS: Their Plans and History, Charles G. Davis. Photos, construction details of schooners, frigates, clippers, other sailcraft of 18th to early 20th centuries—plus entertaining discourse on design, rigging, nautical lore, much more. 137 black-and-white illustrations. 240pp. 6⅛ × 9¼.
24658-2 Pa. $6.95

ENTERTAINING MATHEMATICAL PUZZLES, Martin Gardner. Selection of author's favorite conundrums involving arithmetic, money, speed, etc., with lively commentary. Complete solutions. 112pp. 5⅜ × 8½.
25211-6 Pa. $2.95

THE WILL TO BELIEVE, HUMAN IMMORTALITY, William James. Two books bound together. Effect of irrational on logical, and arguments for human immortality. 402pp. 5⅜ × 8½.
20291-7 Pa. $7.95

THE HAUNTED MONASTERY and THE CHINESE MAZE MURDERS, Robert Van Gulik. 2 full novels by Van Gulik continue adventures of Judge Dee and his companions. An evil Taoist monastery, seemingly supernatural events; overgrown topiary maze that hides strange crimes. Set in 7th-century China. 27 illustrations. 328pp. 5⅜ × 8½.
23502-5 Pa. $6.95

CELEBRATED CASES OF JUDGE DEE (DEE GOONG AN), translated by Robert Van Gulik. Authentic 18th-century Chinese detective novel; Dee and associates solve three interlocked cases. Led to Van Gulik's own stories with same characters. Extensive introduction. 9 illustrations. 237pp. 5⅜ × 8½.
23337-5 Pa. $4.95

Prices subject to change without notice.
Available at your book dealer or write for free catalog to Dept. GI, Dover Publications, Inc., 31 East 2nd St., Mineola, N.Y. 11501. Dover publishes more than 175 books each year on science, elementary and advanced mathematics, biology, music, art, literary history, social sciences and other areas.